FROM SANTA ANNA TO SELENA

Notable Mexicanos *and Tejanos in Texas History since 1821*

Harriett Denise Joseph

University of North Texas Press
Denton, Texas

10 9 8 7 6 5 4 3 2 1

Permissions:
University of North Texas Press
1155 Union Circle #311336
Denton, TX 76203-5017

The paper used in this book meets the minimum requirements of
the American National Standard for Permanence of Paper for Printed
Library Materials, z39.48.1984. Binding materials have been chosen
for durability.

Library of Congress Cataloging-in-Publication Data

Joseph, Harriett Denise, author
From Santa Anna to Selena : notable Mexicanos and Tejanos in Texas
history since 1821 / Harriett Denise Joseph.
pages cm
Includes index.
ISBN-13 978-1-57441-715-9 (cloth : alk. paper)
ISBN-13 978-1-57441-723-4 (ebook)
1. Texas—Biography. 2. Mexico—Biography. 3. Texas—History—19th
century. 4. Texas—History—20th century. 5. Mexicans—Texas—
Biography. 6. Mexicans—Texas—History. 7. Mexican Americans—
Texas—Biography. 8. Mexican Americans—Texas—History.

F385 .J67 2018
976.4/0046872—dc23
2017051198

The electronic edition of this book was made possible
by the support of the Vick Family Foundation.
Typeset by vPrompt eServices.

Dedication

This book is dedicated to Marilyn Payne and Donald Chipman, who inspired my career, and to Lindsey Nicole, Eldee, Simi, Aron, and Hillary, who inspire my life.

Contents

Preface vii

Acknowledgments xi

Introduction 1

1. Antonio López de Santa Anna
    Napoleon of the West 13

2. Erasmo and Juan N. Seguín
    Mexicans or Texans? 53

3. Juan Nepomuceno Cortina
    Crusader or Criminal? 93

4. Adina De Zavala
    The Angel of the Alamo 131

5. Emma Tenayuca
    Passionate Labor Activist 169

6. Jovita González and Edmundo E. Mireles
    Gente Decente 209

7. Raul "Roy" Pérez Benavidez
    The Mean Mexican 245

8. Irma Lerma Rangel
    Latina Legislator 285

9. Selena
    The Tragic Tejana 325

Conclusion 365

Glossary 379

Index 381

Preface

THIS BOOK IS THE result of an evolutionary process that began with two works co-authored with Dr. Donald E. Chipman: *Notable Men and Women of Spanish Texas, 1519–1821 (1999) and Explorers and Settlers of Spanish Texas, 1519–1821* (2001). The first was an award-winning publication with scholarly vocabulary and ample documentation. The latter was designed for secondary students and their teachers with simpler language and no citations. Both volumes used biography as a vehicle to present the history of Texas during the Spanish colonial period, as well as illuminate the roles played by noteworthy men and women during those centuries.

As originally conceived, the current work was intended as a sequel to *Explorers and Settlers of Spanish Texas.* Through the study of carefully selected biographies, middle and secondary school students would learn about important events that occurred in Texas after Mexico declared its independence in 1821. In the process, they would also gain a greater understanding of the critical role that certain Mexicans and Mexican Americans have played in the history of the Lone Star State.

After the project was well underway, valued friend and experienced editor Theresa May suggested that I rethink my target audience. She saw potential for a supplemental college reader for courses in Texas History and Mexican-American Studies. After carefully considering this advice, I redefined the project to produce a manuscript not only for college students but also for the general public. The writing level became a compromise between the extremes of *Notable Men and Women* and *Explorers and Settlers.* Information was presented as clearly as possible, while assuming that the reader had limited prior knowledge of Texas—or Mexican or United

States or Mexican American—history. While still lacking footnotes or endnotes, each chapter would conclude with a bibliographical commentary. Although chapters were designed to stand alone, the whole would be greater than the sum of its parts.

As the revised version was finally nearing completion, the University of North Texas Press published one chapter as part of a larger anthology, *This Corner of Canaan: Essays on Texas in Honor of Randolph B. Campbell* (2013). UNT Press Director Ron Chrisman subsequently read the prospectus for the "From Santa Anna to Selena" book manuscript and indicated interest in the project; however, he advised that documentation was needed. Thus began yet another step in the lengthy process, the endeavor of providing citations for hundreds of pages of material, some of which had been researched and written years earlier. With documentation completed, the manuscript was formally submitted to UNT Press, which sent it to readers for review. After receiving favorable recommendations, Chrisman determined to publish the book on a "fast track." Even so, another eight months were required to get the volume into print by February of 2018, the intended deadline.

Taking the manuscript through the stages described above, while also meeting the demands of my position as a university professor, took much longer than anticipated when the endeavor began in the early 2000s. At that time, one could never have envisioned the events that would follow in the wake of September 11, 2001, or predicted the escalating hostility toward Latinos that have made illegal immigration an increasingly divisive political issue. Ironically, the contents of this book are more relevant now than when the project began. The time devoted to this work will be considered well-spent if it helps readers—whether college students or the general public—to become more appreciative of the contributions that *Mexicanos* (Mexicans) and Tejanos (Mexican Texans) have made to the Lone Star State and, by extension, to the United States.

Lastly, the reader might wonder why a non-Hispanic historian is writing on this topic. Decades ago, as a high school student in a small town in North Central Texas, I was inspired by a gifted Spanish teacher. From Ms. Marilyn Payne, I gained a life-long love of the Spanish language and the people who speak it. That love was nurtured when I was a graduate student in Latin American history at the University of North Texas (then North Texas State University) by my major professor, Dr. Donald Chipman. Thanks in large part to the influence of these two people and to having lived on the Mexican border for more than forty years, *en mi alma soy Mexicana* (in my soul I am a Mexican).

Acknowledgments

WORKLOAD DEMANDS AND MORE urgent projects delayed completion of this manuscript for more than fifteen years. That it has finally come to fruition is because of assistance provided by people and institutions too numerous to mention. However, I would like to recognize at least some of them and extend my apologies for any inadvertent omissions.

A one-semester Professional Development Leave from the University of Texas at Brownsville allowed time away from my professorial duties to initiate this project in the early 2000s. Dean Farhat Iftekharrudin was instrumental in securing that leave, and my colleagues at UTB worked even harder than usual to facilitate it. William Adams, Helmut Langerbein, and Thomas Britten, successive Chairs of the Department of History at UTB and the University of Texas Rio Grande Valley, also provided needed support. Dr. Britten recommended and Dean Walter Díaz approved a reduced teaching load for the fall of 2017 so that I could meet tight deadlines after the manuscript was accepted for publication. Thanks are also owed to the following graduate students for their computer expertise, editorial suggestions, and other assistance: Romeo Revuelta, Alix Riviere, Jordan Penner, and Evan Berg. Among undergraduate students who deserve recognition are Nicholas Poling and Daliarlene Sáenz.

Under the auspices of the Texas State Historical Association, I was awarded a Fred White Jr. Research Fellowship in 2005 for the best manuscript proposal for a book in Texas history focusing on the twentieth century. The funds helped finance research activities.

The staffs of the following repositories and entities deserve special commendations for their gracious assistance with research efforts and obtaining illustrations: The Dolph Briscoe Center for American History, the Nettie Lee Benson Latin American Collection, and the Harry Ransom Center, all housed at The University of Texas at Austin; Texas State Library and Archives Commission in Austin; the State Preservation Board in Austin; the libraries of University of Texas at Brownsville, Texas Southmost College in Brownsville, and the University of Texas Rio Grande Valley in Brownsville and Edinburg; the Brownsville Historical Association; the Mary and Jeff Bell Library Special Collections and Archives at Texas A&M-Corpus Christi; the Willis Library at the University of North Texas in Denton and the TWU Libraries Woman's Collection at Texas Woman's University, also in Denton; San Jacinto Museum of History in Harris County; South Texas Archives at the James C. Jernigan Library at Texas A&M University-Kingsville; the Alamo Complex in San Antonio; the University of Texas at San Antonio Special Collections-Institute of Texan Cultures; The Sisters of Charity of the Incarnate Word Archives and the University of the Incarnate Word in San Antonio; The Wittliff Collections at Texas State University in San Marcos; the *Monitor* in McAllen; the Hearst Corporation; and the Rare Book and Special Collections Division, Library of Congress in Washington, D.C. The family of Roy P. Benavidez generously provided a photograph from their parents' wedding album, and Jerry Thompson of Texas A&M International University in Laredo assisted in locating Juan Cortina images.

Many people associated with the above institutions took time from their busy schedules to assist on short notice with the acquisition of images to enhance this volume. Special thanks go to the following: Ann Hodges, Nathan Lambrecht, Carlos Sánchez, Kimberly Johnson, Shelia Bickle, Tom Shelton, Carlos Cortez, Lori Atkins, Richard Bruce Winders, Ernesto Rodriguez III, Melissa Rucker, Aryn Glazier, Susanna Sharpe, Dylan Joy, Tara Putegnat, Jason Walker, David Parsons, Thomas Hatfield, Katie Salzmann, Lisa Struthers, Ali James, and Laura McLemore.

Although considerable archival research has gone into this endeavor, the book would not have been possible without ideas and information gathered from numerous secondary works in print, as well as various sources on the internet. They are credited in chapter endnotes and bibliographical commentaries. For those contributions, I am also grateful.

Alix Reviere and Jordan Penner served as co-authors of a briefer version of the chapter in this volume that profiles Edmundo Mireles and Jovita González Mireles. It was published by the University of North Texas Press in *This Corner of Canaan: Essays in Tribute to Randolph B. Campbell* (2013). When the prospectus for "From Santa Anna to Selena" subsequently was presented to Ron Chrisman, Director of UNT Press, he expressed strong interest in the project. Throughout the process, his enthusiasm has been key to this work appearing in print. Thank you to the readers to whom the press sent the manuscript for their favorable recommendations for publication. Special credit goes to the press's Assistant Director Karen Devinney, whose editorial expertise and astute observations contributed significantly to the quality of the finished product. The energetic efforts of Marketing Manager Elizabeth Whitby also deserve commendation.

A number of individuals took time from their busy schedules to read all or part of this work while it was in progress. Warmest appreciation goes to my former co-author and longtime mentor, Donald Chipman. He read the entire manuscript, gave critical input, and was unfailingly supportive. Dr. Carlos Blanton of Texas A&M University at College Station provided input on an early version of the Jovita Gónzalez/Edmundo Mireles chapter. Lamberto Álvarez of Denton, Texas, helped me to avoid some pitfalls in the Selena chapter. Andrés Tijerina of Austin Community College provided firsthand information on Tejano Monument, Inc. and the Tejano Monument. Also, my dear friend Yacov Yaacobi, who is a relative newcomer to Texas with an interest in history, served as a guinea pig to read the entire manuscript for clarity and caught some typographical errors in the process.

As explained in the Preface, Theresa J. May's suggestions played a pivotal role in determining the final form of this manuscript. Because of her astute advice, this is a different book than originally envisioned and, hopefully, a better one.

Without the efforts of my daughter, Lindsey Nicole Stephens, meeting the deadlines for this manuscript would not have been possible. She not only helped with locating illustrations, securing permissions, and compiling the index but also provided critical organizational and technical expertise. My grandchildren, Simi and Aron, also helped as needed and proved patient when I had to work instead of spend time with them.

The individuals mentioned above made valuable contributions to this book, but they bear no blame for any omissions, weaknesses, and errors in the final product.

Introduction

IN *GONE TO TEXAS: A History of the Lone Star State*, respected historian Randolph B. Campbell wrote that from prehistoric times to the twenty-first century, "the peopling of Texas by immigrants has never ceased." He also noted that these diverse waves of peoples have often found themselves in conflict with each other.[1] Events in the Lone Star State today seem to support Professor Campbell's thesis. Texans who feel threatened by the changing face of their state with its growing Hispanic population are vocal about the failure of many Latinos to assimilate. They view the immigrant population as a drain on Texas's resources and advocate sealing the borders to stop illegal immigration. Even a cursory look at Texas history reveals the irony of these attitudes.

Although Texas was part of the Spanish empire for centuries before Mexico declared independence in 1821, relatively few Spaniards had immigrated there during the colonial period. The opportunities offered by the Aztec empire in Central Mexico and the Inca empire in South America proved more enticing, as did other areas where mineral wealth was discovered. The Spanish crown tended to consider Texas a low priority except on those occasions when it perceived its claim to the remote borderlands province to be in jeopardy. Consequently, much of the present Lone Star State remained unsettled by Spaniards and underdeveloped by their standards, even though they left impressive legacies that endure to the present.[2]

Hoping to tap into Texas's potential and strengthen its hold on the region, the Mexican government decided to allow foreigners to immigrate into the area in the early nineteenth century. If they agreed to become Mexican citizens and Roman Catholics, aliens were not only welcomed but also were offered generous land grants and other incentives. A depressed economy in the United States drew so many land-hungry Anglo Americans—many of whom came legally, but certainly not all—that they soon outnumbered Tejanos (Mexican Texans).

The rapid increase in Texas's Anglo-American population created alarm in Mexico, as the newcomers drew criticism for not assimilating. Rather than adopting the Mexican way of life, the immigrants continued to speak English; they lived much as they had in the United States; they paid only lip service to Catholicism; and they considered themselves superior to the darker-skinned Mexicans.[3] Also causing strains were the strongly held opinions of the Texians (Anglo Texans) about the desirability of democratic government, the sanctity of constitutional rights, and the need for African-American slavery—issues that were controversial in Mexico. These factors, combined with political instability in Mexico caused in part by the manipulations and ambitions of Antonio López de Santa Anna, led to rebellion in Texas by the mid-1830s. Some Tejanos joined with the Texians in what ultimately became an independence movement. After gaining military victory, Texas functioned as a republic for about a decade, despite Mexico's refusal to recognize the independence of its former possession.

When Texas was annexed to the United States late in 1845 with claims of the Rio Grande as the boundary, Texians once again were part of their country of origin, a highly suitable resolution for almost all of them. For Tejanos, however, being residents of the Lone Star State proved less than satisfactory. Even those who had supported independence could find their loyalty in question and themselves subjects of discrimination because of their ethnicity. The advent of war between the United States and Mexico in 1846, triggered in part by Texas's annexation and a resultant boundary dispute, only served to worsen the situation. Within two years, a defeated Mexico was forced to accept the Rio Grande as the permanent international boundary and to surrender about half of her national territory to the United States. The dominance of Anglo Americans in Texas was assured, as was the second-class status of most of the Tejano population in the state.

To say that the lives of Mexicans and Mexican Americans in Texas after the war proved difficult is an understatement. Those who owned land grants from the Spanish period faced dispossession through a variety of legal, and less-than-legal, tactics. To maintain ownership of even a portion of their ancestral lands was a victory of sorts. Less tangible losses only added to their alienation, which at times led to violent resistance, a case in point being Juan Nepomuceno Cortina, the subject of one of the chapters in this book.

Since the mid-nineteenth century, the majority of *Mexicanos* and Tejanos have been welcome in the Lone Star State—and in the United States—primarily when cheap labor has been in demand. Even under those circumstances, they historically have been exploited and underappreciated. Worse, when the country has experienced economic hardship, as in the Great Depression, Latinos have been shunned by other workers as competitors for scarce jobs. For example, the United States government "from 1929 to 1939 forcibly expelled 469,000 Mexican citizens," as well as some Mexican-Americans, only to put out "the welcome mat" again when World War II caused a labor shortage in the nation.[4] Whatever the situation at any given time, however, their status as a minority has allowed the Anglo majority to have a sense of dominance, superiority, and security.

A new dynamic has come into play in the late twentieth and early twenty-first centuries. As the number of Hispanics in Texas and other parts of the country has grown to previously unheard-of proportions—a trend projected to continue—many Anglos feel threatened. With the traditional majority facing the prospect of becoming a minority, a sense of urgency to stop the "flood" of immigrants has emerged. Much of the hostility evident today is directed toward the more than eleven million of them who are undocumented, as clearly demonstrated in the presidential campaigns in 2016. However, Latinos in general are feeling the weight of increased prejudice based on their ethnicity. In this emotional environment, the fact that people of Hispanic ancestry have been in Texas for almost five centuries and have good reason to consider it their home is often overlooked.

That Mexicans and Tejanos have played a significant role in Texas history before and since the state became part of the United States is beyond dispute. What is being heavily debated is whether their role has been—and is—a positive or a negative one. Ironically, present-day Latinos in the Lone Star State are being criticized for many of the same reasons that Anglo immigrants to Texas were considered suspect during the Mexican period: for not learning to speak the language, for maintaining ties to their country of origin, and for failing to assimilate. Their many contributions are often ignored in this heated discussion.

This volume uses the lives of eleven Mexicans and Mexican Texans to illustrate the importance of these groups in Texas history. To a degree, the decision as to which notables to profile was arbitrary, as countless people were deserving of inclusion. However, limitations of time and space necessitated difficult choices such as the determination that no one still living would be considered. These particular men and women were selected in part for chronological reasons, because their stories collectively cover the period of almost two hundred years since Mexico gained independence from Spain. Achieving gender balance was also a guiding principle, as was introducing major issues in Texas and Mexican-American history through the vehicle of biography. Additional thought was given to the degree to which ethnicity informed and influenced each person's life, as well as the ways in which they responded to their circumstances. The result was the selection of six males and five females whose biographies were deemed particularly compelling and illuminating. They are a varied group, ranging from an infamous Mexican president to an iconic Tejana singer. With one— or possibly two—exceptions, they are sterling examples of the ways in which ethnic diversity has enriched the Lone Star State.

The most notable exception is Antonio López de Santa Anna, one of the most hated Mexicans in Texas history. Readers might wonder why the first chapter in this book is devoted to a man infamous for his brutality as commander of the Mexican army during the Texas Revolution. That hundreds died at his hands at the Alamo or upon his orders at Goliad is only part of his story, however. As the most powerful figure in Mexico from the 1830s to the 1850s, Santa Anna's impact on Texas history cannot be ignored. His actions helped to trigger Texas's war for independence, unintentionally helped the Texas army to attain victory, had negative repercussions for Tejanos, and contributed to the Rio Grande becoming the international boundary. While less than noble, this self-styled Napoleon of the West helped determine the fate of the Lone Star State during his lifetime and beyond.

In stark contrast to Santa Anna are Erasmo and Juan Seguín, a prominent father and son who befriended Anglos settling in Texas in the early nineteenth century. The Seguíns provided needed expertise and assistance to newcomers such as Stephen F. Austin and Sam Houston before, during, and after the Texas Revolution. In the process, they were labeled traitors by many of their countrymen in Mexico, and Juan Seguín fared little better in his subsequent dealings with the Texians. Despite distinguished military service in the revolution, being the only Tejano Senator during the period of the Republic, and holding the office of mayor of San Antonio, the younger Seguín became an object of hostility at least in part because of his ethnicity. An increasingly untenable situation compelled him to seek refuge south of the Río Grande, although he did later return to Texas. Certainly, Juan Seguín deserved better treatment during his lifetime than he received from his fellow Texans, an omission now being rectified by reinstating the long overdue title of hero.

Certainly, one of the most controversial men covered in these pages is Juan Nepomuceno Cortina. Involved in critical events on both sides of the Rio Grande for decades in the 1800s, he was hailed by many Mexicans and Tejanos as a crusader fighting for rights and justice for the oppressed. That he broke numerous laws and terrorized the border region in the course of his "crusades" gained him bitter enemies, especially among Anglos whom he condemned as oppressors. Many Anglo Americans despised Cortina and considered him a common criminal whose true intent was to enrich and empower himself. Those of his ethnicity who perceived him as a savior, however, flocked to his cause and fought by his side. Both the Texas Rangers and the United States Army were unleashed against Cortina with innocent Mexicans suffering in the process. Although subject to widely differing interpretations, the life of this complex man merits our attention.

In the following century, Mexican-born Edmundo E. Mireles waged a different kind of crusade on behalf of Hispanics in Texas. Upset that his people, their language, and their culture were considered inferior, the educator spent decades working to change those attitudes. Committed to improving communication and understanding between Anglos and Hispanics, this exceptional man implemented a program in Corpus Christi's public schools to teach Spanish to English-speaking children. His bilingual program not only garnered praise from many quarters but also became a model for the rest of the state and nation at a critical time when the United States was working to improve relations with Latin America. Mireles, who gained renown for his educational endeavors, benefitted greatly from the support of his wife, the also exceptional Jovita González, who is discussed below.

Another Tejano who gained renown in the twentieth century was Raul "Roy" Benavidez. A belligerent youth angered by prejudice and discrimination, he seemed an unlikely candidate to become a decorated hero or role model. Enlistment in the United States army, coupled with marriage to the right woman, turned Benavidez's life around. Almost killed on two occasions during the Vietnam conflict, the Green Beret was left disabled in body but not in spirit. He later waged another battle to gain appropriate recognition of his military valor. The result was a well-deserved—though considerably belated—Congressional Medal of Honor. After gaining that prestigious honor, he engaged in still a third war to help preserve his badly needed disability benefits and those of others. Known affectionately to his military buddies as the "Mean Mexican," Benavidez displayed a type of courage on and off the battlefield that continues to serve as a source of inspiration to Texans of all ethnicities.

If Medals of Honor were given outside the arena of battle, the women depicted in the following pages would be worthy recipients. Each overcame barriers of ethnicity and gender to pursue her goals, often at a heavy personal price. Their individual and collective accomplishments are truly notable.

Adina De Zavala, whose grandfather Lorenzo de Zavala had served as first vice-president of the Republic of Texas, took pride in her Irish-Spanish ancestry and benefitted from her respected surname. She dedicated her long life (1861-1955) to teaching, publicizing, and preserving the history of the Lone Star State, with special appreciation for its Hispanic heritage. Founder of important organizations in which she assumed a role of leadership, De Zavala demonstrated extraordinary commitment to pursuing goals she deemed worthwhile. Without her fearless efforts, the Alamo—Texas's most visited, albeit controversial, historical site—would almost certainly have been destroyed by commercial interests in San Antonio. Embracing a variety of causes, the "Angel of the

Alamo" battled stronger, wealthier opponents with a determination that did not always insure victory but proved her a worthy successor to her esteemed ancestor.

Another San Antonian, Emma Tenayuca, likewise threw herself into the fray for causes in which she believed. At an unusually early age, she became aware of the exploitation of the working classes by more powerful groups. Not one to be a bystander, the activist embraced radical political movements in her efforts to help labor in the early twentieth century. As she herself later observed, her decisions were not always wise, but her commitment was never in doubt. Whether making speeches to inspire striking workers, walking in a picket line, or going to jail for her beliefs, Tenayuca exhibited courage rare in someone so young. That "the Passionate One" suffered serious consequences because of her activism makes her story even more compelling.

One of the *"gente decente"* (a person of good breeding),[5] Jovita González Mireles used the written word, rather than the picket line, to express passion for her people. Aware that a way of life in South Texas was being lost in the name of so-called progress, González dedicated herself to preserving the folklore of the common people of the border region. A gifted student at The University of Texas and a respected member of the Texas Folklore Society, this Tejana struggled for recognition in a white, male-dominated environment. To survive, she had to learn when to speak and when to submit. These lessons followed her into her marriage to the accomplished Edmundo Mireles, even though she became his companion in their struggle to achieve mutual objectives. Only after her death in 1983 did the contributions of this talented folklorist and author become fully appreciated and extolled.

Irma Rangel enjoyed greater opportunities than Jovita González, in part because she was born in a more enlightened time. After receiving a law degree and working as an attorney, she became the first Latina elected to the Texas House of Representatives, where she served from 1977–2003. Achieving many other "firsts," this member of the Texas Hall of Fame paved the way for others of her ethnicity and gender. Her impact was not limited to Hispanics or women, however. The legislator understood that education, especially at the college and university level, was the key to betterment for all Texans. She worked tirelessly to remove obstacles placed in the path of minorities and to make educational opportunities available to everyone. Her recurring personal battles against cancer did not stop this courageous woman from fighting the good fight on behalf of the people in the Lone Star State.

Fame, not cancer, cost the famous Selena Quintanilla-Pérez her life at a tragically young age. Possibly propelled by the aspirations of her father, who was also her manager, this twentieth-century Tejana spent much of her childhood rehearsing and singing with the family band. Her curious combination of sensuality and wholesomeness led the talented Latina to achieve success, adoration, and awards on both sides of the border. She helped bring a new kind of recognition, as well as respectability, to Tejano music, while instilling pride in Latinos in the process. The price she paid for acclaim proved dear, however, when it led to her murder by "friend" and fan Yolanda Saldívar. Mourned by people throughout the world, Selena became an exploitable commodity in death but achieved a kind of immortality in the process. The endurance of her celebrity and influence is truly remarkable.

For reasons that will be explored, interesting comparisons can be made between the marital situations of the above women and their male counterparts. Finding a suitable mate proved difficult for some of these strong females, and those who did wed faced challenges in maintaining satisfactory relationships. However, all six men were married, some more than once, and they generally benefitted personally, professionally, and/or financially from those unions.

Tragedy and triumph, brutality and heroism, success and failure—all can be found in the lives of the eleven notables profiled in these pages. Even those who were less-than-heroic—a minority within this minority—helped shape the Lone Star State. Their stories remind us that *Mexicanos* and Tejanos, like other waves of immigrants through the centuries, have earned their place in the pages of Texas history.

Bibliographical Commentary

For a single volume that covers the history of Spanish Texas prior to 1821, see Donald E. Chipman and Harriett Denise Joseph, *Spanish Texas, 1519–1821*, rev. ed. (2010). Two works by these same co-authors that provide biographical chapters on select figures from the colonial period are the following: *Notable Men and Women of Spanish Texas, 1519–1821* (1999) and *Explorers and Settlers of Spanish Texas, 1519–1821* (2001). The latter is designed for secondary school students and teachers.

For those wishing to learn more about Texas history, several texts are available. Among these are Randolph B. Campbell, *Gone to Texas: A History of the Lone Star State*, 3rd ed. (2017); Robert A. Calvert, Arnoldo de León, and Gregg Cantrell, *The History of Texas*, 5th ed. (2014); Rupert N. Richardson, et al., *Texas: The Lone Star State* (2010); and the thematically arranged *Texas: Crossroads of North America*, 2nd ed. (2015) by Jesús F. de la Teja, Ron Tyler, and Nancy Beck Young. Because the histories of Texas and Mexico are intertwined, the interested reader can consult one of the following: Michael C. Meyer, William L. Sherman, and Susan M. Deeds, *The Course of Mexican History*, 10th ed. (2014); William H. Beezley and Colin M. MacLachlan, *Mexico: The Essentials* (2015); and Philip Russell, *The Essential History of Mexico* (2015)

General works on Mexican Americans in Texas history include the following: Arnoldo de León, *Mexican Americans in Texas: A Brief History*, 3rd ed. (2009) and Phyllis McKenzie, *Mexican Texans* (2004). *Mexican Americans in Texas History* (2000), edited by Emilio Zamora, Cynthia Orozco, and Rodolfo Rocha, offers essays by various scholars on select topics.

Endnotes

1. Randolph B. Campbell, *Gone to Texas: A History of the Lone Star State* (New York: Oxford University Press, 2003), Preface, ix, quotation.

2. See "The Legacies of Spanish Texas," in Donald E. Chipman and Harriett Denise Joseph, *Spanish Texas, 1519–1821*, rev. ed. (Austin: University of Texas Press, 2010), 256–276.

3. See Arnoldo de León, *They Called Them Greasers: Anglo Attitudes toward Mexicans in Texas, 1821–1900* (Austin: University of Texas Press, 1983).

4. Douglas S. Massey, "Social Sciences: Immigration Statistics for the 21ˢᵗ Century," *The Annals of American Academy of Political and Social Science* 631 (1): 137–139, 1ˢᵗ quotation on 137–138, 2ⁿᵈ quotation on 138. [Sage Publications, Inc. American Academy of Political and Social Science]: 124–140, http:ezhost. utrgv.edu:2110/stable/20744015. Deportees included Mexican Americans as well as Mexican nationals. According to some estimates, as many as one million Mexicans and Mexican Americans in total left the United States by force or voluntarily during the Great Depression. See "INS Records for 1930s Mexican Repatriations," posted March 3, 2014, U.S. Citizenship and Immigration Services, on the official website of the Department for Homeland Security, https://www. uscis.gov/history-and-genealogy/our-history/historians-mailbox/ins-records-1930s-mexican-repatriations.

5. The term "*Gente Decente*" is taken from Leticia Magda Garza-Falcón's *Borderlands Response to the Rhetoric of Dominance* (Austin: University of Texas Press, 1998) and translates as "people of good breeding."

EL ESCMO Sᴿ Gᴬᴸ DE DIVISION D. ANTONIO LOPEZ DE SANTA ANNA.

Presidente de la Republica Mexicana.

El Eccmo. Señor General de División D. Antonio López de Santa Anna
(*His Excellency General of Division Don Antonio López de Santa Anna*),
lithograph by Maurin. San Jacinto Museum of History.

Antonio López de Santa Anna

Napoleon of the West

"FATE HAS DESIRED THAT my history be the history of Mexico since 1821."[1] These words, spoken in the nineteenth century by Antonio López de Santa Anna, accurately describe his role in Mexican history from the 1820s to the 1850s. He was in and out of the office of president numerous times, often exercised command of the Mexican army, and had a major impact on his homeland. Because Texas was so closely tied to Mexico during that era, Santa Anna also helped to shape the fate of the future Lone Star State.

When Mexico declared independence from Spain in 1821, Texas was part of the new nation. Just fifteen years later, Texans successfully fought for their own independence and created a republic that was annexed to the United States in the mid-1840s. Annexation helped trigger a war between the United States and Mexico, which had refused to recognize Texas's independence. In 1848, a defeated Mexico surrendered claims to the Lone Star State, along with significant additional territory. Although Santa Anna spent little time on Texas soil, he played a critical role in all of these events. In the process, he became one of the most despised figures in Texas history.

What did the self-proclaimed "Napoleon of the West," who modeled himself on the French Emperor Napoleon Bonaparte, do to earn the hatred of so many Anglo and Mexican Texans of his generation?[2] Why in the twenty-first century do so many people on both sides of the border still curse Santa Anna's name? Does he deserve the negative image with which he has been portrayed in books and movies? An examination of Santa Anna's life provides insights into these and other questions about arguably the most important Mexican in the history of nineteenth-century Texas.

***

Antonio López de Santa Anna was born to Manuela Pérez de Lebrón in Jalapa, Vera Cruz, Mexico, in 1794, and given his father's name. The family was *criollo*, Spaniards claiming to be pure blooded but born in the New World, which conferred favored status. Nevertheless, top positions in the Americas were reserved for *peninsulares*, those of pure blood born in Spain. Criollos not only enjoyed fewer opportunities but also were viewed as less trustworthy by the Spanish Crown. During Antonio's youth, the Spanish empire was the scene of growing unrest with criollos resenting their second-class status, and other groups disaffected by centuries of exploitation by Spaniards, regardless of their birthplace.[3]

Events in the mother country ignited the flames of rebellion in the early 1800s, when Napoleon Bonaparte of France placed his brother Joseph on the Spanish throne. Loyal Spaniards revolted in both the mother country and the American empire to restore the crown to King Ferdinand VII, whom they considered the legitimate monarch. The American rebellions became complicated by internal power struggles, as some criollos began to talk of independence. Coming to manhood during these turbulent times, Santa Anna faced a difficult decision. Should he defend Spanish rule as a royalist or join the insurgents in their resistance?[4] Demonstrating loyalty to the mother country, the young criollo chose a military career. In 1810, the same year that an unsuccessful uprising headed by Father Miguel Hidalgo erupted in Mexico, sixteen-year-old Santa Anna joined the Spanish army at Vera Cruz as a "gentleman cadet" in a prestigious regiment. Wounded in action in 1811, he was commended for his valor. Promotions followed. By age eighteen with eight military encounters to his credit, the young man attained the rank of lieutenant.[5]

In 1812, the Spanish province of Texas was invaded by filibusters (military adventurers) calling themselves the Republican Army of the North. The leaders were an unlikely pair: Mexican liberal Bernardo Gutiérrez de Lara and former United States military officer, Augustus Magee. The Republican Army managed to conquer the province, and Gutíerrez de Lara declared its independence in 1813. Commandant General Joaquín de Arredondo, under whom Santa Anna served, assumed the mandate of crushing the invaders and became known as "The Butcher" in the process. On August 18, 1813, Arredondo's royalist forces defeated the invaders at the Battle of Medina River, the bloodiest engagement in Texas history. Thirteen of every fourteen rebels were killed during the fighting or executed after being taken prisoner.[6]

Arredondo faulted Texans for not opposing the filibuster movement. At San Antonio de Béxar he executed forty men as suspected insurgents or collaborators. Women and children fared little better with eight dying as a result of mistreatment and others left homeless. Young Santa Anna considered the Butcher's brutal tactics to be an effective response to insurrection. Given the opportunity, he, too, would show no mercy to his enemies. Santa Anna also emerged from this campaign convinced that "the accursed Americans" were not very capable fighters, a miscalculation that would cost him and Mexico dearly in later years.[7]

Another miscalculation was forging the signatures of his superiors, including General Arredondo, to help cover gambling debts. Although Santa Anna made restitution, his reputation suffered. Nevertheless, the young man was captivated by military life, began to wear his hair in the style of Emperor Napoleon Bonaparte of France, and similarly preferred to ride a white horse. Contemporaries described don Antonio as "impulsive, quarrelsome, courageous, disobedient, energetic, despotic, talented, impetuous, arrogant, and good looking."

His ego was fed by honors from the Crown, including "the Shield of Honor and Certificate of the Royal and Distinguished Order of Isabella the Catholic." In 1821, Santa Anna, while still in his twenties, achieved the rank of brevet lieutenant colonel.[8]

That year, another royalist officer, Agustín de Iturbide, betrayed Spain by allying with rebel leader Vicente Guerrero to declare Mexican independence under the Plan of Iguala, which offered something to everyone. The proposed new nation would be governed under a constitutional monarchy; only the Roman Catholic faith would be allowed; and no one "would be discriminated against or persecuted on the grounds that they were Spaniards, castas [mixed race], or Indians." The movement held special appeal for criollos because of turbulent events in Spain that had undermined faith in legitimate authority of the monarch to rule and imposed significant reforms threatening to Mexican conservatives. Iturbide skillfully gained support from Catholic Church leaders, military officers, and large landowners, among others.[9]

Santa Anna cast his lot with the insurrectionists, possibly tempted by the offers of promotion to brigadier general and command at Vera Cruz; however, he later insisted that patriotism motivated his decision. Regardless, his support proved critical to the rebels, "because he was their most effective field commander along the critical route between Vera Cruz and Jalapa." By the early 1820s the young officer was only one of many former royalists who determined that "independence was a viable and desirable option."[10] This would prove the first, but certainly not the last, time that Santa Anna would change allegiance, at least in part to serve his own agenda.

Although initially honored by Iturbide, Santa Anna did not receive the expected promotion and was soon replaced as governor of Vera Cruz. Alienating his subordinate proved a serious miscalculation on Iturbide's part but was only one of many problems plaguing the infant nation. Mexico's economy was in shambles,

the political system was unstable, and most people were unedu-
cated and poor. Over time the independence movement splintered
into factions with "internal struggles between liberals and conservatives, between republicans and monarchists, between federalists
and centralists" that would plague the young nation. Serious divi-
sions existed even within these groups, and their "political ideas—
including those of Santa Anna and his supporters—evolved over
the years as conditions changed."[11] After three centuries of absolutist rule by Spanish monarchs, Mexicans seemed ill-prepared for
self-government.

As individuals and groups vied for power, Iturbide emerged as
emperor in 1822, and Santa Anna threatened to resign his commission unless given military and political command at Vera Cruz.
The emperor granted those appointments, as well as a promotion to
brigadier general. Santa Anna consequently pledged his support
to "immortal Iturbide as Emperor." Less than six months later, a
distrustful Iturbide removed don Antonio from command. As for
the new brigadier general, Santa Anna was increasingly disillusioned
by Iturbide's absolutist rule.[12]

Late in 1822, Santa Anna issued the Plan of Vera Cruz, which
called for the drafting of a constitution based on the principles of
religion, independence, and union. (In this case, religion meant
that only the Catholic faith would be tolerated, continuing the
practice of the colonial period.) Iturbide threw powerful military
forces against the insurgents, and by year's end, the rebel cause
was in jeopardy until the Plan of Casa Mata reversed the situation.
Issued by others, the new pronouncement received support from
Santa Anna, led to the overthrow of the empire, and forced Iturbide
to abdicate in March of 1823. Significantly, don Antonio insisted
"that he was . . . 'the first to proclaim the Republic.'"[13]

This began an unfortunate pattern in which an existing Mexican
government would be overthrown through military force. The stage
was set for trouble, and trouble was what Mexico experienced for

most of nineteenth century. Suffering from civil wars and foreign invasions, the country desperately needed good leadership. For better or worse, what it got was Antonio López de Santa Anna. Only twenty-nine years old in 1823, "he was little more than just another ambitious high-ranking officer at the time." Nevertheless, he would soon gain dominance.[14]

After brief service in Yucatán, Santa Anna returned to Vera Cruz. In 1825, he entered into marriage by proxy with fourteen-year-old Inés García, who came from an affluent Spanish family. "Interested in the financial benefits of the alliance," he used her dowry to acquire a landed estate called *Manga de Clavo* (Clove Spike) that became "a launching pad for revolutions and a refuge" when needed. She managed the estate during don Antonio's absences, and the couple had several children before doña Inés died in her early thirties. Meanwhile, Santa Anna increased his holdings in Vera Cruz and became a major employer in the region. Gambling and cockfighting were among his preferred distractions, as were having amorous affairs and fathering illegitimate children.[15]

Although based in Vera Cruz, Santa Anna did not lose sight of national affairs. Unhappy with the outcome of a presidential election in the late 1820s, he joined with others to place someone more to their liking in the executive office. As a reward, the new president promoted Santa Anna to General of Division, the highest rank in the Mexican army. The *caudillo* (strong man) was also restored as acting governor and military commander of Vera Cruz. That command was soon tested. A long-feared Spanish invasion came in July 1829, with the new general demonstrating impressive abilities to organize local forces, acquire necessary funds, and gather needed supplies. Aided by an epidemic that weakened Spanish forces, Santa Anna received their surrender at Tampico, a victory that forced Spain to accept the reality of Mexican independence. Hailed as a hero, he was credited with "saving the honor of the nation." Don Antonio was transformed "into a living legend."[16]

When Conservatives seized control in 1830, Santa Anna recognized the new government. However, when Centralist domination triggered Federalist revolts, he organized an army to support the insurrection. Victory virtually guaranteed that the hero of Tampico would be elected president in 1833, "although he was below the required age for the office." Rules, constitutional or otherwise, meant little to him, as would become evident. Indeed, the traditional view of the Napoleon of the West is that of an "opportunistic turncoat who changed sides according to necessity." He would be in and out of office many times, and his ability to rebound after failure proved truly remarkable. He became the strong man of Mexican politics for decades. Accordingly, some historians have labeled the period of Mexican history from the 1820s to the 1850s as the Age of Santa Anna.[17]

While Santa Anna was on the ascent in Mexico, significant events were occurring on that country's northern frontier. For centuries Spanish Texas had remained sparsely populated with limited appeal for colonists living to the south. Also, the filibuster invasions of the early 1800s, combined with Joaquín de Arredondo's brutal retaliation, had proven particularly devastating. By 1821, the province "had a non-Indian population of less than 3,000—fewer than the 3,103 reported in the first census of 1777."[18]

During the last decades of the Spanish empire, settlers from the United States had begun illegally infiltrating into East Texas. By adopting a policy allowing for legal immigration, leaders of the newly independent Mexican nation hoped to gain control over the newcomers, while also promoting progress and productivity in the borderlands. Settlers who agreed to become Mexican citizens and Roman Catholics could receive large land grants at low cost with arrangements usually handled by colonization agents, called *empresarios*. By far, the most effective of these was Stephen F. Austin of the Missouri Territory, who brought hundreds and hundreds of Anglo families into Texas in the 1820s and 1830s.[19]

Indeed, Anglo-American colonization proved too successful from Mexico's perspective. By the late 1820s officials faced the reality that Anglos greatly outnumbered Mexicans in Texas. Most of these immigrants came from the Southern United States, where the economy relied heavily on cotton agriculture and slave labor. Slave owners brought their human property with them, even though black servitude was under attack in Mexico. The new settlers, called Texians, differed from the Tejanos (Mexican Texans) in significant ways. Anglo Americans had a different appearance, language, attitudes, religious beliefs, and historical experience. Significantly, these white colonists considered themselves superior to the darker-skinned inhabitants of Texas whom they viewed as less civilized. Also, Texas's geographical isolation prevented the immigrants from having to assimilate to the degree expected, which alarmed the Mexican government.[20]

Ironically, steps to gain greater control over Texas had the opposite effect. In 1829, President Vicente Guerrero issued an order "declaring immediate emancipation everywhere in the republic." Opposition by Stephen F. Austin and others to the proclamation prevented its enforcement in Texas. However, legislation aimed at stopping further Anglo-American immigration, as well as the introduction of more slaves into Texas, became law on April 6, 1830. Colonists were also upset by increased Mexican military presence in their midst and the government's intent to collect import duties on trade. In 1832, some Texans rebelled against a specific official for allegedly abusing his power, but Mexican officials feared that the revolt was a precursor to independence.[21]

Civil war was consuming the heartland of Mexico, as previously noted. In 1832, Texians declared their support for the Federalists, who advocated a republican form of government under the Mexican Constitution of 1824—the cause for which Santa Anna was fighting. Following the overthrow of the Centralist government, don Antonio was elected president in March 1833.

Optimistic Texans prepared a new petition that addressed critical issues such as their desire for separate statehood. Under Mexico's Constitution of 1824, Texas and Coahuila had been combined as a single state. Frustrated at having minimal representation in a distant capital, the petitioners drafted a proposed state constitution. They also asked for renewed Anglo-American immigration.[22] (See Chapter 2 for more detailed information about the creation of the state of Coahuila-Texas.)

In April 1833, Stephen F. Austin headed to Mexico City with the petition, but Santa Anna was absent when the *empresario* arrived. Rather than taking the oath of office, the Mexican leader had instructed his extremist Vice-President Valentín Gómez Farías to assume power. The caudillo himself "did not actually serve as president for more than a few months" from 1833–1836. This began a pattern by the Napoleon of the West of being elected or imposed as president but spending little time in office. While desiring power, he seemingly did not enjoy the day-to-day details of running the country. As a man of action, Santa Anna preferred "to be leading his soldiers into battle rather than waiting idly among the comforts of Mexico City."[23]

The new central government with which Austin dealt was dominated by "radicals, of all shades of liberal opinion from moderate to extreme," with major reforms being espoused. The changes under consideration would almost certainly benefit the Mexican populace, but threatened traditional privileges of "the Church and army, the two most powerful groups in the country." Santa Anna recognized that attempts at rapid change might provoke rebellion. Feigning ill health, he retired to *Manga de Clavo* to distance himself from events in the capital.[24]

Austin's dealings with officials in Mexico City "presented frustratingly mixed signals." That he was stricken by cholera when the disease reached the capital only added to his woes. Politically at least, the situation improved somewhat on those occasions when

Santa Anna chose to make an appearance in the capital. Eventually, he agreed to some of the Texans' requests, most significantly renewed Anglo American immigration—a concession that would cause "emigration from the United States to reach flood proportions." Also, these settlers would be allowed to use the English language and enjoy the benefit of trial by jury. However, distrust of Anglos was too pervasive to allow them separate statehood. Texas must remain joined with Coahuila.[25]

On December 10, 1833, Austin began the lengthy journey back to Texas. En route, however, he was arrested because of an ill-advised letter written while still in Mexico City. In that missive, the frustrated *empresario* had proposed that Texans begin creating "a local government independent of Coahuila, even though the general government withholds its consent." Unfortunately for Austin, some local and state officials viewed the letter as treasonous, as did Gómez Farías when it was forwarded to him. On his orders, the colonizer was returned to the national capital, where he was imprisoned for almost a year without benefit of trial. Even when finally released on December 25, 1834, the Texian was confined to Mexico City until July 1835. The treatment—or mistreatment—of Austin during this period strained his proven loyalty to Mexico.[26]

Austin was not the only person with fraying loyalties. As Santa Anna had anticipated, attacks by the radical Congress against privileged groups such as the church and army were alienating large segments of the population. Fearful that Mexico might suffer the bloody chaos and class warfare unleashed by the French Revolution of 1789, "respectable" citizens were concluding that "the 1824 Constitution had failed to establish a stable, long-lasting political system suited to the needs and customs of the Mexican People." In short, federalism had proven disappointing to men of property in a country plagued by divisive provincialism, bloated bureaucracies, economic recession, and frequent rebellions. Citing his responsibility to prevent a destructive war, Santa Anna cooperated in removing his own government and calling for a Centralist constitution. In the process, he also benefitted himself, as greater power was concentrated in Mexico City. States were replaced by less autonomous units (departments) with hand-picked military officers in charge. Don Antonio's brother-in-law, Martín Perfecto de Cos, was dispatched to Texas with five hundred men to keep order but avoid antagonizing the Texans.[27]

Shocked at Santa Anna's betrayal, disgruntled Federalists took steps to restore constitutional authority. Learning of insurrection in Zacatecas, the Napoleon of the West left *Manga de Clavo* for the capital, where he received "permission to quell the rebellion in person." After inflicting a decisive defeat, he unleashed his soldiers to rape, loot, and kill. Indeed, Santa Anna was proving a worthy successor to his role model, the Butcher.[28]

By fall 1835, Texas was also on the verge of rebellion. Mexican officials feared that a small cannon in possession of the colonists at Gonzales could be turned against their troops should war erupt. Captain Francisco Castañeda was dispatched to seize the weapon. Displaying a banner that read "Come and Take It," the Texians refused to surrender the artillery piece. What happened next "resembled a shoving match more than a pitched battle[,]" and the Mexican officer withdrew his troops—without the cannon. Nevertheless, this clash at Gonzales on October 2, 1835, began the Texas Revolution, as "blood had been shed; a fatal step had been taken. There could be no turning back."[29]

Texans were divided as to the proper course of action, as were their representatives when they assembled in San Felipe in early November. Since 1832, a so-called War Party had favored forceful dealings with Mexico, while the Peace Party had advocated a more cautious course. Generally younger and single, the former tended to be composed of more recent arrivals to Texas. Usually older and married, the latter included settlers of longer duration with stronger ties to Mexico. As the Consultation convened, those present were "more or less evenly divided" between these two parties and a moderate faction. Consequently, by a vote of thirty-three to fourteen the delegates clarified that they were fighting not for independence but for the same reasons as the Zacatecans: loyalty "to the Constitution of 1824 and Mexican federalism."[30]

After the events at Gonzales, volunteers formed an army of sorts. Austin, who returned during this turbulent period, was elected as general with little open opposition and planned a siege of San Antonio. However, the *empresario* would soon head to the United States at the behest of the Consultation to solicit aid in the United States. To command the "nonexistent regular army, the delegates unanimously elected Sam Houston[,]" a former governor of Tennessee who had emigrated to Texas in 1832. His authority did not extend to volunteers, which proved unfortunate. Nevertheless, the Texans managed to force General Cos to surrender in December 1835. The Mexican officer withdrew his men to south of the Rio Grande, and as 1836 dawned, the rebels controlled Texas.[31]

Victory led to over-confidence, as many Texans mistakenly believed that the war was over. The army began to fall apart with men returning to their homes. They underestimated Santa Anna, who brooked no delay in stopping unrest from spreading and keeping Texans from involving other Americans in their defense. Preferring "the hazards of war to the seductive and sought-after life of the Palace," the caudillo determined to "lead the government forces into battle in the remote province of Texas." Neither weather nor distance would stop him from acting against the "ungrateful settlers," regardless of the cost.[32]

Because there was no money for a major military campaign, Santa Anna specified that his officers "were not to be paid but would be given the spoils of war." He promised a special medal, the Legion of Honor, to volunteers but conscripted others into military service. He borrowed thousands of pesos, at times through forced loans, while also confiscating supplies; however, his commitment extended to mortgaging part of his own property. Despite these best efforts, Santa Anna led a force of largely inexperienced men armed mainly with "rifles that dated from the War of Independence." They would be an invading force of less-than-willing soldiers operating in hostile territory. The best course of action, the Napoleon of the West concluded, would be "to have one quick, overwhelming victory that would kill the insurgency in its infancy."[33]

Arriving in San Luis Potosí in December 1835, Santa Anna ordered General Joaquín Ramírez y Sesma to head toward San Antonio to reinforce Cos, not knowing help would arrive too late. Don Antonio told his subordinate that "the Texians had 'audiciously declared a war of extermination to the Mexicans,'" and "should be treated in the same manner." In an interesting twist, Santa Anna's second-in-command was General Vicente Filisola, himself an *empresario* well-known in Texas. After arriving in Saltillo, the Napoleon of the West sent Filisola ahead with orders to assume command of all Mexican troops at and around San Antonio de Béxar. However, "Santa Anna himself wished to be present at the decisive battle[,]" because military victory translated into popularity and power.[34]

As the year ended, Santa Anna marched northward from San Luis Potosí to Texas with more than six thousand men, as well as 2,500 women and children. The *soldaderas* (female soldiers) included wives, cooks, and nurses. During the brutal journey, people and animals died from starvation, disease, cold, and snow-storms. Their commander has been accused of not caring about the casualties, but he "led from the front . . . and thus inspired confidence in his men."[35]

As the Mexican army advanced, James Bowie was sent with a small force to assist James Neill, commander at San Antonio de Béxar. Even so, Sam Houston seemingly did not consider the town defensible. By the time Bowie arrived in mid-January 1836, however, Neill had improved San Antonio's defenses. Possessing hundreds of Mexican muskets, thousands of rounds of ammunition, and a number of Mexican cannon, Neill and Bowie determined to remain but requested reinforcements. Almost one hundred men were in the garrison, when news arrived that Mexican troops were at the Rio Grande. In early February, Lieutenant Colonel William B. Travis arrived at San Antonio with some of his followers, as did former congressman and famous frontiersman David "Davy" Crockett with other Tennessee volunteers.[36]

When family illness prompted Neill to leave in February, command passed to Travis, who held rank in the regular Texas army. However, most of the men at Béxar were volunteers who proceeded to elect Bowie as commander, even as his propensity for alcohol created serious issues. The leaders eventually agreed that Travis would be in charge of the regulars but Bowie would lead the volunteers with orders and correspondence carrying both signatures. Both men also appeared to agree that "the salvation of Texas depends in great measure in keeping Bejar out of the hands of the enemy" to prevent any invading Mexican force from advancing toward the Anglo-American colonies to the east.[37]

On February 23, sooner than expected, Santa Anna arrived at Béxar "and began a 13- day-long siege of the Texan garrison occupying a former Spanish mission known as the Alamo." He offered to allow the rebels "to walk away free as long as they promised never again to take up arms against the Mexican nation." Because Bowie was seriously ill, Travis answered the demand with a single shot from the Alamo 18-pounder. The following day, Travis dispatched a now-famous letter asking "the People of Texas and All Americans in the World" to come to the aid of his men who were faced with a vastly superior enemy. "*I shall never surrender or retreat*," he declared and closed with these words: "VICTORY OR DEATH." Santa Anna responded by ordering "'degüello' (fire and death)." No mercy would be shown to the more than 180 men who stood against the Mexican army at the Alamo, among them Tejanos such as Gregorio Esparza.[38]

The men at the Alamo were "ready to fight to the death if attacked, but still they were not suicidal." They almost certainly were overconfident, because of earlier successes against the Mexicans from whom they had captured a number of cannon. Also, "the Alamo's twelve-foot-high, two-foot-thick walls offered considerable protection . . . , providing that there were enough soldiers to man a defensive perimeter nearly a quarter of a mile long." No doubt, they expected additional reinforcements, particularly Colonel James W. Fannin's force of several hundred at Goliad. Instead, thirty-three men from Gonzales arrived on March 1. A few days later, the defenders learned that Fannin was not coming. Travis reportedly considered surrendering, but only if Santa Anna would assure the safety of his men. Not surprisingly, the Mexican commander offered no guarantees to traitors. Partly from "a romantic concept of honor," the insurgents made the choice to die. They "fought not out of strategic necessity but for reasons perfectly understandable to themselves."[39]

During the siege, Santa Anna awaited reinforcements, strengthened his military position, and encircled the compound. He allegedly also became enamored with a young woman who required marriage before intimacy, whereupon the amorous Mexican arranged for a fake wedding ceremony to be performed. Despite distractions, however, the general was determined "to give a day of glory to the homeland and of satisfaction to the supreme government." On March 6, he ordered a full assault, "rather than waiting a few more days for the siege guns that could have reduced the fort with much smaller losses" among his own troops. Indeed, the Texas rebels killed or wounded hundreds of the enemy, but all died in the process. Santa Anna undoubtedly underplayed the magnitude of his own casualties when he reported having lost "seventy dead and three hundred wounded." The defenders' corpses, whose number the Napoleon of the West greatly exaggerated as being more than six hundred, were burned. Reportedly, only Gregorio Esparza's body was spared, because his brother requested permission to bury him. Santa Anna did allow some women, children, and servants to live.[40]

Since the fall of the Alamo in 1836, Anglo Texans have tended to revere—indeed idolize—the fallen defenders, which helps explain the passionate reaction to a Spanish-language primary source first published in English in 1975. The journal of José Enrique de la Peña, a Mexican officer who served under Santa Anna during the Texas campaign, records that seven men, including Davy Crockett, were captured and executed on Santa Anna's orders. De la Peña expressed disgust at his superior for ordering the killings and at other Mexican officers who "fell upon these unfortunate defenseless men just as a tiger leaps upon his prey." This diary has been attacked as a fake and its contents refuted. While some make a reasoned argument, others react from emotion. Those who worship the larger-than-life heroes of Texas history reject the possibility that any defenders—much less the legendary Crockett—were captured alive. True Texans die fighting! Nevertheless, sound scholarship supports the contention that the journal is an authentic firsthand account by a Mexican participant.[41]

Does the debate over how a handful of the defenders died make their sacrifice any less heroic? All chose to face almost certain death against a superior enemy. They cost the Mexican commander many of his best soldiers and forced the enemy to expend ammunition and supplies. They bought time for Texas delegates, initially including Sam Houston, to assemble at a convention at Washington-on-the Brazos; declare the independence of Texas on March 2, 1836; name Sam Houston as commander of all Texas military forces; and begin the necessary steps to create an interim government. Their deaths helped convince other more cautious Texans that they must unite or die, while the fate of the defenders fostered a thirst for revenge and a battle cry that would have dire consequences for Santa Anna and his men. As one historian has written, "none had reason to be ashamed."[42]

To examine the Mexican commander's motives in making San Antonio de Béxar a priority is also appropriate, given that his own officers questioned that decision. Texas historian Randolph B. Campbell notes that "Santa Anna had no strategic need to take the fort." Biographer Will Fowler claims that the Mexican commander "recognized that the Alamo was not a strategically important objective"; however, he did not dare leave his army exposed to attack from the rear or its supply line vulnerable to disruption as his army advanced into Texas. Another probable factor was Santa Anna's desire to increase the confidence, morale, and experience of his untested army. No doubt, narcissism was another factor. Humiliated by Cos's surrender, the Napoleon of the West wanted to secure revenge, while achieving a dramatic victory. Whatever his motives, Santa Anna committed his resources to the siege, but the cost of taking the Alamo was too high. To quote one of his officers, "With another such victory, we will all go to the devil."[43]

Among Santa Anna's harshest critics was José de la Peña, who wrote the following: "One has been led to believe that only those in command have a right to think. It is taken for granted that men in high posts reason best." The young officer bemoaned the army as being recruited with too much haste and too much force. Many soldiers were too young or too old to withstand the march to Texas. He labelled Béxar "a garrison without any political or military importance" and complained that nothing could convince Santa Anna to alter his plan. In de la Peña's view, a small force should have been used to surveil the Alamo, while the main body of the Mexican army advanced to surprise Sam Houston. Blaming his commander for needless deaths on both sides, the eyewitness asserted that Santa Anna focused on the glory that would accompany military victory.[44]

Santa Anna himself acknowledged that the outcome was "very bloody" but defended his policy of extermination. He declared that his valiant soldiers were defending "the rights of the nation" against a determined enemy. In Santa Anna's version, José María Tornel, the Minister of War and Marine, had ordered foreigners in arms against Mexico to be considered pirates. The penalty for piracy was death. In other words, the Napoleon of the West was just following orders. As before, he deflected blame onto others; but in reality he took orders from no one during the Texas campaign.[45]

Indeed, Santa Anna was the only Mexican leader mentioned by name in the "Texas Declaration of Independence," unanimously adopted by the delegates at Washington-on-the-Brazos on March 2, 1836. Among reasons cited for separating from Mexico was his dismissal of the legitimate constitution and leaving colonists with "the cruel alternative, either to abandon our homes . . . or submit to the most intolerable of all tyranny, the combined despotism of the sword and the priesthood." Condemning the invading army as intent on "a war of extermination," the delegates resolved "that our political connection with the Mexican nation has forever ended." A constitution, similar in many respects to that of the United States, was written. Until formal elections could be held, David G. Burnet was named as interim president with Mexican Liberal Lorenzo de Zavala as vice president.[46]

As commander of military forces for the newly proclaimed Republic, Sam Houston lacked an organized, effective army. The only extant rebel troops were those trapped at the Alamo, some four hundred men under Fannin at Goliad, and various volunteers gathering at Gonzales. When Houston reached Gonzales, he learned of the fall of the Alamo and of a large Mexican army heading in his direction. As the shocking news spread, panicked settlers retreated eastward in the so-called "Runaway Scrape." Bad weather, swollen rivers, and crowded roads created intolerable conditions for the refugees. Government leaders also fled. Meanwhile, Santa Anna determined to end the campaign before his food and supplies were exhausted—and before his army disintegrated. The Napoleon of the West chose to divide his forces. One group stayed at San Antonio, a second under General José Urrea headed to the coast, and a third was sent to the north. Taking the best qualified companies with him, Santa Anna personally led the main body toward the east.[47]

As Urrea's forces headed south, Fannin continued a pattern of delay and indecision. A broken oxcart, straying oxen, and bad weather had prevented him from aiding the men at the Alamo. Then, when Houston ordered a retreat from Goliad, Fannin failed to act promptly. Trapped on open prairie on March 19, the Texas forces attempted an unsuccessful defense. The following day, the wounded Texian officer capitulated his command of several hundred men to General Urrea, who offered only "'surrender at discretion,' but Fannin told his men that their lives would be spared."[48]

José Enrique de la Peña criticized Fannin's "lack of knowledge of the principles of strategy and grand tactics." The Mexican officer did note that both sides had fought valiantly and that Urrea had wanted to spare the prisoners, but guarantees were not within his authority to grant. Santa Anna ordered the immediate execution of all the prisoners. Consequently, on Palm Sunday, March 27, 1836, hundreds of revolutionaries marched down a road on the pretext that "they were on their way to gather cattle or wood, or even to ships to take them away." Instead, almost 350 of the prisoners were slaughtered. Fannin was shot by a firing squad, and his remains were burned along with those of his men.[49]

The burden of command weighed heavily upon Sam Houston. The defeats at the Alamo and Goliad, along with other encounters, had cost more than six hundred lives in three weeks. Houston was the only hope remaining for his countrymen. Relying on one of his strongest qualities—"common sense"—the commander followed an unpopular course. Opening himself to charges of cowardice, he, too, retreated eastward in "a strategic withdrawal away from a numerically superior enemy while building strength and waiting for an opportunity to strike an effective blow."[50]

Fortunately for the Texans, Santa Anna made mistakes, one of which was to underestimate his opponent. Also, following Urrea's victory at Goliad, he worried that his subordinate might emerge as a hero of the Texas campaign and, hence, become a serious rival for power in Mexico. Acting preemptively, the Mexican commander became intent on personally capturing the officials of the Texas government at Harrisburg; nevertheless, they managed to escape from Santa Anna's eastward advance. In the process, the caudillo left himself "overextended and vulnerable." Recalculating, he then decided to target "Houston's 'army of pirates'"—a costly decision, given the outcome.[51]

From captured Mexican messengers, Houston learned that Santa Anna's unit was detached from the rest of his army with both commanders leading roughly equal forces. The time had come to act. "*But, we go to conquest*," Houston declared. "It is wisdom growing out of necessity to meet and fight the enemy *now*." He also inspired his men with a battle cry: "Remember the Alamo! The Alamo! The Alamo!"[52]

As Santa Anna marched toward the San Jacinto River near the mouth of Buffalo Bayou, Houston's troops crossed to the east side of the bayou and hurried to Lynch's Ferry. When the Mexicans arrived on April 20, the Texans already held the best defensive position. Given his opponent's proximity, Houston expected an attack, but none came, possibly because of the Mexican commander's overconfidence. Indeed, when Cos arrived early on April 21 with hundreds of reinforcements, the combined Mexican force totaled more than 1300 to Houston's approximately 900 men. Even though Cos's recruits were exhausted, hungry, and inexperienced, the Texans were at an obvious disadvantage.[53]

At mid-afternoon on April 21, Houston readied his force, which included almost twenty Tejanos. The revolutionary army advanced on the Mexican camp and fired two cannon, known as the Twin Sisters. The actual battle of San Jacinto lasted less than twenty minutes with a decisive Texas victory, but the bloodshed was of longer duration. Vividly remembering the Alamo and Goliad, the Texas troops shot and bayoneted Mexican soldiers, even those trying to surrender. Houston, seriously wounded in the right ankle, was unable to stop the slaughter. Texians and Tejanos killed 630 Mexican soldiers, and an even larger number were captured. In what Houston called "almost a miracle," the Texas army lost fewer than ten men in the victorious surprise attack that "was ultimately to seal the independence of Texas."[54]

Santa Anna cast blame for his defeat far and wide, particularly on fellow officers such as Generals Vicente Filisola and Antonio Gaona. These men had disobeyed his orders not to send written communications, he insisted, and the interception of one such dispatch had provided the enemy with valuable intelligence. The Napoleon of the West also claimed that his subordinates failed to provide reinforcements. Those that did arrive with Cos, as well as Santa Anna's own men, "were hungry and exhausted." Their need for rest "would not have presented a problem had his orders that the sentries posted around the camp remain awake and alert been obeyed." Then, when the Texans did attack, Cos's troops proved "inexperienced and panicked." These excuses, which did hold some truth, failed to prove persuasive to his fellow Mexicans in Congress, who considered him "a curse to the nation."[55]

Despite the above, twentieth-century Mexican historian José C. Valadés agrees that Santa Anna was not responsible for the events at San Jacinto. If the trusted general in charge of camp security had done his duty, the outcome would have been different. Valadés also contends that the Mexican leader was accustomed to fighting against enemies "*con alta dosis de caballerosidad*" (with a high degree of gallantry), whereas Sam Houston was a power-hungry "fox" with dreams of conquest. In other words, the Texas commander committed an ungentlemanly act by attacking when and how he did![56]

A more earthy explanation for the defeat gained popular acceptance. Supposedly, don Antonio was unprepared because he was distracted in his tent by a free woman of color who was a captive of the Mexican army. Although there was such a woman in the camp, many scholars contend that there is more myth than fact in the assertion that she played a key role at San Jacinto. Nevertheless, Emily D. West—"The Yellow Rose of Texas"—gained a place in the pages of Texas lore.[57]

Whatever the reasons for the defeat of the Mexican army at San Jacinto, their commander escaped but only temporarily. Apprehended the following day, his identity was unknown to his captors until he was brought to the Texans' camp, where "captured Mexican officers . . . recognized their commander and exclaimed '*El Presidente*!'" Finding himself at Sam Houston's mercy, the infamous Santa Anna presented himself with these words: "That man may consider himself born to no common destiny who has conquered the Napoleon of the West; and it now remains for him to be generous to the vanquished." Houston replied: "You should have remembered that at the Alamo." Although Houston's men called for the captive to be executed, their commander calculated that "Santa Anna *dead* is no more than Tom, Dick, or Harry *dead*, but living he may avail Texas much."[58]

Houston forced the prisoner to sign an armistice. Consequently, Santa Anna ordered Filisola to return to Béxar and Urrea to Victoria. Second-in-command of Mexican forces in Texas, Italian-born Filisola hoped eventually to "to resume the offensive," but faced challenges that included low morale, internal dissension, scant provisions, scattered troops, and numerous camp followers. Even the weather conspired against the Mexican army with debilitating heat and torrential rains, as they became mired in a "sea of mud." Also significant was the acting commander's concern that the threat of renewed hostilities could constitute a death sentence for Santa Anna and the other prisoners in Houston's custody. Given the realities of

Surrender of Santa Anna by William H. Huddle. This 19th century painting depicts the defeated Santa Anna being brought before a wounded Sam Houston on April 22, 1836, the day after the Battle of San Jacinto. The State Preservation Board, Austin, Texas.

the Texas situation and Mexico's instability, the Mexican army later would withdraw across the Rio Grande.[59]

Aware of the bloodlust among the Texas population, the wounded Houston stayed at San Jacinto to ensure Santa Anna's safety until government officials could arrive. The Mexican general later wrote that he "always recalled with emotions of gratitude how much I owed to this singular man in the saddest moments of my life." Not until early May was the Texas commander able to leave for New Orleans to get treatment for his infected ankle.[60]

When he finally met with David Burnet, the ad interim President of the Republic of Texas, Santa Anna was almost certainly in self-preservation mode. On May 14, 1836, the prisoner signed the Treaties of Velasco: one to be made public, the other to remain confidential. In the former, the Mexican general agreed to remove Mexican troops to below the Rio Grande, exchange prisoners held by the Mexican army, and return any seized property. Certain to provoke outrage among his countrymen should the terms become known, the private treaty contained a pledge "to *try* to have the Mexican cabinet receive a commission from Texas, the purpose of which was to obtain recognition for Texan independence and to set a boundary at the Río Grande." In return, the prisoner was promised "immediate release and reembarkation for Vera Cruz."[61]

Indeed, Santa Anna would be criticized for the concessions in the Treaties of Velasco and accused of betraying his country to save himself. Taking exception to those allegations, a recent biographer argues that the general was operating "on the premise that as a prisoner, he was no longer in a position to act freely, and anything he said or signed would not be validated by Congress." Santa Anna's aim was actually "to deceive the Texans" and, thereby, secure his freedom. In fact, according to this author, the commander wanted his officers to launch another offensive.[62]

Learning of the Mexican general's pending repatriation, Texans were outraged. Recently arrived volunteers from New Orleans forced the removal of Santa Anna from the ship designated to carry him back to Mexico in early June and he was fortunate to escape lynching. Incarcerated during the summer and early fall of 1836, the captive was well aware of his precarious situation. Also, by impeding his release, Texans violated the Treaties of Velasco. Regardless, the Mexican government refused to honor any agreement signed by Santa Anna while a prisoner—as the defeated general had anticipated—and prompted all citizens "to continue the war." Fortunately for the new Republic, instability in Mexico made this a largely empty threat.[63]

Cooler heads in Texas sought a solution to the impasse regarding their prisoner. Possibly at the instigation of Stephen F. Austin, Santa Anna wrote President Andrew Jackson about his plight. Among issues addressed in a letter dated July 4 were the Mexican leader's continuing incarceration and the possibility of renewed warfare, which he presented as interrelated. Insisting that he was "always disposed to sacrifice himself for the glory and well-being" of his country, the prisoner of war also stressed the need for a reasonable person to intervene. He warned that political negotiations were preferable to renewed military action. While noting Santa Anna's lack of official status, Jackson was willing to intercede and help resolve the Texas-Mexico dispute. The U.S. president also wrote his friend Sam Houston to warn that executing the Mexican strongman would be a mistake. As Old Hickory advised: "Let not his blood be shed unless it becomes necessary by an imperative act of just retaliation for Mexican massacres hereafter."[64]

In his capacity as the first elected president of the Republic, Sam Houston was well aware of Santa Anna's precarious situation, given popular sentiment against him. The eventual solution was to send the caudillo back to Mexico by an indirect route, involving "what amounted to a tour through the United States that culminated in Washington, D.C." Apparently, there was some thought that a meeting between the Napoleon of the West and President Jackson might influence the United States to recognize Texas's independence, even if Mexico would not.[65]

According to Andrew Jackson, Santa Anna offered Texas to the United States for a reasonable amount of money, a proposition that the American president did not take seriously. The caudillo's version was that Jackson offered a substantial payment in return for recognition of Texas's independence, but the bribe was refused. Whatever actually transpired in their meeting, don Antonio became an admirer of the president, who treated him well and "gave him a fine dinner before his departure from Washington."[66]

In February 1837, Santa Anna finally returned to Mexico, where he was less than welcome. Ensconced at *Manga de Clavo*, the disgraced leader announced that "all he wanted to do was retire to private life." Far from fading from the public scene, however, Santa Anna would head his country's government on other occasions—his last period in power would be from 1853–1855. In the intervening years, the Napoleon of the West lost his left leg below the knee as the result of a cannonball wound suffered during a brief war with France in 1838. Amputation by a less-than-competent military surgeon left the caudillo in severe pain and forced to use a prosthetic. Significantly, "this 'sacrifice' redeemed Santa Anna's lost honor and restored him to the pantheon of Mexican heroes."[67]

With more political lives than a cat, Santa Anna remained fixated on Texas. Back in the presidential office "in 1841, he made the re-conquest of the province one of the government's priorities." The Congress in Mexico gave him "dictatorial powers in the aftermath of the Santa Fe Expedition" which had been dispatched from Texas to claim that territory for the new republic. Although the incursion failed, Santa Anna retaliated by ordering two separate invasions of Texas in 1842, the first led by General Rafael Vásquez, the second by General Adrián Woll. On both occasions the Mexican military briefly occupied San Antonio before retreating back across the Rio Grande.[68] (See Chapter 2.)

Some three hundred Texans under Colonel W. S. Fisher crossed the river in pursuit of Woll's forces. Following a heated battle at Mier, Mexico, the Texans were captured but later made an unsuccessful attempt to escape with several guards killed in the process. The government ordered their execution. Instead, each prisoner was forced to draw from a container filled with 176 beans of which one in every ten was black. The seventeen unfortunates who drew the black beans were shot. The rest were imprisoned in Mexico, along with the survivors of the 1841 Santa Fe expedition and the prisoners from Vásquez's earlier raid.[69]

Many Texans must have felt a sense of relief when Santa Anna was exiled to Cuba in the mid-1840s for his misuse of money and irresponsible conduct, including throwing a lavish funeral for his own severed leg. Adding to the outrage was the behavior of the fifty-year-old caudillo when his wife of many years died. She had been beloved by the Mexican people, who were disgusted when Santa Anna quickly remarried by proxy fifteen-year-old María Dolores Tosta, "not so much because she was beautiful (which she was) but because she was 'the daughter of very rich entrepreneurs.'" Unlike her predecessor, however, she preferred life in the capital to that at *Manga de Clavo*.[70]

While Santa Anna resided on an hacienda outside Havana, expansionist sentiment pervaded the United States. Adherents of Manifest Destiny, including President-Elect James Polk, believed their nation fated to expand westward to the Pacific. As a result, Texas was annexed on December 29, 1845, which led an infuriated Mexican government to terminate diplomatic relations with the United States. A dispute over the international boundary worsened the tension, with the U.S. supporting Texas's claim of the Rio Grande and Mexico insisting on the Nueces River. After Polk ordered troops into the disputed area, fighting ensued along the Rio Grande in April 1846. The following month Polk asked Congress for a declaration of war on the grounds that "Mexico has passed the boundary of the

United States, has invaded our territory and shed American blood on American soil." Of course, from the Mexican perspective, the U.S. had invaded them and shed blood on Mexican soil.[71]

Aware that the United States had designs on California, Santa Anna negotiated with the Polk administration, which armed the exile with cash and facilitated his return to Mexico. The caudillo tricked Polk "into believing he would bring about a peaceful cession of the territories coveted by the U.S. government . . ."—a bargain he never intended to keep. The Napoleon of the West had no scruples about betraying a country at war with his own. Instead, "he channeled all his energy into fighting the invaders."[72]

Again in command, Santa Anna was hampered by Mexico's political volatility and economic issues. To supply his troops, he resorted to "mortgaging all his properties as well as those of his children." He vigorously engaged American forces at the Battle of Buena Vista near Saltillo in February 1847 but ultimately retreated. Predictably, the caudillo claimed victory despite thousands of Mexican casualties. Likewise, he patriotically, but unsuccessfully, defended Mexico City against a U.S. invasion from the coast. Constantly out-flanked and outgunned, the Mexican forces could not overcome deficiencies in weaponry and training. Santa Anna made such a hasty retreat from the battlefield at Cerro Gordo that he abandoned important papers, an artificial leg, and silver bullion. Nevertheless, when Mexican officials decided to negotiate with the United States, he "was furious with the government for ordering him to put down his arms. . . ." And the cost of defeat was dear. In the Treaty of Guadalupe Hidalgo in 1848, Mexico lost about half of its national territory, including present-day New Mexico, Arizona, and California. Significantly for Texas, the Rio Grande became the permanent international boundary.[73]

Although Santa Anna deserved "credit for his desperate and valiant year-long defense of his country," he was instead accused of being "a despicable traitor, who deliberately lost the war." Exiled a second time, the disgraced leader issued a manifesto announcing his

THE LATE GENERAL LOPEZ DE SANTA ANNA.—Phot. by Gurney.—[See First Page.]

Engraving of the late Gen. Antonio López de Santa Anna. *Harper's Weekly*, July 20, 1867 p. 461, photo by Gurney. 73–1445, UTSA Special Collections—Institute of Texan Cultures.

intent "to retire to a distant country to lament the immense misfortune" that had befallen Mexico. Amazingly, the resilient caudillo would be returned to power by conservatives in Mexico in 1853, but his assumption of a monarchial-style title, exercise of dictatorial powers, and making of lavish expenditures soon alienated his countrymen. Adding to the discord was the decision to sell the United States a strip of Mexican territory in present-day southern Arizona and New Mexico. Forced yet again from his homeland in 1855, Santa Anna was not allowed to return until near death almost two decades later. No crowds greeted the impoverished former president, whose lands "had been confiscated, broken up, and sold." Santa Anna died in the capital on June 21, 1876, at age eighty-two.[74]

***

Antonio López de Santa Anna's role in Texas and Mexican history has been extremely controversial, even in his own country. An obituary published in Mexico City accurately prophesized that "future historians will differ in their judgment of his merits." This can be demonstrated by looking at the titles of just two Spanish-language biographies: *Santa Anna no fué un traidor* (*Santa Anna Was Not a Traitor*) and *Santa Anna: Aurora y ocaso de un comediante* (*Santa Anna: The Dawn and Fall of a Comedian*). Obviously, the first author defended the caudillo, while the second had a low opinion of him.[75]

A balanced view of the Mexican leader falls somewhere between the two extremes, as illustrated in *Santa Anna: A Curse upon Mexico* (2002). Military historian Robert L. Scheina writes that "Few individuals have caused their nation greater pain than . . . Santa Anna." He quotes a high-ranking Spanish official, who early along predicted that "This young man will live to make his country weep." However, Scheina also credits him as a bold, brave soldier who was often victorious in battle. The historian observes that even Santa Anna's enemies were impressed by his obvious courage, organizational ability, and abundant energy.[76]

More recently, biographer Will Fowler has challenged the notion that Santa Anna focused primarily on the acquisition of power. Instead, he argues that the caudillo sought glory. Viewing himself as "above party politics," he "was a soldier first and a politician second." According to Fowler, Santa Anna's "successes, and his failures, his rises and falls and the choices he made were all reflections of the times in which he lived." The end of centuries of monarchial control over Spanish America created a "vacuum that was occupied by the military or regional strongmen . . . of the newly formed republics." Regardless of their political persuasion, Santa Anna was the man on whom Mexicans relied, "the one leader considered capable of restoring peace, order, and safety" when chaos threatened.[77]

As for Santa Anna's view of himself, in his autobiography he complained that envy and hatred had followed him throughout his career, but expressed confidence "that posterity will do me full justice." Admitting to being motivated by thoughts of glory in his youth, don Antonio insisted that in maturity he was occupied "solely with helping Mexico [to] become a nation" and that his ascension to power resulted from his "love of country." One cannot help but wonder if Mexico would have been better served had he loved his nation a little less![78]

During his lifetime, Santa Anna earned the undying hatred of many Texans. His legacy generated antipathy on the part of Texians toward *Mexicanos* in general and Tejanos in particular, for which these groups paid a heavy price long after he disappeared from the scene. For all his faults or because of them, Antonio López de Santa Anna was a pivotal figure in Texas history. Without the self-styled Napoleon of the West, the story of the Lone Star State would read very differently.

Bibliographical Commentary

As a critical figure in nineteenth-century Texas and Mexican history, Antonio López de Santa Anna is the subject of much literature in both English and Spanish. Oakah Jones's *Santa Anna* (1967) is outdated, but still valuable. A more recent revisionist biography by Will Fowler, *Santa Anna of Mexico* (2007), provides new perspectives on the Mexican strongman. Another work by Fowler is *Independent Mexico: The* Pronunciamiento *in the Age of Santa Anna, 1821–1858* (2016). *Santa Anna: A Curse upon Mexico* (2002) by Robert Scheina approaches the topic from a military viewpoint. Works on other key people, whose lives intersected with Santa Anna's, include Gregg Cantrell's *Stephen F. Austin: Empresario of Texas* (1999), Jesús F. De la Teja's *A Revolution Remembered: The Memoirs and Selected Correspondence of Juan N. Seguín* (2002), and Randolph Campbell's *Sam Houston and the American Southwest* (3rd ed., 2007).

Publications on the Texas Revolution include information on that aspect of Santa Anna's career. These include Paul Lack's *The Texas Revolutionary Experience: A Political and Social History, 1835–1836* (1992), Timothy Matovina's *The Alamo Remembered: Tejano Accounts and Perspectives* (1995), Stephen Hardin's *Texian Iliad: A Military History of the Texas Revolution, 1835–1836* (1995), Richard Bruce Winders, *Crisis in the Southwest: The United States, Mexico, and the Struggle over Texas* (2002), William C. Davis, *Lone Star Rising: the Revolutionary Birth of the Texas Republic* (2004), and James Crisp's *Sleuthing the Alamo: Davy Crockett's Last Stand and Other Mysteries of the Texas Revolution* (2005).

Spanish-language sources are significant, and some have been translated into English. Of particular interest is Santa Anna's self-serving autobiography, *The Eagle: The Autobiography of Santa Anna* (1967). A readily available, though controversial, primary source is *With Santa Anna in Texas: A Personal Narrative of the Revolution* (1997), the diary of an officer who served under Santa Anna during the Texas campaign. Among more interesting secondary works by Mexican authors are José Fuente Mares, *Santa Anna: Aurora y ocaso de un comediante* (*Santa Anna: Dawn and Fall of a Comedian*), 3rd ed., 1967, and José Valadés, *Santa Anna y la guerra de Téxas* (*Santa Anna and the War with Texas*), 3rd ed., 1993. However, these works are more difficult to find.

The internet provides an overwhelming amount of resources, some of which are more reliable than others. Many relevant entries can be found in the *Handbook of Texas Online* at the Texas State Historical Association's website, www.tshaonline.org, including "Santa Anna, Antonio López de (1794–1876)," "Texas Revolution," "Alamo, Battle of the," "Goliad Massacre," and "Treaties of Velasco." This website also provides access to many issues of *Southwestern Historical Quarterly*, which contains scholarly articles and primary source materials, some of which relate to Santa Anna's role in Texas history.

Endnotes

1. José Fuentes Mares, *Santa Anna: Aurora y ocaso de un comediante* (México: Editorial Jus, 1967), title page. Translation from the Spanish, "La Providencia ha querido que mi historia sea la historia de México desde 1821."

2. Santa Anna's reference to himself as the "Napoleon of the West" may be found in many sources. See, for example, Thom Hatch, *Encyclopedia of the Alamo and the Texas Revolution* (Jefferson, NC: McFarland & Co., 1992), 163.

3. Oakah L. Jones Jr., *Santa Anna* (New York: Twayne Publishers, 1968), 20–21; Michael C. Meyer, William L. Sherman, and Susan M. Deeds, *The Course of Mexican History*, 10th ed. (New York: Oxford University Press, 2014), 157–159.

4. Wilfrid H. Callcott, *Santa Anna: The Story of an Enigma Who Once Was Mexico* (Norman: University of Oklahoma Press, 1936), 5–7.

5. Robert L. Scheina, *Santa Anna: A Curse upon Mexico* (Washington, DC: Brassey's Inc.: 2002), quotation on 6; Will Fowler, *Santa Anna of Mexico* (Lincoln: University of Nebraska Press, 2007), 20–21, 27–28.

6. Donald E. Chipman and Harriett Denise Joseph, *Spanish Texas, 1519–1821*, rev. ed. (Austin: University of Texas, Press, 2010), 248–251. Joaquín de Arredondo was Commandant General of the Eastern Interior Provinces, which included Texas. He served in that capacity, 1813–1821, idem, 280. For more detailed information, see the chapter titled "José Bernardo Gutiérrez de Lara/ Joaquín de Arredondo" in Donald E. Chipman and Harriett Denise Joseph's, *Notable Men and Women of Spanish Texas* (Austin: University of Texas Press, 1999), 226–249.

7. Chipman and Joseph, *Spanish Texas*, 251; Fowler, *Santa Anna*, 28–29; Jones, *Santa Anna*, 23, as quoted. See Chapter 2 on Erasmo and Juan Seguín for more information on Joaquín de Arredondo's brutal retaliation against the civilian population in Texas.

8. Callcott, *Santa Anna*, 11–12; Scheina, *Santa Anna*, 6; Fowler, *Santa Anna*, 1st quotation on 39, 2nd quotation on 41–42; *Handbook of Texas Online*, Wilfred H. Callcott, "Santa Anna, Antonio López De," 2016, http://www.tshaonline.org/handbook/online/articles/fsa29. [*Handbook of Texas Online* hereinafter cited as *HOT Online*.] Schiena's *Santa Anna* includes a chronology section with early promotions and corresponding dates listed on ix.

9. Will Fowler, *Independent Mexico: The* Pronunciamiento *in the Age of Santa Anna, 1821–1858* (Lincoln: University of Nebraska Press, 2016), 62–72, passim, quotation on 69. For two important works that challenge traditional interpretations of Mexican independence by examining the inconsistencies of the royal government in Spain and how that contributed to the loss of empire, see Timothy E. Anna's *The Fall of the Royal Government in Mexico City* (1978) and *Spain and the Loss of America* (1983).

10. Scheina, *Santa Anna*, 7–8, 1st quotation on 8; Fowler, *Santa Anna*, 2nd quotation on 45.

11. Jones, *Santa Anna*, 30–31; Meyer, Sherman, and Deeds, *Course of Mexican History*, 229, 1st quotation; Peter Santoni, Review of Robert Scheina, *Santa Anna: A Curse Upon Mexico*, in *The Journal of Military History* 67, no. 2 (April 2003): 567, 2nd quotation, Proquest ID 340597851, http://pathfinder.utb.edu:2072/pqdweb?index=41&did=000000340597851. . ..

12. Jones, *Santa Anna*, 32, quotation; Fowler, *Santa Anna*, 58–59.

13. Jones, *Santa Anna*, 34–39; Fowler, *Sana Anna*, 60–61, 65–66, quotation on 66; Fowler, *Independent Mexico*, 97–99.

14. Fowler, *Independent Mexico*, 67, quotation.

15. Scheina, *Santa Anna*, 17; Fowler, *Santa Anna*, 89–93, 351, 1st quotation on 92; Jones, *Santa Anna*, 43–45, 2nd quotation on 45.

16. Scheina, *Santa Anna*, 15–20; Wilfred Hardy Callcott, *Santa Anna: The Story of an Enigma Who Once Was Mexico* (Hamden, CT: Archon Books, 1964), 71–76, 1st quotation on 76; Fowler, *Santa Anna*, 120–123, 2nd quotation on 123.

17. Jones, *Santa Anna*, 52–56, 1st quotation on 56; Meyer, Sherman, and Deeds, *Course of Mexican History*, 249; Fowler, *Santa Anna*, Intro., xx, 2nd quotation; Jones, *Santa Anna*, Preface, np. For an overview of the traditional view and portrayal of Santa Anna, see Fowler, *Sana Anna*, Introduction, viii–xxiv. Aspects of Fowler's revised interpretation of Santa Anna have been incorporated into the narrative in this chapter.

18. Chipman and Joseph, *Spanish Texas*, rev. ed., quotation on 255. For detailed information on the history of colonial Texas from 1519–1821, see the volume just cited.

19. Campbell, *Gone to Texas: A History of the Lone Star State*, 2nd ed. (New York: Oxford University Press, 2012), 98–106, passim; Randolph B. Campbell, *An Empire for Slavery: The Peculiar Institution in Texas, 1821–1865* (Baton Rouge: Louisiana State University Press, 1989), 12–13. In the late Spanish period, Moses Austin initiated efforts to gain approval for legal immigration of Anglo Americans into Texas; however, he died in 1821, the same year that Mexico declared independence. Moses's son, Stephen Fuller Austin, assumed responsibility for the colonization venture and found himself dealing with a rapidly changing situation in Mexico. An award-winning work on the subject is Gregg Cantrell's *Stephen F. Austin: Empresario of Texas*.

20. Campbell, *Empire for Slavery*, 12–18; Campbell, *Gone to Texas*, 114–115, 130–132; Arnoldo de León, *They Called Them Greasers: Anglo Attitudes toward Mexicans in Texas, 1821–1900* (Austin: University of Texas Press, 1983), 20, 24.

21. Campbell, *Empire for Slavery*, 25–26, quotation on 25; Gregg Cantrell, *Stephen F. Austin: Empresario of Texas* (New Haven: Yale University Press, 1999), 220–221; Campbell, *Gone to Texas*, 116–118. A reprint of "The Law of April 6, 1830" can be found in *Texas Voices: Documents and Biographical Sketches*, written and edited by Keith J. Volanto, 34–36.

22. Michael P. Costeloe, "Santa Anna and the Gómez Farías Administration in Mexico, 1833–1834," *The Americas* 31, no. 1 (July 1974): 18–22; "The Turtle Bayou Resolutions of June 13, 1832," reprinted in Volanto, *Texas Voices*, 37–38; Campbell, *Gone to Texas*, 121, 123.

23. Cantrell, *Stephen F. Austin*, 267–270; Costeloe, "Santa Anna and Gómez Farías," 22–23; Fowler, *Santa Anna*, 142–144, 354, 1st quotation on 143, 2nd quotation on 354; Jones, *Santa Anna*, 56.

24. Costeloe, "Santa Anna and Gómez Farías," 1st quotation on 23, 2nd quotation on 25; Fowler, *Santa Anna*, 142–146.

25. Cantrell, *Stephen F. Austin*, 269–275, 299, 1st quotation on 270, 2nd quotation on 299; Campbell, *Gone to Texas*, 123.

26. Cantrell, *Stephen F. Austin*, 271, 275, 277–278, 282, 289, 296, 305; Campbell, *Gone to Texas*, 124, 129.

27. Fowler, *Santa Anna*, 154–157; Michael P. Costeloe, *The Central Republic in Mexico, 1835–1846: "Hombres de Bien" in the Age of Santa Anna* (New York: Cambridge University Press, 1993), 1st quotation on 107; Fowler, *Independent Mexico*, 2nd quotation on 172; Michael P. Costeloe, "Federalism to Centralism: The Conservative Case for Change, 1824–1835," in *The Americas* 45, no. 2 (Oct. 1988): 177; Scheina, *Santa Anna*, 25–26. For more detailed information on the factors precipitating the change in governments, as well as Santa Anna's role in these events, see both the Costeloe article, "Federalism to Centralism," and his book, *The Central Republic*, cited in this note.

28. Fowler, *Independent Mexico*, 171–172, quotation on 172; Callcott, *Santa Anna*, 114–116.

29. Winders, *Crisis in the Southwest: The United States, Mexico, and the Struggle Over Texas* (Wilmington, DE: Scholarly Resources Inc., 2002), 18, 1st quotation;

Stephen L. Hardin, *Texian Iliad: A Military History of the Texas Revolution, 1835–1836* (Austin: University of Texas Press, 1994), 7–13, passim, 2nd quotation on 12, 3rd quotation on 13.

30. Cantrell, *Stephen F. Austin*, 298–299, 323, all quotations; Paul D. Lack, *The Texas Revolutionary Experience: A Political and Social History, 1835–1836* (College Station: Texas A&M University Press, 1992), 44–49, passim.

31. Cantrell, *Stephen F. Austin*, 316–317, 325–326, quotation on 325; Randolph B. Campbell, *Sam Houston and the American Southwest*, 3rd ed. (New York: Pearson Longman, 2007), 51, 60, 62, 64.

32. Hardin, *Texian Iliad*, 91; Fowler, *Santa Anna*, 163, 1st and 2nd quotations; William C. Davis, *Lone Star Rising: The Revolutionary Birth of the Texas Republic* (New York: Free Press, 2004), 199; *Suplemento al número 79, noticia oficial de Texas* (Supplement to Number 79, Official Notice from Texas), March 21, 1836, 3rd quotation, [Transcript of Letter from Antonio López de Santa Anna, March 21, 2836], https://texashistory.unt.edu/ark:/67531/metapth217058/m1/1/?q=Antonio%20Lopez%20de%20Santa%20Anna, University of North Texas Libraries, The Portal to Texas History, texashistory.unt.edu, crediting CAH. [Hereinafter cited as Santa Anna, *Noticia Oficial*].

33. *General Vicente Filisola's Analysis of José Urrea's Military Diary: A Forgotten 1838 Publication by an Eyewitness to the Texas Revoluton*, ed. Gregg J. Dimmick, trans. by John R. Wheat (Austin: Texas State Historical Association, 2007), Prologue, xiii [Hereinafter cited as *Filisola's Analysis*]; Jones, *Santa Anna*, 65; Davis, *Lone Star Rising*, 200–210, 203, 2nd quotation on 203; Winders, *Crisis in the Southwest*, 23; Fowler, *Santa Anna*, 1st quotation on 164.

34. *HOT Online*, "Ramirez Y Sesma, Joaquin," http://www.tshaonline.org/handbook/online/articles/fra22; Davis, *Lone Star Rising*, 202–203, quotations on 203; *Filisola's Analysis*, prologue, xiv–xv; Paul Calore, *The Texas Revolution and the U.S.-Mexican War: A Concise History* (Jefferson, NC: McFarland & Company 2014), 55.

35. Hardin, *Texian Iliad*, 102–105; Campbell, *Gone to Texas*, 140; Fowler, *Santa Anna*, quotation on 165.

36. Paul D. Lack, *The Texas Revolutionary Experience: A Political and Social History, 1835–1836* (College Station: Texas A&M University Press, 1992), 119; Campbell, *Gone to Texas*, 139–141; Hardin, *Texian Iliad*, 107–111, 117.

37. Lack, *Texas Revolutionary Experience*, 119; *HOT Online*, William R. Williamson, "Bowie, James," http://www.tshaonline.org/handbook/online/articles/fbo45; *HOT Online*, Stephen L. Hardin, "Alamo, Battle of The," http://www.tshaonline.org/handbook/online/articles/qea02; Thomas Ricks Lindley, *Alamo Traces: New Evidence and New Conclusions* (Lanham, MD: Republic of Texas Press, 2003), 13, as quoted.

38. *HOT Online*, Archie P. McDonald, "Travis, William Barret," http://www.tshaonline.org/handbook/online/articles/ftr03; Winders, *Crisis in the Southwest*, 23–24, 1st quotation on 23; "The Battle of the Alamo Siege Chronology: Day One-Tuesday February 23, 1836," http://www.tamu.edu/faculty/ccbn/dewitt/adp/history/1836/the_battle/chronology.html; Fowler, *Santa Anna*, 165–166, 2nd quotation on 166, 6th quotation on 165; "Travis' Letter of February 24, 1836," *Documents of Texas History*, 2nd ed., eds. Ernest Wallace, David M. Vigness, and George B. Ward (Austin: State House Press, 1994), 96,

3rd through 5th quotations; *HOT Online*, Jesús F. de la Teja, "Tejanos and the Siege and Battle of the Alamo," http://www.tshaonline.org/handbook/online/articles/qst01.

39. Campbell, *Gone to Texas*, 141–145, 1st quotation on 144, 2nd quotation on 142, 3rd and 4th quotations on 145; Hardin, *Texian Iliad*, 132–133, 135.

40. Fowler, *Santa Anna*, 166–167, 3rd quotation on 166; Santa Anna, *Noticia Oficial*, 1st quotation; Campbell, *Gone to Texas*, 140–146, 2nd quotation on 145; Timothy M. Matovina, *The Alamo Remembered: Tejano Accounts and Perspectives* (Austin: University of Texas Press, 1995), Intro. 4, 33–34. For detailed information on the survivors of the Alamo, see Crystal Sasse Ragsdale, *Women and Children of the Alamo* (Austin: State House Press, 1994). Santa Anna's written report on the battle of the Alamo can be found in the *Noticial Oficial* (Official Notice of March 21, 1836) cited in this note.

41. José Enrique de la Peña, *With Santa Anna in Texas: A Personal Narrative of the Revolution*, Expanded ed., (College Station: Texas A&M University Press, 1999), quotation on 53. For a well-supported argument confirming the authenticity of the de la Peña diary, see James E. Crisp, *Sleuthing the Alamo: Davy Crockett's Last Stand and Other Mysteries of the Texas Revolution* (New York: Oxford University Press, 2005). For a refutation of the diary's authenticity, see Bill Groneman, *Death of a Legend: The Myth and Mystery Surrounding the Death of Davy Crockett* (Plano, TX: Republic of Texas Press, 1999).

42. Campbell, *Gone to Texas*, 145–147; Fowler, *Santa Anna*, 166; Davis, *Lone Star Rising*, 224; Hardin, *Texian Iliad*, 149, 157, quotation on 149.

43. Campbell, *Gone to Texas*, all quotations on 145; Fowler, *Santa Anna*, 165–166; Davis, *Lone Star Rising*, 220; Hardin, *Texian Iliad*, 136, 155.

44. De la Peña, *With Santa Anna*, Prologue, xxix, 8–9, 18–19, 43, 45, 54–55, 67, 1st quotation on xxix, 2nd quotation on 18.

45. Santa Anna, *Noticia Oficial*, quotations; Fowler, *Santa Anna*, 167–168.

46. "The Texas Declaration of Independence, March 2, 1836," in *Documents of Texas History*, 98–99, 1st quotation on 98, 2nd and 3rd quotations on 99; Campbell, *Gone to Texas*, 145–147. A copy of "The Constitution of the Republic of Texas, March 17, 1836" can also be found in *Documents of Texas History*, 100–106.

47. Campbell, *Sam Houston*, 71–74; Jones, *Santa Anna*, 67; Gregg J. Dimmick, *Sea of Mud: The Retreat of the Mexican Army after San Jacinto, An Archaeological Investigation* (Austin: Texas State Historical Association, 2004), 30, 35.

48. Campbell, *Sam Houston*, 72; Winders, *Crisis in the Southwest*, 24–25; Campbell, *Gone to Texas*, 149–150, quotation on 149.

49. De la Peña, *With Santa Anna*, 72–75, 1st quotation on 72; Davis, *Lone Star Rising*, 237–238, 2nd quotation on 238; Hardin, *Texian Iliad*, 173–174.

50. Davis, *Lone Star Rising*, 249–250; Campbell, *Sam Houston*, 73, 78–79, 87, 199, 1st quotation on 199, 2nd quotation on 87.

51. Winders, *Crisis in the Southwest*, 27, 1st quotation; Davis, *Lone Star Rising*, 253–255; Fowler, *Santa Anna*, 169–170, 2nd quotation on 170.

52. Fowler, *Santa Anna*, 170; Callcott, *Santa Anna*, 135; Campbell, *Sam Houston*, 80–81, all quotations on 81.

53. Campbell, *Sam Houston*, 80–83; Davis, *Lone Star Rising*, 266–268; Fowler, *Santa Anna*, 170–171.

54. Campbell, *Sam Houston*, 83–85, 1st quotation on 85; Fowler, *Santa Anna*, 2nd quotation on 172.

55. Fowler, *Santa Anna*, 1st, 2nd and 3rd quotations on 73; Jones, *Santa Anna*, 4th quotation on 75.

56. José C. Valadés, *Santa Anna y la guerra de Téxas*, 3rd ed. (México: Editorial Diana, 1993), 202, quotations.

57. For factual information on Emily D. West, as well as how this story came to be part of Texas lore, see *HOT Online*, Margaret Swett Henson, "West, Emily D.," http://www.tshaonline.org/handbook/online/articles/fwe41.

58. Jones, *Santa Anna*, 69–70, 1st quotation on 70; Campbell, *Sam Houston*, 85; Campbell, *Gone to Texas*, 156–158, 2nd and 3rd quotations on 156, 4th quotation on 158.

59. *Filisola's Analysis*, xi, xiii, xvi–xix, 200–201, 297, 1st quotation on xix; Dimmit, *Sea of Mud*, 5, 29, 35, 317, 320, 2nd quotation on 5; Campbell, *Gone to Texas*, 156. For more detailed information on the retreat of the Mexican forces after the Battle of San Jacinto, as well as the factors that prevented their retaking the offensive, see Gregg J. Dimmick's *Sea of Mud: The Retreat of the Mexican Army after San Jacinto, an Archaeological Investigation*.

60. Antonio López de Santa Anna, *My Memoirs, Written in My Last Exile*, excerpt from 7th chapter, as quoted in "Santa Anna's Captivity," http://www.tamu.edu/faculty/ccbn/dewitt/santaanna4.htm; Campbell, *Sam Houston*, 85–86; Campbell, *Gone to Texas*, 157–158.

61. Jones, *Santa Anna*, 70, quotations.

62. Fowler, *Santa Anna*, 176–178, 1st quotation on 176–177, 2nd quotation on 176.

63. Albert A. Nofi, *The Alamo and the Texas War of Independence, September 30, 1835 to April 21, 1836: Heroes, Myths, and History* (Boston: Da Capo, 1992), 167; Jones, *Santa Anna*, 71–72, quotation on 72; José María Tornel, Ministry of War and Marine, to Division General Don Vicente Filisola, June 25, 1836, in *Filisola's Analysis*, 214–215.

64. Antonio López de Santa Anna to President Andrew Jackson, July 4, 1836, 1st quotation, https:texashistory.unt.edu/ark:/67531/metapth217006/m1/1/?q=Antonio%20Lopez%20de%20Santa%20Anna, accessed Aug. 23, 2016, University of North Texas Libraries, The Portal to Texas History, texashistory.unt.edu, crediting the Dolph Briscoe Center for American History; Fowler, *Santa Anna*, 180–181; Schiena, *Santa Anna*, 33–34, 2nd quotation on 34.

65. Winders, *Crisis in the Southwest*, 34, quotation; Campbell, *Gone to Texas*, 160–161.

66. Jones, *Santa Anna*, quotation on 74.

67. Jones, *Santa Anna*, 74–75, quotations on 75; Lesley B. Simpson, *Many Mexicos*, 4th ed. (Berkeley: University of California Press, 1967), 244–245; Winders, *Crisis in the Southwest*, quotation on 35. Scholarly sources disagree as to how many times Santa Anna actually held the office of president of Mexico. Oakah Jones in *Santa Anna* (1939) gives the number as five; Robert Scheina in *Santa Anna: A Curse upon Mexico* (2002) says eleven times, as cited in many other sources; and Will Fowler in *Santa Anna and Mexico* (2007) says that he held the office on six occasions.

68. Sam W. Haynes, *Soldiers of Misfortune: The Somervell and Mier Expeditions* (Austin: University of Texas Press, 1990), 10–23, passim; Fowler,

Santa Anna, 1ˢᵗ quotation on 183; Winders, *Crisis in the Southwest*, 51–56, passim, 2ⁿᵈ quotation on 51.

69. Haynes, *Soldiers of Misfortune*, 122–127, passim; Winders, *Crisis in the Southwest*, 60–62.

70. Callcott, *Santa Anna*, 184–187, 193, 200–201; *HOT Online*, Callcott, "Santa Anna"; Jones, *Santa Anna*, 90–91; Fowler, *Santa Anna*, 228–229, quotation on 229.

71. Winders, *Crisis in the Southwest*, 71–72, 77–88, 92, 95–96; Meyer, Sherman, and Deeds, *Course of Mexican History*, 257–258, as quoted on 258. For the message that the president sent to Congress, see James K. Polk, Special Message to the Senate and the House of Representatives, May 11, 1846, http://www.dmwv.org/mexwar/documents/polk.htm.

72. Callcott, *Santa Anna*, 238–239; Fowler, *Santa Anna*, 251–256, quotations on 251.

73. Scheina, *Santa Anna*, 55–76, passim; Fowler, *Santa Anna*, 256–285, passim, 1ˢᵗ quotation on 261, 2ⁿᵈ quotation on 280; Winders, *Crisis in the Southwest*, 122–123.

74 Fowler, *Santa Anna*, 281–284, 344–345, 1ˢᵗ quotation on 284, 2ⁿᵈ quotation on 282, 4ᵗʰ quotation on 344; Antonio López de Santa Anna, *Manifesto del General de División, Benemérito de la Patria, Antonio López de Santa-Anna, a sus conciudadanos* (Mexico: Imprenta de Navarro, 1848), reproduction by ULAN Press, 3ʳᵈ quotation on 12; Jones, *Santa Anna*, 122–127, 129, 131; "Antonio López de Santa Anna (1794–1876)," New Perspectives on the West, PBS, http://www.pbs.org/weta/thewest/people/s_z/santaanna.htm (accessed March 6, 2006).

75. "Antonio López de Santa Anna," Sons of DeWitt Colony Texas, Wallace L. McKeehan, obituary as quoted, http://www.tamu/edu/ccbn/dewitt/santaanna.htm. See José Fuentes Mares, *Santa Anna: Aurora y ocaso de un comediante*, and Juan Gualberto Amaya, *Santa Anna no fué un traidor* (Mexico: Cicerón, 1952).

76. Scheina, *Santa Anna*, 3, 87–90, 1ˢᵗ quotation on 3, 2ⁿᵈ quotation on 90.

77. Fowler, *Santa Anna*, 346–368, passism, 1ˢᵗ quotation on 356, 2ⁿᵈ quotation on 352, 3ʳᵈ quotation on 347, 4ᵗʰ quotation on 347–348, 5ᵗʰ quotation on 363. The final chapter of Fowler's biography, cited in this endnote, offers a concise overview of his revisionist interpretation of Santa Anna.

78. Antonio López de Santa Anna, *The Eagle: The Autobiography of Santa Anna*, ed. Ann Fears Crawford (Austin: State House Press, 1988), 3–5, 249, 1ˢᵗ quotation on 249, 2ⁿᵈ quotation on 5, 3ʳᵈ quotations on 3.

CONSTITUCION

FEDERAL

DE LOS ESTADOS UNIDOS

MEXICANOS,

Sancionada por el Congreso General Constituyente, el 4. de Octubre de

1824.

Imprenta del Supremo Gobierno de los Estados-unidos mexicanos, en Palacio.

The Federal Constitution of the United Mexican States, sanctioned by the General Constituent Congress, 4th of October, 1824. Erasmo Seguín served as Texas's representative to the Congress that produced Mexico's first constitution. Image of Mexican Constitution of 1824 Courtesy of the Rare Book and Special Collections Division, The Library of Congress, Washington, DC.

Erasmo and Juan N. Seguín

Mexicans or Texans?

THE CONTRIBUTIONS OF JUAN José María Erasmo de Jesús Seguín and his son Juan Nepomuceno to the birth of the Texas Republic in the nineteenth century are unequaled by any other Hispanic-Tejano family. Nevertheless, their story—especially that of the younger Seguín—is filled with controversy that spills over into present times.

Texans of Mexican ancestry faced many challenges in the first half of the 1800s. The last decades of Spanish colonial rule in Texas were disturbingly unstable as a result of invasions from without and rebellions from within. In each instance, Tejanos had to decide whether to remain loyal to their mother country or ally with the insurgents. For Mexican Texans, this was a "no win" situation, regardless of which choice they made. As a respected public servant in San Antonio, for example, Erasmo helped defeat a major threat against the Spanish crown in 1811, only to find his loyalty suspect a few years later and his property confiscated.[1]

When Mexico gained independence from Spain in 1821, its citizens found conditions little improved. Texas in particular was "drained of human resources and in economic ruins," while instability and conflict remained the norm for the young nation as a whole. As the Mexican period progressed, Tejanos soon found themselves a minority in their own land because of legalized immigration from the United States. "A strong proponent of

Anglo-American settlement," Erasmo Seguín formed close bonds with the newcomers and provided valuable services to Stephen F. Austin, the leading *empresario* (colonization agent) in Mexican Texas.[2] Son Juan followed his father's lead.

For both Texians (Anglo Texans) and Tejanos, however, changing conditions in Mexico in the 1830s posed a new set of challenges. Intent on gaining and keeping power, Antonio López de Santa Anna's political inconsistencies helped plunge the nation into conflict by mid-decade. Resistance against his increasingly authoritarian policies contributed significantly to Texans rebelling in 1835 and declaring independence in 1836.[3] Juan and Erasmo Seguín risked their own lives, their family's safety, and their material possessions by supporting the revolutionary cause, and each made singular contributions to the movement.

These men should have been embraced as honored citizens of the Republic of Texas, and for a time they were, with Juan serving as one of only four Tejanos in the Texas Congress. Unfortunately for Tejanos, however, continuing tensions between Mexico and Texas served to reinforce already-existing prejudices and make their loyalty suspect. For these and other reasons, animosity toward Juan Seguín became so pronounced that he felt compelled to relocate with his family to Mexico in the 1840s. During his years of exile, he not only participated in an invasion of Texas but also fought against the United States in a war that began mid-decade. This former hero of the Texas Revolution became a traitor in the eyes of many in the Lone Star State. Although Juan eventually returned to Texas, his reputation was tarnished.

Both Juan and Erasmo lived long lives but died insufficiently appreciated for their myriad contributions. Only long after their deaths would they again be accorded the acclaim they merited. This chapter addresses a fascinating Tejano family who played a critical role at a critical time in Texas history.

***

Seguín ancestors dated back to the earliest years of Spain's settlement of the future Lone Star State. Santiago, a soldier stationed at
San Antonio de Béxar in the 1720s, was "the first Seguín in Texas."
Two decades later he was joined by a relative named Bartolomé,
who prospered as a carpenter, land-owner, and farmer. Despite the
dangers of frontier life, Bartolomé outlived three wives and died in
1791 at about seventy years of age.[4]

Bartolomé's only son from his first marriage was Santiago
Seguín, the father of Erasmo and grandfather of Juan. Rather than
following his parent into carpentry, Santiago was fortunate enough
to inherit "his maternal grandfather's farming and ranching interests and parlayed them into enough wealth to join the ranks of
San Antonio's prosperous." Still, Santiago ran into trouble—a fore-
shadowing of the difficulties later experienced by his grandson Juan.
At age twenty-four, the recently married Santiago was arrested for
stealing cattle from the herd of one of San Antonio de Béxar's five
missions. Although the charge was quickly dropped, the rancher's
various problems with Spanish officials continued into the 1790s.
After the governor of Texas labeled Santiago's behavior as "scandal-
ous," he left Béxar early in the nineteenth century and moved south
of the Rio Grande to Saltillo for a fresh start.[5]

The Seguín family name continued in San Antonio with Santiago's
third son, Juan José María Erasmo, who was born on May 26,
1782. A young man of perhaps twenty-one years of age when his
father left Béxar, Erasmo later would become one of the most
respected Tejanos in Texas history. He is remembered for the
unusual distinction of holding office under three governments—the
Spanish Crown, the Mexican Republic, and the Texas Republic—
a rare accomplishment.[6]

For Texas, confusion and crisis marked the period from 1800
to 1821. In 1803, the United States bought the vast Louisiana
Territory from France, which had acquired it from Spain just a
few years earlier. The exact boundaries of the newly purchased

lands were vague, particularly to the west, and the United States attempted to claim present-day Texas as part of the bargain. The Spanish crown, however, strongly repudiated those claims. Aware of the threat posed to Texas by land-hungry citizens of the United States, Spain sent hundreds of soldiers to San Antonio and Nacogdoches, and war between the two nations appeared imminent. Armed conflict was narrowly avoided by the signing of an agreement in 1806 that created a neutral buffer zone between Texas and Louisiana. This accord kept the peace but created other problems, as lawless elements drifted into the so-called Neutral Ground, which was not under the direct authority of either claimant. These settlers were so disreputable that were called the "refuse of both Texas and Louisiana."[7]

Spain soon faced much bigger issues that overshadowed the Texas problem but had repercussions for that province. Intent on spreading his power in Europe, Napoleon Bonaparte of France imposed his brother Joseph on the Spanish throne in 1808. Revolts ensued in the mother country and flowed over into Spanish America, including a movement initiated by Father Miguel Hidalgo in Mexico in 1810 that would follow a convoluted path to independence slightly more than a decade later. The Hidalgo revolt reached Texas by 1811, but Royalists, who favored remaining under the Spanish flag, reestablished control in short order.[8]

Contributing to instability were military adventurers from the United States, called filibusters, who invaded Texas bent on acquiring land and wealth. Joining them was Bernardo Gutiérrez de Lara, a rancher and merchant from Revilla in Nuevo Santander province. Gutiérrez allied with William Augustus Magee, and they co-led an invasion of Texas in 1812. Magee was a citizen of the United States, but no ordinary invader. Instead, he was a graduate of the United States Military Academy at West Point and a disgruntled former artillery officer in the U.S. Army. These two men led some three hundred volunteers into Texas under the banner of the

"Republican Army of the North," which overran San Antonio and captured the young Spanish governor. Then, on Gutiérrez's order, Governor Manuel Salcedo was murdered along with sixteen others who had remained loyal to Spain.[9]

To avenge the brutal murders and crush the growing invasion, a huge Spanish army under the command of Commandant General Joaquín de Arredondo marched on Texas. At the Battle of Medina River in August 1813, Arredondo's royalist forces killed approximately thirteen of every fourteen rebels who opposed them. This included not only combat deaths but also more than one hundred men who had surrendered. The rebel death toll may have been as high as 1,300 men, making this the bloodiest battle in Texas history.[10]

Arredondo then marched on a defenseless San Antonio, where he executed another forty men who had joined the rebels or were suspected collaborators. Their mothers, wives, and children were packed into makeshift compounds, where eight of them died of suffocation. One of Arredondo's lieutenants also marched toward Nacogdoches and en route executed another seventy-one men who were suspect. Although this officer never reached the East Texas town—he was fatally stabbed by one of his own men near the San Marcos River—the threat of Spaniards carrying out summary executions was enough to cause the near total abandonment of Nacogdoches over the next six or seven years. As one historian has written, "By 1821 it must have been difficult to tell whether royalists or rebels had done the most harm." As another noted, "Although Colonel Arredondo kept Texas Spanish, he all but ruined it."[11]

Nacogdoches, with more than six hundred settlers in the early 1800s, "had been nearly abandoned" by 1821. Indeed, the entire province of Texas had declined from 3,103 as reported in its first census of 1777, to a non-Indian population of less than 3,000 on the eve of becoming part of a newly independent Mexico.

These depressing conditions, combined with instability in the mother country, made it easier for Texans to consider alternatives to remaining within the Spanish empire. And helping pave the way was Erasmo Seguín.[12]

In 1800, Seguín had married María Josefa Becerra, "a talented woman who could read and write." The couple had three children, including the eldest Juan Nepomuceno who was born in October 1806. The following year, Erasmo began his public career as San Antonio's postmaster, a job he would hold with few interruptions until 1835. Facilitated by having a wife who could be entrusted "with the family's business interests in his absence," he also became involved in ranching with hundreds of head of livestock. Erasmo remained loyal to Spain when San Antonio briefly came under the control of rebels—as mentioned, an offshoot of the Hidalgo movement in 1811. He helped suppress the revolt and restore Spanish authority. At this time, Erasmo's loyalty to Spain was unquestioned, but that would change after the Gutiérrez-Magee expedition.[13]

As Arredondo regained control of Spanish Texas, Erasmo Seguín lost his postmaster position and his property, under suspicion of abetting enemies of Spain. With his family homeless, he was fortunate not to be placed in front of a firing squad. Declining an offer of general amnesty, Erasmo "preferred to prove his innocence before a court." Successful in that endeavor, he received a pardon from the Spanish government in 1818. Although the family house and ranch were recovered, about $8000 of other confiscated property was not. Erasmo's restored reputation was evidenced by his election in 1820 as *alcalde* of San Antonio, an office often compared to that of a mayor in the United States, but in reality one of much greater power and prestige. *Alcaldes* were presidents of city councils, but they also had judicial powers and could issue laws for their municipalities.[14]

Following Moses Austin's visit to Texas in 1820 and the somewhat delayed approval of his plan to recruit three hundred

Anglo-American families to settle in the province, Governor Antonio Martínez selected Erasmo Seguín to lead a small delegation to inform the colonizer. Journeying toward the Texas-Louisiana border region, Erasmo managed by late March to get a message to Austin, who had headed back to Missouri. The Tejano then spent several months in the remote town of Natchitoches on the Red River awaiting the return of the *empresario.*[15]

The Austin who did appear on July 1 was not Moses, but his son Stephen Fuller, who brought news of his father's serious illness but indicated his own willingness to fulfill the colonization contract. As the party headed toward San Antonio, they learned that Moses Austin had died of pneumonia. Erasmo Seguín then pledged his support to Stephen F. Austin in an endeavor that would "open a new page in Texas history," and the two began "a close friendship, economic partnership, and crucial political alliance" that would continue for the next fifteen years until the colonizer's death.[16]

Like higher-ranking officials, Erasmo Seguín recognized in Stephen F. Austin and Anglo-American settlers the best possibility for offsetting the poverty, depopulation, and insecurity that had plagued Texas during Mexico's struggle for independence. Certainly, he could not have foreseen the negative long-term consequences that significant immigration from the United States would have on people of his ethnicity. As for Austin, who did not speak Spanish, Seguín would provide invaluable advice and support for his colonization efforts, as well as serve as a source of funds when needed. Erasmo also extended personal kindness to Austin by taking Stephen's younger brother into his household, where he could learn Spanish in a family atmosphere.[17]

Despite the complexities involved, Stephen F. Austin received conditional permission from Spanish officials to fulfill his father's colonization contract, and that agreement subsequently was honored by the newly independent Mexican nation. Erasmo Seguín

Portrait of Juan Seguín by Thomas Jefferson Wright, 1798–1846. The State
Preservation Board, Austin, Texas.

fulfilled a vitally important role for both Tejanos and Texians as
their agent to the Congress in Mexico City that would draft the
country's first constitution. In his early forties at the time, the delegate was "widely read, patriotic, and progressive." And again he
spent time away from home and family in service of Texas.[18]

In the Congress's deliberations, a major issue for Seguín and his constituents was the status of Texas within the new nation. Statehood was the ideal, but Erasmo "recognized that by itself Texas lacked sufficient resources and population to support a state government, much less fight off hostile Indians, or control westward-moving Anglo Americans." A realist, he considered territorial status as an option. One consideration was that the federal government would provide Texas with "the necessary resources for development." Another was his desire to counter a proposal that Texas be united with Coahuila as a state, because he feared such a union would lead to Texas being dominated by a capital in far-off Saltillo—fears that proved well-founded. Furthermore, both Tejanos and Texians would have to pay taxes to support the entire state of Coahuila-Texas, as well as send money to Mexico City.[19]

During his tenure in the national capital, Seguín was privy to a "bad, very bad" situation in which daily "the number of conspiracies increases, and everyone is out to undo the government's orders." Given that environment, Erasmo ultimately determined that the best of bad choices for Texas was union with Coahuila, which was formally approved on May 7, 1824. Although San Antonio would lose its status as a provincial capital, there was also relief that Texas would retain control of its public lands. Also, Seguín did secure a clause in the decree of union that Texas had the right to petition for separate statehood when it attained sufficient population. Even combined, however, Coahuila-Texas was considered the poorest state in the new nation.[20]

Although the above issue was a focal point of Seguín's efforts in Congress, he also paid heed to concerns expressed by his friend Stephen Austin regarding strong anti-slavery sentiment in Mexico. The colonizer "had enticed a number of slaveholders to bring cotton culture to Texas" and warned that fewer would come in the future if their preferred labor institution was in jeopardy. Erasmo himself believed that "preservation of slavery was the means to assuring the immigration of wealthy men who could do much to further regional development." He articulated that reality to fellow congressmen, and both Tejanos and Texians were relieved that the Mexican Constitution of 1824 contained not one word about slavery.[21]

Despite a subsequent attempt by the Mexican government in 1829 to abolish slavery throughout the nation, Tejanos assisted Austin in getting an exemption that prevented the decree from being enforced in Texas. Increasingly, the question of African-American slavery in Mexico was an issue dealt with at the state level until April 5, 1837, when the central government issued a law that freed slaves "'without any exception' throughout the Republic." By that time, Texas had declared its independence from Mexico and was not affected by the legislation.[22]

After Erasmo Seguín returned from his duties in Mexico City in 1824, he spent most of his time on local matters and resumed his duties as postmaster of San Antonio. The Tejano continued to join Austin in opposing attempts to eliminate slavery in Coahuila-Texas, and he worked at softening the requirement that settlers in Texas practice the Catholic faith. Within less than a decade, however, Erasmo would turn his interests elsewhere. In the early 1830s, the elder Seguín relocated with his family to a more rural setting, where he prospered with interests in livestock and agriculture. By 1834 he had a home that was described by a visitor as "admirably situated on a rising ground, . . . [near] the river San Antonio, . . . They [the Seguíns] have made a species of fortification as a precaution against the Indians. It consists of a square, palisadoed [*sic*] round, with the houses of the families residing there forming the sides of the square. . . . They have begun to sow cotton, which thrives very well. . . ."[23] Erasmo's impressive resources would prove valuable for the Texas revolutionaries when war broke out in 1835.

As matters worsened between Texas and Mexico in the late 1820s and early 1830s, Erasmo's elder son began to take center stage. At the time of Juan's birth in the early 1800s, there were very few opportunities for formal education in the borderlands province. Schools that did exist did not last long, and teachers at Béxar often resigned because they received no salary whatsoever. Bad as these conditions were, they deteriorated during the Mexican struggle for independence. By the end of the colonial period in 1821, "not a school in all Texas survived." Therefore, it is not surprising that the younger Seguín had little, if any, formal education. However, Juan did learn to read and write at the urging of his father, who probably served as his teacher.[24]

At age nineteen, Juan married María Getrudis Flores de Abrego, who was a member of one of San Antonio's most prominent ranching families, but probably illiterate because of the limited educational opportunities noted above. The couple would have a large family of ten children. The most notable among their offspring were a son who would become mayor of Nuevo Laredo and Juan Jr., an officer in the Mexican army in the 1860s and 1870s.[25]

Following in Erasmo's footsteps, Juan Seguín got his first experience by helping his mother run the post office while his father served in Congress in Mexico City from 1823–1824. Shortly after he was relieved of this responsibility, the younger Seguín took advantage of the easing of trade restrictions that had existed under Spanish rule to make a business trip to New Orleans. His travel companion was Juan Martín Veramendi, a future governor of Coahuila-Texas, suggesting that the twenty-year-old moved in elite circles. While in Louisiana, Juan purchased some one thousand pesos of merchandise, which was transported over-land by mule train to Austin's colony at San Felipe and sold there for profit. Erasmo's concern for his son led him to send him fresh horses, as well as asking Austin and his colonists to look after Juan's well-being, which they did.[26]

Again emulating his paternal role model, Juan Seguín sought public office. In 1829, at only twenty-two years of age, he was elected as one of San Antonio's two city councilmen, or *regidores*. He gained additional experience by occasionally serving as *alcalde* when the person who held that office was absent on other business. In such instances, Erasmo's son served as judge and heard minor cases involving civil misconduct or criminal activity.[27] All in all, these were particularly impressive accomplishments for someone of his age.

As the younger Seguín gained experience in city government and earned the trust of his fellow Bexareños, problems rose with Texas being linked to Coahuila. Texas had only one representative in the state legislature, whereas Coahuila had ten. This translated into the interests of Texans being frequently ignored or their issues being outvoted in the state capital. Furthermore, it took several days on horseback to travel from San Antonio or Austin's colony to Saltillo, and the dissemination of information was slow as well. More importantly, Texas had begun to grow rapidly in population by 1830, and being bound to Coahuila became less and less acceptable.[28]

The new, overwhelmingly Anglo-American population in Texas numbered around ten thousand in 1830. Despite having agreed to become Mexican citizens, these Texians conducted their business in English, as well as maintaining close ties to the United States. By then Texas's ethnic make-up more closely resembled a state in the southern United States than that of any in Mexico. Most of the new colonists came from the states in closest proximity to Texas, such as Louisiana, Arkansas, Mississippi, and Missouri. They not only brought African-American slaves with them but also were Protestant in their religious orientation. Although required to convert as a condition of immigration, many were unwilling to practice the Roman Catholic faith. The colonists, however, easily got around this requirement, because Texas did not have a single priest to minister to them until 1831. When one did appear, he was so indulgent that Texians overwhelmingly remained Protestants at heart, if not in name.[29]

These realities did not escape the attention of the government in Mexico City, which understandably feared the eventual loss of Texas. On April 6, 1830, the national Congress passed an act designed to terminate all immigration from the United States and prohibit the introduction of more slaves into Texas. Texians were understandably agitated by these prohibitions, which they sought to change. Stephen F. Austin was convinced that Texas would not continue its population expansion or make economic progress unless Mexican officials repealed the objectionable legislation. Changes taking place in Mexico City facilitated that objective, as the officials who had enacted the Law of April 6, 1830, were soon replaced by others willing to change it, or simply not enforce it.[30]

In the early 1830s, Stephen F. Austin worked at getting Tejanos to cooperate with Texians to achieve needed reforms, including separate statehood for Texas within the Mexican nation. On one occasion, the Anglo colonizer went to San Antonio to meet with Erasmo Seguín and other local leaders. He stressed to them "an exact description of the evils that are retarding the progress of Texas." With the support of Erasmo and Juan, the San Antonio *cabildo* (city council) lashed out at the state government in Saltillo and the national government in Mexico City for its treatment—or mistreatment—of Texas.[31]

A convention held in 1833 prepared a petition to formalize the concerns of the Texans. Among their demands, the delegates called for repeal of the Law of April 6, 1830, and for Texas to become a separate Mexican state. Although committed to the institution of slavery, they resolved to not import any new slaves

from Africa. The three men selected to take the petition and resolutions to Mexico City were Stephen F. Austin, Erasmo Seguín,
and Dr. James B. Miller. Even though Seguín had not been a
participant in the convention, Austin believed that a show of
Tejano support was critical to success. The colonizer headed to
San Antonio to inform his friend of the appointment and acquaint
him with the proceedings of the convention.[32]

To Austin's distress, Mexican Texans in San Antonio responded
with little enthusiasm to the news he brought. They knew that the
Constitution of 1824 stipulated that only a state legislature could
petition the national congress. Aware also that an earlier Texas
petition had been ruled illegal, Tejanos saw no reason to believe
that this second attempt would fare any better. Considering separate statehood to be a remote possibility, some thought a more
realistic aim would be to seek relocation of the capital of Coahuila-
Texas to San Antonio. An overarching—and realistic—concern for
these Tejanos was "that revolution was brewing in the colonies
and that they would be caught in the crossfire of an Anglo revolt
and a vengeful central government." Consequently, only Erasmo
Seguín sanctioned the convention's petition.[33]

Despite his public posture of support, Seguín asserted "that his
'private affairs' made it impossible for him" to make the lengthy trip
to the interior of Mexico. Because Texas was experiencing a cholera
outbreak, Dr. Miller also remained behind. Stephen F. Austin,
therefore, was the sole representative who traveled to Mexico
City to present the colonists' grievances. Once in the national
capital, the *empresario* was eventually able to attain a number of
significant government concessions, including repeal of the provi-
sion of the Law of April 6, 1830, that had prohibited Anglo-
American immigration.[34] But, the wheels of government in Mexico
turned slowly, and these efforts took time.

While Austin was away, Juan Seguín's political career made
impressive advances. He was elected *alcalde* of San Antonio to be

inducted into office on January 1, 1834. That same day, however, the Tejano learned that the political chief for the entire region had resigned. The twenty-seven year old, consequently, "assumed the top administrative office" for a substantial jurisdiction until the state governor "could appoint a permanent replacement." Just a few days later troubling news came that Stephen F. Austin, while returning to Texas from Mexico City, had been arrested in Saltillo.[35]

After making headway in opposing the anti-immigration law while in Mexico City, the *empresario* had focused on the issue of separation from Coahuila but made little progress in that regard. The situation worsened when a cholera epidemic caused thousands of casualties in the nation's capital, and Austin learned that family and friends were dying from the same disease in Texas. Depressed and frustrated, he penned a letter to the San Antonio city council, headed by Juan Seguín. The colonizer urged the formation of a separate state government, even though formal permission had not yet been granted. The *cabildo*, hesitant to follow Austin's question-able recommendation, forwarded the letter to Saltillo. Generally distrustful of Texians, Mexican officials there feared that Austin was fomenting revolution, and these fears were not without justifica-tion. They in turn forwarded his letter to Mexico City, which led to the order for the colonizer's arrest.[36]

Austin spent the better part of 1834 in prison. In early spring, Antonio López de Santa Anna made a brief return to the capital and assumed his duties as president. Although unwilling to free the *empresario*, the Napoleon of the West did sponsor some notable concessions, including increasing the number of Texas's represen-tatives in the state legislature from one to three. Also, "English became an official language in the state, and its citizens received the right to trial by a jury, a practice unique in all of Mexico."[37]

While Austin languished in prison and Juan Seguín exercised power in Texas, profound changes were occurring in Mexico.

Concerned by growing instability, Santa Anna recognized that sentiment was turning against the liberal Federalist government he headed and its "radical attack on church and army." As a result, he switched his allegiance to the Centralists (conservatives), who demanded "a strong national government and continued privileges for the clergy and military. . . ."[38]

That conservatives "were on their way to overturning the 1824 Constitution" was not immediately obvious. However, local militias were demobilized, and the various states in the Mexican Republic were replaced by military departments under officials appointed by and loyal to Santa Anna. Federalists rebelled against these and other reactionary measures with the earliest uprising taking place in Zacatecas. Personally leading the troops that crushed that insurrection, Santa Anna "rewarded his centralist soldiers by allowing them two days of rape and pillage . . . , during which more than two thousand noncombatants were killed." Worsening an already volatile situation, by late October 1835 the Constitution of 1824 had indeed been abolished.[39] But, what did this mean for Texas?

Like many other citizens of Mexico, Anglo and Mexican Texans initially were unsure how to interpret Santa Anna's actions. They knew that Santa Anna had previously been a supporter of the Constitution of 1824, which provided significant rights to the various states. He had also conceded to some of the requests incorporated in the 1833 petition. Nevertheless, as the reactionary intentions of the *caudillo* (strong man) became more apparent, Texas started down the dangerous road to revolution with the backing of the Seguíns.

Juan Seguín began his military career just months before the Texas Revolution erupted. In spring 1835, he led a small troop to Monclova, where the state government was under threat from Centralist forces commanded by Santa Anna's brother-in-law, General Martín Perfecto de Cos. All too aware of what had taken place at Zacatecas, however, the governor prudently decided against opposing Cos's army, whereupon an angry Seguín withdrew his men. Upon his return to San Antonio, the Tejano determined "to use all our influence to rouse Texas against the tyrannical government of Santa Anna." Given the sizable Anglo-American population in Texas, he recognized that any chance for success required their support.[40]

Texians became actively involved when General Cos demanded that several of their leaders be turned over to him for punishment after they forcibly removed a Mexican officer from his post without permission. Cos also informed the colonists that they must accept all laws emanating from Mexico City, particularly those removing their locally elected officials. The Texians not only refused to submit to these orders but also resisted the Mexican army's attempt to remove a cannon from the town of Gonzales. In the famous "Come and Take It" incident of October 2, 1835, violence erupted in what proved to be the beginning battle of the Texas Revolution.[41]

The events at Gonzales united the Anglo and Mexican Texans against Santa Anna and the Conservatives. Elected commander of the Texas army, Stephen Austin appointed Juan Seguín, whom he considered devoted to the Constitution, to the rank of captain. The *empresario* hoped "to reduce the dangerous possibility that the conflict would become defined strictly in ethnic or racial terms." Tejano participation also helped legitimize the argument that "the revolt was being fought against centralism, not for independence. . . ." The newly appointed captain was instructed to recruit other Tejanos to the cause, a task which he took seriously. The resultant recruits were experienced on horseback, had familiarity with the countryside, and were destined to play an important role in the ensuing revolution. In Austin's own words: "Cap. Seguín and his men were at all times ready and willing to go on any service they were ordered. They uniformly acquitted themselves to their credit. . . ."[42]

By November Cos was entrenched in San Antonio with hundreds of Mexican soldiers. Concluding that a hasty attack would be ill-advised, Austin decided to lay siege to the city. He wisely utilized Tejano support. Juan Seguín's men kept a vigilant watch for any reinforcements that might come to Cos's aid and burned the grass along the roads outlying San Antonio to prevent the enemy from being able to graze their horses. The Tejanos also proved capable in "foraging for supplies from the ranches for the troops at Bexar and Goliad." Among those providing major support was Erasmo Seguín, whom Cos had expelled as postmaster and forced to flee on foot from San Antonio. The Mexican general's mistreatment of the elder Seguín "helped to solidify that family's influence for the federalist side," and Erasmo subsequently "recruited men to help patriots win the Siege of Bexar." Also, evidence indicates that the younger Seguín—and certainly some of his men—participated in the eventual fighting that forced Santa Anna's brother-in-law to withdraw and retreat by the dawn of 1836.[43]

Having a family with deep roots in Texas, Juan Seguín "identi-fied his first loyalty with the land that was his by birth and blood for generations." Indeed, Juan had been raised "in a tradition of public service and independent thinking, and in a climate in which revolution was a way of life." Furthermore, given their federa-list inclinations, the Seguíns shared the Texians' frustration over Santa Anna's usurpation of power. Thus, their support for the restoration of legitimate government in Mexico was understand-able. Within months, however, the fight would take a radically different turn and lead to separation from Mexico. Understand-ably, many Mexican Texans had reservations about involvement in a revolutionary movement. Their fears that independence would mean being "woefully outnumbered by *norteamericanos* [Anglo Americans] and thus relegated to minority status in a land domi-nated by foreigners . . . " would prove well-founded. However, the Seguíns saw little future in remaining part of a nation as plagued by turmoil, instability, and poverty as Mexico—and they had economic ties to the United States.[44] Ultimately, both father and son would choose to take their chances in an independent Texas, and only later would the younger Seguín come to rue that decision.

With Mexican troops temporarily removed from Texas soil, Juan Nepomuceno attained the position of judge at San Antonio early in 1836. However, his tenure in that position proved brief, because Santa Anna was marching on Texas with a massive army. Seguín would again became captain of cavalry troops and actively coordinate defensive efforts. He also helped oversee the election in which two Tejanos, José Antonio Navarro and José Francisco Ruiz, were chosen as delegates to the convention at Washington-on-the-Brazos that would declare Texas's independence on March 2, 1836.[45]

The month before the historic convention made its fateful declaration, Seguín's scouts reported the presence of the first of Santa Anna's forces across the Rio Grande. Some Texian leaders reacted with skepticism, as alarming rumors were not uncommon. Also, a general distrust of the loyalty of Tejanos made their reports suspect. Unfortunately for all Texans, this time the information was correct. When the advance units of Santa Anna's army arrived at Béxar (San Antonio) on February 23, Juan Seguín was present. More than half a century later, he wrote about the early days of the Mexican siege. The Tejano noted that Colonel William "Travis resolved to concentrate all his forces within the Alamo, which was immediately done." On February 24, Santa Anna's troops began a bombardment. Within a few days, the besieged defenders found themselves "in such a desperate situation" that Travis decided to send a messenger to seek reinforcements, but Mexican soldiers had effectively encircled the Alamo.[46]

To attempt to leave, Seguín recounted, "was the same as to encounter death." Since no one wanted to run the risk, the men voted. Juan Seguín was selected, because his ethnicity and language would work in his favor. He also had the advantage of familiarity with the area. However, according to the Tejano, Travis opposed his accepting the commission, because his "presence in the Alamo might become necessary in case of having to treat with Santa Anna." Nevertheless, the others insisted that he accept the mission. Accompanied by his aide, Antonio Cruz, the Tejano captain made his way through the Mexican sentries. In Seguín's own words, "I arrived safely at the town of Gonzalez [*sic*], and obtained at once a reinforcement of thirty men, who were sent to the Alamo, and I proceeded to meet Sam Houston."[47]

Gathering a small company, Seguín then headed back to aid those under siege at the Alamo but neared the city shortly after the garrison had fallen. Travis had arranged to fire a signal gun periodically to let anyone approaching know that the defenders were still holding out against the numerically superior enemy. Hearing no signal, Seguín reluctantly recognized what the silence meant. Leaving to take the tragic news to Sam Houston, he had two men remain behind. Within a few days, they confirmed that the Alamo had indeed fallen.[48]

The fall of the Alamo and death of the defenders created panic in Texas. The forces Houston commanded were insufficient and unprepared to confront the Mexican army. To buy time, he made the difficult—and unpopular—decision to retreat. Similarly, frightened civilians, including Juan's own family, "fled eastward in advance of Santa Anna's legions. . . ." At that juncture, "Houston put [Juan] Seguín in command of the rearguard of his little army, with special instructions to help keep these civilians out of the way of advancing enemy columns, a role Seguín continued to play for some weeks." The capture of Colonel James Fannin and his troops at Goliad only escalated the panic, particularly when news came that almost four hundred of these prisoners had been slaughtered on Palm Sunday in late March 1836.[49]

Houston finally found the opportunity he sought, when he determined to attack Santa Anna's weary force on the afternoon of April 21, 1836, on "a point of land where Buffalo Bayou met the San Jacinto River." Seguín, who held the rank of colonel, commanded the only Tejano military company that would fight in the decisive battle for Texas's independence. At this moment in history, there could be no doubt where the loyalties of this Seguín and his followers lay.[50]

Fearing that in the heat of battle the loyal Tejanos might be mistaken for the hated enemy, Sam Houston decided that Seguín's company should not participate at San Jacinto. Reminding his commander that Tejanos had died defending the Alamo, Seguín heatedly countered that Mexican Texans had ample reason to hate Santa Anna and that they "wanted in on the kill." Furthermore, the Tejano officer and the surviving members of his company could not return to their homes in San Antonio until the Mexican army was ousted. Houston acquiesced but took precautions. To protect the Tejanos from friendly fire, he had them place pieces of cardboard in their hat bands. A popular version is that they used a deck of playing cards for that purpose.[51]

In the brief, but gory, Battle of San Jacinto, Seguín's men proved as bloodthirsty as their Texian counterparts. During the fighting, one of Santa Anna's officers recognized a Tejano acquaintance, Antonio Menchaca. When the Mexican begged for mercy, Menchaca exclaimed, "No, damn you, I'm no Mexican. I am an American." Then he instructed an Anglo soldier to shoot the man. That enemy officer was only one of hundreds of Santa Anna's men to die at the hands of Anglo *and* Mexican Texans at San Jacinto.[52]

Seguín's valor earned Sam Houston's "warmest regard and esteem." The Texas commander took the time to inform Erasmo about his son's "brave and gallant bearing in the battle of San Jacinto, with that of his men." Houston also had sufficient confidence in the young Tejano to entrust him with overseeing the withdrawal of the Mexican army from Texas and recovering property belonging to its citizens.[53]

While garnering praise from his commander, Juan Seguín's role in the revolution earned criticism from officers in the Mexican army. Among these was José Enrique de la Peña who served on Santa Anna's staff during the Texas campaign. While acknowledging Seguín as an intelligent man, de la Peña vilified him as a traitor to Mexico, "a label both ugly and deserved." Similarly, Vicente Filisola, commander of the Mexican army following Santa Anna's capture, complained about the Tejano's fulfilling the very mission he had been assigned by Sam Houston. The Mexican General noted that Seguín with a rebel force had appeared at the rear of retreating Mexican artillery troops. The Tejano declared his intent "to reclaim the property and slaves that might be in the possession of members of the army and belonged to Texas owners, according to what had been agreed to in the armistice. . . ." Seguín also strongly urged a hasty withdrawal, because "those under his command had no discipline and . . . he was hard put to control them"—a not very subtle threat.[54] That the Tejano was labelled a traitor by de la Peña and Filisola is understandable, but ironic, given that within six years his loyalty would be questioned by fellow Texans.

The Mexican officers cited above almost certainly would have taken perverse satisfaction at the more immediate personal cost Seguín paid for fighting against their country. As soon as he was able—which would not be until mid-July—Juan went to escort his family home from East Texas, where they had fled for safety. The journey proved arduous, as all were ill from the lingering effects of an epidemic. And upon his return, the Tejano officer "found my ranch despoiled; what little was spared by the retreating enemy, had been wasted by our own army; ruin and misery met my return to my unpretending home."[55]

Before making the above-mentioned trip, Seguín had to fulfill orders to take possession of San Antonio and organize some ninety men for its defense. Recruiting efforts fell far short of the goal, however, and his command proved troubled and short. For all practical purposes, Bexareños were living under virtual military rule, and some were upset at the policies Seguín instituted. Backed by a force of fewer than twenty-five men, he was unable "to make his decisions respected." With vivid memories of General Cos's occupation of Béxar, and of more recent events, local residents declined to take up arms against their former homeland, instead favoring the safer course of remaining neutral. The arrival of well over two hundred Anglo reinforcements from outside only served to further alienate the Bexareños. Before the end of June 1837, Seguín made the decision to vacate the city. Before leaving, he chastised Tejanos with the following words: If you continue as "mere lookers-on; if you do not abandon the city, and retire [to] the interior of Texas, that its army may protect you, you will, without fail, be treated as real enemies, and will suffer accordingly."[56] His advice was appropriate, although almost certainly unappreciated.

After the furlough to bring his family back from East Texas, Seguín was promoted to lieutenant colonel by President David G. Burnet, instructed to recruit a battalion, and again given command at San Antonio. Once more "controversy and turmoil" ensued. Felix Huston, the new commander of the Texas army, thought Seguín unfit for the job "because 'he cannot speak our language.'" This was truly an affront, given that it came from a man who had not migrated to Texas until after the Battle of San Jacinto. To his credit, newly elected president of the Republic Sam Houston came to the Tejano's defense. Taking steps to counter Huston's order, he assured his trusted subordinate that "no intention has been entertained to wound your feelings or compromise your honor!"[57]

Yet another issue between Huston and Seguín required the intervention of the president. For reasons that are subject to debate, Huston ordered Seguín's troops to "depopulate San Antonio and to remove its citizens more than a hundred miles east beyond the Brazos River." Perhaps the Texian commander thought the city

too vulnerable should another Mexican invasion occur. Allegations surfaced, however, that Huston wanted to remove the city's
overwhelmingly Tejano population to prepare the way for Anglo
investors "to move in and take over. . . ." President Houston coun-
termanded Huston's order.[58]

Juan Seguín's problems were just beginning. As Texians realized that Mexico had not and would not accept the loss its territory, the loyalty of Tejanos became increasingly suspect because
of their ethnicity, language, and religion. In 1836, none other
than Stephen F. Austin had condemned Mexicans as members of
a "mongrel Spanish-Indian and Negro race, against civilization
and the Anglo-American race." What a betrayal those words were
to the Seguíns, who had done so much for Texas—and for Austin,
himself. That the colonizer's sentiments were shared by a rapidly
increasing Anglo-American population in Texas did not bode well
for inhabitants of Mexican descent.[59]

Adding to the Tejano's concerns was the failure of the army to
provide support for his regiment. "Short of money and supplies,"
he took drastic measures that alienated his fellow Bexareños.
The officer resorted to raiding city coffers, as well as seizing horses
and mules owned by private citizens. The explanation that he needed
mounts and pack animals for his troops was small consolation to
those who received only receipts as compensation for their livestock.
Privately, Seguín began engaging in land speculation, a practice that
would generate even more animosity toward him.[60]

Despite his issues with Huston and other Texans, Seguín was
chosen to provide appropriate honors to the men who had died at
the Alamo. He found their ashes in three piles and placed the two
smaller heaps in a casket. On February 25, 1837, it was taken in a
formal procession from the Béxar parish church to where "the ashes
had been collected." After volleys were fired, "the coffin was then
placed upon the large heap of ashes." Seguín delivered a eulogy in
Spanish, and a speech was given in English by Major Thomas Wester.

"The coffin and all the ashes were then interred," and more volleys were fired. Afterwards, the battalion marched back to Béxar "with music and colors flying." Seguín later reported that "every honor was done within the reach of my scanty means."[61]

The words that Seguín spoke on the above occasion were translated and published in the press. He praised "the valiant heroes who died in the Alamo" for preferring "to die a thousand times rather than submit themselves to the tyrant's yoke." Citing "Travis, Bowie, Crockett, and others" as exemplary, the Tejano declared that they deserved a place in the annals of history. He called the enemy barbaric for their treatment of these heroes, whose feet were bound and who were "dragged to this spot, where they were reduced to ashes." Seguín ended with the declaration that "Texas shall be free and independent or we shall perish in glorious combat."[62] At that moment, his sincerity and trustworthiness surely must have been evident, even to his detractors.

Later that year, Seguín again conducted business in New Orleans. During his absence, the voters of Béxar elected him to serve in the Texas Congress—the only Tejano to hold a Senate seat during the duration of the Republic. Upon his return to San Antonio in March 1838, he consequently terminated his military service and received payment in land grants, the only commodity available to the "cash poor" Texas government to compensate veterans. During these post-revolutionary years, land speculation was rampant with financially distressed Tejanos being exploited in a system full of fraud and abuse. Whether Seguín participated in "fraudulent practices cannot be determined"; nevertheless, he was "a small-scale but enthusiastic player in this and other questionable money-making ventures."[63]

Whatever irregularities he might have committed in his private life, Juan Seguín acquitted himself well in the Texas Congress. Despite limited knowledge of English, he chaired the Committee on Military Affairs and sponsored legislation to assist orphans and widows of the defenders who sacrificed their lives at the Alamo.

He also advocated having "the laws of the new republic printed in Spanish" out of concern "that Tejanos were being shut out of participation in, or even understanding of, the new government." Nevertheless, in 1840, Juan resigned from his Senate seat to aid Federalist General Antonio Canales militarily and financially in what proved to be "an abortive campaign against the Centralists" in Mexico. On a more positive note, that same year the Texas Congress approved paying Erasmo more than three thousand dollars for supplies provided during the Revolution.[64]

Juan Seguín's tenure in the Senate was not the only evidence that he was held in high regard by many fellow Texans. In the 1830s, Anglo families began to settle on land about thirty-five miles to the northeast of San Antonio. Late in the decade, the town of Walnut Spring was established in that region, and in February of 1839 the name was changed to Seguin, in honor of the war hero. Still another sign of the Tejano's prominence was his election as mayor of San Antonio at the end of 1840.[65] Yet, Juan Nepomuceno's downfall would come within two years.

Mexico's refusal to recognize Texas's independence, much less the Rio Grande as the international boundary, created a volatile situation. Sam Houston's less-cautious successor in the presidency, Mirabeau B. Lamar, wanted "to extend the limits of the republic" and planned an expedition to Santa Fe "to bolster Texas's claim to New Mexico." Seeking critical Tejano support, the president went to San Antonio in 1841, where he was honored with an impressive ball. One guest later wrote that the function "opened with Lamar dancing with Mrs. Juan Seguin [sic], the mayor's wife" and observed that she "was so fat that the president could hardly get a firm hold on her waist. . . ."[66] The important point is not that Juan's wife was rotund but that the Seguíns' status was such that the president accorded her the first dance. Ironically, an unintended consequence of Lamar's resultant 1841 Santa Fe expedition was undermining the Tejano's standing to an alarming degree.

That the resilient Antonio López de Santa Anna regained power as president of Mexico in the early 1840s did not bode well for Texans in general or Juan Seguín in particular. The Santa Fe Expedition, despite being a disastrous failure, had the effect of waving a red flag in front of a bull. An infuriated Santa Anna would twice dispatch Mexican armies into Texas in 1842, the first headed by Colonel Rafael Vásquez, the second by General Adrián Woll. Each time the invaders would target San Antonio. (See Chapter 1.) These frightening incursions served to exacerbate Texians' prejudice against Tejanos, who found themselves in increasingly difficult circumstances.[67]

Preceding the first raid, General Mariano Arista offered protection and amnesty to those who offered no resistance but warned that "the sword of justice" would be unleashed on anyone who resisted. These words were particularly directed at Tejanos. An obstinate Juan Seguín informed Sam Houston, who had again become president of the Republic, "of his suspicions that the Mexicans were planning a raid into San Antonio." However, the government's response was that "the impoverished condition of our country renders it almost helpless," so no aid would be forthcoming. The mayor then made the realistic decision to evacuate the town and advised other residents to do the same. Ironically, when Vázquez briefly captured San Antonio, he claimed that Seguín "had assisted him in his advance into Texas." Anglo settlers of longer duration tended to discount the allegations. However, newer arrivals from the United States welcomed a chance to undermine the mayor who had alienated them through his efforts "to protect the interests of the citizens of San Antonio against the [Anglo] adventurers." Juan's attempts to refute Colonel Vásquez's allegations proved futile.[68]

Already existing resentment created by Seguín's aforementioned "questionable money-making ventures" only compounded his woes, as did burdensome debts that he resorted to smuggling to pay. Being "hunted by bands of armed Anglo-Americans,"

Col. Juan Nepomuceno Seguín. *A Comprehensive History of Texas*, edited by Dudley G. Wooten, published by William. G. Scarff, 1898, p. 395, v. 1. 074–0268, UTSA Special Collections—Institute of Texan Cultures.

the Tejano found himself "a foreigner in my native land." For his own protection and that of his family, he resigned as mayor of San Antonio and fled with them to Mexico shortly after the Vásquez invasion. Not surprisingly, the former war hero held tremendous resentment against those Texians who had forced him to leave his place of birth and anger at being made a victim of "the wickedness of few men."[69] Also, he had a large family to support, no matter which side of the Rio Grande he chose for his residence.

Mexico did not prove a safe haven for Juan Seguín, who was imprisoned after crossing the border because of his role in the Texas Revolution. According to the Tejano's later accounts of his six-year exile, he was given the choice of "loathsome confinement or to accept military service." Recognizing that the former would leave his family without resources, he reluctantly chose the latter. In his own words, "the father triumphed over the citizen: I seized the sword that pained my hand." Whatever his motives, Seguín's subsequent actions made him even more despised by his fellow Texans. Compelled to participate in the second invasion of Texas, led by Adrián Woll in September 1842, Seguín "performed his duties with the Mexican army as conscientiously as he had with the Texas army." In fact, Woll commended Seguín not only for marching "in the vanguard to explore and direct the scouting in all directions" but also for performing meritoriously in the fighting to capture San Antonio.[70]

While widely condemned for betraying Texas and killing innocent civilians, Juan Seguin still had at least one true friend in the Republic. Sam Houston went out of his way to console Erasmo, who, unlike his son, did not face such intense, prolonged accusations of disloyalty. The president sent these comforting words to a troubled father: "I pray, Sir, that you will not suppose for one moment, that I will denounce Colonel John [Juan] N. Seguín, without a perfect understanding of his absence."[71]

During Juan Nepomuceno's period of voluntary exile, Texas was annexed to the United States, which precipitated a war with Mexico in 1846. In an ironic twist, this same Tejano who had fought against Santa Anna at the Battle of San Jacinto was now a colonel under his command. Texas Rangers who participated in General Zachary Taylor's invasion of northern Mexico made serious, but futile, attempts to capture the hated Seguín. Had they succeeded, his life would almost certainly have been forfeited. Regardless, even before Mexico's defeat and concession of territory in 1848, the Tejano resigned his commission. The "care worn & *thread-bear* [*sic*]" Tejano decided to risk returning to Texas, where he and his family settled on land near his father's *Casa Blanca* (White House) Ranch in the San Antonio region near present-day Floresville.[72]

Used to being publicly active, Juan Seguín soon tired of life on the ranch. Despite his recent infamy, he again became involved in San Antonio politics. Twice elected justice of the peace for heavily Hispanic Bexar County in the 1850s, he also played a prominent role in establishing the local Democratic Party there. Seguín found himself again working closely with Texians. Not all, however, were willing to forgive his participation in Woll's invasion, much less his having fought against the U.S. during the recent war. Accused of "barbarous and unworthy deeds[,]" the Tejano defended himself by penning his memoirs in 1858. One doubts that his detractors were moved to sympathy by Seguín's version of events or rationale for his actions. At any rate, the Tejano would hold only one more elective position, that of Wilson County judge in the 1860s.[73]

Shortly before Juan wrote his memoirs, his father Erasmo died on October 30, 1857, and was laid to rest in the family plot at his ranch. No longer young himself, Juan spent decades seeking various forms of compensation for himself and the men who had served with him in the Texas army. Persevering despite rejections along the way, in 1874 he was awarded "a pension for his service to the Republic."[74]

This man, who had been both acclaimed and reviled during his lifetime, would spend his final decades in retirement at Nuevo Laredo, Mexico. Juan Nepomuceno died there on August 27, 1890, in his eighty-third year of life with "no obituaries, no ceremonies, no notice of his passing." The better part of a century would pass before the Tejano's reputation was resurrected and his body returned to his native soil. On July 4, 1976, Juan Seguín's remains were buried with ceremony at a park in Seguin, Texas, now "the site of annual celebrations honoring the war hero."[75]

* * *

Without question, Erasmo Seguín, son Juan, and other Tejanos who supported the Texas Revolution later became the unfortunate victims of racial prejudice. The Texas Republic from 1836 to the beginning of Texas statehood in late 1845 was increasingly dominated by Anglo Americans convinced of their superiority. That domination would continue throughout Seguín's life and well beyond his death. With it came racial discrimination.[76] Nothing sets people apart quite so much as those in a minority being *different* from the majority. Those differences can be matters of appearance, language, religion, and even levels of income and education. Juan suffered from several, albeit not all, of these liabilities.

During his lifetime, Juan Seguín experienced charges of disloyalty to both Texas and Mexico, and they often came at the same time! What was he to do? What might anyone have done in his situation? His family had been in Texas for generations. His father Erasmo was a man of accomplishment in both the public and private sectors, someone respected by Tejanos and Texians alike. Son Juan also served Texas well. He not only demonstrated his loyalty on and off the battlefield but also held offices ranging from mayor to senator. Nevertheless, a complex web of circumstances forced him into years of exile, and at the end he did not die on his native soil. "Of all the patriots of the Texas Revolution, it was perhaps Juan Seguín who had the most troubled relationship with the land he helped to found."[77] A review of his life seems to underscore the cliché that "no good deed goes unpunished."

Significant time would pass before the Seguíns would be widely appreciated for their contributions. Twentieth-century attention to the role of Tejanos in the history of the Lone Star State appropriately led to greater homage being accorded to these two notable men. As early as 1908, a pamphlet by J.M. Woods carried an extremely long, but telling, title: *Don Erasmo Seguin: A Spanish aristocrat, a trusted agent of Governor Martinez, a counselor of Stephen F. Austin, an able Deputy of the Mexican State of Texas to the National Congress, a patriot of the Republic of Texas and loyal citizen of the American Commonwealth.* More than sixty years later a *San Antonio Express-News* article enumerated Erasmos's many impressive accomplishments, while bemoaning that *Casa Blanca* had fallen into ruin with the exact location of his grave unknown, despite efforts by descendants to locate it. Significantly, that same article labelled son Juan as one of Texas's "greatest patriots and heroes."[78]

In the late twentieth and early twenty-first centuries, publications ranging from scholarly works, to comic books, to children's books began to extol the exploits of the younger Seguín. Significantly, a "10-foot high equestrian monument was unveiled on October 28, 2000 in Seguin, Texas, providing a long-overdue tribute to an overlooked Texas hero. . . ." A decade later, the Texas Education Agency adopted standards requiring students in public middle schools to learn about the contributions of both father and son, thereby insuring their place in the annals of Texas history.[79]

Descendants of the Seguíns can still be found in the Lone Star State and in Mexico. Those who live in Texas can point with pride to not one but two principled ancestors—Erasmo and Juan Seguín—who were honorable men, honorable Tejanos, and honorable Texans.

Bibliographical Commentary

The Texas State Historical Association's *Handbook of Texas Online* at www. tshaonline.org has succinct, but reliable, entries by Jesús F. de la Teja on "Seguín, Juan José María Erasmo de Jesús (1782–1857)" and "Seguin, Juan Nepomuceno (1806–1890)," as well as related topics. Also, the Texas State Libraries and Archives Commission has a page on Juan Seguín that includes three embedded images of primary sources on which the viewer can click to retrieve those documents.

　　Among published works on the Seguíns, those of Jesús F. de la Teja are particularly noteworthy. He edited an important collection of primary sources in *A Revolution Remembered: The Memoirs and Selected Correspondence of Juan N. Seguín* (2002) and is also editor of *Tejano Leadership in Mexican and Revolutionary Texas* (2010). De la Teja also authored various articles and book chapters reproduced in *Faces of Béxar: Early San Antonio and Texas* (2016). Greg Cantrell's *Stephen F. Austin: Empresario of Texas* (1999) is especially helpful in understanding the Seguíns' relationship with Austin and their role in Anglo-American colonization. Also noteworthy are Timothy Matovina's edited work, *The Alamo Remembered: Tejano Accounts and Perspectives* (1995), and Andrès Tijerina's *Tejanos and Texas under the Mexican Flag, 1821–1836* (1994). To a lesser degree, material can be found in Raúl Ramos's *Beyond the Alamo: Forging Mexican Ethnicity in San Antonio, 1821–1861* (2008), Randolph Campbell's *Sam Houston and the American Southwest*, 3rd ed. (2007), and Paul Lack's *The Texas Revolutionary Experience: A Political and Social History, 1835–1836* (1992). For more general coverage of race relations in nineteenth-century Texas, see *They Called Them Greasers: Anglo Attitudes toward Mexicans in Texas, 1821–1900* (1983) by Arnoldo de León.

　　Less traditional literature includes comic books by Jaxon, pseudonym for noted illustrator and historian Jack Jackson. Among these are *Recuerden el Alamo: The True Story of Juan N. Seguín and His Fight for Texas Independence* (1979) and *Tejano Exile: The True Story of Juan N. Seguín and the Texas-Mexicans after San Jacinto* (1980). Works geared to younger readers include Rita Kerr, *Juan Seguín: A Hero of Texas* (1985); Robert Hollman, *Juan Seguín* (2007); William R. Chemerka, *Juan Seguín* (2012); and Kathy Gause, *Arnie Armadillo and the Texas Heroes—Juan N. Seguín* (2014).

Endnotes

　　1. For an overview of the turbulent events in the late Spanish period and their impact on the province of Texas, see Chapter 11, "The Twilight of Spanish Texas, 1803–1821," Donald Chipman and Harriett Denise Joseph, *Spanish Texas, 1519–1821*, rev. ed. (Austin: University of Texas Press, 2010), 230–255, passim.

　　2. Jesús F. de La Teja, *Faces of Béxar: Early San Antonio and Texas* (College Station: Texas A&M University Press, 2016), 30, 182, 1st quotation on 182, 2nd quotation on 30.

　　3. See Chapter 1 of this book on "Antonio López de Santa Anna: 'Napolean of the West.' "

4. De la Teja, *Faces of Béxar*, 28, quotation.

5. De la Teja, *Faces of Béxar*, 28, 1ˢᵗ quotation; Jesús F. de la Teja, ed., *A Revolution Remembered: The Memoirs and Selected Correspondence of Juan M. Seguín* (Austin: Texas State Historical Association, 2002), 2–3, 2ⁿᵈ quotation on 3.

6. De la Teja, *Revolution Remembered*, 3; *Handbook of Texas Online*, Jesús F. de la Teja, "Seguín, Juan José María Erasmo De Jesús," http://www.tshaonline.org/handbook/online/articles/fse07. [*Handbook of Texas Online* hereinafter cited as *HOT Online*.]

7. Randolph B. Campbell, *Gone to Texas: A History of the Lone Star State*, 2ⁿᵈ ed. (New York: Oxford University Press, 2012), 84–85; Odie B. Faulk, *The Last Years of Spanish Texas, 1788–1821* (The Hague: Mouton, 1964), 125.

8. Michael C. Meyer, William L. Sherman, Susan M. Deeds, *The Course of Mexican History*, 10ᵗʰ ed. (New York: Oxford University Press, 2014), 216–217, 220–229, passim; Chipman and Joseph, *Spanish Texas*, 246.

9. Chipman and Joseph, *Spanish Texas*, 247–250; Félix D. Almaráz, *Tragic Cavalier: Manuel Salcedo of Texas, 1808–1813* (Austin: University of Texas Press, 1989), 171.

10. Donald E. Chipman and Harriett Denise Joseph, *Notable Men and Women of Spanish Texas* (Austin: University of Texas Press, 1999), 226–227; see also Ted Schwarz, *Forgotten Battlefield of the First Texas Revolution: The Battle of the Medina, August 18, 1813*, ed. and annot. Robert H. Thonhoff, (Austin: Eakin Press, 1985), 82, 89, 102.

11. Chipman and Joseph, *Notable Men and Women*, 245, 247; David J. Weber, *The Mexican Frontier, 1821–1846: The American Southwest under Mexico* (Albuquerque: University of New Mexico Press, 1982), 10, 1ˢᵗ quotation; John L. Kessell, *Spain in the Southwest: A Narrative History of Colonial New Mexico, Arizona, Texas, and California* (Norman: University of Oklahoma Press, 2002), 365, 2ⁿᵈ quotation.

12. See Alicia V. Tjarks, "Comparative Demographic Analysis of Texas, 1777–1793, *Southwestern Historical Quarterly* 77 (January 1974): 299.

13. Robert Kerwin, "Juan Nepomuceno Seguín" (Master of Arts Thesis, University of Texas Pan-American, December 2008), 9, 1ˢᵗ quotation; de la Teja, *Revolution Remembered*, 4, 2ⁿᵈ quotation.

14. Kerwin, "Juan Nepomuceno Seguín," 11; de la Teja, *Revolution Remembered*, 4–5, quotation on 5.

15. Weber, *The Mexican Frontier*, 160–161; Gregg Cantrell, *Stephen F. Austin: Empresario of Texas* (New Haven: Yale University Press, 1999), 85–86; de la Teja, *Revolution Remembered*, 6. For additional information on Moses Austin, see David B. Gracy II, *Moses Austin: His Life* (San Antonio: Trinity University Press, 1969).

16. Cantrell, *Stephen F. Austin*, 88–90; de la Teja, *Revolution Remembered*, 6, 1ˢᵗ quotation; Andrés Reséndez, *Changing National Identities at the Frontier: Texas and New Mexico, 1800–1850*, reprint (Cambridge: Cambridge University Press, 2006), 69, 2ⁿᵈ quotation.

17. Cantrell, *Stephen F. Austin*, 86, 110; Kerwin, "Juan Nepomuceno Seguín," 46.

18. Randolph B. Campbell, *Gone to Texas*, 101–104; Weber, *Mexican Frontier*, quotation 20.

19. Weber, *Mexican Frontier*, 24, 1ˢᵗ quotation; de la Teja, *Faces of Béxar*, 184–185, 2ⁿᵈ quotation on 185. For more detailed information on the complex issue of determining Texas's status within the new nation, how it came to be united with Coahuila as a single state, and Erasmo Seguín's efforts on behalf of his fellow Texans, see Charles A. Bacarisse, "The Union of Coahuila and Texas," *Southwestern Historical Quarterly* 61, no. 3 (Jan. 1958): 341–349.

20. De la Teja, *Revolution Remembered*, 9, quotations; de la Teja, *Faces of Béxar*, 184–86.

21. Cantrell, *Stephen F. Austin*, 160; de la Teja, *Faces of Béxar*, 186–187, 1ˢᵗ quotation on 186, 2ⁿᵈ quotation on 186–187.

22. Andrés Tijerina, "Under the Mexican Flag," in *Tejano Journey, 1770–1855*, Gerald E. Poyo, ed. (Austin: University of Texas Press, 1996), 40–41; Cantrell, *Stephen F. Austin*, 215–216; Josefina Z. Vázquez, "The Texas Question in Mexican Politics, 1836–1845," *Southwestern Historical Quarterly* 89 (January 1986): 317, quotation.

23. De la Teja, *Revolution Remembered*, 5–6, 10–11, quotation on 5–6; de la Teja, *Faces of Béxar*, 187–188; *HOT Online*, "Seguín, Erasmo." For more on the religious issue, see Timothy M. Matovina, *Tejano Religion and Ethnicity: San Antonio, 1821–1860* (Austin: University of Texas Press, 1995).

24. Max Berger, "Education in Texas during the Spanish and Mexican Periods," *Southwestern Historical Quarterly* 51 (July 1947): 42–43, quotation on 42–43; *HOT Online*, Jesús F. de la Teja, "Seguin, Juan Nepomuceno," 2ⁿᵈ quotation, http://www.tshaonline.org/handbook/online/articles/fse08.

25. Jesús F. de la Teja, ed., *Tejano Leadership in Mexican and Revolutionary Texas* (College Station: Texas A&M University Press, 2010), 216; de la Teja, *Revolution Remembered*, 17–18, 52; *HOT Online*, "Seguin, Juan Nepomuceno."

26. De la Teja, *Tejano Leadership*, 216; de la Teja, *Revolution Remembered*, 16–17; Reséndez, *Changing National Identities*, 94–100, passim. In the 1820s and 1830s, Juan Seguín was only one of numerous Anglo and Mexican Texans capitalizing on more open trade policies, coupled with economic opportunities provided by the proximity of the borderlands to the United States. For more detailed coverage of this phenomenon, see the just-cited *Changing National Identities at the Frontier: Texas and New Mexico, 1800–1850* by Andrés Reséndez.

27. De la Teja, *Revolution Remembered*, 18–19.

28. Campbell, *Gone to Texas*, 104–105, 115; Cantrell, *Stephen F. Austin*, 192–193, 230; *HOT Online*, "Census and Census Records," http://www.tshaonline.org/handbook/online/articles/ulc01. According to the just-cited census entry in the *HOT Online*, "the colonization period of 1821–1831 brought many settlers; the population was estimated at 20,000 in 1831."

29. Campbell, *Gone to Texas*, 108–109.

30. Cantrell, *Stephen F. Austin*. 219–223, 275; Campbell, *Gone to Texas*, 114–116, 118, 123. The Fredonian Rebellion, a short-lived revolt in Texas in the mid-1820s, contributed to increasing suspicion on the part of the Mexican government toward Anglo Texans, even though Stephen F. Austin and his colonists opposed the movement. See *Handbook of Texas Online*, Archie P. McDonald, "Fredonian Rebellion," http://www.tshaonline.org/handbook/online/articles/jcf01.

31. Davis, *Lone Star Rising: The Revolutionary Birth of the Texas Republic* (New York: Free Press, 2004), 94–95, quotation on 94.

32. Davis, *Lone Star Rising*, 99; Cantrell, *Stephen F. Austin*, 267–268. See "Memorial to the Congress of the United Mexican States" [English]/04–13–1833/ Edward Eberstadt Collection in *Focus on Texas History: Colonization through Annexation*, exhibit, Dolph Briscoe Center for American History, https://www.cah.utexas.edu/texashistory/annex/anglo/exhibit.php?s=33.

33. Cantrell, *Stephen F. Austin*, 268, quotation; Davis, *Lone Star Rising*, 99–101.

34. Davis, *Lone Star Rising*, 100–101, quotation on 100; Campbell, *Gone to Texas*, 123.

35. De la Teja, *Revolution Remembered*, 20, quotations.

36. Cantrell, *Stephen F. Austin*, 270–273; Campbell, *Gone to Texas*, 123–124.

37. Campbell, *Gone to Texas*, 124, quotation.

38. Will Fowler, *Independent Mexico: The* Pronunciamiento *in the Age of Santa Anna, 1821–1858* (Lincoln: University of Nebraska Press, 2016), 169–171, 1st quotation on 169; de la Teja, *Revolution Remembered*, 21, 2nd quotation.

39. Fowler, *Independent Mexico*, 171–172, 1st quotation on 171; Meyer, Sherman and Deeds, *Mexican History*, 251; Okah Jones, Jr., *Santa Anna* (New York: Twayne Publishers, Inc., 1968), 62; Zacatecasinsider.com: Travelers Guide to Zacatecas, 2nd quotation, http://www.zacatecasinsider.com/zacatecas-history.asp.

40. De la Teja, *Tejano Leadership*, 223–224, quotation on 223.

41. Campbell, *Gone to Texas*, 128–130.

42. Fane Downs, "The History of Mexicans in Texas, 1820–1845" (Ph.D. Dissertation, Texas Tech University, 1970), 233; de la Teja, *Revolution Remembered*, 214–215; Cantrell, *Stephen F. Austin*, 319, 1st and 2nd quotations; Davis, *Lone Star Rising*, 214–215; Paul D. Lack, *The Texas Revolutionary Experience: A Political and Social History, 1835–1836* (College Station: Texas A&M University Press, 1992), 185, 3rd quotation.

43. De la Teja, *Revolution Remembered*, 25; Downs, "Mexicans in Texas," 236, 1st quotation; "Erasmo Seguin [sic]-Texas Historical Markers on Waymarking.com," Marker 4633, 3rd quotation, http://www.waymarking.com/waymarks/WMABJ3_Erasmo_Seguin; Lack, *Texas Revolutionary Experience*, 165, 2nd quotation.

44. Davis, *Lone Star Rising*, 215–216, 1st quotation on 215, 2nd quotation on 216; Stephen L. Hardin, "Efficient in the Cause," in Gerald E. Poyo, *Tejano Journey, 1770–1850* (Austin: University of Texas Press, 1996), 58, 3rd quotation; Reséndez, *Changing National Identities*, 158–169, passim, 268.

45. De la Teja, *Revolution Remembered*, 25; David McDonald, *José Antonio Navarro: In Search of the American Dream in Nineteenth-Century Texas* (Denton: Texas State Historical Association, 2010), 150.

46. Garland R. Lively, "Gonzales: Crucible of the Texas Revolution," MilitaryHistoryOnline.com, http://www.militaryhistoryonline.com/19thcentury/articles/Gonzales.aspx, accessed Aug. 29, 2016; James Donovan, *The Blood of Heroes: The 13-Day Struggle for the Alamo—and the Sacrifice That Forged a Nation* (New York: Little, Brown and Company, 2013), 100, 102; Juan Seguín to William Winston Fontaine, Nuevo Laredo, June 7, 1890, in de la Teja, *Revolution Remembered*, 194, as quoted. For information on the Spanish mission that became the site of

the famous battle, see *HOT Online*, Susan Prendergast Schoelwer, "San Antonio De Valero Mission," http://www.tshaonline.org/handbook/online/articles/ uqs08. For concise coverage of the historic battle, see *HOT Online*, Stephen L. Hardin, "Alamo, Battle of The," http://www.tshaonline.org/handbook/online/ articles/qea02.

47. De la Teja, *Revolution Remembered*, 194–195, 1ˢᵗ quotation on 194, 2ⁿᵈ quotation on 194–195, 3ʳᵈ quotation on 195; Hardin, "Efficient in the Cause," in Poyo, *Tejano Journey*, 57.

48. Davis, *Lone Star Rising*, 223.

49. Downs, "Mexicans in Texas," 246; Lack, *Texas Revolutionary Experience*, 181, 1ˢᵗ quotation; Davis, *Lone Star Rising*, 243, 2ⁿᵈ quotation; Randolph B. Campbell, *Sam Houston and the American Southwest*, 3ʳᵈ ed. (New York: Pearson-Longman, 2007), 75, 77.

50. "Interpretative Guide to: San Jacinto Battleground State Historic Site," Texas Parks and Wildlife, quotation, https://tpwd.texas.gov/publications/ pwdpubs/media/pod_br_p4504_0088.pdf. Also, see the previous chapter, "Santa Anna: 'The Napoleon of the West,'" infra, for details of the Battle of San Jacinto, as well as the contributions of Juan Seguín and other Tejanos.

51. Hardin, *Texian Iliad*, 209, quotation. The story that Juan Seguín's men placed playing cards in their hatbands at San Jacinto can be found in numerous sources on the internet. As examples, see the following: "Remembering the Alamo-Floor Remarks-Congressman Ted Poe," February 24, 2015, http://poe.house.gov/floor-remarks?ID=D0074954-2105-43D5-8B16-04B225E5D180 and "All Texas Newcomers Need to Know about Us," by LASHBY, March 24, 2016, http://theleadernews.com/all-texas-newcomers-need-to-know-about-us/.

52. Hardin, *Texian Iliad*, 213, quotation.

53. De la Teja, *Revolution Remembered*, 27–28, quotations on 27.

54. José Enrique de la Peña, *With Santa Anna in Texas: A Personal Narrative of the Revolution*, ed. and trans., Carmen Perry, expanded ed. (College Station: Texas A&M University Press, 1999), 4, 1ˢᵗ quotation; *General Vicente Filisola's Analysis of José Urrea's Military Diary: A forgotten 1838 Publication by an Eyewitness to the Texas Revolution*, ed. by Gregg J. Dimmick, trans. by John R. Wheat (Austin: Texas State Historical Association, 2007), 162–163, 2ⁿᵈ and 3ʳᵈ quotations on 163.

55. Lack, *Texas Revolutionary Experience*, 202; Downs, "Mexicans in Texas," 246, quotation.

56. De la Teja, *Revolution Remembered*, 28–29, all quotations on 29; Lack, *Texas Revolutionary Experience*, 181–182, 201.

57. De la Teja, *Revolution Remembered*, 29–31, quotations on 31.

58. James E. Crisp, *Sleuthing the Alamo: Davy Crockett's Last Stand and Other Mysteries of the Texas Revolution* (New York: Oxford University Press, 2005), 46, 1ˢᵗ and 2ⁿᵈ quotations; Downs, "Mexicans in Texas," 252.

59. David J. Weber, *The Spanish Frontier in North America* (New Haven: Yale University Press, 1992), 339, quotation. For a seminal work that examines race relations in Texas during the nineteenth century, see Arnoldo de León's *They Called Them Greasers: Anglo Attitudes toward Mexicans in Texas, 1821–1900* (Austin: University of Texas Press, 1983).

60. De la Teja, *Revolution Remembered*, 31 quotation; Edited Memoirs, in *Revolution Remembered*, 87; "Juan Seguín," Texas State Library and Archives Collection, https://www.tsl.texas.gov/treasures/giants/seguin/seguin-pratt-1. html. See also Juan Seguín to Captain Pratt, Mar. 26, 1837, A.J. Houston Collection, Archives and Information Services Division, Texas State Library and Archives Commission, https://www.tsl.texas.gov/treasures/giants/seguin/seguin-pratt-1. html. In the just-referenced letter, the Tejano officer commands Pratt to impress horses and mules but to provide the owners with receipts.

61. Juan N. Seguín to General Albert Sidney Johnston, March 13, 1837, in Timothy M. Matovina, *The Alamo Remembered: Tejano Accounts and Perspectives* (Austin: University of Texas Press, 1995), 19–20, all quotations on 20.

62. Juan N. Seguín's oration, translated and published in *Columbia Telegraph and Texas Register*, 4 April 1837, in Matovina, *The Alamo Remembered*, 20–21, 1st through 3rd quotations on 20, remaining quotations on 21.

63. "Juan Seguín," Areas of Interest, Texas State Library and Archives Commission, 1st and 3rd quotations, https://www.tsl.texas.gov/treasures/giants/seguin/seguin-01.html; de la Teja, *Revolution Remembered*, 33, 38, 2nd quotation on 38. [Texas State Library and Archives Commission hereinafter cited as TSLAC.] As Roberto R. Calderón notes in the entry on "Tejano Politics" in the *HOT Online*, only four Tejanos were elected to Congress during the period of the Republic, and all were from the heavily Hispanic Bexar district.

64. De la Teja, *Revolution Remembered*, 33, "Juan Seguín," TSLAC, 1st and 2nd quotations; *HOT Online*, "Seguín, Juan Nepomuceno," 3rd quotation; *HOT Online*, "Seguin, Erasmo."

65. *HOT Online*, John Gesick, "Seguin, Texas," http://www.tshaonline.org/handook/online/articles/hes03. Jerry Robins in his thesis, "Juan Seguín," claims that the town was named for Erasmo; however, the *HOT Online* and the website for Seguin, Texas, [http://www.seguintexas.gov/visitors/category/seguin_history/] state that the name honors the son, Juan Nepomuceno.

66. Richard Bruce Winders, *Crisis in the Southwest: The United States, Mexico, and the Struggle over Texas* (Wilmington, DE: Scholarly Resources Inc., 2002), 48–49, 1st quotation on 48, 2nd quotation on 49; Downs, "Mexicans in Texas," 85, 3rd and 4th quotations; Reséndez, *Changing National Identities*, 205.

67. Campbell, *Gone to Texas*, 175–177; Winders, *Crisis in the Southwest*, 49–56, Downs, "Mexicans in Texas," 263; Arnoldo de León, *They Called Them Greasers*, 78–79.

68. Brigadier General John C.L. Scribner, "The Texan Republic: Part 2," Texas Military Forces Museum, Camp Mabry, Texas, 1st quotation; "Juan Seguín," TSLAC, 2nd quotation; William Pack, "Seguín: The Painful Tale of a Texas Patriot," *San Antonio Express-News*, Jan. 23, 2015, updated Feb. 19, 2015, http://www.expressnews.com/150years/leaders/article/segu-n-The-painful-tale-of-a-Texas-patriot-6035629.php; Joseph Milton Nance, *Attack and Counterattack: The Texas-Mexican Frontier, 1842* (Austin: University of Texas Press, 1963), reprint placed online by H. David Maxey, 2008, 11, 3rd quotation; Winders, *Crisis in the Southwest*, 52; Jerry D. Robins, "Juan Seguín," (M.A. thesis, Southwest Texas State College, August 1962), 74, 4th quotation; Downs, "Mexicans in Texas," 263.

69. "Juan Seguín," TSLAC, 1st quotation; *HOT Online*, "Seguin, Juan," 2nd quotation; Matovina, *Tejano Religion*, 32, 2nd quotation; de la Teja, *Edited*

Memoirs, *Revolution Remembered*, 74, 3rd and 4th quotations; Robins, "Juan Seguín," 58–59, 75.

70. De la Teja, Edited Memoirs, *Revolution Remembered*, 74, 1st quotation, 97–100; Robins, "Juan Seguín," 65–66, 3rd and 4th quotations on 65; Phyllis McKenzie, *The Mexican Texans* (College Station: Texas A&M University Press, 2004), 2nd quotation on 55.

71. Robins, "Juan Seguín," 66–67; *HOT Online*, "Seguín, Erasmo"; de la Teja, *Revolution Remembered*, 49, quotation.

72. Robins, "Juan Seguín," 70–71; de la Teja, *Revolution Remembered*, 50, quotation; Pack, "Seguín," *Express-News*. Previously cited *Crisis in the Southwest* by Bruce Winders is excellent, especially for the reader who wants to understand the role that Texas played as a causative factor in the war between the United States and Mexico. An older, but still valuable, book on the U.S.-Mexican War is John S. D. Eisenhower's *So Far from God: The U.S. War with Mexico, 1846–1848*.

73. De la Teja, *Revolution Remembered*, 50–51, quotation on 1. The previously cited *A Revolution Remembered: The Memoirs and Selected Correspondence of Juan N. Seguín*, edited by Jesús F. de la Teja, contains both edited and unedited versions of these memoirs.

74. *HOT Online*, "Seguín, Erasmo"; Fane Burt, "Seguín's Mansion Now Only Rubble," San Antonio *Express-News*, Mar. 16, 1969, https://www.tamu.edu/faculty/ccbn/dewitt/adp/archives/newsarch/casa.html; de la Teja, *Revolution Remembered*, 51, quotation.

75. De la Teja, *Revolution Remembered*, 56, 1st quotation; Pack, "Seguín," *Express-News*, 2nd quotation.

76. See Arnoldo de León, *They Called Them Greasers: Anglo Attitudes toward Mexicans in Texas, 1821–1900* (1983) for a scholarly look at the racial perceptions Anglos had of the Mexican population and the impact those attitudes had in Texas in the nineteenth century.

77. "Juan Seguín," TSLAC, quotation.

78. J.M. Woods, *Don Erasmo Seguin: A Spanish aristocrat, a trusted agent of Governor Martinez, a counselor of Stephen F. Austin, an able Deputy of the Mexican State of Texas to the National Congress, a patriot of the Republic of Texas and loyal citizen of the American Commonwealth* (Stockton, CA: Gaylord Bros., Inc., 1908), https://archive.org/stream/donerasmoseguins00woodrich/donerasmoseguins00woodrich_djvu.txt; Burt, "Seguín's Mansion," *Express-News*, quotation.

79. "Juan Seguín Memorial," Stevens Art Foundry, quotation, http://stevensartfoundry.com/notable-projects/juan-seguin-memorial/; TEKS Clarification, Social Studies, Grade 7, http://www.teksresourcesystem.net/module/content/search/~/item/678489/viewdetail.ashx.

Photograph of Juan Nepomuceno Cortina by Louis De Planque 1866. Taken the year following the end of the U.S. Civil War. 73–842, UTSA Special Collections—Institute of Texan Cultures.

Juan Nepomuceno Cortina

Crusader or Criminal?

JUAN NEPOMUCENO CORTINA, BORN in northern Mexico three years after that country declared independence from Spain, was a complex man who lived in complex times. During his lifetime, his homeland was plagued by internal and external conflict. Increasing frustration with the instability in Mexico, the manipulations of Antonio López de Santa Anna, and a host of other factors led Texans to rebel in the mid-1830s. Despite the success of the revolution and the creation of the Republic of Texas, Mexico refused to recognize the independence of its former possession. Texas's annexation to the United States a decade later helped trigger a war that cost Mexico dearly. Little more than a dozen years later, Mexico's northern neighbor was the victim of its own costly Civil War (1861–1865). That same decade, France invaded Mexico to impose an Austrian nobleman as emperor. Although Maximilian was eventually overthrown, Mexico's instability continued until Porfirio Díaz became president in the 1870s. He brought order at the cost of decades of dictatorial rule. The tumultuous events described above shaped Juan Cortina's life; for, he "was nothing if not a product of the social and political forces of his time and region."[1] The role he played in affairs on both sides of the border was truly remarkable.

Action-oriented Juan Cortina was passionate about politics, war, and women. He championed justice for his people, as well as power and wealth for himself. When committed to a goal, he used any means—legal or illegal—to achieve it. Cortina was also a man of contradictions. Minimally literate, he issued impressive proclamations that he could not have written himself. Sometimes he was a respected leader, but on other occasions he was a fugitive fleeing from authorities on both sides of the border. During times of war, he would switch his loyalty from one side to the other for practical or idealistic reasons.

Cortina was very lucky; some would say blessed. Indeed, he was convinced that God was on his side, and many of his followers concurred. As proof, they pointed to the more than thirty battles he fought without suffering a single wound. Like a magnet, he attracted people to his various causes. However, his forceful personality and violent methods also created bitter enemies. To some he was a savior, to others an outlaw. In short, he was not a man about whom people could be neutral, then or now. Much has been written about this complex, contradictory figure. Presenting dramatically contrasting views, these writings make it even more difficult to draw valid conclusions about the man.

To apologists, Juan Cortina was a hero like the legendary Robin Hood of England who stole from the rich to help the poor, a crusader bent on punishing those who abused his people. But, were his motives truly selfless or was he an unscrupulous bandit, as his detractors claim? Did he use injustices against Mexican Texans as an excuse to break the law, enrich himself, and gain power? Almost certainly, the real Juan Nepomuceno Cortina falls somewhere in between these extremes. An examination of his dramatic life helps us understand why he was and is a polarizing figure.

***

Juan Cortina's mother, María Estéfana Goseascochea, had Spanish ancestors who came with the famous colonizer José de Escandón in the mid-1700s to settle the province of Nuevo Santander, today part of northern Mexico and South Texas. One of those forbears, José Salvador de la Garza, was the recipient of the large Espíritu Santo land grant that over time became divided among his many heirs. Estéfana eventually inherited thousands of acres in the lower Rio Grande Valley.[2]

Estéfana and husband, Francisco Cavazos, had two children: a boy named Sabas and a girl, Refugio. After Cavazos died, Estéfana married Trinidad Cortina[s]. Their first child, Juan Nepomuceno, was born on May 16, 1824, near the Rio Grande in Camargo, Mexico. Two more children, José María and Carmen, resulted from that marriage. Trinidad, a lawyer, became *alcalde* (mayor) of Camargo when Juan was young. Sadly, Estéfana was widowed again when her husband died early in the 1840s.[3]

"Strong and fearless," Estéfana was adept in politics and business. Some of these qualities passed on to her son, for whom she was a strong influence. Nevertheless, his failings would cause the two to become estranged. The widow moved the family to the part of her Espíritu Santo grant north of the Rio Grande near present-day Brownsville, Texas. Juan, therefore, observed first-hand the lives of people on both sides of the river and witnessed the mistreatment that Mexicans received at the hands of Anglo Americans settling in the area in the 1840s.[4]

Juan Cortina seems an unlikely champion for poorer Mexicans along the border. While not one of the common people, he did not fit well into the upper class image either. Spending little time in school, the youth was expelled more than once for "beating some boy terribly." Barely able to read or write, Juan became "a black sheep in the family." Also, the green-eyed Cortina with his "reddish-brown" hair" was not a stereotypical Mexican.[5] Neverthe-less, a careful look at his early years helps to explain the unlikely choices he made.

Young Juan learned his most valuable lessons not in school but in real life. He enjoyed "the rough and exciting life of a common vaquero [cowboy]" more than the pursuits of the elite class to which his family belonged. Working with employees on the family ranch, Cortina evidenced an interest in their welfare, and they fondly nick-named him *Cheno*. He developed the ability to interact comfortably with lower-class Hispanics and in so doing earned their loyalty and respect, talents that would serve him well later in life.[6]

Cortina was influenced by disturbing events in the future Lone Star State. At the time of his birth, Anglos from the United States had begun to migrate to Texas, although not yet to the lower Rio Grande Valley. Most came legally with permission of the govern-ment, which wanted the northern frontier to become more popu-lated and productive. Settlers were offered incentives in return for accepting Mexican citizenship and Roman Catholicism. Suffering from the negative economic impact of the Panic of 1819 in the United States, Anglos were seeking new opportunities. Southerners in particular were attracted to a region that offered cheap, fertile land suitable for cotton agriculture.

Texians (Anglo Texans) soon outnumbered Tejanos (Mexican Texans). Ethnic, religious, philosophical, and other differences between the two groups created the potential for trouble. Making matters worse, because of their "whiteness," the Anglos viewed themselves as superior to the darker-skinned *Mexicanos* (Mexicans) of whom they tended to have negative stereotypes.[7] Also, Texians were committed to African-American slavery, an unpopular institu-tion in Mexico. When Texans finally rebelled in 1835, however, unstable conditions in Mexico and the actions of Mexican President Antonio López de Santa Anna were the more immediate causes.

As explained in previous chapters, Santa Anna controlled a badly divided nation at the time of the Texas Revolution. Although he had become president as a leader of the liberals, changing politi-cal circumstances led him to switch his support to the conservatives, overthrow the liberal Mexican Constitution of 1824, and impose increasingly dictatorial rule. Liberals reacted by rebelling in some twelve Mexican states, and Santa Anna reacted with great brutality to these challenges to his authority.

Fighting began in Texas in October 1835, and on March 2, 1836, liberal Texians and Tejanos declared Texas's independence. At the Alamo and later at Goliad, hundreds of Texans died in battle or were shot as prisoners on Santa Anna's orders. The Mexican leader was determined to regain control of Texas at any cost; however, after a relatively brief war, General Sam Houston and the Texas Army defeated the "Napoleon of the West" at the Battle of San Jacinto in April 1836. Despite Mexico's reluctance to recognize the independence of its former territory, Texas functioned as a separate republic for about a decade.

Once the decision for independence had been made, most Anglo Texans favored annexation to the United States—their country of origin—for myriad reasons, including military protection from Mexico. However, the initial request for annexation was rejected, because to do otherwise would almost certainly have led to war. Also, Texians supported slavery at a time when the institution was an increasingly divisive issue in the United States. Anti-slavery forces in the North strongly opposed adding a large slave-holding territory to their nation. Nevertheless, Manifest Destiny, the spirit of expansionism sweeping through the United States, finally led to Texas's being annexed in December 1845.

Never having officially recognized Texas's independence, an angry Mexico severed diplomatic relations with its northern neighbor. Adding to the tension was a boundary dispute in which the United States claimed the Rio Grande as the international dividing line, while Mexico insisted on the Nueces River. Significantly, the disputed territory between the two rivers was where Juan Cortina lived and military conflict would soon begin. The desire of many Americans to acquire California from Mexico only exacerbated the situation, especially after attempts by the James K. Polk administration to purchase that western territory in the mid-1840s proved futile. California could only be acquired by force—a war with Mexico.

President Polk elected to send American troops under General Zachary Taylor to the disputed region between the Nueces River and the Rio Grande. Considering this an invasion of its territory, Mexico dispatched General Mariano Arista to Matamoros, just south of the river claimed by the U.S. as the boundary. In April 1846, Mexican troops crossed the Rio Grande and exchanged fire with some of Taylor's men. Subsequently asking the United States Congress for a declaration of war, Polk recounted many grievances against Mexico but emphasized that the Mexican army had invaded U.S. territory and "shed American blood on the American soil." A majority of the Senate and House of Representatives voted for war in June 1846.[8]

During the United States-Mexican War, Juan Cortina, who was in his twenties, fought on the side of Mexico. He joined a National Guard company called the *Defensores de la Patria* (Defenders of the Homeland). Fighting alongside Arista's forces, Cheno participated in the early battles at Palo Alto and Resaca de la Palma, north of the Rio Grande.[9] Taylor's army not only won both of these early encounters but also gained control of Matamoros on the Mexican side of the river. From there the American troops, accompanied by Texas Rangers and other volunteers, headed deeper into Mexico.

The war began only ten years after Texas had fought for independence. Memories of Antonio López de Santa Anna's savagery remained vivid in the minds of many Anglos, particularly Texas Rangers who wanted to avenge their fallen comrades. The invading Americans perpetrated brutal acts not only against enemy soldiers but also against Mexican civilians. In Matamoros, some U.S. troops committed "murder, robbery, and rape." In Camargo, Cortina's birthplace, murders and violence happened so frequently that they reportedly did not attract much notice. While American military personnel committed some of these acts, General Taylor complained more about his Texas volunteers. He described them as difficult to control and guilty of abuses against peaceable Mexicans. General Winfield Scott, who led an invasion of Central Mexico, complained that on the northern border women had been raped "in the presence of tied-up males" from their families. The officer was distressed by acts that would "make Heaven weep and every American of Christian morals blush." In an ironic twist, General Santa Anna voiced similar sentiments when he complained that American soldiers had "looted several cities and abused women."[10] Whether or not Juan Cortina personally witnessed such violent acts against his people, he must have been aware of them. Furthermore, if he and his countrymen thought that the end of the war would put an end to abuses, they were wrong.

Despite valiant attempts by Mexicans to defend their country against the *Yanquis* (Yankees), Mexico lost every major military campaign of the war and had to accept terms dictated by the victor. The Treaty of Guadalupe Hidalgo, signed in February 1848, officially recognized Texas as part of the United States with the Rio Grande as the international boundary. Mexico was also forced to surrender territory stretching from Texas to California, an area known as the Mexican Cession.

While not heavily populated, the conquered borderlands were home to perhaps 100,000 Mexicans for whom Mexico attempted to gain protections. The U.S. government conceded that people in the newly acquired territories would be given one year to decide whether to remain. Those making that determination would be granted citizenship with accompanying Constitutional guarantees such as "the right to vote, testify in American courts, . . . hold elected office, and all other political privileges of Americans." Significantly, their ownership of all kinds of property would be respected, a fact that influenced the decision of those with land holdings on the U.S. side of the Rio Grande.[11] Whether these guarantees would be honored remained to be seen.

Among Mexicans accepting the offer of citizenship was Juan Nepomuceno Cortina, an acquisition from the war that U.S. authorities might have preferred to have done without! With favorite pastimes that included gambling and cockfighting, Cheno had unsavory associates. Cortina himself was a suspect in the murder of an Anglo American, and when formal charges were filed, he fled into the interior of Mexico. Interestingly, no one attempted to arrest him after he later returned to the border. Possible explanations are that local officials may have cleared his name, were hesitant to act because of his family's prominence, or his own popularity may have made the Tejano difficult to prosecute.[12]

Shortly after the war, Cortina began working with the U.S. Quartermaster Corps, which provided food and supplies to American troops. He was in charge of more than a dozen Mexican herders managing the livestock for a large wagon train formed on the border in Matamoros to take supplies overland into Texas. En route, Cheno got into a heated argument with an Anglo wagon driver who had not only ignored his authority but also struck him, whereupon Juan almost killed the man. Even though the military officer who had hired the Tejano did not blame him for the incident, Cheno soon quit and returned home to a rapidly changing lower Rio Grande Valley.[13]

Anglos in increasing numbers were migrating into South Texas during the post-war period and major changes were occurring as a consequence. Juan tried to adapt to the new reality. Receiving some land from his mother, he established *El Rancho de San José* (San José Ranch). Living nearby was his half-brother, Sabas Cavazos. Needing horses and cattle for his ranch, Juan Cortina allegedly acquired stolen animals. In one instance, a Mexican national claimed to be the rightful owner of some of the rustled livestock on Cortina's land. Again, local authorities failed to act.[14]

Threats to family landholdings soon demanded more of Cortina's attention. Early in the war with Mexico, the U.S. had established a military post that came to be known as Fort Brown, directly across the Rio Grande from Matamoros. As the town of Brownsville developed nearby, land in the area appreciated. Actual ownership of property was often unclear because of confusion over titles, which led to lengthy, complicated lawsuits. Over time, "the old Mexican landholding families frequently had their titles challenged by Americans, and if the Mexicans did not lose in the courts they lost through the legal chicanery of their American lawyers." Charles Stillman, a founder of Brownsville, "managed to take over a valuable portion" of the land in question.[15]

As owners of the Espíritu Santo grant where Brownsville was located, "Cortina's family became embroiled in the most celebrated land dispute of the 1850s." To afford legal fees incurred while defending their claims, they resorted to selling part of their property. In 1853 both a local judge and the Texas legislature supported the legitimacy of the family's ownership of their ancestral grant; nevertheless, expensive litigation continued to plague them. Compromise seemed the wisest alternative. At one point, Cheno's mother reportedly "signed away her right to the Brownsville tract . . . for the sum of one dollar." Ultimately, the U.S. Supreme Court confirmed the de la Garza heirs as the owners of what was left of the Espíritu Santo Grant, and Doña Estéfana got "the upper one sixth" as her share of the property.[16]

Realistically, Juan Nepomuceno's mother was fortunate to retain even part of her ancestral land grant. Seeing his family cheated of much of its birthright, an angry, embittered Juan Nepomuceno held special resentment against Charles Stillman and his cohorts. That the de la Garza heirs were not the only ones suffering such injustices made Cheno even more livid. He saw Tejanos as "pawns in the political game" being played in South Texas and concluded that the group "with the most money, guns, alcohol, and promises of spoils was destined to control Brownsville and Cameron County."[17]

To Juan's disgust, the situation was no better in the rest of Texas, where most Tejanos had become second-class citizens in a state run primarily by and for Anglos. Again playing a key role, Texas Rangers gained "a well-earned reputation for violence against the Mexican community." According to one author, "the Rangers were used by the Anglo ranchers and merchants who controlled South Texas" to help keep Hispanics at "the lowest levels." In 1857, even the governor of Texas openly recognized that Mexicans in the state did not receive justice.[18]

Still worse, the problem was not confined to Texas. In 1859, a United States military officer reported that whites were in the process of "exterminating or crushing out the inferior [Mexican] race" on the border. Clearly, the guarantees provided at the end of the Mexican War were not being enforced. President James Buchanan expressed the prevailing attitude of his countrymen, when he spoke of "the destiny of our [white] race to spread themselves over the continent of North America." That this was happening at the expense of darker-skinned peoples was the price of "progress." Not surprisingly, Cheno found this state of affairs to be unacceptable.[19]

Ironically, Estéfana and her sons were among the more fortunate border residents after the war, because Anglo Americans were open to accommodations with the Tejano elite whom they held in higher esteem than lower-class Mexican Americans. Sabas Cavazos was respected as a successful rancher, while José María attained prominence in local politics. For a price, Juan Nepomuceno would "lead the lower-class *Tejanos* to the polls and show them how to vote." He also used his political influence in 1858 to help half-brother José María gain election to the post of tax assessor and collector. Note that while Cheno was angered by the wrongs perpetrated against Mexican Americans, he was not above using them to his own or his family's advantage. Juan Cortina's political sway and his family's status also help explain "why for a decade arrest warrants sworn against him for cattle theft and even murder went unserved."[20]

To Cortina, being among the Tejano elite proved frustrating. By the late 1850s, he was convinced "that life in south Texas offered little opportunity for any Mexican who aspired to a position of leadership and authority." He concluded that "Americans had little use for any Mexican who did not accept second class status and subordination." These conclusions led Cheno to consider Mexico as a viable alternative.[21]

The decision to relocate was difficult for Cortina, as Mexico was again racked by turmoil. Shamed by their nation's loss in the recent war and determined to make significant changes in their homeland, liberals in 1855 forced Antonio López de Santa Anna into his final exile. A series of subsequent Reform Laws attacked the traditional privileges of the Roman Catholic Church and military. A democratic constitution enacted in 1857 not only incorporated much of that legislation but also "emphasized individual liberty and . . . property rights," as well other guarantees for the populace. These measures alienated conservatives, particularly the clergy and the military, who determined to restore the old order. As the War of the Reform raged in Mexico from 1858–1861, a Zapotec Indian named Benito Juárez emerged as the leader of the liberal cause.[22]

Some evidence suggests that conservative leaders tried to entice Juan Cortina by providing him with "money and provisions to put an army in the field" in northern Mexico. At the same time, Cheno seems to have been willing to negotiate with liberals by offering his services for a price. He allegedly accepted financial and other resources from both sides in the War of the Reform but did not actively participate in the conflict at this point. Instead, he used those resources to strengthen "his personal power base along the Lower Rio Grande."[23] In this regard the Tejano exhibited an opportunistic bent not dissimilar to that of the deposed *caudillo* Santa Anna.

Matters changed when Cortina came to Brownsville on July 13, 1859, just as the town marshal was arresting a drunk, unruly old man—a former employee of Cheno's mother. Juan objected to Marshal Robert Shears pistol-whipping the *vaquero* (cowboy). After the marshal reportedly cursed Cortina for interfering, he twice shot Shears who "lay in the street gravely wounded and bleeding profusely." Cheno then "swung the elderly vaquero up behind him on his pinto horse and galloped out of town" to the cheers of nearby Mexicans. Although the sheriff would eventually recover, Juan Nepomuceno was again a wanted man. He tried to resolve the matter by offering money to the injured marshal, but the two could not agree on an amount. Unable to return to his ranch, the fugitive angrily vowed to shoot Shears again.[24]

Also on the growing list of Juan's enemies was Adolphus Glavecke, a German immigrant who had come to Texas in 1836 and married into the Cortina family. Cheno considered Glavecke "an opportunist and opponent of Mexican rights." The enmity was mutual, as the German reportedly availed himself of every opportunity to cause trouble for Cortina such as accusing him of stealing livestock. This was particularly ironic, given that the two men at times reportedly had been partners in that specific criminal activity.[25]

Among others deserving retribution in Cortina's opinion were William P. Neale and George Morris, who supposedly "had killed Mexicans recently and were still free to kill more." The time had come, Cortina decided, "to see that justice, long delayed, came to those who were allowed no justice" in South Texas. Getting disaffected members of the poorer classes to join in this crusade was not difficult for the charismatic Cheno. Planning to punish "wicked men," the Tejano formed a raiding party of more than three dozen followers. The *Cortinistas* rode into Brownsville in the early hours of September 28, 1859. At a local pawnshop, they seized the arms and ammunition; however, their leader supposedly paid for these items. This enabled later apologists to insist that the raid was not intended for the purpose of looting, as his enemies alleged.[26]

The *Cortinistas* attacked the town with shouts of "Death to the Americans" and "Long Live Mexico." More than willing to kill his enemies, Cheno did not want to hurt innocent people—an unrealistic expectation. Jailer Robert Johnson refused to hand over the keys so that they could free five incarcerated men. Instead, Johnson took refuge in a store belonging to Viviano García. When the *Cortinistas* attacked the establishment, both the jailer and the proprietor were killed. With the keys taken from Johnson's body, Cortina's men then released the prisoners.[27]

By raid's end, several people had been shot. Although two were innocent casualties, others who died that day were among Cortina's prime targets—William Neale and George Morris. Glavecke and Shears escaped. The former, awakened by the noise of the raid, joined others in a building that Cortina, out of respect for the owner, considered off limits. Glavecke later complained that he missed a chance to shoot Cortina when someone knocked his shotgun away just as he was ready to fire. As for Marshal Shears, he supposedly proved less than heroic by hiding in a large oven.[28]

After the *Cortinistas* captured Brownsville, some of the town's leaders asked authorities in Matamoros, Mexico, for help. Answering the call were several men, including one of Cortina's cousins, who persuaded the raiders to withdraw from the town. However, two days later, September 30, 1859, Cortina issued an eloquent statement in both English and Spanish addressed to the people of Brownsville and the rest of Texas. Regardless of who actually penned the document, the ideas were almost certainly his. "Orderly people and honest citizens" need have no fear, the proclamation pledged. The raid was directed at villains who had gone unpunished for crimes against people guilty of nothing more than being Mexican. Cortina stated his satisfaction that "criminal, wicked men" had died but regretted that "innocent blood" had also been shed.[29]

The document also condemned Brownsville's leaders, lawyers, and others who had cheated Mexicans of their lands. Adolphus Glavecke was specifically named in that category for using his role as deputy sheriff to terrorize Hispanics to get them to leave the country. As for Marshal Shears, Cortina labeled him as an "assassin" who had committed "a thousand misdeeds." While hoping to spare innocent lives, the Tejano insisted that justice would be achieved.[30]

Cortina's proclamation particularly resonated with the common people, who joined him in ever greater numbers. Whether the Tejano intended to use his army to fight in Mexico or to engage "in a race war with the Americans" was unclear. Given that U.S. troops had been withdrawn from lower South Texas months earlier, he "had Brownsville at his mercy." Nevertheless, Cheno began to move his livestock—and reportedly many stolen cattle as well—across the Rio Grande. In early October, he entered Matamoros with some two hundred and fifty followers to a hero's welcome.[31]

Prominent people of Brownsville were still fearful. Town guards were appointed and barricades created to impede raiders. Also, local residents again asked Mexican authorities in Matamoros for help. Consequently, fifty militiamen were sent across the river "to protect U.S. citizens from an irregular army of Mexicans being led by a man who considered himself a U.S. citizen."[32] How confusing!

Brownsville's leaders formed a Committee of Public Safety, which appealed to officials in Washington, D.C. to return troops to their region. A similar plea went to the state government in Austin. Local residents also determined to protect themselves. In October a posse led by Sheriff James Browne captured elderly *Cortinista* Tomás Cabrera, who was jailed in Brownsville. Cheno warned that the town would be turned to ashes unless his subordinate were released. When the demand was refused, dozens of Cortina's men began firing on Brownsville at night. Their leader pledged to leave the country with his followers, but only if Cabrera went with him. Refusing this demand, the Committee of Public Safety went on the offensive. Joined by Matamoros militiamen, some twenty volunteer Anglos—calling themselves the Brownsville Tigers—headed toward the Tejano's camp. After encountering some of the *Cortinistas* at Rancho del Carmen, however, the panicked Tigers fled back to Brownsville and lost their cannon in the process. By late October, the townspeople were desperate.[33]

In November 1859, Governor Hardin R. Runnels made a decision that proved ill-advised when he authorized Captain William Tobin to take Texas Rangers into the troubled region. The arrival of these unruly men provided a measure of safety for the leading people of Brownsville but did the opposite for Mexicans and Tejanos. Just one night after the Rangers' arrival, Tomás Cabrera was taken from the Brownsville jail and hanged in Market Square, supposedly by a vigilante mob. However, "there can be little doubt that the Rangers not only participated in the mob action but actually incited it." The lynching "plunged the Lower Rio Grande Valley into a firestorm of violence and death." Cheno responded by ambushing a squad of Rangers and killing three whose bodies were reported to have been "stripped and mutilated." Tobin, in turn, went after Cortina; however, when the two groups exchanged fire less than ten miles from Brownsville, the Rangers were the ones who retreated.[34]

Border Hispanics paid for the actions of the *Cortinistas*. Texas Rangers allegedly "sacked, plundered, and burned any ranch thought to be owned by a Mexican-American assisting Cortina." Nevertheless, the *campesinos* (peasants) did not turn against their leader. Instead, hundreds "of the economically deprived and politically disenfranchised" enlisted in his crusade, as the Tejano emerged "as a warrior chief battling the oppression of the Anglo minority." Needless to say, the rebels committed depredations of their own by "ravaging many of the larger farms and ranches in the Lower Valley." According to one author, "violence and killing had become a way of life between Texans and Mexicans." [35]

Cortina was well aware of the precariousness of his situation. To gain information, the Tejano captured mail intended for Brownsville and had an American prisoner read the contents to him. Worthy of note is that he subsequently not only freed the captive but also returned the stolen letters. These gestures, however, failed to allay the fears of local Anglos who were greatly outnumbered by *Mexicanos* and Tejanos along the Rio Grande. Hoping to "attract attention and aid from Washington and Austin," citizens of Brownsville exaggerated events in their region, as well as portraying the insurgents as Mexican nationals and dangerous criminals. Wild rumors spread through the United States about the violence along the border. Newspapers advised that the rebellion must be suppressed. Indeed, "the people of Brownsville truly did need help," but they also knew that a return of U.S. troops to the border region would be economically beneficial for businesses in the area.[36]

Justifying his actions in a second proclamation, dated November 23, 1859, Cortina condemned the "flocks of vampires" who had come to South Texas to rob, jail, and kill Mexicans. Anglos escaped punishment, while Mexicans were treated like "wild beasts." According to Cheno, "breaking the chains" of his people's slavery was his God-given mission. He asked recently elected governor Sam Houston for help and assured that the way to end the violence in the Rio Grande Valley was clear—end crimes committed against innocent Tejanos and *Mexicanos*.[37]

Predictably, most officials in Austin and Washington, D.C. considered the Cortinistas to be common criminals and reacted accordingly. A new company of Texas Rangers entered the picture. Under John Salmon "Rip" Ford, these men were more disciplined than Tobin's but had the same goal of ending the rebellion. Significantly, arriving at the same time as these Rangers were United States troops commanded by Major Samuel P. Heintzelman. This officer kept a daily journal while in Texas, and Ford later wrote his memoirs. These provide firsthand perspectives into events on the border in 1859. Of special interest was the major's opinion of the Texas Rangers, for whom he held little respect. He believed that their "killing of *Mexicanos* and *Tejanos*" had contributed to the trouble along the lower Rio Grande, but this did not deter Heintzelman from following orders to crush Cortina's movement. Indeed, he believed that action was imperative, because "the whole country from Brownsville to Rio Grande City . . . has been laid waste" and "business as far up as Laredo . . . has been interrupted or suspended for months." However, the major recognized that stopping Cortina would be difficult, because he had "the sympathy and aid of the population."[38]

With several hundred disorganized and undisciplined raiders, Cheno moved upriver with soldiers and Rangers in pursuit. When the two sides finally engaged in battle at Rio Grande City in late December, more than a dozen Texas Rangers were wounded, but a much higher number of the raiders were killed. Reportedly, "Cortina's line dissolved in retreat, abandoning baggage, equipment, and half-cooked breakfast." Estimates of the dead insurgents ranged from sixty to two hundred killed, depending on who was tallying the body count.[39]

Cheno lost even more supporters as they deserted to save themselves but was not ready to abandon the fight. With the remnants of his band, Cortina camped about thirty-five miles from Brownsville at La Bolsa, on the Mexican side of the river. Ford was convinced that he had chosen that location to attack an American steamboat carrying thousands of dollars in gold. Crossing into Mexico, the Rangers attacked. In a brief, heated battle, the rebels were defeated and again fled. Ford reported that Juan Nepumeceno had been shot at repeatedly. His saddle, his hair, his bridle, and his horse's ear had been hit; yet, "he galloped off unhurt." Twenty-nine of his men with fatal wounds had not been so lucky.[40]

While across the Rio Grande, Ford ordered his command not to molest the civilian population. However, several Mexican *jacales* (huts) were burned, probably by Tobin's men. Mexico protested the

presence of the Rangers on its soil and wanted payment for property destroyed. In early February 1860, Heintzelman responded
that Cortina's forces were being supplied from south of the river.
Mexican authorities had a responsibility to "put a stop to these
outrages," the officer insisted, because the raiders intended to
"rob and murder" in Texas. Their failure to act necessitated the
American reaction.[41]

The Rangers' actions increased Cortina's appeal to the lower
classes, but his efforts to protect them—if that were indeed his
motive—had the opposite effect. Rather than securing justice,
poorer Mexicans became the objects of more "hatred and persecu-
tion than ever before." Significantly, Cortina's mother fared better
than many others during the Cortina War, not only because of her
elite status but also because Rip Ford offered her his protection.
Despite their enmity, Cheno appreciated the courtesy and would
later repay the favor.[42]

After the defeat at La Bolsa, Cortina was in no position to
address the abuse of *Mexicanos* and Tejanos, because U.S. troops
under Colonel Robert E. Lee had been dispatched to critical military posts along the border. Sanctioned to act "beyond the limits
of the United States" if needed, Lee warned Mexican officials of
serious consequences if banditry continued. Those authorities
assured that they would take steps to provide security in the future.
Lee's arrival "signaled the temporary end of the 'quasi war.'" In
the meantime, the U.S. government had sent Duff Green to Texas
to gather accurate information. In his reports, Green observed
"that Texans were as guilty as Mexicans in creating havoc along
the border." Regardless of where blame should be assigned, the
Cortina War had cost some 200 lives "and an estimated $340,000
in damages."[43]

Although free, Cortina retreated to the mountains in the
interior and became little more "than a fugitive and wanderer in
Mexico." During this period of exile, he supposedly abandoned

his wife, Rafaela Cortéz, an act that alienated his mother. That her son reportedly had a string of mistresses in subsequent years only intensified her disapproval.[44]

Those who viewed the lusty Cheno as an outlaw dreaded the thought of his returning to Texas, just as those who considered him a hero hoped for that eventuality. Indeed, Cortina's role in Texas history was far from over. New wars were on the horizon for both the United States and Mexico. Juan Nepomuceno would become involved in those conflicts and would again wield power along the Rio Grande.

By late 1860, the United States was on the brink of Civil War. Serious sectional differences, many directly or indirectly related to the slavery issue, threatened the Union. When Republican Abraham Lincoln was elected president in 1860, matters quickly worsened. Slave-holding states were mistrustful of the newly elected president and his northern party, which was committed to stopping the spread of slavery in the United States. Even before Lincoln's inauguration, several states began to secede from the Union and form a new nation, the Confederate States of America. As Southerners with a vested interest in slavery, Anglo Texans chose to join the Confederacy. Shortly after Lincoln assumed office, the Civil War began in April 1861. Texas's isolated geographic position as the westernmost of the seceded states initially kept it from being a major Union target. That situation would change as the war progressed with Texas functioning as an increasingly important supply line for the Confederacy.

The war brought Juan Nepomuceno back to the border, perhaps because he thought the unsettled conditions would work in his favor. A Second Cortina War ensued, this time upriver from Brownsville where the political machine controlling Zapata County worked to intimidate the poorer people within their jurisdiction to support secession. In the month the war started, a group of several dozen Tejanos and Mexicans rebelled against "boss rule in the county." Union sympathizers, led by a *Cortinista*, threatened to kill the Anglos in the county and attempted to prevent local officials from swearing loyalty to the Confederacy. Armed with warrants, "a hastily organized Confederate company" gunned down the insurgents, even though purportedly "not a single shot was fired in defense." Among those who died were several alleged noncombatants, possibly unarmed.[45]

Cheno wanted revenge for those who died in the above Clareño Massacre, but had to contend with John S. Ford, commander of the Confederate troops along the border. Cortina's old enemy entrusted Santos Benavides, who was destined to become the highest-ranking Tejano in the Confederacy, to protect Zapata County. As during the first Cortina War, rumors exaggerated the threat posed by the *Cortinistas*, whose forces were said to be increasing by the hour. Despite fear that "it was only a matter of time before Cortina swept the Rio Grande clean of Americans," Benavides was able to rout the raiders "in a running fight." Initially, seven of Cheno's men were killed, and more died attempting to cross the river into Mexico. Almost a dozen captured insurrectionists were executed, because Benavides—in the tradition of Antonio López de Santa Anna— had ordered his men to "kill all of the bandits that should fall into their hands." Although Cortina survived, "the Mexican military and civilian authorities [were] cooperating with the Confederates" against him by the summer of 1861.[46]

Having failed in Texas, Cheno again directed his attention to the country of his birth, which was being torn apart by internal conflicts and facing external threats as well. In typical fashion, Cortina jumped into the fray with both feet. After Mexico's War of the Reform ended in 1861 with victory for Benito Juárez and the liberal cause, the country desperately needed peace and stability. Unfortunately, the government could not pay its debts, some of which were owed to European nations, including France. Using debt collection as a justification, Emperor Napoleon III sent thousands of troops to conquer Mexico. The invading force had the support of many Mexican conservatives, who hoped to strengthen their position should the invasion succeed. However, the French suffered a major defeat on May 5, 1862, at Puebla—later celebrated as *Cinco de Mayo,* a national holiday in Mexico. Nevertheless, the French recruited a new army, triumphed the following year, and occupied Mexico City. The *Juaristas* were forced to flee to northern Mexico.[47]

Joining the fight against the French, Cortina gave every sign of being a loyal *Juarista.* He had been among his country's defenders at Puebla in 1862 and fought there again in the following year. His valor earned him the rank of lieutenant colonel in the Mexican cavalry and an assignment on the border. Juaréz needed financial assets to maintain the republic, and the customs house in Matamoros produced significant revenue. Cheno's familiarity with the region, his desire for power, and his popularity with the *campesinos* again propelled him to prominence.[48]

Returning to the border by 1864 provided Cortina with an opportunity to reconcile with his mother. According to a member of his staff, Estafania and her son met on the Mexican side of the Rio Grande. On that occasion, she reportedly whipped Cheno with his own riding crop and gave him a hug, whereupon the two moved beyond the bitterness of the past.[49]

Cortina not only improved relations with his mother but also made a power play in Tamaulipas by removing Governor Manuel Ruiz from office late in 1863. While not immediately taking the position himself, Juan Nepomuceno had "effective control of Matamoros and most of Tamaulipas." Early the following year, Cortina did officially declare himself governor and military commander of the state at a critical time when Union and Confederate forces were vying for control of South Texas. He became involved in that struggle and "did everything a gentleman could for Rip Ford's wife" who had taken refuge in Matamoros.[50]

Part of the U.S. strategy during the Civil War was imposing a blockade of the Confederate coastline to prevent exportation of cotton and importation of goods. This led to the increased importance of the Brownsville-Matamoros border region. "Matamoros [Mexico] furnished a medium for Confederate-European trade as well as a good market for the sale of cotton and the acquisition of arms and war matériel."[51] Disrupting this trade became a priority for the Union.

Cheno was in Matamoros when U.S. forces occupied Brownsville on November 1, 1863, the reason for Rip Ford's wife having relocated to Mexico. Given Brownsville's role in Confederate commerce, the South had no recourse but to recapture the town. Both sides recognized the value of having Cortina as an ally, and he adeptly manipulated the situation to his advantage. As one historian has noted, "Cortina had multiple, contradictory allegiances during the 1860s." He persuaded the Union to provide him with military supplies "to stop Confederate commerce in northern Mexico." While pledging to assist in any action against the Confederates, he allowed Southern cotton "to pass unmolested through his territory." Rip Ford observed that Cortina "was known to be friendly to the Union, yet he was not adverse to allowing his friends to earn an honest penny by supplying Confederates." Cooperation with the latter was also a practical matter, since Ford's troops recaptured Fort Brown and most of South Texas in the summer of 1864.[52]

Interpretations as to the motives behind Cortina's duplicity vary significantly. One twentieth century advocate asserted that the Tejano's "overriding motivation was no less than to survive the political turbulence and to use it to continue his people's struggle." A more critical historian labelled Juan Nepomuceno as "a caudillo constantly seeking new sources of wealth" who formed alliances based on self-interest and convenience.[53] Both interpretations most likely contain a grain of truth.

Given his declarations about social justice and Mexico's antipathy toward slavery, Cortina almost certainly sympathized with the Union. Only through a Northern victory could the millions of slaves in the South hope for an end to their bondage. Furthermore, events in Mexico served to increase Cortina's hostility towards the Confederacy. With the eventual success of the French invasion, Napoleon III had imposed Austrian nobleman Ferdinand Maximilian as emperor of Mexico in 1864. With Benito Juárez and his followers fighting to restore the integrity of the republic, Confederate attempts to establish ties with French Imperialists must have distressed Cortina.[54]

As a *Juarista*, Cortina used control of the ports of Matamoros and Bagdad to help with the flow of supplies and weapons to the cause. He also directed some of the customs duties collected along the border to provide badly needed funds for the liberals. However, when French imperialists eventually targeted Tamaulipas, Juan Nepomuceno found himself "shut up in a circle of bayonets." Ever the pragmatist, he decided to switch sides, "a decision that would haunt him for the rest of his life." He later insisted that the move was meant to be temporary and that he did his best to avoid military encounters with liberal forces. Nevertheless, Cortina's service for the French made him vulnerable to charges of treason and cowardice.[55]

In April 1865, the same month that the Civil War ended in the United States, Cheno officially declared himself against Maximilian's empire. Again claiming the posts of state governor and military commander in Tamaulipas, Cortina engaged in brutal, all-out guerrilla warfare against French troops in northern Mexico and gained control of almost "the entire Mexican side of the border." The notable exception was Matamoros, which remained under Imperialist control. In response, Cortina laid siege to the city.[56]

While in power in Tamaulipas, the commander was criticized by other liberal officers for being too independent and opportunistic.

One general informed President Benito Juárez that "Cortina was not a patriot and worked for no one but himself." Complaints against Cheno, coupled with his own actions, led to his being replaced as governor of the state in spring of 1866. Nevertheless, Cortina remained involved in internal power struggles among Mexicans liberals, as well as in the war with the French. The fight was going well for the *Juaristas* early in 1867, and a discouraged Napoleon III decided to remove his forces from Mexico. Cortina and his troops joined other liberals who encircled the Austrian-born emperor and his key officers at Querétaro. A two-month siege ended with the capture of Maximilian in May and his execution in June of 1867.[57]

Perhaps predictably, the border region remained chaotic with several caudillos, including Juan Nepomuceno, vying for control. Juárez was convinced "that Mexico could not progress as a nation until the power of these independent war lords had been broken." Despite an attempt to remove Cortina, by late 1870 he was back in control in Tamaulipas and "was at the peak of power." Ironically, the American press applauded him during this period and expressed hope that he would bring calmer conditions to the unstable border.[58] At this moment, Cortina was preferable to chaos, at least in their eyes.

Forty-one of Juan Nepomuceno's advocates in South Texas—mostly Mexican Texans from Starr County—sent a petition to the state government in Austin. As governor and commander-in-chief along the Rio Grande, they wrote, Cortina had supported the Union during the Civil War. He had provided "important protection to all American citizens" and was helping to maintain "the peace and Harmony on this Frontier." The petitioners asked that "a full and complete pardon be granted" so that he could return home to South Texas. Significantly, the signers included even the mayor of Brownsville at the time of the 1859 raid.[59]

The petition ultimately failed—in large part because of Cortina's enemies. They portrayed him as a hardened criminal deserving of punishment, not compassion. The anti-Cortina rhetoric became so exaggerated that he "was held responsible for nearly every head of cattle that disappeared from Texas," in addition to other crimes. Similarly, in 1872 Rip Ford headed a federal grand jury in Cameron County that denounced Cortina and other Mexicans for conducting "'a reign of terror' from the Rio Grande to the Nueces River." Pleading for federal involvement, the jurors accused Cortina of writing "the history of his career on this side of the Rio Grande in letters of blood and fire."[60]

Responding to public pressure, the U.S. government in the early 1870s dispatched a three-man commission to Texas to study the criminality in that state, determine the identity of the guilty parties, and define "the character and value of the property destroyed or carried away." Among the crimes investigated by the Robb Commission was rustling all along the Rio Grande, and twenty-two witnesses testified that Cortina played a prominent role in the cattle raids in South Texas. The commissioners also addressed the larger issue of the Cortina War and its legacy. They concluded that Juan Nepomuceno was responsible for "a history of the wrongs and outrages . . . committed with impunity . . . on our southwestern frontier." Responsibility for lawlessness was attributed to "the powerlessness of 'civil authorities on the right bank'" of the river. Mexico was labelled a country "rent with civil commotion, conspiracy, and insurrections." The solution was "the employment of a sufficient force of cavalry to enforce law and protect life and property on the Rio Grande."[61]

For its part, the Mexican government not only ordered Cortina to report to the nation's capital but also sent its own team of investigators to the border late in 1872. These three men disputed the Robb Commission's conclusions regarding Juan Cortina, "the object of the severest criticism along the whole length of the Mexican line." They labeled the focus on the Tejano as a pretext on the part of a few people who desired to produce conflict with

Mexico and justify "the territorial expansion of a covetous nation." Furthermore, "the Cortina War was no more than a revolt" that had originated in Texas, was led by a U.S. citizen, and was linked to "evils that American citizens of Mexican birth endured."[62]

Regarding rustling, the committee insisted that "*Mexicanos* on the Mexican side of the river also suffered from theft." Cheno's fault lay in not being careful enough about the background of his men, because "the bad reputation of some of them caused a lot of suspicion to fall on Cortina." Nevertheless, he was not responsible for cattle theft along the border but "had been the victim of a smear campaign conducted by Texans with ulterior motives." Some of the witnesses against him were themselves thieves or enemies, so their testimony was filled with lies. The committee also alleged that Texans had an ulterior motive for blaming international bandits— to receive compensation by forcing "the Mexican government to assume responsibility for the theft of Texas cattle."[63]

As the above investigation was transpiring, President Benito Juárez died, which facilitated Cortina's returning to Tamaulipas and regaining power in Matamoros. During his tenure as *alcalde* (mayor), border conditions deteriorated. All sorts of crimes and abuses were being perpetrated against Mexicans in Texas. For their part, Mexican raiders were killing, looting, and terrorizing. When Texas Rangers under Cpt. Leander H. McNelly were dispatched to the border, they themselves were "responsible for numerous executions." Two investigators sent by the governor of Texas "confirmed the wide-scale assassination of Mexican Texans," while noting that Texans who committed these acts "did not think it a crime to kill a Mexican."[64]

Cheno was again accused of cattle rustling and worse. The U.S. Congress sent yet another committee to investigate, and these men claimed to have proof that Cortina was "the number one cattle thief in the Lower Rio Grande Valley." Fueling the fire was the recovery of stolen cattle near Brownsville by Texas

Rangers who killed a number of the rustlers. The bodies were identified as "men who had served in Cortina's force." Indeed, American officials were convinced that he was the "head and protector of all the cattle thieves and murders from Camargo to the mouth of the Rio Grande" and demanded action from the Mexican government. In early May of 1875, President Sebastián Lerdo de Tejada finally ordered the regional caudillo to report to the capital. Because he procrastinated, Cheno was placed under arrest two months later.[65]

The prisoner protested his innocence, and sources disagree on his culpability. Ranger Captain McNelly himself observed that for months after the caudillo left the border "cattle rustling remained a booming business along the Lower Rio Grande," implying that accusations against Cortina were exaggerated. A prominent historian contends that Cheno was behind "the theft of more cattle in Texas than any man ever; yet, he was accused of hundreds of other crimes . . . , none of which he could conceivably have committed." Still another researcher argues that Juan Nepomuceno was probably not guilty of the crimes of which he was accused from 1868–1871 but did sponsor "cattle raids into Texas from 1872–1875." Whatever the truth, the usual pattern prevailed. Cortina was not brought to trial and managed to escape from prison the following year, at which time he left Mexico City.[66]

By the time Cortina fled, Mexico was in renewed turmoil with a new power player on the scene. Porfirio Díaz started a rebellion that overthrew the Lerdo de Tejada government. Supporting the Díaz movement, Cortina returned to the border region. Forming an army, he forced Lerdo's followers from several towns south of the river by year's end. Matamoros, however, was captured by other supporters of the *Porfirista* revolt. Nevertheless, when Cheno and his men arrived, they were welcomed with "military honors."[67]

Photograph of Juan Cortina in Mexican Army uniform. The Brownsville
Historical Association Archival Collection.

Many thought that Cortina once more had "as much influence and authority as at any time within the past ten years." They were proved wrong, because the United States insisted on his removal from the border. There is also evidence to support allegations that prominent men in Brownsville bribed the newly installed Mexican president to take action against Juan Nepomuceno. Also influencing Cortina's fate was his life-long enemy, Servando Canales, who became governor of Tamaulipas. Possibly fearing a renewed power struggle, Díaz ordered Cheno to report to Mexico City.[68]

Cortina again delayed leaving Tamaulipas and almost forfeited his life as a consequence. In February 1877, Governor Servando Canales placed his longtime nemesis under arrest. A military trial was held with little doubt as to the outcome: a death sentence. How Cheno avoided being executed is unclear. Some sources claim that Sabas Cavazos successfully appealed to Porfirio Díaz on his half-brother's behalf. Also, Rip Ford used this opportunity to repay his former enemy for the protection afforded Addie during the Civil War. The former Ranger met with Canales to warn that killing Cortina would "be a stain on your memory for all time to come." Whatever the reasons, the execution was canceled. Instead, Juan Nepomuceno was sent to the Mexican capital, where he did not fare well.[69]

Initially, the border caudillo was incarcerated at Santiago Tlatelolco Prison in Mexico City and allowed no contact with his family, friends, or lawyers, an experience that badly damaged his health. Although released in 1878, for the remainder of his life Cortina was either incarcerated or confined to the Mexico City region—with one exception. As an elderly man, he received permission for a brief visit to Matamoros in 1890. With him was a recently acquired young wife, and a banquet was held in Matamoros to honor the couple. Despite their history of enmity, Cortina reportedly agreed that Adolphus Glavecke could be invited, and "the two old men talked, broke bread, and forgave." Soon after, Cortina returned to Mexico City to be visited the following year by Rip Ford. The former Confederate commander was "received courteously by Cortina and his wife." Pleasantries ended, however, when Díaz suspected the old border caudillo of "attempting to incite another revolutionary uprising against the government." Imprisoned yet again in 1893, Cortina was freed from jail early the following year. Realistically, by that time he was too old and frail to pose a threat to anyone. [70]

On October 30, 1894, Cheno's luck and life ran out. The seventy-year-old former rebel, soldier, and governor died of pneumonia. Perhaps hoping to exploit the memory of the popular heroic figure, President Díaz arranged a full-honors military funeral for Juan Nepomuceno, who was laid to rest in the capital at the *Panteón de Dolores* (Pantheon of Sorrows). Early in the twentieth century the Cortina family attempted to have Juan's body moved to Texas to rest beside his mother's remains. Because those efforts failed, his grave today is weed-infested and his "tombstone has been vandalized."[71]

* * *

When Juan Nepomuceno Cortina died, the *Brownsville Herald* carried a story about this man who was so famous or infamous, depending on one's perspective. A quotation from that article illustrates the complexity of his life: "That his memory will long be cherished and cursed on the lower Rio Grande, there is no doubt, for if some people have cause to love him because of his former kindly acts, others have equal cause to hate him because of his evil deeds. Cortina was never a saint, but with his evil nature there was a certain amount of good, and the poor people loved him because of the charity he used to bestow."[72]

As the above obituary so aptly illustrates, Juan Nepomuceno Cortina elicited strong reactions from his contemporaries. Likewise, scholars have long been divided in their treatment of this larger-than-life figure. In the 1920s and 1930s, folklorist

Photograph of Juan Cortina and his third wife, María de Jesús López, at their home in Azcapotzalco, taken in Mexico ca. 1891. Courtesy of Nettie Lee Benson Latin American Collection, University of Texas Libraries, The University of Texas at Austin.

J. Frank Dobie and historian Walter Prescott Webb, relying heavily on the accounts of Cortina's enemies, presented him "as a ruthless bandit" who was "an architect of the lawlessness and violence" along the border. Mid-century, Charles Goldfinch used Cortina family papers and other documents to tell a very different story. The revisionist wrote of an intelligent, dynamic leader who served "as a convenient device for Brownsville merchants and residents" to benefit their region economically by soliciting the return of U.S. troops to the border. Little more than twenty years later, Michael Webster in a well-researched dissertation described "Cortina as a leader of a people who were forced to confront the violence associated with American manifest destiny." Also writing in the 1970s, noted scholar and folklorist Americo Paredes rejected the Robin Hood image of Juan Nepomuceno but saw him as a man who sought to bestow social justice and dignity on all Mexican Texans. Beneficiary of earlier scholarship, as well as decades of his own research efforts, Jerry Thompson in *Cortina: Defending the Mexican Name in Texas* (2007) credits his subject for being a "'social bandit' in his early struggle for equality and justice in Texas"; however, the biographer also acknowledges that the Tejano's quest for power and fame led him to become "a rugged, fearless, and, at times, ruthless frontier caudillo."[73]

Unlike the above authors, many people in the twenty-first century have never heard of Juan Nepomuceno Cortina, but he is well remembered along the Rio Grande. *Corridos* (Spanish language ballads) with Cheno as the theme began to appear as early as mid-nineteenth century, and interest in his exploits continues to the present. As recently as 2004, a musical play written by professor Milo Kearney was presented on the campus of the University of Texas at Brownsville. Entitled "The Red Beard of the Rio Grande," the production took a semi-serious, semi-humorous look at the life of one of the most significant men in nineteenth-century South Texas and Northern Mexico.[74] Crusader, criminal, or both, Juan Nepomuceno made his mark on the history of two nations.

Bibliographical Commentary.

Because of the controversy surrounding Juan Cortina's life, much has been written about this man—often by authors with an agenda. The most impressive scholarly works are those of Dr. Jerry Thompson, whose contributions range from *Sabers on the Rio Grande* (1974) to *Juan Cortina and the Texas-Mexican Frontier, 1859–1877* (1994) to *Cortina: Defending the Mexican Name in Texas* (2007), the last a definitive biography. Thompson's more recent *José de Santos Benavides and the History of the Texas-Mexico Borderlands, 1823–1891* (2017) profiles another significant figure, one who was an enemy of Cortina's, but in the process offers insight into the interactions between the two Tejanos. For valuable primary sources in print, written by contemporaries, that cast much light on Cortina from their perspectives, see *Fifty Miles and a Fight: Major Samuel Peter Heintzelman's Journal of Texas and the Cortina War*, edited by Jerry Thompson, and *Rip Ford's Texas*, edited by Stephen B. Oates.

Although an online search for Juan Nepomuceno Cortina yields many hits, one must be thoughtful in evaluating information found on these sites, given how controversial this man remains to the present. The reliable *Handbook of Texas Online* (www.tshaonline.org) has a short piece titled "Cortina, Juan Nepomuceno (1824–1994)" by Jerry Thompson, as well as entries on many of the major people and significant events in his life such as the following: Jerry Thompson's "Benavides, Santos (1823–1891)," Seymour V. Connor's "Ford, John Salmon [Rip] (1815–1897)," Thomas W. Cutrer's "Heintzelman, Samuel Peter (1805–1884)," and Zelime Vance Gillespie's "Tobin, William Gerard (1833–1884)."

For the more dedicated researcher, archival materials can be found at the Dolph Briscoe Center for American History and the Benson Latin American Collection, both located on the campus of The University of Texas at Austin.

Endnotes

1. James Ridley Douglas, "Juan Cortina: *El Caudillo de la Frontera*" (master's thesis, The University of Texas at Austin, 1987), Intro., 3, quotation.

2. Charles W. Goldfinch, "Juan N. Cortina, 1824–1892: A Reappraisal" (Chicago, 1949), reprinted in *Juan N. Cortina: Two Interpretations* (New York: Arno Press, 1974), 10, 13–14; *Handbook of Texas Online*, Jerry Thompson, "Cortina, Juan Nepomuceno (1824–1894)," http://www.tshaonline.org/handbook/online/articles/fco73, published by the Texas State Historical Association. [*Handbook of Texas Online* hereinafter cited as *HOT Online*.]

3. Goldfinch, "Cortina," 17.

4. Carlos Larralde and José Rodolfo Jacobo, *Juan N. Cortina and the Struggle for Justice in Texas* (Dubuque, IA: Kendall/Hunt Publishing Co., 2000), 4, quotation; Douglas, "Cortina," 11.

5. John Salmon Ford, *Rip Ford's Texas*, ed. by Stephen B. Oates (Austin: University of Texas Press, 1987), 261, 1st and 2nd quotations; Samuel Peter Heintzelman, *Fifty Miles and a Fight: Major Samuel Peter Heintzelman's Journal of Texas and the Cortina War*, ed. with Intro. by Jerry Thompson (Austin: Texas State Historical Assn., 1998), Intro., 18, 3rd quotation.

6. Douglas, "Cortina," 11–12, quotation on 12.

7. See Arnoldo de León, *They Called Them Greasers: Anglo Attitudes toward Mexicans in Texas, 1821–1900* (Austin: University of Texas Press, 1983).

8. See James K. Polk, President of the United States at Washington, D.C., to the Congress of the United States, A special message calling for a declaration of war against Mexico, Washington, May 11, 1846, http://www.dmwv.org/mexwar/documents/polk.htm.

9. *Juan Cortina and the Texas-Mexico Frontier*, ed. with Intro. by Jerry Thompson (El Paso: Texas Western Press, 1999), Intro., 1.

10. Llaralde and Jacobo, *Cortina*, 12–15, 1st quotation on 12, 2nd through 4th quotations on 14.

11. Omar S. Valerio-Jiménez, *River of Hope: Forging Identity and Nation in the Rio Grande Borderlands* (Durham, NC: Duke University Press, 2013), 239–240, quotation on 239.

12. Goldfinch, "Cortina," 22.

13. Ford, *Rip Ford's Texas*, 262–264.

14. Goldfinch, "Cortina," 33; Thompson, "Cortina, Juan Nepomuceno (1824–1894)," *The New Handbook of Texas*, vol. 2 (Austin: The Texas State Historical Association, 1996), 343.

15. Douglas, "Cortina," 18, 1st quotation; Llaralde, *Cortina*, 29–30, 2nd quotation on 29.

16. Douglas, "Cortina," 18, 1st quotation; Jerry Thompson, *Cortina: Defending the Mexican Name in Texas* (College Station: Texas A&M University Press, 2007), 31–32; Goldfinch, "Cortina," 37, 2nd and 3rd quotations.

17. Douglas, "Cortina," 20; Goldfinch, "Cortina," 40–41, 1st quotation on 40; Heintzelman, *Fifty Miles*, Intro., 18, 2nd quotation.

18. Goldfinch, "Cortina," 40–41; Llaralde and Jacobo, *Cortina*, 25–27, 1st quotation on 25, 2nd quotation on 26, 3rd quotation on 27.

19. Llaralde and Jacobo, *Cortina*, 1st quotation on 18, 2nd quotation on 33.

20. Valerio-Jiménez, *River of Hope*, 148, 234, 238; Goldfinch, "Cortina," 39; Ford, *Rip Ford's Texas*, 264; Heintzelman, *Fifty Miles*, Intro, 18, 1st quotation; Robert M. Utley, *Lone Star Justice: The First Century of the Texas Rangers* (Oxford: Oxford University Press, 2002), 107–109, 2nd quotation on 109.

21. Douglas, "Cortina," 21, 1st quotation, 29, 2nd quotation.

22. Michael C. Meyer, William L. Sherman, Susan M. Deeds, *The Course of Mexican History*, 9th ed. (New York: Oxford University Press, 2011), 284–288, quotation on 287.

23. Douglas, "Cortina," 24–26, all quotations on 25.

24. Thompson, *The Texas-Mexican Frontier*, 10–12; Douglas, "Cortina," 35; Thompson, *Cortina*, 37–38, all quotations on 37.

25. Goldfinch, "Cortina," footnote 2, 12; Llaralde and Jacobo, *Cortina*, 31, quotation; Thompson, *Cortina*, 27–28.

26. Goldfinch, "Cortina," 43–44, 1st and 2nd quotations on 43; Douglas, Cortina," 37–38, 3rd quotation on 37.

27. *HOT Online*, Thompson, "Cortina, Juan Nepomuceno"; Douglas, "Cortina," 3; Thompson, *Texas-Mexican Frontier*, 12; Thompson, *Cortina*, 43.

28. Douglas, "Cortina," 38; Thompson, *Texas-Mexican Frontier*, 12; Goldfinch, *Cortina*, 44–45.

29. *HOT Online*, Thompson, "Cortina"; Ford, *Rip Ford's Texas*, 264; Thompson, *Texas-Mexico Frontier*, 12–16, 1st quotation on 14, 2nd quotation on 15, 3rd quotation on 16. The actual proclamation issued from Rancho del Carmen on 30 September 1859 is presented as Document No. 1 in the last source referenced here.

30. Thompson, *Texas-Mexico Frontier*, 16–18, quotations on 16.

31. Douglas, "Cortina," 41–42, 1st quotation on 41, 2nd quotation on 42; Heintzelman, *Fifty Miles*, Intro., 25–26.

32. Thompson, *Texas-Mexico Frontier*, 19, quotation.

33. Thompson, *Texas-Mexico Frontier*, 19, 21; Heintzelman, *Fifty Miles*, Intro., 26; Manuel Callahan, "Mexican Border Troubles: Social War, Settler Colonialism and the Production of Frontier Discourses, 1848–1880" (Ph.D dissertation, The University of Texas at Austin, August 2003), 178.

34. Robert M. Utley, *Lone Star Justice: The First Century of the Texas Rangers* (Oxford: Oxford University Press, 2002), 110–111, 1st quotation on 111; *HOT Online*, Thompson, "Cortina,"; Douglas, 46, 2nd quotation; Heintzelman, *Fifty Miles*, 32, 3rd quotation.

35. Jerry Thompson, *Sabers on the Rio Grande* (Austin: Presidial Press, 1974), 189, 1st quotation; "*A Shared Experience's* Historical Survey: Juan Nepomuceno Cortina," 2nd quotation, www.rice.edu/armadillo/Past/Book/Part2/cortina. html; Utley, *Lone Star Justice*, 119, 3rd quotation; Heintzelman, *Fifty Miles*, Intro., 28, 4th quotation; Douglas, "Cortina," 62, 5th quotation.

36. Douglas, "Cortina,"47–48, 59–60, 1st quotation on 47, 2nd on 48; Thompson, *Mexican Name in Texas*, 58–62; Llaralde and Jacobo, *Cortina*, 67; Heintzelman, *Fifty Miles*, 28, 30; Valerio-Jiménez, *River of Hope*, 223, 228, 230, 232.

37. "*Pronunciamiento*, 23 November 1859," in Thompson, *Texas-Mexico Frontier*, 23–28, 1st quotation and 2nd quotations on 25, 3rd quotation on 27.

38. *HOT Online*, Thompson, "Cortina"; Heintzelman, *Fifty Miles*, Intro, 3, 34, 1st quotation on 3; "The Cortina Raid in 1859–'60," Official Report of Major Heintzelman, H. Ex. Doc. 81, 36th Cong., 1st Session, pp. 75–81, Appendix B, in Index to the Reports of the Committees of the House of Representatives for the First and Second of the Forty Fifth Congresses, 2nd and 3rd quotations on p. 81; J. Fred Rippy, "Border Troubles along the Rio Grande, 1848–1860," *Southwestern Historical Quarterly* 23, no. 2, 109, 4th quotation. For published editions of the accounts mentioned, see Heintzelman, *Fifty Miles and a Fight*, and Ford, *Rip Ford's Texas*.

39. Douglas, "Cortina," 48; Utley, *Lone Star Justice*, 113, quotation; Ford, *Rip Ford's Texas*, 274–275.

40. Ford, *Rip Ford's Texas*, 278, 280–281, 283–286, quotation on 286.

41. Douglas, "Cortina," 54; Heintzelman, *Fifty Miles*, 191, ftn. 4, quotations.

42. Goldfinch, *Cortina*, 50, 1st quotation; Jerry Thompson, "Juan Nepomuceno Cortina and the Texas-Mexico Ranching Frontier," 12th Annual Ranching Heritage Symposium, Texas A&M University-Kingsville, February 20, 2004.

43. Utley, *Lone Star Justice*, 117, 1st quotation; Ford, *Rip Ford's Texas*, 305–306; Callahan, "Mexican Border Troubles," 2nd quotation on 181; Richard B. McCaslin, *Fighting Stock: John S. "Rip" Ford of Texas* (Fort Worth: TCU Press, 2011), 96, 3rd quotation; Thompson, *Sabers*, 190, 4th quotation.

44. Goldfinch, *Cortina*, 50, 67, 67n1, quotation on 50.

45. Thompson, *Cortina: Defending the Mexican Name*, 96–99, 1st and 2nd quotations on 98, 3rd quotation on 98–99.

46. Thompson, *Cortina: Defending the Mexican Name*, 99–102, 1st through 3rd quotations on 100; 4th quotation on 102. See also, Jerry Thompson, *Vaqueros in Blue and Gray*, New Edition (Austin: State House Press, 2000), 14–24, passim. Also born in the 1820s in Mexico, Santos Benavides provides an interesting contrast to Juan Cortina. See Jerry Thompson's *Tejano Tiger: José de los Santos Benavides and the Texas-Mexico Borderlands, 1823–1891* (Fort Worth: Texas Christian University Press, 2017).

47. Meyer, Sherman, and Deeds, *Mexican History*, 9th ed., 290–292.

48. Douglas, "Cortina," 79; Thompson, *Cortina:Defending the Mexican Name*, 106.

49. Goldfinch, *Cortina*, 67n1.

50. Douglas, "Cortina," 80–82; Ford, *Rip Ford's Texas*, 351, quotation.

51. Thompson, *Cortina: Defending the Mexican Name*, 106; Ford, *Rip Ford's Texas*, xxxvii, quotation.

52. Thompson, *Cortina: Defending the Mexican Name*, 110; Ford, *Rip Ford's Texas*, 351; Llaralde and Jacobo, *Cortina*, 82, 1st quotation; Douglas, 85–86, 2nd quotation on 86, all other quotations on 85.

53. Llaralde and Jacobo, *Cortina*, 82, 1st quotation; Douglas, "Cortina," Intro., 5, 2nd quotation.

54. Llaralde and Jacobo, *Cortina*, 76, 78; Meyer, Sherman, and Deeds, *Mexican History*, 292–296, passim.

55. Llaralde and Jacobo, *Cortina*, 73–74; Thompson, *Texas-Mexico Frontier*, 58–62, 1st quotation on 58; Thompson, *Cortina: Defending the Mexican Name*, 145, 2nd quotation.

56. Douglas, "Cortina," 94, quotation; Thompson, *Texas-Mexico Frontier*, 68.

57. Douglas, "Cortina," 97–98, quotation; Meyer, Sherman, and Deeds, *Mexican History*, 294–297, passim; Thompson, *Texas-Mexico Frontier*, 68.

58. Douglas, "Cortina," 100–101, quotation on 101; Thompson, *Texas-Mexico Frontier*, 68.

59. Thompson, *Defending the Mexican Name*, 199, 3rd quotation; Goldfinch, *Cortina*, 53, all other quotations. The original petition and the resulting Senate Joint Resolution # 26 (October 16, 1871) are reproduced in Goldfinch, 54–57.

60. Goldfinch, *Cortina*, 58, 1st quotation; McCaslin, *Fighting Stock*, 217, 2nd and 3rd quotations.

61. Callahan, "Mexican Border Troubles," 279–283, 1st quotation on 279, 3rd and 5th quotations on 282, 4th quotation on 283; Goldfinch, *Cortina*, 58–59, 2nd quotation on 59.

62. Callahan, "Mexican Border Troubles," 283, 294–296, 1st and 2nd quotations on 294, 3rd quotation on 295, 4th quotation on 294–295.

63. Callahan, "Mexican Border Troubles," 292, 1st quotation; Douglas, "Cortina," 118–119, 4th quotation; Goldfinch, *Cortina*," 59–60, 2nd and 3rd quotations on 59.

64. Douglas, "Cortina," 120; Thompson, *Cortina: Defending the Mexican Name*, 219–225, passim, 1st quotation on 224, 2nd quotation on 224–225, 3rd quotation on 225.

65. Douglas, "Cortina," 120, 1st quotation; Goldfinch, *Cortina*, 60–62, 2nd quotation on 61; Thompson, *Cortina: Defending the Mexican Name*, 225–228, 3rd quotation on 225.

66. Douglas, "Cortina," 123–124, 1st and 3rd quotations on 123; Thompson, *Texas-Mexico Frontier*, 2, 2nd quotation.

67. Thompson, *Texas-Mexico Frontier*, 87, 91, quotation on 91.

68. Thompson, *Texas-Mexico Frontier*, 91, 93, as quoted on 91; Callahan, "Mexican Border Troubles," 191–192; Ford, *Rip Ford's Texas*, 412.

69. McCaslin, *Fighting Stock*, 231; Llaralde and Jacobo, *Cortina*, 131; Ford, *Rip Ford's Texas*, 413–414, quotation on 413.

70. Llaralde and Jacobo, *Cortina*, 132–133, 2nd quotation on 133; Thompson, *Texas-Mexico Frontier*, 93; Thompson, *Defending the Mexican Name*, 243, 1st quotation.

71. Thompson, *Defending the Mexican Name*, 245; Llaralde and Jacobo, *Cortina*, 134; Thompson, "Juan Nepomuceno Cortina," Ranching Heritage Symposium, quotation.

72. Llaralde and Jacobo, *Cortina*, 134, as quoted.

73. Callahan, "Mexican Border Troubles," 169–171, 1st, 2nd, and 4th quotations on 169, 3rd quotation on 170; Thompson, *Cortina: Defending the Mexican Name*, 4, 251, 5th and 6th quotations on 251.

74. Llaralde and Jacobo, *Cortina*, 135; Program, Patron of the Arts, The University of Texas at Brownsville and Texas Southmost College Bravo Opera Company Gala, "The Red Beard of the Rio Grande," by Milo Kearney, April 17–18, 2004.

Photograph of Adina De Zavala. This image was printed on the front cover of the sheet music entitled "Remember the Alamo," composed by Jessie Beattie Thomas and dedicated to Adina De Zavala. Courtesy of The Sisters of Charity of the Incarnate Word Archives and the University of the Incarnate Word.

Adina De Zavala

The Angel of the Alamo

THE DE ZAVALA NAME was a distinguished one in Texas when a baby girl named Adina was born into the family in 1861, and having that surname shaped her life and career. Paternal grandfather, Miguel Lorenzo Justiniano de Zavala y Sáenz, was a noted Mexican Liberal who helped write his country's first constitution, served as governor of the state of Mexico, represented his native state of Yucatán in the Mexican Congress, and held a diplomatic post in France.[1]

A prominent Creole of Spanish ancestry, Lorenzo de Zavala played a significant role in Texas history as well. When Antonio López de Santa Anna began to establish centralized control over Mexico in the mid-1830s, as described in the first chapter of this book, Lorenzo denounced the overthrow of legitimate government in his homeland. Tying his future to that of Texas, he was a delegate to the convention that declared Texas's independence on March 2, 1836. Attaining the prestigious post of interim vice-president of the Republic of Texas, he undoubtedly would have provided other valuable services had he not died late in 1836. While the people of Mexico viewed Zavala as a traitor, future President Mirabeau B. Lamar lauded him as an "unwavering and consistent friend of liberal principles and free government." More than a century after Lorenzo's death, English-language publications referred to him as a "Texas Patriot" and as "Freedom's Champion."[2]

Being the descendant of such a prominent figure was consequential for Adina who took great pride in her ancestry and benefitted from it. Living to be in her nineties, she devoted herself to teaching, researching, and preserving Texas history—and exalting the de Zavala name, spelled with a capital "D" by her lifetime. Although these activities might not sound very dramatic, they led the strong-willed woman to become embroiled in heated battles over causes to which she was deeply committed. A true descendant of her grandfather, she refused to be intimidated. A dramatic example was her struggle to preserve the site of the battle of the Alamo from destruction in the service of commercial development. Thanks in large part to Adina's courage and perseverance, this and other historic treasures still exist as reminders of the state's proud heritage.

Had Lorenzo de Zavala lived long enough to know his granddaughter, he would have been as proud of her as she was of him. Called the "Alamo Crusader" and "The Angel of the Alamo," Adina also earned a place in the annals of Texas history.

* * *

Adina De Zavala was the first child of Augustine De Zavala and Julia Tyrrell. Augustine was Lorenzo de Zavala's son by his second wife, Emily West of New York. Julia Tyrrell, although originally from Ireland, was educated in Galveston, Texas. The couple married in New York City in March of 1860 but made their home in the Lone Star State. They resided at Zavala Point on Buffalo Bayou, close to the home of Augustine's widowed mother and the location of the Battle of San Jacinto—the definitive engagement in the Texas Revolutionary War. Here Adina was born in 1861. Augustine and Julia later would have five other surviving children: Florence, Mary, Zita, Thomas, and Augustine, Jr.[3]

Adina was born at a critical time in American history, shortly before the Civil War began in the United States. Newly elected Republican President Abraham Lincoln was determined to preserve the Union; nevertheless, eleven Southern states voted to secede and formed a separate nation: the Confederate States of America. In essence, these Southerners were declaring their independence. Just as his father had fought for Texas's right to break away from Mexico twenty-five years earlier, Augustine De Zavala supported the Confederate cause in the 1860s. As for his role in the war, Adina later "claimed that her father had served as a blockade runner" who smuggled supplies past the Union ships patrolling the Texas coast. According to a recent master's thesis, however, military records indicate that "he enlisted as a private in . . . Madison's Regiment, Texas Cavalry" and was "mustered out as a corporal." His daughter's version has by far been the more widely publicized.[4] Either way, the war had profound consequences for the family.

The efforts of men like Augustine De Zavala proved insufficient, because a defeated Confederacy surrendered in April 1865. The Federal Union was preserved, and the Thirteenth Amendment to the U.S. Constitution freed millions of slaves. The De Zavalas were among those who lost the labor of their human property and also the capital investment those slaves represented. Adding to their concerns was Augustine's deteriorating health, as he suffered from "a rather severe condition of arthritis and disabling rheumatism." For these and other reasons, the family relocated to Galveston after the costly conflict ended.[5]

Despite the outcome, Adina took great pride in the role of her father and other relatives during the Civil War—whether or not she romanticized those exploits. Later in life she became a member of the United Daughters of the Confederacy, and one of her prized possessions reportedly was a Confederate flag.[6]

Despite the trauma of the war and its aftermath, Adina had what some would consider a privileged childhood. As a De Zavala, she was exposed to notable men who had helped shape the Lone Star State. The girl loved to hear tales of their adventures, which made a lasting impression. A gifted reader, she preferred books that focused on the past. As she got older, Adina and her sister would enact plays that were "always scenes from history."[7]

Being a De Zavala also provided access to a better education than was available to most women of her ethnicity and generation. The bright child was tutored by "her mother and her grandmother, followed by family governesses." After the family settled in Galveston, Adina was able to attend Ursuline Academy from 1871–73, an experience that deepened her devotion to Catholicism. In the early 1870s, the family was uprooted again, because the coastal climate proved detrimental to Augustine's medical issues. They settled on a ranch several miles from San Antonio but also maintained a home in town. Eldest daughter Adina apparently remained in Galveston for a time but soon joined the rest of the family at their new home, where she helped take care of her younger siblings.[8]

In 1879, Adina enrolled at Sam Houston Normal Institute (now Sam Houston State University) in Huntsville, Texas, where her studies included algebra, Latin, and astrology. Two years later, she was "a member of that school's first graduating class." After garnering "a permanent certificate of the first rank and diploma Master of Instruction," the young woman began her teaching career in Terrell, Texas, in the mid-1880s "with her salary apparently serving as family support." However, she soon returned to San Antonio where she taught elementary school for about two decades.[9]

Although a "fragile-looking wisp of a black-haired, blue-eyed woman," Adina did not hesitate to speak her mind or pursue her own agenda. In 1900, she forcefully complained at a meeting of the San Antonio School Board about her low salary, after which the board ruled that teachers' complaints must be presented "only in writing." This did not stifle the educator, who became "the first woman [1st] vice president of the Texas State Teachers' Association." In 1904, Adina was reprimanded by the superintendent for missing a month of school without providing proper notice. Her belated explanation was "that she had been 'studying Mexican history in Mexico.'" She was also chastised for missing mandatory teachers' meetings, to which she responded "that she 'attended . . . when she had nothing more urgent'" to do. A few years later, the headstrong educator was "censured by the school board for being too strict with pupils[,]" as well as for being too "'independent and insubordinate. . . .'" These reprimands and strictures almost certainly factored into her decision to resign as of 1907.[10]

While still in the classroom, Adina used creative methods to inform children about their state's past. As an example, in 1900, she wrote a short play entitled "The Six National Flags That Have Floated Over Texas." She wanted students to understand that Texas had belonged to Spain's empire, the French empire, Mexico, the Republic of Texas, the United States, and the Confederacy.[11] Six Flags over Texas, the popular theme park that opened decades later in Arlington, Texas, is based on that same concept.

Teaching history in a classroom or writing a play about historic events was not enough for the Tejana. She passionately believed that the past needed to be integrated into the present. "If people—especially children—can actually see the door through which some noble man or woman passed," she wrote, "or some object he or she touched, they'll be impressed." Then, "they'll remember, they'll be inspired to read . . . about that man or woman." She insisted that people would copy the "high ideals" of Texas heroes, once they learned about their exploits.[12] Therefore, she dedicated her life to recording and preserving the history of her beloved Lone Star State.

The Tejana's strong personality, along with her prestigious family surname, made her effective as a leader and organizer. Around 1889, she "began gathering a group of local 'patriotic' women to discuss ways to arouse interest in Texas history." Among the aims of The De Zavala Daughters—named for Lorenzo, of course—were "to keep green the memory of the heroes, founders, and pioneers of Texas," foster interest in the care and restoration of historic structures, awaken the "dormant patriotism" in the Lone Star State, and encourage "a more general display of the Texas flag."[13]

In 1891, more than a dozen "ladies" in Houston organized a somewhat similar society, the Daughters of the Republic of Texas (DRT). Their aspirations resembled those of the De Zavala Daughters, such as preserving "the memory and deeds of the men and women, who, amid the conflict of battle, laid the foundation of the great commonwealth of Texas." Preservation of historic sites was also on the agenda, as was promoting the annual celebration of significant dates in the state's history. The exclusive organization restricted membership to women related to someone who had played a role in Texas history prior to annexation in early 1846.[14] Obviously, Adina met that criterion.

In 1893, the year before Adina's father died, The De Zavala Daughters joined the DRT as the De Zavala Chapter, again to honor Lorenzo "whose name carried important historic weight." As the dominant force in the San Antonio branch, Lorenzo's granddaughter was elected president in 1893, an office that she held for the next sixteen years. Her surname "gave her a degree of credibility" and amount of influence she would have lacked otherwise.[15]

One of the first projects of the San Antonio Chapter was to honor Ben Milam, who had been killed in the Texas Revolution. The members' efforts resulted in a monument being placed on his grave, which was located in the old city cemetery. Beginning on March 6, 1897, they also "organized an annual Texas Heroes Day observance at the spot." March 6 was selected for commemoration, because on that date in 1836 the Alamo had fallen to General Antonio López de Santa Anna's army with the loss of many lives. Just four days earlier, Texas officially had declared independence from Mexico; so, women of the De Zavala chapter encouraged official recognition of March 2 as well. Additionally, they were responsible for the placement of "a marble tablet" at the Alamo in 1901. (See Chapters 1 and 2 for more detailed information about the siege and capture of the Alamo.)[16]

Adina De Zavala found still another way to recognize significant figures from Texas's past. When she began her teaching career at Ward School No. 5 in San Antonio, the city's schools had numbers instead of names. She and her chapter sought to have the names of those institutions changed to commemorate Texas heroes, and they succeeded in that endeavor in the early 1900s. Ward School No. 5 became David G. Burnet Elementary in honor of the second vice-president of the Republic of Texas, and another was named after her grandfather.[17]

Another of De Zavala's special concerns was to save historic sites in and around San Antonio. A devout Catholic, she was distressed that the five old Spanish missions in the area "were falling into ruin" by the late nineteenth century. This was partly the result of decay and age. However, some destruction was caused by tourists breaking off pieces of carvings and doors or stealing religious figures from the old structures. Elected to the State Executive Committee of the DRT in 1902, Adina pushed the state organization to help conserve these historic church buildings. Much was accomplished as a result, although the efforts were "always handicapped by lack of funds."[18]

The preservationist worked closely with Elizabeth di Barbieri, wife of Italian-born sculptor Pompeo Coppini. The two women called on local businessmen to solicit donations of "bricks, lumber, cedar posts, or wire." These materials were used to repair and fence Mission San José, where graves "were being trampled down," and a man was hired by the women's society to care for that property. In even worse condition was the San Juan mission complex for which the Roman Catholic Church in 1902 granted the De Zavala Chapter a lease for five years. The agreement stipulated that the mission must remain open for public worship, but the DRT were authorized to undertake restoration efforts—at their own expense. Costs could be offset by charging admission fees to the public for touring the property.[19]

Indeed, by the early twentieth century tourism was a growing industry in San Antonio and was one of the reasons that the city was increasingly "a target for capitalist expansion." Commercialization threatened historic structures in the area and led to Adina De Zavala's greatest crusade, involving the site of the Battle of the Alamo. The mission proper had been established by the Spaniards in 1718 under the name San Antonio de Valero. Also constructed was a long two-story building, called at various times "the convent, monastery, long barrack, or fortress." It served to house religious personnel. Later a chapel that became known as the Alamo was erected near the fortress. A wall enclosed the mission and environs.[20]

When Santa Anna laid siege to the Alamo in late February 1836, those inside faced certain death for rebelling against his government and defying his authority. Initially, the Texans tried to defend the outer walls of the mission, but almost certainly retreated to the long barrack, where many of them died at the hands of the Mexican troops. In ensuing decades, the property changed owners numerous times and "lost its identity as an integrated complex." In 1883, the Catholic Church sold the old chapel, which was erroneously "accepted by many . . . as the whole and only theatre of the siege . . . and holocaust," to the state of Texas. It was then turned over to "the city of San Antonio for a museum." [21]

The long barrack had a more complicated history. The owner, grocer Honoré Grenet, had covered the stone structure with wood in 1878 to make it look like a fort, and over time "many forgot that the original structure of the long barracks were still extant." When Grenet died in the early 1880s, his heirs sold the building to another grocery concern, Hugo & Schmeltzer (H&S). The property was used as a warehouse to store inventory that included alcoholic beverages. By the turn of the century, much nearby real estate was also privately held.[22]

Those more invested in Texas's past than in commercial development wanted to preserve the Alamo. However, this proved more challenging than anticipated, as even the preservationists involved in the endeavor could not agree on exactly what comprised the original mission or what part of the site was of historical import. These differences of opinion ultimately led to a prolonged series of contentious events known as "The Second Battle of the Alamo," and Adina De Zavala was one of the major combatants involved.[23]

Early in the twentieth century, the De Zavala chapter of the DRT created a group known as the Congress of Patriotism to help maintain the Alamo church, as well as the H&S warehouse. The ultimate goal was to utilize the property as a "Texas Hall of Fame—a Museum of History, Literature, and Relics." Persons of good moral character who shared that vision were eligible to participate in the endeavor.[24]

A sense of urgency arose in 1903, when investors with plans to erect a hotel purchased the lot behind the H&S building. Their intention to create a park nearby threatened the existence of the long barrack (convent). Having anticipated such an eventuality, Adina years earlier had secured an oral pledge from the grocery concern that the property would not be sold without the De Zavala Daughters being given "the opportunity to acquire it." Alerted by Pompeo Coppini, De Zavala recognized the imperative of attracting significant capital or the old convent would be lost. Their first strategy involved appealing to the self-interest of the owners of the Menger Hotel, which was situated near the Alamo and would be in competition with the proposed new enterprise. Unfortunately, the hoped-for allies were out of the country.[25]

Undeterred, the two preservationists developed an alternate plan upon learning that "the daughter of a wealthy, elite Corpus

Christi family" was a guest in residence at the Menger. Providentially, Clara Driscoll had travelled in Europe, where she had acquired an appreciation for historic sites. The young woman had publicly expressed her distress at the "shabby condition" and "unsightly surroundings of the Alamo Chapel." Not surprisingly, then, when De Zavala and Coppini approached her, Driscoll agreed to become involved in the Alamo project. She also joined the De Zavala Chapter of the DRT for which she could easily qualify, since at least one of her grandfathers had fought at the Battle of San Jacinto.[26]

In mid-March 1903, serious talks ensued between owner Charles Hugo and the two women hoping to acquire the grocery warehouse for the DRT. The former agreed to let the organization have a thirty-day option on the $75,000 property, in return for which Clara Driscoll wrote a personal check for $500. Another payment of $4,500 was due within thirty days or the deal was off. Despite enthusiastic fund-raising efforts by DRT chapters, only slightly more than $1,000 was raised by the deadline, at which time Driscoll personally paid the remainder. The $5,000 expended bought time—until February 1904—to secure the next, larger payment of $20,000. The fate of the historic structure was still far from certain.[27]

Treasurer of the De Zavala Chapter, Clara Driscoll also became its Chair of the Committee on Alamo and Mission Improvements. Predictably, Adina was chapter president. Attempts to raise money included chain letters, door-to-door solicitations, and "other customary methods," but only produced around an additional $6,000. Again, Driscoll stepped in to meet the shortfall. She also signed personal notes for the $50,000 balance, due in five annual payments of $10,000 plus interest. Although these transactions were done in Driscoll's name as security for her expenditures, she clearly was making the purchase on behalf of the DRT. In turn, the Executive Board "recognized this as a debt of honor and pledged themselves to work unceasingly" to repay her.[28]

The DRT contended that Texans were "of the opinion that the State should become the purchaser of the property" and pressured the controlling Democratic Party to that end. Initial efforts proved unsuccessful because of opposition by the governor. Early in 1905, however, he succumbed to pressure by signing an act to repay Driscoll "and put title of the property in the name of the State of Texas." The new law entrusted custodianship of both the H&S building and the Alamo church to the DRT "to be maintained by them in good order and repair without charge to the State."[29]

Adina fully expected that she and the De Zavala Chapter would be named custodians of the newly acquired property, and for a time that seemed possible. Ultimately, however, the Executive Committee would accord that responsibility—and honor—to Driscoll. In an explanatory letter, "the powerbrokers of the DRT" wrote of "the debt we owe to Clara Driscoll" who had asked for "a little return for my work in this matter." The purpose of the missive was to discourage De Zavala from opposing the decision to grant custodianship to her counterpart. That Driscoll left the state for years and "handled much of her association with the DRT by long distance" must have been even more galling to Adina.[30]

That Driscoll's plan for the long barrack was diametrically opposed to De Zavala's soon became clear. The young Anglo woman considered it "an eyesore that detracted from what she saw as 'the Alamo'—the church—and should be removed to create a park." Adamant that "Little blood had been shed in the Alamo chapel," De Zavala insisted that the H&S warehouse contained "'a large part' of the original convent, significant to both mission and battle." She took an unrelenting stand against its destruction. These contrary positions proved irreconcilable and divisive. For a while, the matter was moot, because she retained possession of "the keys to and relics from the Alamo" chapel. She leveraged this into a "very public and highly emotional battle" regarding the site. Under threat of a lawsuit by the DRT, however, Adina reluctantly surrendered the keys to Driscoll.[31]

Problems intensified in 1906, with a letter from Charles M. Reeves, acting on behalf of the St. Louis hotel group that owned the property by the Alamo. Extolling the plan to build a "splendid structure" there, he required a guarantee from De Zavala that the grocery warehouse would be replaced by a park. In reply, the preservationist unequivocally reiterated that the structure in question was an integral part of the Alamo and after restoration should be designated as a Hall of Fame. Reeves's second letter added fuel to the fire, when he declared hers an impractical plan that would "only result in disappointment." No businessman, he proclaimed, would be influenced "by a misguided sense of patriotism" to preserve an unsightly structure.[32] One has to admire his honesty, if not his message.

Well before the annual meeting in 1906, the DRT was divided into opposing factions. At those proceedings, Driscollites and De Zavalans contested issues that ranged from custodianship of the Alamo to the purchase of a portrait of Davy Crockett. At the Austin convention the following year, hostility escalated as the competing parties vied for control of the state organization. Two separate Executive Committees emerged, each of which claimed legitimacy. Adina openly represented the one she headed as "acting for Daughters of R. Of Texas." For her part, Driscoll resigned from the DRT, but that failed to resolve the crisis, which divided "practically all of Texas."[33]

The Driscollites used the legal system to stop the De Zavala Chapter's "interfering tactics until rightful officers could be determined by the courts." Suing the San Antonians, the DRT argued that the H&S building had never been blessed "by the blood of heroes of Texas." Instead it was watered by "good, bad, and indifferent whiskey" stored at the warehouse. The ugly structure should be replaced with "a park, museum or something else."

Adina would lose this battle with the state's Attorney General later "stating that an elected executive committee—not Adina's committee—was the only body authorized by the Legislature to take care of the property."[34]

Prolonged stress took a toll on De Zavala, physically and emotionally. She bemoaned "that she no longer knew her friends from her enemies." At least one who still counted herself as a friend worried that Adina had "more on her mind and heart than any mere human ought to be burdened with." And the Alamo war was far from over. The lease held by the H&S firm expired on February 10, 1908, with the DRT to take possession of the warehouse the following day. Around that time, a disturbing newspaper report alleged that the building was going to be rented for theatrical purposes, which distressed De Zavala. However, she feared even more that it would be razed. Remembering Davy Crockett's words, "'Be sure you are right—then go ahead,'" Adina did.[35]

On February 10, Adina De Zavala took possession of the H&S structure to which she had again acquired the keys. Later that day a DRT attorney, business syndicate agents, and law enforcement officials came to the premises. They expelled three guards Adina had hired, but the defiant woman barred the doors—barricading herself inside the building. As she later explained, "There was nothing else for me to do but hold the fort. So I did." This was especially gutsy, given that the building had few amenities but did have rodents. "Electric and telephone lines were cut" to discourage her staying.[36]

The next day a local newspaper reported that an injunction had been secured to force the recalcitrant woman to vacate the old fortress. However, De Zavala "refused to accept a copy" and "stopped her ears with her fingers" when the sheriff attempted to read it to her. Frustrated officials attempted to keep anyone from bringing her food and water, but no amount of deprivation could deter Adina. To the contrary, she informed the press that "my immortal forefathers suffered every privation to defend the freedom of Texas. I, like them, am willing to die for what I believe to be right." While overly dramatic, these words encapsulated Adina's strong connection to Texas's past and determination to preserve it. Fortunately for the Tejana, public scrutiny convinced the sheriff to restore electricity to the building, but she apparently repaired the phone line herself. Friends also managed to get some nourishment to her.[37]

The standoff was settled after three days and three nights, but only after state officials intervened. Even that resolution was not easily achieved, however, as the preservationist and her adversaries differed over the exact terms by which De Zavala would agree to evacuate the premises. Finally, with assurances that "nothing would be done to the building" until legal proceedings were completed, she surrendered it on February 13 to the state superintendent of public buildings.[38]

A district court determined that the Driscollites were the legal officers of the DRT. Not surprisingly, Adina and her supporters appealed to a higher Texas court, but to no avail. On March 10, 1910, the Alamo property was entrusted to the DRT, then firmly under the control of the opposing faction. The De Zavala Chapter also received notice that they were no longer members of the state organization. In defiant response, the San Antonio contingent recast themselves as an independent society, the De Zavala Daughters and Sons of the Heroes of the Republic of Texas.[39]

In 1911, Governor Oscar Colquitt "intervened in the dispute on the side of the preservationists" by agreeing that many of the walls in the H&S warehouse predated the Texas Revolution. Applauding his "determination to restore the main building of the Alamo," Adina wrote the governor that his decision made her "happy and encouraged." Her happiness proved short-lived, however. Not only did the state restoration funding prove inadequate but also, when Colquitt was out of the country in 1913, the lieutenant governor allowed the Long Barrack's second story to be removed.[40]

The heartbroken preservationist condemned the act as "a sacrifice to private greed." Nevertheless, she persevered. Around 1917 De Zavala authored a book entitled *History of the Alamo and Other Missions in San Antonio* in honor of the members of the De Zavala Daughters. She called them "Noble, Loyal, unselfish, Patriotic Women in Whose Veins course the Blood of the Heroes, Statesmen, Patriots, Pioneers, and Founders of Texas." Conversely, she condemned her opponents as "selfish and ambitious persons." Adina assured readers that she and her followers were "still engaged in patriotic and unselfish labors" to save the Alamo. And engage in that battle she did decade after decade.[41]

Still presenting her case almost twenty years later, Adina publicly decried the fact that money budgeted for the Alamo during the Texas Centennial (1936) was going to be spent largely to beautify the church. Governor James Allred, she bemoaned, "like most of our people does not appear to understand that the church of San Antonio de Padua is not the Alamo, but just a small part of it, and not where the heroes died. . . ." The frustrated preservationist asked Texans to pressure the governor to restore "the real Alamo" and not allow it to "fall into ruins." Despite De Zavala's admirable efforts, her long-cherished dream of the monastery being fully restored and dedicated as a museum would not be realized during her lifetime. Notably, however, many of Adina's arguments regarding the Alamo were proven correct with time. Her stubborn efforts certainly saved more of the site than otherwise would have been rescued, given Clara Driscoll's designs for the site.[42]

Though Adina lost the struggle for control of the historic site, she did gain national prominence in the process. One company published a song called "Remember the Alamo" with the preservationist's photograph at the top of the sheet of music. The events of February 1908 made headlines nationally with the press portraying De Zavala as a heroine: "'The Angel of the Alamo' and 'The Sweetheart of Texas.'" While admiring her courage, reporters acknowledged that the issue had torn Texas apart and made friends into enemies. One newspaper opined that the Second Battle of the Alamo involved "warfare quite as determined as the defense of the Alamo in 1836."[43]

De Zavala's tremendous energy was not directed solely at preserving the Alamo. In 1912, she helped found the Texas Historical and Landmarks Association (THLA) when historic preservation was relatively new. This organization permitted membership to women who could not meet DRT requirements, and men were also eligible. Chapters were established in San Antonio and several other towns. Adina "was the leader of the group, the state president, and usually the *de facto* president." From 1922 to 1935 the organization researched and marked almost thirty historic sites in San Antonio and ten elsewhere in the state.[44]

The preservationist became particularly focused on an old stone building located on the Military Plaza in San Antonio. Researching its history, she erroneously concluded that it had served as the headquarters for the Texas government during the Spanish colonial period. Consequently, De Zavala undertook yet another crusade, to save the "Ancient Government Palace," as she referred to the dilapidated structure. Adina contended that the Governor's Palace, as it was also known, had been "the residence of the representative of the King of Spain," a rare treasure that should be saved from vandalism.[45]

Early efforts to salvage the Governor's Palace coincided with World War I, and numerous military personnel were stationed in San Antonio. Consequently, Adina and her THLA colleagues developed a plan "to restore the . . . building and use it as a school and meeting place for soldiers." "Rooms for reading, writing, music, and the playing of games" would be situated around a patio with a fountain. Combining patriotism with preservation maximized the chance for effective fund-raising but still failed to produce the necessary "down payment goal of $10,000." After the war ended, efforts to solicit donations continued, including a Tag Day, sponsored by a committee under the leadership of Adina De Zavala and Mattie Dittmar. Booths were placed at various locations around the city, including the post office, the Menger Hotel and the Grand Opera House. Dozens of women sold tiny replicas of the Texas flag to raise money.[46]

Adina availed herself of every opportunity to write about the Governor's Palace in particular and local history in general. In December 1919, a local magazine, the *Interstate Index: A Journal of Progress*, notified readers that De Zavala had agreed to be editor of the Texas history section. Praising the exceptional woman, the journal listed her many memberships and offices—as remarkable in number as in variety. A sampling included the following: former vice-president of the Folk Lore Association of Texas, ex-vice-president of the San Antonio Art League, Treasurer for the Council of National Defense of Texas, Director of the San Antonio Women's Club, ex-vice-president of San Antonio Women's League for Betterment of the Life of Women, honorary member of the Texas Press Association—and on and on. The announcement also credited her for establishing a large library at the Burnet School and helping to organize the only Patriotic Carnival ever held in San Antonio. Appropriately, pictures of Adina, her grandfather Lorenzo, and her grandmother graced the article.[47]

The history editor used the *Interstate Index* as a forum to address her key project. The December 1920 issue contained an article entitled "Save the Ancient Government Palace" in which the historian-preservationist declared that "It would be a disgrace to the State of Texas to permit the destruction of so important a building!" Pleading with readers to be heroes "by coming to the relief of the history of Texas," she pledged that contributors' names would be inscribed in a "The Roll of Honor" to be kept in the restored building.[48]

The Palace crusade proved lengthy and frustrating—not a new experience for De Zavala. In 1920, she spoke to the Lions Club about "new plans for restoring the building and making it a 'Texas Hall of Fame' as well as a 'museum for Texas relics, art, and literature.'" Her vision for the Alamo site had been transferred to the Governor's Palace, as she emphasized the need to act before any other city created "a state history museum."[49]

In 1922, the *San Antonio Express* recounted the lengthy efforts undertaken by De Zavala and her two organizations, the THLA and the Daughters of the Heroes of Texas, to prevent the historic building from being razed. According to the newspaper, appeals had gone out in "thousands of letters to individuals, societies and clubs and to the press." Listing Adina as Trustee of the "Ancient Government Palace Purchase Fund," these missives advised that "A good name is to be prized above riches" but noted that it was not easy to enter "the pages of Texas . . . history." However, "Promoters" who collected or donated $1,000 could have "a name designated by them placed on a bronze tablet on the outside of the building." Similarly, $10,000 "Benefactors" could have a room named for them or a person of their choice, a more fitting tribute than "a monument in a cemetery."[50]

Adina must have experienced a sense of deja-vu, as she again found herself in competition and conflict with others. In 1924, the San Antonio Conservation Society was founded by Emily Edwards and Rena Maverick Green. An irate De Zavala informed them that "preservation was 'her field,' and 'there was just room for nobody else.'" The possibility of the new organization working with the THLA came to naught, with Adina's arbitrary attitude almost certainly a contributing factor. Still another parallel occurred in 1924, when the owners of the Government Palace contemplated selling the building for commercial purposes. Insisting that the THLA had an option on the property, Adina urged the city to intervene. Acting separately, the City Federation of Women's Clubs added their voices to pressure San Antonio to purchase the structure. The combined efforts did prevent a sale at least temporarily.[51]

With renewed urgency, the preservationists pursued their fundraising but fell far short of the $57,000 needed to purchase the structure. De Zavala openly chastised city commissioners for spending so much for "industrial and commercial development" but "doing nothing to preserve the spiritual and historical side of San Antonio." Her voice was only one of many that in 1928 finally led the city to dedicate $55,000 in a larger bond issue to buy the building and grounds. Another $30,000 would be provided to restore the structure to good condition.[52]

As with the Alamo, De Zavala anticipated that her groups would control the project. Instead San Antonio's mayor formed an advisory board of representatives from several local organizations "to oversee restoration and administration of the Governor's Palace." One can only imagine how she felt when rival Rena Maverick Green of the Conservation Society was appointed chair. That the mayor had served in the state senate with Rena's late husband may have influenced his decision, but Adina's headstrong personality assuredly did not help her cause. At any rate, a petition labelling the mayor's actions unfair did not bring satisfaction, and she remained marginalized.[53]

Despite setbacks, Adina and her collaborators attempted to influence the architect's design for the restoration project. Her insistence that the historic palace had been a two-story structure put her at odds with architect Harvey Smith, who produced a single-story design. The rehabilitated Governor's Palace was officially opened to the public on July 7, 1930, with the Conservation Society in charge of operations. "Although Adina De Zavala had lost control of the restoration of the building and of the museum inside," she received well-deserved credit for her role. Newspapers and magazines lauded her as the person who "Launched [the] Palace Movement" and called her "the keeper" of tradition. A 1935 publication referred

Adina De Zavala in the Chapel Room at The Governor's Palace. Adina De Zavala Papers, di_11068, The Dolph Briscoe Center for American History, The University of Texas at Austin.

to the restored structure as "one of the great sight-seeing attractions in America today" and cited Adina as still advocating full restoration with "the upper tiers of rooms and arcades added."[54]

Adina and the De Zavala Chapter of the THLA did manage to put an imprint on the front of the Governor's Palace, when a plaque was installed in 1938. Encapsulating her view, it read: "WHERE

TRADITIONS OF GLAMOROUS DAYS, ROMANCE, AND TRAGEDY STILL LINGER." The restored building allowed citizens of San Antonio "to embrace the Hispanic heritage of the city, and to make it part of their modern identity."[55] Ironically, later research revealed that the misnamed Governor's Palace was not actually the official residence of Spanish governors, as De Zavala had contended. Instead, it most likely housed colonial military commanders, the series of captains in charge of the presidio (fort) at San Antonio. Also, some documentation supports Harvey Smith's contention that it was historically a one-story structure. Regardless, his architectural blueprint was not as true to the original as it might have been, because features were borrowed from buildings elsewhere in the Southwest.[56]

While engaged in the struggle over the Governor's Palace, the indomitable De Zavala was multi-tasking, as always. In 1923, she was appointed by the governor to the Texas Historical Board. A pet project during that decade was to commemorate the "Six Flags That Have Floated Over Texas" by having homes from each of those periods renovated. To this end, she worked more cooperatively with the San Antonio Conservation Society, an effort facilitated by that fact that her friend Anna Ellis headed that organization in 1927 and 1928.[57]

Commemorating significant occasions in Texas history also remained a high priority. De Zavala served on the committee that designed a medal to honor San Antonio's 200th anniversary in 1931. Mid-decade, the preservationist-historian served on the advisory board for Texas's Centennial Committee, as the state celebrated events in which her grandfather had played a significant role a century earlier.[58]

Lorenzo de Zavala's granddaughter revered the Spanish and Mexican heritage of the Lone Star State; yet finding her place in Texas during her lifetime proved challenging. A recent graduate thesis notes that she was "Three-quarters Anglo, one-quarter Spanish," in

effect "an Anglo with a Mexican last name." The author provoca-
tively argues that her "blue eyes, [superior] education, rudimentary
Spanish, and lofty aspirations" would have prevented acceptance into
Tejano culture, while "her name and relatively limited financial status"
impeded fully integrating into elite Anglo society. Almost certainly,
this created a difficult course for the woman to navigate.[59]

In an illuminating letter written late in life, De Zavala
complained about the "neglect and abuse of our early settlers and
their descendants—the real owners of the soil before our arrival."
She argued that people of Mexican heritage in Texas "know they
are NOT Mexicans," despite being repeatedly told they are. She
insisted that these "Americans" should be recognized as "Texans
and fellow citizens. . . ." Particularly noteworthy, however, is that
she seems to write from the perspective of one who is not part of
the disadvantaged group being referenced. As one scholar notes,
she considered herself "a Texan, an American."[60]

Indeed, among likely reasons cited for the decision made by
either Adina or her father to begin capitalizing the "D" in De
Zavala were to Anglicize it and make it appear more aristocratic.
Whether or not she identified with being a Tejana, she emphasized
her grandfather's and father's accomplishments whenever possible.
However it was spelled, her family name provided access, opportunities, and respect not usually accorded to Mexican-Americans from
the 1860s through 1950s.[61]

Adina and her relations had hoped that being Lorenzo's descendants would provide more tangible benefits as well. As early as the
1880s, the extended family began what would prove a disappointing
half-century quest to get "remuneration for the important services
that Big Papa [Lorenzo] had provided to the Texas cause in the most
critical period of its public existence. . . ." His granddaughter became
involved in those frustrating efforts, not only by using her skills as a
researcher to gather documentation to support those claims but also
by corresponding with state officials to elicit their support.[62]

While taking advantage of her prestigious ancestry for whatever benefits it did provide, Adina De Zavala did not perpetuate the bloodline. That she never married or had children merits examination. Her mixed ancestry could have complicated finding a spouse, as it did other aspects of her life, or perhaps she resisted the idea of giving up the De Zavala name. However, in Mexican culture married women could keep their own surname, while adding their husband's, so other factors must have affected her marital status. Not to be overlooked was the impact of the Civil War, which cost the lives of hundreds of thousands of men—Union soldiers and Confederates troops alike. Young women reaching maturity in the decades after that traumatic conflict faced the reality of a drastically reduced pool of prospective mates.

Notably, De Zavala's strong ego, sharp tongue, and uncompromising opinions were readily apparent in her well-publicized personal and professional battles. One doubts that she behaved differently in more private situations. How men of her generation would view those qualities is difficult to assess, but sources suggest that the Tejana was enamored of a "Boy" who married another woman and that she rejected the overtures of an older man who pursued her.[63]

Another factor could have been familial responsibilities. Remember that Augustine suffered from ill health almost from the time of Adina's birth, which placed an added burden on the eldest daughter. After her husband's death in 1894 and until her own demise in 1918, mother Julia lived with daughters Adina and Mary in their residence on Taylor Street. By then the former was well past the age at which women commonly married, but her sister also remained single.[64]

Conjecture aside, the reasons for De Zavala's remaining single cannot be known with certainly. We do know that she forcefully insisted that teachers—primarily women—deserved higher wages, as well as exhibiting considerable independence while in that occupation. She also served as an officer for the San Antonio Women's League for Betterment of the Conditions of Life for Women, and her personal library contained issues of *The Texas Woman* and similar publications covering topics such as suffrage. While not liberated in the modern sense, the preservationist possibly believed that marriage was not necessary for fulfillment, would place limits on her independence, and would distract from her other aspirations. Affectionately known as "Miss Adina," this woman "by choice or circumstance"[65] demonstrated what an educated, determined, outspoken—but unwed—female could accomplish.

Those accomplishments were lauded in 1917, when the Tejana was listed in a publication entitled *Who's Who among the Women of San Antonio and Southwest Texas* that recognized the work done by "pioneer women . . . who laid the foundations" for others of their gender. The Adina De Zavala entry noted that from an early age she had been involved in "educational, philanthropic and patriotic work." Among the many memberships listed were the Woman's Texas Council for National Defense (Treasurer), the San Antonio Woman's Parliament, the Committee Buy-It Made-in-Texas, the Texas Woman's Press Association, Woman's Texas Council for National Defense (Treasurer), and many others.[66]

Adina's vigorous and varied service continued to garner accolades. In 1925, the Texas Historical and Landmarks Association celebrated History Week with a luncheon honoring its founder and longtime president. The event was "one of the largest attended and most enjoyable . . . held the present season." Presented with a corsage, the honoree also received numerous letters and telegrams from those unable to attend. In one such message, she was called "the most patriotic woman in Texas. . . ." During the luncheon Sarah King spoke of the bravery of pioneer women in the Lone Star State, citing the honoree as a prime example, and Elizabeth Maverick presented the guest of honor with a platinum wristwatch. Appropriately, the function ended with a one-act play, "Christmas

Legend in Old San Antonio," authored by none other than Adina De Zavala.[67]

Another organization benefitting from and rewarding the Tejana's contributions was the Texas State Historical Association (TSHA). De Zavala was a charter member of the group when it was founded in 1897—and it still exists today. During her almost sixty years of affiliation, she rarely missed an annual meeting. Adina served on the Executive Council for thirty-five years, and in 1945 was selected as the first TSHA Honorary Life Fellow, based "on special aptitude for historical investigation." Five years later, the Antonio Conservation Society also paid tribute to the ninety-year-old woman by presenting her an award in a ceremony at the Spanish Governor's Palace.[68]

The elderly De Zavala must have been gratified to receive so many accolades for her many and varied contributions. However, with advanced age came infirmities. After suffering a fall, this last surviving member of her family died on March 1, 1955. During her funeral on March 5, a Texas flag covered the coffin, and the procession fittingly passed the Alamo on the way to St. Mary's Cemetery, where she was interred. Shortly thereafter, the Texas Legislature lauded De Zavala's "major role in preserving the Alamo and the Spanish Governor's Palace." Lawmakers praised the preservationist for putting historic markers on forty sites, encouraging the flag to be flown on March 2, and helping name public schools after Texas heroes. An official resolution declared that "in her memory an appropriate plaque [should] be placed in the Alamo, . . . in grateful recognition of her services to the history of Texas."[69]

The actual placing of the memorial marker took decades, because the bitter conflict between Adina De Zavala and Clara Driscoll was far from forgotten. This was true even though the latter (Mrs. Henry Sevier) had died a decade earlier than her rival. Notably, Driscoll's body had been allowed to lie in state in the

Alamo Chapel, a special privilege not accorded to De Zavala. The title of a 1991 DRT pamphlet, "Clara Driscoll Rescued the Alamo," speaks for itself. While acknowledging the significance of the Long Barrack, guess whose story was omitted from the booklet.[70]

That same decade the Daughters of the Republic of Texas—whom De Zavala had at one time called "the Daughters of Santa Anna"—began to show at least limited "signs of genuine reconciliation" with their long-deceased rival. In 1994, that organization held a ceremony at her grave to dedicate a special "Commemorative Marker." Later that same year the DRT Board of Management also agreed that a bronze marker with the names of both Clara Driscoll and Adina De Zavala should be "placed in the court yard of the 'long-barracks[,]' " since "each in her own way" played a critical role in preserving the historic site.[71]

Also in 1994, the Texas Historical Commission determined to honor the Tejana with a marker, but months passed "before it was placed inconspicuously on Alamo Plaza." Not until the twenty-first century would appropriate national recognition again be accorded to this exceptional woman. One reason for her resurrection was Andrew Carroll's publication, *Here Is Where: Discovering America's Great Forgotten History*, which contained an illuminating passage relating De Zavala's determined battle "to save the Long Barrack." Reawakened interest in her exploits led to a special ceremony in 2014 at the Menger Hotel, "where a plaque was placed to commemorate her residency there while she fought her good fight." The inscription aptly called Adina "an early hero in the national movement to save historical American landmarks."[72]

On display at the Menger during the above ceremony was a painting of the deceased preservationist, commissioned by the Alamo Mission Chapter of the DRT and dedicated two years earlier at Alamo Hall. At that time the chapter president

Marker honoring Adina De Zavala and Clara Driscoll on the grounds of the Alamo. Photograph by Ernesto Rodriguez III. The Alamo Collection, San Antonio/Archives and Records Program, Texas General Land Office, Austin.

publicly acknowledged that "we've not done enough for Adina." The "overdue goodwill gesture" was cited by some as "part of a sea change" in an organization that not only had neglected De Zavala but also had been "long accused of not recognizing Tejano contributions to Texas history." The DRT's intent was to have the Stuart Seal portrait of De Zavala placed on permanent display in the Long Barrack—where Driscoll's had been placed in 1987. However, those efforts have not succeeded to date. In an ironic series of events, the latter picture was removed when the building underwent renovations, so neither woman's portrait is currently on display there. However, both are "represented in a historical context in exhibit panels."[73]

Despite losing control of "day-to-day management" of the Alamo site to the Texas General Land Office in 2015, the DRT continues to find ways to honor the two figures most responsible for its survival. In recent years on the anniversary of the organization's founding, members of multiple San Antonio chapters visit St. Mary's Cemetery "to place a wreath at De Zavala's grave" but also "do the same at Driscoll's mausoleum nearby at the Masonic Cemetery."[74] Perhaps it is fitting that these two rivals in life are honored jointly in death.

**

To be born in the year that the Civil War began and live for almost a century is an accomplishment in and of itself. What Adina De Zavala did with that time was the true measure of her worth. Had she been born with a different surname or with a different temperament, perhaps she would have taken a more traditional path. However, being Lorenzo de Zavala's granddaughter helped define her life, one spent teaching, recording, and preserving the legacy of the Lone Star State. Although she operated within Anglo society, she paid special homage to the Spanish and Mexican heritage of Texas. While doing so may have benefitted her personally—given her ancestry—it also had significant results for posterity.

That the past spoke to Adina was not a contrivance on her part. Indeed, these words written in 1904 eloquently express her sentiments: "Our written history, though sufficient to keep one well and profitably employed for years, is not the history which so fascinates me—it is the unwritten that strongly appeals; that which seems to whisper from every stone of our old ruins, landmarks, and spots famed for historic deeds. It calls to me from every relic of the past—though I do not always understand its meaning."[75]

In pursuit of the written and unwritten past, Adina De Zavala had the courage of her convictions. If she made enemies along the way, she was willing to pay that price. This teacher-historian-preservationist chose her battles and fought them to the best of her ability. She might not have gained custodianship of the Alamo once it became an official historic site, but her efforts to that point prevented it from being destroyed. Likewise, the Governor's Palace might have been misnamed and not restored exactly as the preservationist desired, but without her persistence this "sole example of eighteenth-century residential architecture in the Spanish province of Texas" would not have been preserved at all.[76]

That De Zavala lost control of the Alamo to the Daughters of the Republic of Texas had long-term consequences that she could not have envisioned. During their more than one-hundred-year custodianship, the site became "a shrine to Anglos" in a city with a majority Hispanic population. There the DRT memorialized a past that glorified the Anglo-Americans defenders such as James Bowie, while seemingly perpetuating negative racial stereotypes of Mexicans as treacherous, villainous, and murderous. Also, their focus was on the thirteen dramatic days during which the Alamo was besieged and captured by the Mexican Army to the neglect of its significant Hispanic heritage. To be fair, the legislation that entrusted the site to the organization mandated that it "be maintained as a sacred memorial to the Alamo heroes of the 1836 battle." Nevertheless, criticism of the DRT's interpretation of those historical events and proprietary attitude toward the property almost certainly factored into the state's recent decision to end its conservatorship of "the most visited historic landmark in Texas and one of the top tourist destinations in America."[77] Adina De Zavala, herself a heroic defender of the Alamo, should not be faulted for the actions of a group with which she went to war but ultimately lost.

Without a doubt, this remarkable woman proved herself deserving of the esteemed De Zavala name. As one obituary aptly noted,

"When on March 1, 1955, her frail body was committed to the soil of her beloved Texas, her spirit became a part of Texas History, along with her distinguished ancestors."[78]

Bibliographical Commentary

A good starting point for information is L. Robert Ables's entry on "Zavala, Adina Emilia de (1861–1955)" in the *Handbook of Texas Online* (www.tshaonline.org). The *Handbook* also has an entry on her grandfather, "Zavala, Lorenzo de (1788– 1836)." An internet search will locate numerous other sources as well, although some are more reliable than others.

Not surprisingly, much that has been written about Adina De Zavala focuses on the Second Battle of the Alamo and her rivalry with Clara Driscoll; however, some works take a wider biographical approach. The above-referenced Robert Ables did his master's thesis on De Zavala at *Centro de Estudios Univer- satrios*, Mexico City College, in 1955. Among his subsequent writings on the preservationist are "Adina De Zavala," in *Keepers of Our Past* (1965), edited by Clifford L. Lord, and "The Second Battle of the Alamo," in *Southwestern Historical Quarterly* 70, no. 3 (January 1967). Later articles include Frank W. Jennings and Rosemary Williams, "Adina De Zavala: Alamo Crusader" published in *Texas Highways* 42, no. 3 (March 1995) and Scott Zesch, "Adina De Zavala and the Second Siege of the Alamo," *CRM: The Journal of Heri- tage Stewardship* 5, no. 1 (Winter 2008). Additional print sources containing at minimum a section or a chapter on this notable woman include *Women in Early Texas*, edited by Evelyn M. Carrington (1994); Michelle and Barbara Bennett's *Twenty-Two Women: Strong, Tough, Independent* (1996); Gale Hamilton Shif- frin's *Echoes from Women of the Alamo* (1999); and Andrew Carroll's *Here Is Where: Discovering America's Great Forgotten History* (2013).

Books on topics related to De Zavala's life and career also offer considerable information. Examples would be Lewis F. Fisher, *Saving San Antonio: The Precari- ous Preservation of a Heritage* (1996), and Laura Lyons McLemore's *Adele Briscoe Looscan: Daughter of the Republic* (2016). As yet unpublished but available on the internet is Suzanne Seifert Cottraux's "Missed Identity: Collective Memory, Adina De Zavala and the Tejana Heroine Who Wasn't," a University of Texas at Arlington master's thesis (2013). For works that offer insights into the Alamo's place in collective public memory, as well as the DRT's stewardship of the site, see W. Fitzhugh Brundage, ed., *Where These Memories Grow: History, Memory, and Southern Identity* (2000) and Richard R. Flores, *Remembering the Alamo: Memory, Modernity, and the Master Symbol* (2003).

An exact reproduction of Adina De Zavala's book, *History and Legends of the Alamo and Other Missions In and Around San Antonio*, is available for purchase on websites such as www.amazon.com. An original copy is part of the "Adina De Zavala Papers," donated by the preservationist to The University of Texas at Austin and housed at the Briscoe Center for American History. Other archival materials are in the Sisters of Charity of the Incarnate Word Archives at the University of the Incarnate Word in San Antonio. Baylor University in Waco, Texas, also has a "De Zavala Collection."

Endnotes

1. Peter Boyd Wells, "Lorenzo de Zavala: Mexican Traitor or Texas Idealist?" *The Texas Gulf Historical and Biographical Record* 21, no. 1 (Nov. 1985): 17, 20; *Handbook of Texas Online*, Raymond Estep, "Zavala, Lorenzo de," https://tshaonline.org/handbook/online/articles/fza05. [*Handbook of Texas Online* hereinafter cited as *HOT Online*.]
2. Raymond Estep, "Lorenzo de Zavala and the Texas Revolution," *The Southwestern Historical Quarterly* 57, no. 3 (Jan. 1954): 323, 330–335, passim, 1st quotation on 335; J. M. Woods, "Lorenzo De Zavala, Texas Patriot," *Frontier Times*, 14, no. 10 (July 1937): 433, 2nd quotation; Mary Waurine Hunter, "Freedom's Champion: First and Last," *Texas Parade* 6, no. 10 (Mar. 1942): 14, 3rd quotation. For more detailed coverage on Adina De Zavala's grandfather, see Margaret Swett Henson, *Lorenzo de Zavala: The Pragmatic Idealist* (Fort Worth: Texas Christian University Press, 1996).
3. Virginia Taylor, "Adina De Zavala (1861–1955)," in *Women in Early Texas History*, ed. Evelyn M. Carrington (Austin: Jenkins Publishing Company, The Pemberton Press, 1975), 303–304; Frank W. Jennings and Rosemary Williams, "Adina De Zavala: Alamo Crusader," *Texas Highways* 42, no. 3 (Mar. 1995): 16; Gale Hamilton Shiffrin, *Echoes from Women of the Alamo* (San Antonio: AW Press, 1999), 97.
4. Suzanne Seifert Cottraux, "Missed Identity: Collective Memory, Adina De Zavala and the Tejana Heroine Who Wasn't" (master's thesis, University of Texas at Arlington, 2013), 27, quotations. Among the many sources containing the version that Augustine was a blockade runner are the previously cited Taylor, "Adina De Zavala" and Erin Cassidy, "Miss Adina De Zavala, Angel of the Alamo," Musings from Sam Houston's Stomping Grounds Podcast Series, Episode 43: July 1, 2009, Newton Gresham Library at Sam Houston State University.
5. Taylor, "Adina De Zavala," 304; Shiffrin, *Echoes*, 108, quotation.
6. Pearl Howard, "Texas' Most Distinguished Best Loved Woman," reprinted from *Holland's Magazine* (Dec. 1935), in *Frontier Times* 30 (July-September 1953): 333, Center for American History, University of Texas at Austin. [Center for American History hereinafter cited as CAH.]
7. Howard, "Best Loved Woman," 332, quotation.
8. Teresa Palomo Acosta and Ruthe Winegarten, *Las Tejanas: 300 Years of History* (Austin: University of Texas Press, 2003), Foreword, x; Shiffrin, *Echoes*, 107–109, quotation on 107; Jennings and Williams, "Adina De Zavala," 16; Cottraux, "Missed Identity," 31; Taylor, "Adina De Zavala," 304–305.
9. Cassidy, "Adina De Zavala," 1st quotation; Taylor, "Adina De Zavala," 305; Clarence R. Wharton, author and ed., "Miss Adina De Zavala," in *Texas Under Many Flags*, vol. 4 (Chicago: The American Historical Society, 1930), 37, 2nd quotation; *HOT Online*, L. Robert Ables, "Zavala, Adina Emilia De," http://www.tshaonline.org/handbook/online/articles/fzafg [hereinafter cited as *HOT Online*, Ables, "Zavala"]; Cottraux, "Missed Identity," 32, 3rd quotation.

Although many sources, including some cited in this endnote, indicate that De Zavala attended a school of music in Missouri, Suzanne Seifert Cottraux in the previously cited thesis states that "no documentation of her attendance at such a school, nor the existence of one, can be located" (31).

10. Jennings and Williams, "Adina de Zavala," 15, 1st quotation; L. Robert Ables, "The Second Battle of the Alamo," *Southwestern Historical Quarterly* 70, no. 3 (Jan. 1967): 373–374, 2nd and 4th quotations on 373, 5th quotation on 374; Wharton, "Miss Adina De Zavala," 37, 3rd quotation; Susan Shumaker, "Adena [*sic*] De Zavala, Untold Stories from America's National Parks," Part 2, 38, 6th and 7th quotations, http://www-tc.pbs.org/nationalparks/media/.../tnp-abi-untold-stories-pt-02-de-zavala.pdf.

11. Jennings and Williams, "Adina De Zavala," 20.

12. Howard, "Best Loved Woman," 332, all quotations. Adina De Zavala capitalized the De in de, a practice either she or her father began.

13. Lewis F. Fisher, *Saving San Antonio: The Precarious Preservation of a Heritage* (Lubbock: Texas Tech University, 1996), 44, 1st quotation; Adina De Zavala, *History of the Alamo and Other Missions in San Antonio,* [no publ. info.], 212, 2nd through 4th quotations, CAH.

14. S.B. Maxey, [Mrs. J.J. Mckeever, Jr.], *Inception, Organization and Work of the Daughters of the Republic of Texas,* 1904, 5–7, 1st quotation on 5, 2nd quotation on 6–7, https://texashistory.unt.edu/ark:/67531/metapth29772/, University of North Texas Libraries, The Portal to Texas History, texashistory.unt.edu; crediting Star of the Republic Museum; "Membership Eligibility," The Daughters of the Republic of Texas, http://www.drtinfo.org/membership-2-membership.

15. Fisher, *Saving San Antonio,* 44; "Augustine de Zavala, Sr.," Find a Grave, http://www.findagrave.com/cgi-bin/fg.cgi?page=gr&GRid=133156486; Cottraux, "Missed Identity," 3, 66–67, 1st quotation on 67, 2nd quotation on 3; *Work of the Daughters,* 14; "Miss Adina De Zavala," *Interstate Index: A Journal of Progress* 13, no. 6 (Dec. 1919): 1, CAH.

16. Fisher, *Saving San Antonio,* 46, all quotations; Jennings and Williams, "Adina de Zavala," 16.

17. Jennings and Williams, "Adina De Zavala," 16; Cottraux, "Missed Identity," 87; Taylor, "Adina De Zavala," 305.

18. Cottraux, "Missed Identity," 2; Jennings and Williams, "Adina De Zavala," 16, 18, 1st quotation on 16; Laura Lyons McLemore, *Adele Briscoe Looscan: Daughter of the Republic* (Fort Worth: TCU Press, 2016); Shiffrin, *Echoes,* 113, 2nd quotation.

19. Jennings and Williams, "Adina De Zavala," 18; *HOT Online,* Caroline Remy, Jean L. Levering, Eldon S. Branda, rev. by Kendall Curlee, "Coppini, Pompeo Luigi (1870–1957)," http://www.tshaonline.org/handbook/online/articles/fco67; Fisher, *Saving San Antonio,* 47, 51, quotations on 47.

20. Cottraux, "Missed Identity," 70, 1st quotation; Bennett and Bennett, "Adina De Zavala," 5; L. Robert Ables, "Adina De Zavala," in *Keepers of the Past,* ed. Clifford L. Lord (Chapel Hill: The University of North Carolina Press, 1965), 205, 2nd quotation [hereinafter cited as Ables, "Adina De Zavala"].

21. Elda Silva, "Split over Alamo Soured Friendship," *San Antonio Express-News,* Feb. 5, 2015, updated Feb. 6, 2015, accessed June 16, 2106; *HOT Online,* Susan Prendergast Schoelwer, "San Antonio de Valero Mission," 2nd quotation,

http://www.tshaonline.org/handbook/online/articles/uqs08; McLemore, *Looscan*, 108; Adèle B. Looscan, "The Work of the Daughters of the Republic of Texas in Behalf of the Alamo," *The Quarterly of the Texas State Historical Association* 8 (July 1904–April 1905): 79, 1ˢᵗ quotation, texashistory.unt.edu/ark:/67531/ metapth101033/m1/81/?q=Adina%20de%20Zavala, University of North Texas Libraries, The Portal to Texas History, texas history.unt.edu, crediting TSHA.

22. Cottraux, "Missed Identity," 73, quotation; McLemore, *Looscan*, 108; Shiffrin; *Echoes*, 117; Ables, "Adina De Zavala," 205.

23. See above-cited article by Ables entitled "The Second Battle of the Alamo," in *Southwestern Historical Quarterly*.

24. Fisher, *Saving San Antonio*, 54–55, quotation on 55.

25. Cottraux, "Missed Identity," 75; Ables, "Second Battle," 378, quotation; Ables, "Adina De Zavala," 206–207; Shiffrin, *Echoes*, 165; Jennings and Williams, "Adina De Zavala," 19.

26. McLemore, *Looscan*, 117, 1ˢᵗ quotation; Shiffrin, *Echoes*, 163–164, 188, 2ⁿᵈ quotation on 163 and 3ʳᵈ quotation on 118.

27. McLemore, *Looscan*, 117–118; Fisher, *Saving San Antonio*, 55; Cottraux, "Missed Identity," 77–78.

28. Cottraux, "Missed Identity," 75; Jennings and Williams, "Adina De Zavala," 19; Looscan, "Work of the Daughters," 80–81, 1ˢᵗ quotation on 81, 2ⁿᵈ quotation on 80; McLemore, *Looscan*, 120; Shiffrin, *Echoes*, 170–171, 188.

29. Looscan, "Work of the Daughters," 81–82, 1ˢᵗ quotation on 81; Fisher, *Saving San Antonio*, 55–56, 2ⁿᵈ quotation on 56; *Inside These Gates*, "The Daughters of the Republic of Texas: 105 Years of Alamo Custodianship," Feb. 4, 2010, 3ʳᵈ quotation, https://drtlibrary.wordpress.com/2010/02/04/the-daughters-of-the-republic-of-texas-105-years-of-alamo-custodianship/.

30. McLemore, *Looscan*, 123–124; Cottraux, "Missed Identity," 80, 1ˢᵗ through 3ʳᵈ quotations; Ables, "Adina De Zavala," 208; Shiffrin, *Echoes*, 174, 4ᵗʰ quotation.

31. Silva, "Split over Alamo," 1ˢᵗ and 3ʳᵈ quotations; Cottraux, "Missed Identity," 72, 2ⁿᵈ quotation; Fisher, *Saving San Antonio*, 56; Shiffrin, *Echoes*, 171; Cottraux, "Missed Identity," 82, 4ᵗʰ and 5ᵗʰ quotations.

32. Adina De Zavala, *History of the Alamo and Other Missions in San Antonio*, [1917], 216–218, 1ˢᵗ quotation on 216; McLemore, *Looscan*, 138; Ables, "Adina De Zavala," 290, 2ⁿᵈ and 3ʳᵈ quotations.

33. McLemore, *Looscan*, 133, 145–146; Ables, "Adina De Zavala," 209; Cottraux, "Missed Identity," 84, 1ˢᵗ quotation; Scott Zesch, "Adina De Zavala and the Second Siege of the Alamo," *CRM: The Journal of Heritage Stewardship* 5, no. 1 (Winter 2008), 2ⁿᵈ quotation, https://www.nps.gov/CRMJournal/Winter2008/article2.html.

34. Ables, "Adina De Zavala," 209–210, 1ˢᵗ quotation on 209, 2ⁿᵈ through 4ᵗʰ quotations on 210; Cottraux, "Missed Identity," 84, 5ᵗʰ quotation.

35. McLemore, *Looscan*, 140, 146, 148, 155, 1ˢᵗ quotation on 148, 2ⁿᵈ quotation on 155; Cottraux, "Missed Identity," 85; Ables, "Adina De Zavala," 210, 212, 3ʳᵈ quotation on 212; Zesch, "Adina De Zavala"; Fisher, *Saving San Antonio*, 57.

36. Howard, "Best Loved Woman," 327, 1ˢᵗ quotation; Shiffrin, *Echoes*, 121; Zesch, "Adina De Zavala," 2ⁿᵈ quotation.

37. Jennings and Williams, "Adina De Zavala," 20, 1st and 2nd quotations; Fisher, *Saving San Antonio*, 57–58; Zesch, "Adina De Zavala"; Andrew Carroll, *Here Is Where: Discovering America's Great Forgotten History* (New York: Three Rivers Press, 2013), 3rd quotation.

38. Fisher, *Saving San Antonio*, 58; Shiffrin, *Echoes*, 122, quotation; Zesch, "Adina De Zavala."

39. Fisher, *Saving San Antonio*, 59; Ables, "Adina De Zavala," 212; Taylor, "Adina De Zavala," 307.

40. Introduction to "Adina de [sic] Zavala to Colquitt, August 25, 1911," Records of Oscar B. Colquitt, Texas State Library and Archives Commission, 1, 1st quotation, https://www.tsl.texas.gov/governors/rising/colquitt-alamo-1. html; Fisher, *Saving San Antonio*, 58; Adina De Zavala Chapter to Oscar B. Colquitt, Aug. 25, 1911, 2nd and 3rd quotations, https://www.tsl.texas.gov/ governors/rising/colquitt-alamo-1.html; Zesch, "Adina De Zavala."

41. Adina De Zavala, *History of the Alamo*, dedication, 215–219, 1st and 4th quotations on 219, 2nd quotations in dedication, 3rd quotation on 215.

42. "Group Carries on Fight for Rebuilding of the Real Alamo," *San Antonio Light*, June 28, 1936, quotations; Zesch, "Adina De Zavala"; Zavala to Colquitt, 1911, Intro.; Cottraux, "Missed Identity," 77; Shiffrin, *Echoes*, 153; eayala@ express-news.net [Elaine Ayala], "The Long Road to Giving Adina De Zavala Due Credit at the Alamo," *San Antonio Express-News*, June 17, 2014, http://www. mysanantonio.com/saculture/conexion/article/The-long-road-to-giving-Adina-De-Zavala-due-5555537.php. In 1968, thirteen years after De Zavala's death, preparations for a months-long international HemisFair in San Antonio finally led to the Long Barrack being restored and becoming the one-story museum that exists today. See Shiffrin, *Echoes*, 150, and "Welcome to HemisFair '68 Online," www.worldsfair68.info.

43. Jennings and Williams, "Adina De Zavala," 20; Ables, "Adina De Zavala," 210–211, 2nd quotation on 211; Howard, "Best Loved Woman," 327, 1st quotation.

44. Jennings and Williams, "Adina De Zavala," 20; Taylor, "Adina De Zavala," 307, quotation; Fisher, *Saving San Antonio*, 77.

45. Kenneth Hafertepe, "The Romantic Rhetoric of the Spanish Governor's Palace," *The Southwestern Historical Quarterly* 107, no. 2 (October 2003): 239, 246–248, 2nd quotation on 247; "Says City Should Awake; Save the Ancient Palace," *San Antonio Express*, May 28, 1922, 1st quotation, CAH.

46. Hafertepe, "Romantic Rhetoric," 250–251, 1st quotation on 250, 2nd quotation on 251; Fisher, 78, 3rd quotation; "Our Own State—Texas: Texas, One and Indivisible," ed. Adina De Zavala, "Tag Day for the Ancient Government Palace," *Interstate Index: A Journal of Progress* 2, no. 4 (Oct. 1920): 13, CAH.

47. "Miss Adina De Zavala," *Interstate Index: A Journal of Progress* 13, no. 6 (Dec. 1919): 1, CAH.

48. "Our Own State—Texas: Texas, One and Indivisible," ed. Adina De Zavala, "Save The Ancient Government Palace," *Interstate Index: A Journal of Progress* 2, no. 5 (Dec. 1920): 20–21, all quotations, CAH.

49. Hafertepe, "Romantic Rhetoric," 254, quotations; Fisher, *Saving San Antonio*, 78.

50. "Says City Should Awake," *San Antonio Express*, all quotations.

51. Hafertepe, "Romantic Rhetoric," 254–256, quotations on 254; Fisher, *Saving San Antonio*, 125.

52. Hafertepe, "Romantic Rhetoric," 256; Fisher, *Saving San Antonio*, 125, 129, all quotations on 125; Ables, "Adina De Zavala," 213.

53. Fisher, *Saving San Antonio*, 125–126, quotation on 125; Cottraux, "Missed Identity," 93.

54. Hafertepe, "Romantic Rhetoric," 269, 272–274, 1st through 3rd quotations on 274; Shiffrin, *Echoes*, 134; *HOT Online*, Tim Draves, "Spanish Governor's Palace [Comandancia]," https://tshaonline.org/handbook/online/articles/ccs03; Howard, "Best Loved Woman," 331, 4th and 5th quotations.

55. Hafertepe, "Romantic Rhetoric," 275, all quotations.

56. Draves, "Spanish Governor's Palace"; Fisher, *Saving San Antonio*, 129; Hafertepe, "Romantic Rhetoric," 276.

57. Bennett and Bennett, "Adina De Zavala, 9–10; Jennings and Williams, "Adina De Zavala," 20.

58. Taylor, "Adina De Zavala," 307; *HOT Online*, Ables, "Zavala."

59. Cottraux, "Missed Identity," 3, 103–105, 1st quotation on 103, 2nd and 3rd quotations on 104, 4th quotation on 105.

60. Shumaker, "Adena [*sic*] De Zavala," 44, all quotations; Cottraux, "Missed Identity," 103.

61. Summary Information, "Adina E. De Zavala Papers," The Texas Collection, Baylor University, http://www.baylor.edu/content/services/document.php/195681.pdf; Cottraux, "Missed Identity," 56, 58, 60, 103. Sources disagree as to whether Augustine or daughter Adina began the practice of using a capital D in their De Zavala surname.

62. Lorenzo de Zavala Jr. to Adina De Zavala, Mar. 24, 1891, quotation, texashistory.unt.edu/ark:/67531/metapth3425/m1/3/?q=Adina%20de%20Zavala, University of North Texas Libraries, The Portal to Texas history.texashistory.unt.edu, crediting University of Texas at Arlington library; Cottraux, "Missed Identity," 35, 49–56 passim. *Papá Grande* (Big Papa) was apparently an affectionate family name for Lorenzo de Zavala.

63. Cottraux, "Missed Identity," 35, 37–38, 42, quotation on 42.

64. Cottraux, "Missed Identity," 33, 38; Star of the Republic Museum, "Lorenzo de Zavala Family Tree," Second Generation, Family of Manuel Lorenzo Justiniano de Zavala & Emily West, http://www.starmuseum.org/signers_descendants/Zavala/rr01/rr01_003.htm; Find A Grave Memorial, "Julia Byrne Tyrell De Zavala," http://www.findagrave.com/cgi-bin/fg.cgi?page=gr&GRid=133156826.

65. "De Zavala, Miss Adina," *Who's Who Among the Women of San Antonio and Southwest Texas*, ed. Marin B. Fenwick (San Antonio, 1917), Preface [np], 48; P.I. Nixon, "Adina De Zavala," *Southwestern Historical Quarterly* 59, no. 1 (July 1955): 94, 1st quotation; Cottraux, "Missed Identity," 33, 2nd quotation. The Adina De Zavala Papers at the Center for American History contain publications from her library, including *The Texas Woman*.

66. Fenwick, "De Zavala, Miss Adina," Preface, 48, 1st quotation in Preface, 2nd quotation on 48, CAH.

67. "History Week Celebrated by Texas Historical and Landmarks Association, Dec. 3" *The Pioneer Magazine of Texas* 6, no. 4 (Dec. 1925): 5, all quotations, CAH.

68. P.I. Nixon, "Adina De Zavala," *Southwestern Historical Quarterly* 59, no. 1 (July 1955), quotation on 95; Jennings and Williams, "Adina De Zavala," 20.

69. Ables, "Adina De Zavala," 214; Jennings and Williams, "Adina De Zavala," 10, 21, quotations on 10; Cassidy, "Miss Adina De Zavala." According to Shiffrin in *Echoes*, in the early 1950s, the historian-preservationist offered her "large accumulation of papers, documents, and relics" (141) to The University of Texas at Austin, and much of that material can be found there. Upon her death, however, De Zavala had provided that "all she owned was to go to the Sisters of Charity of the Incarnate Word" (147), so some archival materials found their way to the University of the Incarnate Word. Also, some of De Zavala's papers are housed at Baylor University.

70. *HOT Online*, Dorothy D. DeMoss, "Driscoll, Clara (1881–1945)," https://tshaonline.org/handbook/online/articles/fdr04; Shiffrin, *Echoes*, 150–151.

71. Zesch, "Adina De Zavala," 1st quotation; Jennings and Williams, "Adina De Zavala," 21, 2nd and 3rd quotations; eayala@express-news.net, "Long Road"; Shiffrin, *Echoes*, 175, 4th and 5th quotations.

72. Zesch, "Adina De Zavala," 1st quotation; Silva, "Split over Alamo"; eayala@express-news.net, "Long Road," 2nd and 3rd quotations; eayala@express-news.net [Elaine Ayala], "Adina De Zavala, Key S.A. Preservationist Gets National Recognition," *San Antonio Express-News*, June 11, 2014, updated June 12, 2014, 4th quotation. See Texas Historical Sites Atlas, "Details for Adina De Zavala: Historical Marker—Atlas Number 5029000086," atlas.tch.state.tx.us/Details/5029000086. See also Andrew Carroll, *Here Is Where: Discovering America's Great Forgotten History* (New York: Three Rivers Press, 2013).

73. Elaine Ayala, "Alamo's Long Barrack Savior to Get Her Due," *San Antonio Express-News*, updated Feb. 25, 2012, 1st through 4th quotations, http://www.mysanantonio.com/news/local_news/article/Honor-a-century-in-the-making-3360169.php; Silva, "Split over Alamo"; Richard Bruce Winders to Harriett Denise Joseph (email), Aug. 10, 2016, 5th quotation.

74. Sarah Rumpf, "Texas Assumes Control of Alamo; Daughters of the Republic of Texas 'Will Always Be Honored,'" Breitbart, March 3, 2015, 1st quotation, http://www.breitbart.com/texas/2015/03/13/texas-assumes-control-of-alamo-daughters-of-the-republic-of-texas-will-always-be-honored/; Scott Huddleston, "DRT Ousted from Alamo," *San Antonio Express-News*, Mar. 12, 2015, http://www.expressnews.com/news/local/article/DRT-ousted-from-Alamo-613098.php; Silva, "Split over Alamo," 2nd and 3rd quotations. The Texas General Land Office assumed control from the DRT on July 10, 2015. In addition to the Breitbart and Huddleston sources cited in this note, see the DRT's "The Alamo Legacy of the Daughters of the Republic of Texas," Inside the Gates, July 3, 2015, https://drtlibrary.wordpress.com/2015/07/03/the-alamo-legacy-of-the-daughters-of-the-republic-of-texas/.

75. Adina de Zavala, "Texas History—Written and Unwritten," *Texas Talks* (June 1904) 4, quotation, CAH. [*Texas Talks* was published monthly by the Texas Talks Publishing Co., Galveston, Texas.]

76. Hafertepe, "Romantic Rhetoric," 277, quotation.

77. W. Fitzhugh Brundage, "No Deed but Memory," in *These Memories Grow: History, Memory, and Southern Identity*, ed. W. Fitzhugh Brundage

(Chapel Hill: University of North Carolina Press, 2000), 17; Holly Beachley Brear, "We Run the Alamo, and You Don't: Alamo Battles of Ethnicity and Gender," in Brundage, *These Memories Grow*, 299, 301–302, 314, 1st quotation on 299, 2nd quotation on 314; Richard R. Flores, *Remembering the Alamo: Memory, Modernity, and the Master Symbol* (Austin: University of Texas Press, 2003), xvi, xix, 21, 33–34; Carroll, *Here Is Where*, 430, 3rd quotation;
78. Nixon, "Adina De Zavala," 95, quotation.

Emma Tenayuca in Bexar County Jail, June 29, 1937. ©San Antonio *Light* Collection/Zuma, UTSA Special Collections—Institute of Texan Cultures, L-1575-C. Gift of the Hearst Corporation.

Emma Tenayuca

Passionate Labor Activist

FEW TEJANAS BORN IN the early twentieth century had a life as turbulent or interesting as that of Emma Tenayuca, particularly in her youth. She reached adolescence just as the Great Depression hit the United States. Demonstrating maturity beyond her years, she not only knew the pangs of hunger herself but cared about others who felt those pangs as well. Unwilling to ignore the exploitation of people of her ethnicity, she chose to act. Encouraging the working poor to organize and to strike, Tenayuca made their battles her battles. Speaking out at a time when women and minorities were subordinate, this remarkable young woman earned the nickname of "*La Pasionaria*" (The Passionate One) for her fearless leadership as a labor activist in her hometown of San Antonio in the 1930s. That she paid a high price for her efforts only serves to make her story more compelling.

While Emma Tenayuca's life serves as an inspiration, it is also a cautionary tale. In her quest to help the "poor and powerless,"[1] she embraced radical movements, some of which during the first half of the twentieth century were considered controversial at best and subversive at worst. For her actions, she was at various times placed under arrest, threatened with bodily harm, and prevented from working. The well-known public figure not only was forced to withdraw from the limelight but also had to leave Texas for an extended period. Only years later was the Mexican American woman able to return to the Lone Star State, where she received long overdue appreciation for her role in the labor movement in San Antonio.

Emma Tenayuca's degree of empathy, concern, and involvement would have been unusual in a person of any age during any time period, much less a Tejana during the 1930s and 1940s. What influences made her so different from a typical teenager, particularly one of her ethnicity? Why was she so admired by the exploited workers inspired by her speeches, yet successfully targeted by the conservative establishment and coerced into relinquishing her public role in the labor movement? Later in life when she achieved recognition as a significant figure in Texas history, what regrets—if any—did she express for the decisions of her youth? These and other questions can be answered by a look at the life of this very uncommon woman.

*　*　*

Born on the South Side of San Antonio to Sam Teneyuca and Benita Hernández Zepeda on December 21, 1916, Emma was one of eleven children. Possibly because of an error on her baptismal certificate, she went through life with her surname (Tenayuca) spelled differently from the rest of her family. Her father was a "*puro indio*" (pure-blooded Indian) from the southern part of the state, while her mother's family traced their roots back to early Spanish settlers in Texas. According to the Tejana, her maternal grandparents "wanted my sister and me to live with them." As a result, she did not have much contact with her Indian relatives to whom the "lighter-skinned" Zepedas felt superior.[2]

The Zepedas' assumption of superiority was not surprising, given that historically in both Mexico and the United States whites considered darker-complexioned people to be inferior. The latter were subject to discrimination, injustice, exploitation, and poverty. Being the product of racially mixed parentage and bearing an Indian surname helped define Emma Tenayuca's life. As she later declared, "it was the combination of being a Texan, being a Mexican, and being more Indian than Spanish that propelled me to take action."[3]

The South Side of San Antonio was composed of "modest working-class homes" with a mix of people of different nationalities, unlike other parts of the city where Anglos, Mexicans, and Tejanos tended to be segregated from each other in their own neighborhoods. Unskilled people of Hispanic ethnicity tended to cluster in the West Side of the city, allegedly "the worst slums . . . in the nation." As a consequence of her upbringing, the girl was exposed to and part of two worlds—Anglo and Hispanic. She learned to speak the languages of both, which gave her an important advantage that more recent immigrants from Mexico did not have.[4]

The adults in Emma's family took pride in being American citizens. To them, one of the most important benefits of having citizenship was the franchise, the right to vote. However, to exercise that right in Texas a person had to pay a fee known as a poll tax. Historically, these taxes were one of several tactics utilized by the Anglo power structure to lessen the political voice of minorities. Despite limited financial means, Emma's parents and grandparents paid so that they could participate in local, state, and national elections. They also spent considerable time reading and talking about politics, especially the girl's maternal grandfather, Francisco Zepeda. Later in life, she recalled that he had voted for Miriam Amanda Ferguson, the first woman to be elected governor of Texas. Consequently, Emma grew up understanding the importance not only of being politically active but also aware that women could aspire to public life.[5]

The Tejana deeply loved her Grandfather Francisco, was interested in what he had to say, and aspired to please him. Zepeda, who worked as a carpenter in a lumberyard, was concerned about the plight of disadvantaged groups in American society, especially

Mexican Americans and Mexicans, since the latter were coming to the United States in ever increasing numbers because of deteriorating conditions in their homeland.[6]

After achieving independence in 1821, Mexico was a nation long plagued by internal turmoil, severe inequality, and widespread poverty. Increasing frustration on the part of the populace and some of their leaders erupted in a lengthy, bloody revolution in the early 1900s. Ironically, the Mexican Revolution of 1910 did not solve the nation's problems, as conditions in Mexico worsened instead of improving. The revolutionary movement had too many leaders with conflicting ideas and strong egos, as well as too many opponents unwilling to accept significant changes in the political, economic, and social arenas. For many years, therefore, Mexico continued to be torn by civil wars and economic difficulties. These conditions caused many Mexicans, some of whom embraced radical ideologies, to flee from their homeland. Seeking a better life, they looked to their northern neighbor, the United States. "For geographical, cultural, and economic reasons," thousands chose to resettle in San Antonio, which "acted as a magnet for these immigrants."[7]

Founded in the early 1700s when Texas was part of the Spanish empire, San Antonio two centuries later was "a city of Mexicans." Some of these people were Mexican Americans, such as Emma Tenayuca. Many others were recent arrivals, who hoped that their lack of English language skills would not prove too great a handicap in South Texas. They were also attracted by the city's proximity to Mexico. While carving out new lives in the Lone Star State, these immigrants still maintained strong ties to their homeland. Certainly, some hoped to return to their country of origin when— and if—stability returned.[8]

The life that Mexican immigrants found in San Antonio was far from the ideal envisioned. Unskilled Mexicans and Tejanos had access to service and industrial jobs but were forced to do the least desirable work for the lowest wages. Living in "floorless shacks . . . mostly without plumbing, sewage connections or electric lights," they suffered from poverty, hunger, and disease. In fact, the West Side of San Antonio was notorious for having "the highest infant death rate in the nation." Most "bosses" (business owners and political leaders), however, seemed more interested in exploiting these workers than helping to improve their lives. Indeed, the presence of so many thousands of Mexicans and Mexican Americans in San Antonio in the 1920s created a low-wage labor market that "encouraged the expansion of nonmechanized industrial work in the city." [9]

Handicapped by both race and gender, Hispanic women in the job market faced even more hardships. Among the employment options available to them were "piece work from garment factories" and "pecan shelling for candy factories." In piece work women were given cloth to make items of clothing and paid a flat rate for each garment they produced. In the case of shelling, the workers were paid by the pound for shelled pecans with higher rates for pecan halves than for broken pieces. In either case, they received less than a living wage but composed most "of the labor force in the lowest paying industries in Southwestern cities such as San Antonio." Realistically, it was the presence of so many of these women skilled in embroidery and sewing that stimulated "the establishment of garment factories in San Antonio."[10]

Even though piece work and pecan shelling did not pay well, Hispanic women took these jobs, because of the absence of other options, the demands of "household responsibilities," and a number of cultural factors. Stay-at-home workers faced heavy demands on their time. They had to do the required work for their employers, while still being expected to fulfill their duties as wives and mothers. The situation was arguably worse for those employed outside the home. In the factories, they were exposed to "horrible, unsafe conditions," and if they had husbands and babies, they tended to them when they returned home after long hours in the workplace.[11]

Rather than hiding the realities of life from his granddaughter, Francisco Zepeda wanted the girl to know what was happening around her. A bright child, she learned to read at a very young age. When her grandfather was reading the newspaper, she would read the back side of the page he was holding. He would talk to her about local and national events. Almost certainly, those topics included conversations about the plight of disadvantaged groups in society. Emma also accompanied Francisco on Sundays when he went to the Plaza de Zacate at Milam Park, a major gathering place for *Mexicanos* and Tejanos in San Antonio. People would go there to relax, see friends, make contacts, seek work, and hear speeches. While enjoying an ice cream cone, Emma was very attentive to what was happening around her and paid particular attention to the speakers, who included proponents of out-of-the-mainstream ideologies such as anarchism and socialism.[12]

Convinced that governments were tools by which the wealthy and powerful exploited the working class, Anarchists condemned governmental power as undesirable and unnecessary. They advocated "a society based on voluntary cooperation and free association of individuals and groups." Socialists called for a different approach to reform. They favored a system in which the "means of production are owned by the state, community, or the workers." Socialism called for cooperation among people, rather than competition for wealth and power, as occurred in a capitalist economy such as that found in the United States.[13]

Regardless of their agendas, the speakers at the plaza shared a common goal—to mobilize the oppressed. Another commonality was the negative reaction of the white establishment to the unwelcome messages these reformers were espousing. Those who exercised political, economic, and social control felt threatened by talk of meaningful changes to the status quo. The young Tenayuca, on the other hand, was receptive to the ideas being espoused. Early along, her actions indicate that she internalized the stirring declarations against inequality and exploitation.

As an adolescent in high school, Emma actively participated in a book club. An avid reader, she was drawn to controversial publications, including the writings of Karl Marx. Marx was the founder of a provocative political and economic system known as Communism, which advocated eliminating private property with goods being "owned in common" and made "available to all as needed." Marx's writings contained revolutionary ideas similar to some of those being spread at Plaza del Zacate. Probably "only books equaled the influence of Francisco Zepeda on Tenayuca's life" and contributed to the formation of her strong ideas.[14]

The high school student joined the Ladies Auxiliary Chapter of the League of United Latin American Citizens (LULAC) when it was formed in San Antonio in the early 1930s—the original all-male organization having been founded in 1929 in reaction to rampant discrimination against *Mexicanos* and Tejanos. She met some prominent leaders in the movement and even spoke at some of their venues. Emma soon became disillusioned, however, because "their policy . . . was one of Americanization." LULAC "encouraged U.S. Mexicans to distinguish themselves from Mexicans of foreign birth." The young Tejana felt that "Mexicans needed to unite, not divide on the basis of citizenship, class, or educational status." At some point she also disagreed with the organization's policy of segregating women into auxiliary chapters, and Tenayuca was not hesitant to voice her opinions on these and other issues.[15]

The articulate teenager soon became known as a dynamic speaker with other students listening raptly to her discourses. Unfortunately, no matter how well she performed in class or how powerfully she spoke, the Tejana could not overcome the reality of her ethnicity. A victim of racism in high school, the teenager refused to let prejudice defeat her. Instead, she became determined to try to change the world for the better. Understanding the importance of education, she planned to go to college with her grandfather's financial assistance.[16] That dream collapsed with the coming of the Great Depression.

After the stock market crashed in 1929, the United States experienced the longest and worst economic crisis in its history. Businesses and banks failed; people lost their jobs, homes, and savings; and hardship spread throughout the country. Among the victims was Emma's grandfather. The bank in which he had placed his savings failed in 1932, and Francisco lost his money—money that almost certainly would have helped pay for Emma's college education. The teenager apparently was the only one in the family whom her grandfather told about the loss, which must have been a weighty secret for her to carry. She experienced great anger, not that her own future was jeopardized but that so many like her grandfather "lost everything they had."[17]

During these hard economic times, the Teneyucas and Zepedas did not always have enough to eat. Despite occasional hunger, however, Emma knew that her family was more fortunate than many others. The Teneyucas owned land on the West Side of the San Antonio River on which some homeless people were living. The teenager was deeply affected by the sight of these "people from the east, people from a lot of places, right there in broken down cars and so forth. I remember that there was no water there[,] so they would take water from us and we paid for it. They didn't have any money. They didn't have anything." The young Tejana began to think about ways to help those less fortunate than herself.[18]

Not everyone was as compassionate as Emma. As unemployment increased during the Depression, many Anglos began to resent the presence of so many Mexicans in the United States. They felt that these aliens were taking jobs away from "real" Americans, were a drain on the nation's resources, and should go back where they belonged. Even worse, hostility was not directed solely at Mexican nationals but also at Mexican Americans. Ultimately, the U.S. Immigration Bureau deported hundreds of thousands of people of this ethnicity—many of whom were from Texas and some of whom were American citizens.[19]

The cigar industry provided a dramatic example of the grim situation of even those Hispanics fortunate enough to have employment during the 1930s. The Finck Cigar Company had come to San Antonio before the Depression, attracted by the availability of skilled labor at low wages. Despite significant layoffs, in 1933 more than three hundred women were still employed by Finck, but these workers complained that their pay was too low—an accurate accusation. The National Recovery Administration (NRA), created early in President Franklin Roosevelt's administration, was establishing "codes of fair practices that would set . . . minimum wages . . . within each industry." Despite these codes, Finck employees were receiving weekly compensation of $2 to $7 weekly, well below the $12 minimum. Adding to their distress was a poor work environment that included "industrial hazards" and "faulty plumbing and leaky roofs."[20]

Finck proved unreceptive to repeated appeals for "increased pay, better working conditions, and union recognition." Under the leadership of Mrs. W. H. Ernst, a Mexican-American, the women determined that the major weapon in their arsenal was to strike: to refuse to work until their demands were met. In 1933, the Tejanas walked out of the workplace. Unfortunately for the workers, their first strike failed to achieve the desired results. Committed to their cause, they began a second strike the following year and then a third in 1935.[21]

What the cigar workers failed to understand was that they had little chance of success no matter what tactics they used. Because of the Depression, Finck Cigar Company was in such financial distress that pay increases were not a realistic option for the owners, who were considering selling the business. Also, employees lacked a well-conceived plan or enough funds to sustain a strike for very long. Consequently, the demands of the cigar workers "were never met, and the strike was eventually broken." This was done in part through the hiring of scabs, people who took the place of striking workers but were bitterly resented by those being replaced. Attempting to keep a business from being able to operate during a walkout, the strikers and their supporters would form picket lines around the building. The protestors would carry signs with a variety of pro-labor slogans and attempt to keep anyone else entering the workplace, as the Finck cigar workers did.[22]

As picketers quickly learned, the San Antonio political machine that included Mayor Charles Quin and police chief Owen Kilday sympathized with the factory owners, not the distressed workers. To participate in a picket line meant that a person might be arrested or even assaulted. Not surprisingly, strike leaders were usually among those taken to jail, and some lost their jobs in retaliation for their activities. When the Finck walkouts began, Emma Tenayuca was only a teenager. Excited by news of the workers' resistance, she wanted to experience a strike firsthand but got more than she expected. Half a century later, the Tejana told an interviewer that she had intended only "to observe," but was angered by the sheriff's declaring that he was going to greet the strikers with his "brand new pair of boots." The thought of women being kicked was counter to Tenayuca's "basic underlying faith in the American idea of freedom and fairness." Joining the picket line, she "landed in jail and learned how difficult it would be to make this [San Antonio] a union town." This was only the first of several times that the young woman would be arrested.[23]

What did Tenayuca mean when she talked about making San Antonio a union town? Formal labor organizations, unions, attempted to convince workers in certain crafts or industries to join ranks to pursue common objectives. Union members paid dues in return for benefits received. When a union was sufficiently strong, it would negotiate on behalf of its members. Workers' demands might involve higher salaries, reasonable working hours, and improved working conditions. If employers refused to comply, the union could threaten to declare a strike. A union-organized work stoppage was a powerful weapon that could paralyze a business. As previously discussed, however, business owners also had powerful weapons at their command, including their ability to fire workers, hire scabs, and have picketers arrested.

The prospect of strikes alarmed many people in the community, not only because of the threat to business interests but also because walkouts sometimes led to violence. Hoping to neutralize Tenayuca, both the press and the police labeled her an "outside agitator," because she was not employed in the industry. Their efforts failed, however, at least in the short term. Notably, the same factors that turned local officials and business owners against the Tejana caused the workers to welcome her as a valuable ally. Despite threats of retaliation, she voluntarily chose to join them in their resistance to exploitation. How could the workers not admire "the little girl who confronts men" and look "to her for leadership"? Also, the young woman's eloquence in English and some Spanish, combined with her being so well-read and knowledgeable, made her an even more valuable asset.[24]

The young labor leader's youth and dedication were particularly impressive. She did not graduate from high school until 1934 at which time she briefly worked at the Gunter Hotel as an elevator operator. Nevertheless, in the mid-1930s, she "supported almost every strike in the city, writing leaflets, visiting homes of strikers, and joining them on picket lines." During these years, Emma worked tirelessly to organize the industrial workers of the West Side "until violence at the end of the decade effectively ended her abilities to lead," as will be shown.[25]

The radical actions of labor organizers and frustrated workers fed the flames of hostility directed at them. The mayor and the chief of police took steps to stop even peaceful workers' protests. Especially alarming was a threat by San Antonio officials to deport troublesome Mexicans. Furthermore, not only *Mexicanos* but also Mexican American workers faced opposition "from the Anglo press, . . . from civil authorities, and sometimes from the Catholic Church." Raised as a Catholic herself, Tenayuca was especially upset at the Church's lack of support for labor. Also, she learned "early that state and federal officials rarely came to the defense of Tejanos." She was convinced that change would come only when the working classes and minority groups mobilized to help themselves. [26]

Emma was searching for answers, for effective ways to address the problems she observed around her. At least in part because of her youth, she experimented with a number of different political movements. Trying one and then another, Tenayuca made some choices that she later regretted. "For a while . . . I was probably very much of an anarchist," she later explained. "I had their ideas. I felt that the labor movement was the way: you organize the laborers and they'd change the situation." She also declared that "People, as a relief in order not to go through another Depression, turned to organization. . . . This is the way the workers responded and they had a right to respond that way."[27]

The Tejana activist wanted to help the Finck Cigar Company strikers, especially those who were fired from their jobs. She knew that many others in San Antonio were unemployed or under-employed as well, such as migrant or seasonal workers. As the term indicates, migrant workers lived a life on the move. Part of the year, they traveled down to South Texas or up to the northern states to pick crops and do other labor-intensive, poorly compensated jobs. In "late fall and early winter"—the off-season— they returned to San Antonio, where they hoped to find supplemental employment.

Sometimes they succeeded, sometimes not—often the latter as the Depression worsened. Out of desperation, "Chicanos took work when and where they could get it."[28] Emma threw herself into helping the disadvantaged, particularly those of her ethnicity. For her efforts she would be vilified by the power brokers in the city.

The bilingual Tenayuca exhibited a special "ability to bridge the gap between the West Side Hispanic workers and the Anglo officials of national labor unions." She went with organizers to "the homes of Mexican women and talked to the people about joining the union." Her efforts helped in forming local branches of the International Ladies' Garment Workers Union (ILGWU) in San Antonio in the mid-1930s. Initially, hand sewers, embroiders, and machine workers were recruited, although their interests later diverged. The Tejana also played a role when the employees of Dorothy Frock Company went on strike in 1936 and again the following year when the seamstresses for the Texas Infant Dress Company demanded higher wages. Ironically, much of what Emma knew about organizing labor she learned from books. In 1936, however, she went to Mexico City to study at the newly founded Workers' University, an institution dedicated to training people "to better orient their fight" in service of "the interests of the working class." She later acknowledged that she stayed there only a few months, because she was so young and her "Spanish was not very good."[29]

As for those without jobs, Emma worked at first through the West Side Unemployed Council on their behalf, but soon her efforts were increasingly directed to the larger Workers' Alliance (WA). Formed in the mid-1930s, the WA was led by Socialists and Communists. The organization sought legislative action such as "a minimum wage and hour law" and higher taxes, with the money to be used to assist the unemployed. The WA insisted that its major goal, however, was not welfare but "jobs."[30]

Joining the Workers' Alliance (WA) in 1936, Tenayuca and Mrs. Ernst organized the San Antonio branch, which was composed of unemployed pecan shellers and agricultural workers, among others. As the numbers of the jobless increased, "so did the ranks of the Workers Alliance." Soon the local WA "numbered fifteen branches with three thousand members, making it one of the strongest such organizations in the country." Despite her youth, Emma presided over the San Antonio chapters from 1936 to 1938, and at one point was "general secretary of at least ten chapters" in that city. Not surprisingly, all of this activity took a toll, as the activist began to suffer from physical problems and "nervous exhaustion."[31]

Undeterred, Emma helped exploited Mexicans not only to organize but also to define and articulate their issues, a number of which related to the Works Progress Administration. This federal program under President Franklin D. Roosevelt operated in conjunction with the states to provide employment on public works projects. Among other demands, the WA wanted more equal allotment of WPA jobs, "revision of WPA minimum-wage guidelines," better WPA distribution of food to the unemployed, and "the right of Mexican workers to organize without fear of deportation."[32]

Besides conducting a vigorous "writing and telegram campaign to New Deal officials in Washington," the young activist helped organize marches on Mayor Charles Quin's office, a sit-in at city hall, and a demonstration at the Gunter Hotel. The last was held "to protest the layoff" of workers employed by the WPA. Police response to these activities was aggressive. Tenayuca later told an interviewer that she and four others were arrested for their activities at the Gunter. The Tejana was the first taken to trial. Charged with inciting to riot, she retained her freedom because Everett Looney, the state's assistant attorney general, represented her *pro bono* (without charge). While expressing appreciation for his assistance, she bemoaned that fact that "the police went into the Workers Alliance hall [in 1937] and broke every bit of furniture." Even worse, two Hispanic men were injured during that intrusion.[33]

In 1937, Emma's selfless advocacy for labor led to an appointment as a member of the WA National Executive Committee. When a WA request to hold a parade in San Antonio was refused, the defiant Tejana called for a mass demonstration to be held in San Pedro Park on May Day—a date celebrated by some as International Workers' Day. The rally was to protest her earlier arrest, the removal of WA members from a sit-in at City Hall, and the city's refusal to grant the parade permit. Because this gathering of thousands was scheduled in a public venue without legal permission, San Antonio officials were furious. However, "not one person was arrested"—at least on this occasion.[34]

Just as the San Antonio political machine was increasingly antagonized by Tenayuca's actions, she was increasingly angry with the situation in San Antonio and elsewhere. Too many people were suffering; not enough was being done to alleviate that suffering. She especially resented the "tremendous amount of repression . . . against the labor movement" and the way that "any effort of the Mexicana workers to organize was met with brutal force." Equally upsetting was the exclusion of people of her ethnicity "from membership in most traditional unions." For these and other reasons, in 1937 the Tejana chose to join the very controversial Communist Party, a decision that would cost her dearly in both her public and private lives.[35]

By 1937 a young man named Homer Brooks was a leader in the Texas Communist Party. "An intellectual from Pennsylvania who had attended college for a few years," he had been sent to the Lone Star State to recruit new members to the cause. When Brooks and Tenayuca met, chemistry sparked. Although from very different backgrounds, the pair decided to get married in 1937. However, after a brief time living with her husband in Houston, the Tejana returned to San Antonio. Whether this was to continue her organizational and labor activities in her hometown, since Brooks was doing considerable travelling in pursuit of his Communist activities, or caused by early discord in the marriage—or a combination of these and other factors—is unclear. What is certain is that early the following year Tenayuca is quoted as saying, "I love my husband and am a good cook," despite what a magazine writer described as a "marital life confined to irregular week-ends." Her declaration of love aside, the couple would divorce in 1941. She later acknowledged that she "wasn't ready for marriage," while also noting that Brooks was an "inflexible" Communist with no sense of humor. However, Tenayuca described their union as one "of tremendous passion" and confessed that "it was a long time before I could get him out of my mind."[36] Apparently, Emma was a passionate person in all facets of her life.

During her marriage, the activist continued to direct her energies to the labor movement in her hometown. Again in need of her leadership were the shellers, numbering 10,000 to 20,000 of whom at least 80 percent were women. San Antonio was the "world's largest pecan shelling centre," and it depended "upon the family labor of Mexicans and Tex-Mexes (U.S.-born Mexicans)." Employees "worked in unsanitary conditions: the workrooms lacked proper ventilation, workers sat on backless benches, and the only tools they had for crushing shells were their own hands." Some plants lacked bathrooms, as well as running water. Also, these laborers were susceptible to widespread health issues, including tuberculosis, possibly related to the small particles of pecan dust in the workplace environment.[37]

Even shellers who managed to stay relatively healthy were desperate because of the "exploitative" methods being used. The best example would be Julius Seligmann's Southern Pecan Company, a major employer, with shelled pecans "valued at more than 1 million dollars" annually. In the 1930s, Seligmann was using a system in which contractors purchased whole pecans from him on credit for around 10 cents a pound. They then operated the pecan-processing facilities and handled labor issues.

The company repurchased the shelled pecans for around 30 to 36 cents a pound. For workers, this system translated into a life of dire poverty. According to a government report, the average income in 1938 for shellers from all sources was "$251 for a family of 4.6 persons"— or "69 cents per day . . . for food, clothing, shelter, and incidentals." They had the dubious honor of receiving some of the lowest wages in the country.[38]

Seligmann's Depression strategy was to "simply cut wages to ensure his pecans sold at a profit." The announcement of more wage reductions on January 31, 1938, "sparked an explosive atmosphere that had developed over years." Instead of seven cents per pound for halves, shellers would receive six cents, and the price for pieces dropped from six to five cents. Those who cracked the pecans "were cut from fifty cents to forty cents per one hundred pounds." *Time* magazine reported that even the "owners of the shelleries" recognized that the lower wages were "miserable" but claimed that they could not afford to pay more. Adding insult to injury, representatives of Seligmann's Company publicly argued that the workers "did not care to make much money. They were satisfied to earn little, and besides, they had a nice warm place to work and could go visit their friends while they earned." Exhibiting stereotypical racist attitudes of that period, they rationalized that workers who received higher wages would be inclined to "leave work early and fritter away their money on tequila."[39]

Even though two earlier strikes in 1934 and 1935 had failed to produce the desired results, distressed pecan shellers felt that their only option was to try again. Spontaneously, perhaps as many as two-thirds of the "workers walked out of pecan plants . . . on January 31." Thus began San Antonio's "longest and most bitter strike of the Depression"—which was also the largest in that city's history. As Tenayuca later noted, "What started out as a movement . . . for equal wages turned into a mass movement against starvation, for civil rights, for a minimum-wage law, and it changed the character of West Side San Antonio."[40]

Related to the decision to strike and the strength of the movement was increased attention to the San Antonio area by national labor organizations in the 1930s. Progress had been slow in coming for various reasons, including anti-Mexican attitudes expressed by some local union leaders. Not only had Mexican immigration had been blamed for "San Antonio's low wages and high unemployment" but also some whites held Mexicans responsible for most minor crime in the city. Therefore, West Side *Mexicanos* and Tejanos were understandably suspicious of labor organizers. Nevertheless, some shellers had joined the Congress of Industrial Organizations (originally the Committee for Industrial Organization), formed in the mid-1930s to unite "unskilled workers in mass production industries." More workers recognized the advantage of union support after the strike underway, as the number paying dues to the local CIO-affiliated United Cannery, Agricultural, Packing, and Allied Workers of America (UCAPAWA) soon reached three thousand.[41]

According to a local Spanish-language newspaper, major leaders of the movement included local union officers Minnie Rendón and Leandro Avila; however, Emma Tenayuca's name was also listed. Despite not being a sheller, she did play a key role in this struggle—at least initially. Although the strikers were almost certainly uncomfortable with her Communist affiliation, many were Workers Alliance members, well-aware of the Tejana's compassion, commitment, and competence. Consequently, they "elected Emma Tenayuca Brooks honorary strike chairman." Despite being a "5-foot, 2-inch, tiny woman," Emma exercised temporary leadership and in the process "became known as '*La Pasionaria*' for her fiery speeches." She committed herself to the cause, one that "shook the city and the state—and thrilled the working class." Tenayuca Brooks's ties to Communism and her radical husband, however, created problems for the movement, as did the Communist label often applied to the CIO by its opponents.[42]

Covering the dramatic events in San Antonio, *Time* magazine in February 1938 described Tenayuca as "a slim, vivacious labor organizer with black eyes and a Red [Communist] philosophy" who was "up to her small ears" in the strike. Portraying her as a puppeteer without using that term, the article alleged that the Tejana was pulling the strings of the workers. It also referenced her long-running feud with the chief of police, which had "landed her in jail on countless occasions"—and that feud would only intensify as events progressed.[43]

Convinced that the Pecan Shellers were part of a "Communist Revolution," both Mayor Charles Quin and Chief Owen Kilday vowed to stop what they viewed as anti-American activities in their city. Kilday was determined not to "let any reds [Communists] get mixed up in this strike" and asserted that "the police would arrest anyone caught picketing who was not a worker." Significantly, as the work stoppage progressed, even the strikers found themselves targets of the police, who were at times armed with tear gas. Hundreds of people were arrested for blocking the sidewalks and "carrying signs in public without permits" with the prisoners taken to city and county jails that soon became badly overcrowded. Some picketers were fined as much as $10, a heavy burden for anyone during the Depression, much less disadvantaged minorities. Labor leaders Tenayuca and Rendón were among the first taken into custody, although the former later noted that "they didn't hurt me or anything like that."[44]

"Red-baiting" proved an effective tactic. Referring specifically to Tenayuca, Mayor Quin insisted that her presence "would cost the strikers public sympathy." These words proved prophetic, as even the "moderate voices in both the Hispanic and Anglo communities of San Antonio spoke out against the strike and communist influences." These voices included the Roman Catholic archbishop.

Officials in the CIO and UCAPAWA quickly determined that
"removing Tenayuca from a visible leadership role seemed the safer
route for the union." Ironically, they enlisted her husband—himself
a staunch Communist—to persuade her to step down. According to
Emma, Homer Brooks came to her with a typed statement already
prepared "to remove me from the [strike] leadership."[45] One can
only imagine the sense of betrayal the Tejana must have felt with
her church, her colleagues, and her spouse.

Decades later Tenayuca told an interviewer that she was infuriated by the demand that she withdraw, because "I organized that
strike, led it." Nevertheless, she recognized that her presence was
hurting the workers' cause. Concerned with the greater good, the
activist agreed to vacate her public role, even though she "was enthu-
siastically supported by strikers and was endorsed by *La Prensa*,
San Antonio's [major] Spanish newspaper." On February 6, the
Tejana resigned "as Chairman of the strike committee . . . and had
no more direct influence on strike decisions or direction."[46]

Tenayuca continued to support the laborers privately from the
Workers Alliance headquarters, as she "still held daily meetings,
produced and distributed circulars, and sent strikers to picket lines."
Among her other contributions was helping feed families of strikers
who were in jail. She later stated her conviction that she "would have
done a good job" leading the strike but acknowledged that "I would
have needed the help of someone who had experience."[47]

Facing so much opposition, Emma and the strikers must have
welcomed a message from Congressman Maury Maverick indicating
his support for the strike. This proved especially significant, because
Maverick would soon become mayor of San Antonio. Important
help also came from the American Civil Liberties Union, an organization that attempted to protect the right to strike and provide
legal representation for the arrested participants. Additionally, on
March 19 a rally was held at Military Plaza to celebrate the release of
some strikers from jail and raise money for the shellers' cause.[48]

Complaints of San Antonio police abusing their power drew the attention of Governor James Allred, who instigated an investigation; the union unsuccessfully went to court to file for an injunction "to prevent police from stopping picketing at the west side pecan plants"; and labor leaders continued their efforts to disassociate the movement from the taint of Communism. The governor helped persuade "Julius Seligman . . .and the union to arbitrate the dispute." The strikers agreed on March 8 "to return to work . . . pending the determining of a fair wage scale" by a three-member arbitration board. By mid-April negotiations were underway throughout the industry. Through this this process, an agreement was reached for temporary pay of 5½ cents per pound for pieces and 6½ cents for halves with more comprehensive negotiations to follow. Although both sides felt they had won, in reality the outcome "favored employers over the shellers."[49]

What appeared a hopeful sign for labor occurred in October 1938, with the implementation of the Fair Labor Standards Act (FLS). The new federal law "mandated a minimum wage of twenty-five cents an hour" for industrial labor. Initially optimistic, pecan shellers ultimately suffered from unintended consequences of the FLS legislation. Both Seligmann and the union failed in attempts to get shellers classified as agricultural workers so that they would be exempt from the mandated minimum. Unwilling or unable to pay the higher wages, Southern Pecan and other companies temporarily "closed their doors in protest" and laid off workers. When they reopened, some producers tried to find ways to circumvent the law, but most mechanized their operations which meant less manpower was needed. For thousands of shellers, low income was replaced by no income.[50]

While the above events were transpiring, Tenayuca continued to be committed to labor activism and to helping her people improve their lives. She also remained a target of the San Antonio political machine. In April of 1938, police had raided Workers Alliance headquarters, where the Tejana was running a school for some of the younger workers. The authorities "seized Communist literature" and arrested several people, some of whom where Mexican citizens threatened with deportation.[51]

At the end of the decade, Emma and Homer Brooks continued their efforts to mobilize minorities to become more active in the fight for rights and justice. As part of that effort, they co-authored a seminal essay, "The Mexican Question in the Southwest," which was published in *The Communist* in March 1939. Significantly, the Tejana is often credited as the primary force behind this treatise, which has been labeled "the most lucid and accurate analysis of Mexican people ever produced" by representatives of the Communist Party. Rather than distinguishing Mexican nationals residing in the United States from Mexican Americans born in that country, the authors approach them as one people who must unify to "free themselves from the special oppression and discrimination in all its phases that have existed for almost a century." Referencing the strikes that had already occurred in Texas and elsewhere, Emma and Homer Brooks presented union organization as the "surest guarantee for the full and successful development of the people's movement."[52]

The couple was heartened by changes that were occurring at the municipal level in San Antonio by the late 1930s. Representative Maury Maverick, a progressive politician, lost a bid for reelection to Congress because of unsubstantiated charges that he was "the friend and ally of Communism." The opponent making those allegations was Paul Kilday, brother of the San Antonio chief of police. Maverick responded by announcing his candidacy for mayor of San Antonio—an office held by his grandfather a century earlier—and thereby challenging the political bosses who held "a big majority of the offices in the city and county government." Promising "good government," he courted Mexican-American voters and received support from the local Pecan Shellers Union.

Because of Maverick's sympathy toward labor, Homer Brooks welcomed his victory as "an opportunity to bring back efficient, democratic government to San Antonio."[53]

Taking advantage of the more open atmosphere in San Antonio, Brooks and other radicals planned to hold a major meeting at the Municipal Auditorium on August 25, 1939. Tenayuca personally penned a note to the new mayor to ask for a city permit, a request that Maverick granted. Opposition was quick in coming from varied groups, including the Roman Catholic Church, veterans' organizations, the San Antonio press, and the Ku Klux Klan—all demanding the permit be cancelled. A strong believer in civil liberties, Maverick cited the U.S. Constitution, specifically the rights of free speech and freedom of assembly, to justify his refusal to give in to these demands.[54]

Tensions grew as the date for the rally drew near. Aware that anti-Communist feeling was strong, Tenayuca and some other organizers became concerned about the lack of support they had received and questioned the wisdom of holding the proposed function. She later claimed that she tried to persuade Brooks to cancel the event, but "wasn't listened to." He insisted on going forward as planned. Submitting to her husband's wishes, Emma prepared her remarks for the event, since she was the "elected chair person of the Communist Party USA in Texas and was . . . scheduled to speak."[55]

Anticipating trouble, Maverick deployed policemen and firemen to the venue, where "Led by tiny Mrs. Emma Tenayuca Brooks," between 100 and 150 attendees entered the Municipal Auditorium. They were vastly outnumbered by angry citizens congregating outside. After burning the mayor in effigy, the "screaming, angry, stone-hurling crowd" of 5,000 to 8,000 anti-Communist protesters forced their way into the building, despite police efforts to stop them with "tear gas and streams of water." In the ensuing riot, injuries were sustained, windows in the building were broken, and the interior of the auditorium was damaged. Ironically,

Emma and Homer Brooks, along with other rally participants, escaped from the mob's fury, because "police officers guided those inside to safety using a tunnel that extended from the auditorium to the San Antonio River nearby."[56]

Targeting the mayor for permitting the rally, some of the mob headed to his house. Maverick's son later explained that "On the night of the riot, the police hid my parents and me for fear that we would be murdered. The next morning a police escort took us home. Throughout the day, people would drive by shouting insults." When Maverick later ran for re-election as mayor of San Antonio, he lost at least in part because of his support of "Emma's Reds," a fact that she deeply regretted. Perhaps predictably, C. K. Quin regained the mayor's office.[57]

Maverick was not the only person to suffer as a result of the disastrous Communist rally. For the Tejana, it marked "the end of her public role of political activist." The target of intense hostility, the twenty-three-year-old woman found herself "hounded, harassed, and threatened," as well as being unable to find employment in her hometown. Tenayuca's life was falling apart. All of these stresses, combined with problems in the marriage, caused Homer and Emma to separate. Even before their divorce was finalized in 1941, she relocated temporarily to Houston. There "she worked various office jobs under the alias 'Beatrice Giraud,' and attended night classes at the University of Houston."[58]

In the 1940s, Tenayuca would break away not only from Brooks but also from the Communist Party. A number of factors, such as the Municipal Auditorium riot and resultant fallout, influenced this decision. Notably, she was one of many who felt betrayed when Communist leaders in the Soviet Union "signed a nonaggression pact" with Nazi Germany in 1939 that facilitated Hitler's invasion of Poland and the beginning of World War II. Nevertheless, the Tejana remained a party member as the new decade began, because she still believed that it "offered the best avenue for social change."

In 1940, she was state chairman of the Communist Party of Texas, as well as its candidate for the 20th District (San Antonio) Texas congressional seat. By mid-decade, however, a "disillusioned" Tenayuca "concluded that the party had lost touch with the powerless and decided to leave it."[59] In short, she lost faith in the Communist Party, just as she had in her husband.

As if the Tejana did not have enough problems after the disaster at the Municipal Auditorium, she also had to deal with a serious health issue. By the early 1940s, she was "suffering the lingering effects of tuberculosis." Despite this affliction, cement, garment, and laundry workers reportedly still solicited her help when they went on strike.[60]

Spending at least part of World War II in San Antonio, the Tejana attempted to join the Women's Army Corps. After a provisional acceptance, however, her application was rejected without explanation. Tenayuca contended that the reason was her membership in the Communist Party, and she was probably correct. The FBI had been maintaining a file on her since 1939 because of those affiliations, although she may have been unaware of that surveillance. What she did know was that she was blacklisted, which made finding work extremely difficult. To her distress, even the Catholic Church "turned its back on her." This was undoubtedly one of several reasons why Emma decades later wrote that she had "once dropped the church" and at times felt "spiritually bankrupt." Interestingly, the Tejana was able to survive only because she was finally hired by "a Jewish garment manufacturer of US Army officer uniforms who had sympathized with her community work."[61]

Weighed down by her past, Tenayuca supposedly regretted that her limited financial resources prevented her from helping her numerous siblings, and she "was beginning to miss more and more meals" herself. Hoping for a fresh start far from Texas, Emma moved to Los Angeles in the mid-1940s, around the same time that she left the Communist Party. After a short period,

Emma Tenayuca and her son Frank, in 1953. Emma Tenayuca Papers, 1940s–1990, Mss420 Box 16. Courtesy of the TWU Libraries Woman's Collection, Texas Woman's University, Denton, TX.

she relocated yet again, this time to San Francisco. Paying her own way through San Francisco State University, she received a bachelor's degree with high honors in 1952—much later than she would have graduated from college had the effects of the Great Depression not been so devastating for her grandfather and others. Also in 1952, Emma gave birth to a son, Francisco "Frank" Tenayuca Adams, whom she raised as a single parent and in whom she took great pride.[62]

The Tejana finally decided to move back to San Antonio late in the 1960s, the same decade during which her mother died. Despite having lived far from Texas for many years, the former Communist feared that her past would be resurrected and that she would have to maintain a low profile. As will be seen, however, the second phase of her life in the Lone Star State proved very different from the first. Although she still held strong convictions, the mature Tenayuca found acceptable, mainstream ways to express them, as indicated by her membership in "the League of Women Voters, the American Civil Liberties Union, and the Democratic Party."[63]

Another difference was Emma's ability to obtain employment. Despite her earlier estrangement from the church, she was hired to teach at St. Gerard's Catholic School in San Antonio but soon switched to the public school system. Determined to continue her own education as well, she earned a master's degree from Our Lady of the Lake University. In 1982, the Tejana retired from teaching in the Harlandale School District, located on the South Side of San Antonio. Developing Alzheimer's toward the end of her noteworthy life, Emma Tenayuca died on July 23, 1999, at age eighty-two.[64]

In Emma's last decades before her mental faculties began to decline, she was active in local political affairs. Changes occurring in San Antonio were personified by Henry Cisneros, who was

Portrait of Emma Tenayuca later in life. Emma Tenayuca Papers, 1940s–1990, Mss420 Box 16. Courtesy of the TWU Libraries Woman's Collection, Texas Woman's University, Denton, TX.

elected mayor in the early 1980s—the first Latino in that office since Juan Seguín in the mid-nineteenth century and one of the first in a major city in the United States in the twentieth century. Correspondence between Cisneros and Tenayuca reveals her involvement in garnering petition signatures, distributing political literature, and philanthropic fund-raising efforts during his multiple terms in office in the 1980s. In one missive, the mayor wrote the aging woman that he was "truly grateful for your friendship and your work on behalf of the growth and progress of our city."[65]

Cisneros was not the only person to benefit from the strides that Latinos were making in the second half of the twentieth century. Upon returning to Texas, Emma had received "a heroine's welcome" from residents of the West Side who remembered her sacrifices on their behalf. The labor activist also "became the subject of much attention from Chicana activists who were inspired" by her story and subsequently publicized her exploits. Accolades began to pour her way. Tenayuca became one of the "outstanding Texas Women" highlighted in an exhibit at the Institute of Texan Cultures in San Antonio in 1981, was one of the first women publicly honored by the National Association for Chicano Studies in 1984, was nominated for the Texas Women's Hall of Fame in 1985, and "was inducted into the San Antonio Women's Hall of Fame in 1991." Three years prior to that induction, Bob Bullock, Texas Comptroller of Public Accounts, had written the Tejana that "your know-how and political savy are now legend. You have every right to be proud. . . ." Honors would continue posthumously into the twenty-first century, including the placement of "a Texas historic marker at Milam Park" on the date that "would have been Tenayuca's 95th birthday."[66] Times had indeed changed!

**

Emma Tenayuca was an extraordinary woman. As an adolescent, she made the conscious, courageous choice not to be a bystander but instead to address actively the injustices all around her. With the recklessness of youth, she took great risks for the causes in which she believed. That she was not always wise in the paths she chose does not lessen the courage behind her actions or the price she paid.

Tenayuca's role in gains made by Hispanics is difficult to measure. In a real sense, her youthful efforts as a labor organizer did not accomplish many concrete results and her radicalism aroused widespread opposition. Nevertheless, she was arguably, "the single figure in San Antonio in the 1930s who could mobilize the West side." Strikers were uplifted when the passionate Tejana would stand at a microphone and exhort them to continue the struggle. They were also inspired by her willingness to go to jail for her beliefs and their cause. She "empowered and inspired people who never [before] had any hope of changing their situation."[67]

When stories about Tenayuca appeared in the national press during the 1930s, events and conditions in San Antonio were brought to the country's attention. By the end of that decade, government investigators were condemning the "dreadful living conditions on the West Side and the exploitation of the community's labor force." Without her presence, this might not have happened. The young woman helped show "the path for [later] Tejanos and Tejanas to follow."[68]

At Tenayuca's funeral in 1999, hundreds honored this courageous woman. Mourners "offered pieces of metal in tribute because . . . she was made of steel." Noted Chicana writer, Carmen Tafolla, composed a poem for the occasion, which included the following excerpt: "*La Pasionaria*, we called her, because she was our passion, because she was our corazón [heart]—*defendiendo a los pobres* [defending the poor], speaking out at a time when neither Mexicans nor women were expected to speak at all."[69]

Influenced by "her grandfather, her extensive reading, her personal experiences, and her observations[,]" Tenayuca played an important role not only in Chicano history but also in Texas history as well. To the activist, her actions were simply a matter of "helping her community through the rough times of the Depression." Less than ten years before her death, she explained in an interview that she saw her support of labor "as perhaps something I could do to help." She posed the following question to the interviewer: "If you saw people that were hungry, if you saw children crying for milk, what would you do if you could do something?" Hopefully, all of us would have the courage to follow Emma Tenayuca's example—to "do something," even if it cost us as dearly as it did this notable Tejana.[70]

Bibliographical Commentary

Brief information on Emma Tenayuca can be found in general sources on Mexican Americans, such as *Las Tejanas: 300 Years of History* (2003) by Teresa Palomo Acosta and Ruthe Winegarten. Articles focused more specifically on this Tejana activist include Roberto R. Calderón and Emiliano Zamora, "Manuela Solis Sager and Emma Tenayuca: A Tribute" in Teresa Córdova, Norma Cantú, et al., *Chicana Voices: Intersections of Class, Race, and Gender* (3rd printing, 1993); "Emma Tenayuca: Vision and Courage" by Julia Kirk Blackwelder in *The Human Tradition in Texas* (2001), edited by Ty Cashion and Jesús F. de la Teja; "Carolina Munguía and Emma Tenayuca: The Politics of Benevolence and Radical Reform" by Gabriela González in *Frontiers: A Journal of Women Studies* 24, nos. 2 and 3 (2003); and "Tejana Radical: Emma Tenayuca and the San Antonio Labor Movement during the Great Depression" by Zaragosa Vargas in *Texas Labor History*, edited by Bruce A. Glasrud and James C. Maroney (2013). Also available in print is Carmen Tafolla's and Sharyll Tenayuca's bilingual children's book, *That's Not Fair! Emma Tenayuca's Struggle for Justice/¡No Es Justo! La lucha de Emma Tenayuca por la justicia!* (2008). For juvenile readers, Sammye Munson's *Our Tejano Heroes: Outstanding Mexican Americans* (1989) includes a brief section on Tenayuca.

Works on the 1938 pecan shellers' strike in San Antonio also prove informative. Examples would include the following: Patricia E. Gower, "Unintended Consequences: The San Antonio Pecan Sheller Strike of 1938," *The Journal of South Texas* 17, no. 2 (Fall 2004); Laura Cannon, "A Careful Balance: Changing Tactics of the Mexican American Business Community in the 1938 San Antonio Pecan Shellers' Strike," *The Journal of South Texas* 29, no. 1 (Fall 2015); Laura Cannon Dixon, "Police Brutality Makes Headlines: Retelling the Story of the 1938 Pecan Shellers' Strike" (M.A. thesis, Indiana State University, 2010); and Matthew Jerrid Keyworth, "Poverty, Solidarity, and Opportunity: The 1938 San Antonio Pecan Shellers' Strike" (M.S. thesis, Texas A&M University, December 2007).

Internet resources include audio and transcribed versions of two oral interviews with Emma Tenayuca that have been digitized by the University of Texas at San Antonio. Jerry Poyo's 1987 interview is accessible at http://digital.utsa.edu/ cdm/ref/collection/ p15125coll4/id/1172, and an interview conducted by Luis R. Torres in 1987 or 1988 can be found at https://medialibrary.utsa.edu/ Play/9046. The *Handbook of Texas Online* (www.tshaonline.org) offers a short biographical entry titled "Tenayuca, Emma Beatrice" that includes a *Texas Talks* video clip (6:35) in which Emilio Zamora and Andrés Tijerina discuss Tenayuca's role as a labor organizer. Another biographical sketch can be found at National Bibliography Online (www.anb.org/articles/15-15-01312.html).

For archival research, the Emma Tenayuca Collection can be found in the Woman's Collection, housed in the Blagg-Huey Library at Texas Woman's University in Denton, Texas. A June 1986 interview with Tenayuca, conducted by Emilio Zamora (with Oralia Cortez), can be found in MS420, Box 11, Folder 5 of that collection.

Endnotes

1. Julia Kirk Blackwelder, "Emma Tenayuca: Vision and Courage," in *The Human Tradition in Texas*, edited by Ty Cashion and Jesús F. de la Teja (Wilmington, DE: Scholarly Resources Inc., 2001), 195, quotation [Hereineafter cited as Blackwelder, "Tenayuca"].

2. Blackwelder, "Tenayuca," 192; Gabriela González, "Carolina Munguía and Emma Tenayuca: The Politics of Benevolence and Radical Reform," *Frontiers* 24, no. 2/3 (2003): 209–210, 1st quotation on 209, 3rd quotation on 210; Emma Tenayuca, interview by Emilio Zamora with Oralia Cortez, June 1986, 2nd quotation, Emma Tenayuca Collection, MS420, Box 11, Folder 5, Texas Woman's Collection, Blagg-Huey Library, Texas Woman's University, Denton, Texas [Hereinafter cited as Zamora, Interview, Emma Tenayuca Collection hereinafter cited as ETC]; "Transcript of Interview with Emma Tenayuca," interview by Jerry Poyo, February 21, 1987, University of Texas at San Antonio Libraries Digital Collections, http://digital.utsa.edu/cdm/ref/collection/p15125coll4/id/1172 [hereinafter cited as Poyo, Interview]; "Emma Tenayuca," *La Voz de Aztlan*, March 13, 2000, http://www.aztlan.net/default6.htm [hereinafter cited as "Tenayuca," *Aztlan*, 2000].

3. Roberto R. Calderón and Emilio Zamora, "Manuela Solis Saeger and Emma Tenayuca: A Tribute," in *Chicana Voices: Intersections of Class, Race, and Gender*, Teresa Córdova, Norma Cantú et al., eds. (Albuquerque: University of New Mexico Press, 1993), 31, 37–38; Blackwelder, "Tenayuca," 192, quotation; "Tenayuca," *Aztlan*, 2000.

4. Blackwelder, "Tenayuca," 192–193, 1st quotation on 192, 2nd quotation on 193.

5. Blackwelder, "Tenayuca," 192; Zamora, Interview, ETC; Miriam Ferguson was twice elected governor of Texas, first in 1924 and again in 1932.

6. Emma Tenayuca, interview by Luis R. Torres, ca 1987–1988, José Angel Gutiérrez Papers, University of Texas at San Antonio Library, https://medialibraryutsa.edu/Play/9046 [hereinafter cited as Torres, Interview]; Blackwelder, "Tenayuca," 195; Poyo, Interview; Dedra McDonald, "Chicanas at the Forefront of Labor Organization: A Look at Emma Tenayuca's Role as a Labor Activist," paper presented at "Mexican Americans in Texas History: A Conference," Texas Lutheran College, July 26, 1990 (copy at Briscoe Center

for American History, University of Texas at Austin), 2. [Briscoe Center hereinafter cited as CAH].

7. Matthew Jerrid Keyworth, "Poverty, Solidarity, and Opportunity: The 1938 San Antonio Pecan Shellers' Strike" (M.S. Thesis, Texas A&M University, December 2007), 3, 1st quotation; Julia Kirk Blackwelder, "Texas Homeworkers in the Depression," in *Texas Labor History*, Bruce A. Glasrud and James C. Maroney, eds. (College Station: Texas A&M University Press, 2013), 282, 2nd quotation.

8. Blackwelder, "Tenayuca," 193, quotation.

9. Blackwelder, "Tenayuca," 193, 2nd quotation; Teresa Gutiérrez, "Workers' Hero," *Workers' World*, 3rd quotation; Audrey Granneberg, "Maury Maverick's San Antonio," *Survey Graphic: Magazine of Social Interpretation*, July 1939, 1st quotation, http://newdeal.feri.org/survey/39a07.htm; Blackwelder, "Texas Homeworkers," 282, 4th quotation.

10. McDonald, "Chicanas," 3rd quotation on 5; Barbara J. Rozek, "The Entry of Mexican-American Women into Urban Based Industries: Experiences in Texas During the Twentieth Century," in *Women and Texas History*, edited by Fane Downs and Nancy Baker Jones (Austin: Texas State Historical Association, 1993), 22, 1st and 2nd quotations; Blackwelder, "Texas Homeworkers," 282, 4th quotation.

11. Blackwelder, "Texas Homeworkers," 285, 287, 1st quotation on 287; Rozek, "Mexican-American Women," 22; Teresa Gutiérrez, "Workers' Hero," reprinted from Aug. 13, 1999 issue of *Worker's World* newspaper, 2nd quotation, http://www.workers.org/ww/1999/emma0819.html.

12. Torres, Interview; McDonald, "Chicanas," 2; Zamora, Interview; Poyo, Interview; "Emma Tenayuca," UTSA, http://lonestar.utsa.edu/ldalby/tenayuca.htm [hereinafter cited as "Emma Tenayuca," UTSA].

13. "Women's History from the Helaine Victoria Press Collection: Emma Tenayuca," *Jocelyn's Web Site*, http://www.jocelyn.com/wom03.html; "anarchism," 1st quotation, www.merriam-webster.com/disctionary/anarchism; "anarchism," www.encyclopedia.com/topic/anarchism.aspx; "socialism," 2nd quotation, www.merriam-webster.com/dictionary/socialism; Alia Hoyt, "How Socialism Works," 2016, money.howstuffworks.com/socialism.htm.

14. González, "Tenayuca," 210; Poyo, Interview; "Communism," 1st and 2nd quotations, www.merriam-webster.com/dictionary/communism; McDonald, "Chicanas," 2, 3rd quotation.

15. Zamora, Interview; Cynthia E. Orozco, *No Mexicans, Women, or Dogs Allowed* (Austin: University of Texas Press, 2009), 208–215, passim; González, "Tenayuca," 210, all quotations. To learn more about Emma Tenayuca's views on the need for unity among Mexicans, see the following article that she co-authored with Homer Brooks: "The Mexican Question in the Southwest," *The Communist*, March 1939.

16. Blackwelder, "Tenayuca," 195; McDonald, "Chicanas," 3.

17. Blackwelder, "Tenayuca," 192; McDonald, "Chicanas," 2–3; Poyo, Interview; Torres, Interview, quotation; Zamora, Interview.

18. McDonald, "Chicanas," 3–4, quotation, as quoted.

19. Laura Cannon, "A Careful Balance: Changing Tactics of the Mexican American Business Community in the 1938 San Antonio Pecan Shellers' Strike," *The Journal of South Texas* 29, no. 1 (Fall 2015): 91–92.

20. Blackwelder, "Tenayuca," 195–196; "The National Recovery Administration," Digital History ID 3442, 1st quotation, www.digitalhistory.uh.edu/disp_textbook.cfm?smtlD=2&psid=3442; Judith N. McArthur and Harold L. Smith, "Not Whistling Dixie: Women's Movements and Feminist Politics," in David O'Donald Cullen and Kyle G. Wilkinson, eds., *The Texas Left: The Radical Roots of Lone Star Liberalism* (College Station: Texas A&M University Press, 2010), 141; Arnoldo de León, "More Than a Somnolent Type: Tejanos Resist the Rule of Dominance," in *The Texas Left*, 200, 2nd and 3rd quotations.

21. Zaragoza Vargas, "Tejana Radical: Emma Tenayuca and the San Antonio Labor Movement during the Great Depression," in *Texas Labor History*, ed. Bruce A. Glasrud and James C. Maroney (College Station: Texas A&M University Press, 2013), 223, quotation; McDonald, "Chicanas," 6; *Handbook of Texas Online*, R. Matt Abigail and Jazmin León, "Tenayuca, Emma Beatrice," http://www.tshaonline.org/handbook/online/articles/fte41; Blackwelder, "Tenayuca," 195–199, passim. [*Handbook of Texas Online* hereinafter cited as *HOT Online*.]

22. Blackwelder, "Tenayuca," 196–197, 199; Julia Kirk Blackwelder, *Women of the Depression: Caste and Culture in San Antonio, 1929–1939*, 2nd ed. (College Station: Texas A&M University Press, 1984), 135, quotation; McDonald, "Chicanas," 7.

23. Vargas, "Tejana Radical," 22; McDonald, "Chicanas," 6; Geoffry Rips, "Living History, Emma Tenayuca Tells Her Story," *The Texas Observer*, October 28, 1983, 9, all quotations; Blackwelder, "Tenayuca," 196. Sources disagree as to whether Tenayuca's labor involvement began with the first or second Finck strike; however, in the Rips interview cited here, Tenayuca says it was the second.

24. Blackwelder, "Tenayuca," 196, 1st quotation; Winegarten, *Las Tejanas*, 143; Vargas, "Tejana Radical," 223, 2nd and 3rd quotations".

25. *HOT Online*, Abigail and León, "Tenayuca"; "Tenayuca," *Aztlan*, 2000; Blackwelder, "Tenayuca," 197, 2nd quotation; "Emma Tenayuca," Jocelyn Cohen, last modified August 4, 2008, 3rd quotation, http://www.jocelync.com/wom03.html.

26. Blackwelder, "Tenayuca," 195, 197, 200, 1st quotation on 200, 2nd on 197; Winegarten, *Las Tejanas*, 143.

27. McDonald, "Chicanas," 7, as quoted.

28. Blackwelder, "Texas Homeworkers," 282, quotations.

29. Blackwelder, "Tenayuca," 199, 1st quotation; Rips, Interview, 10, 2nd quotation; Blackwelder, "Texas Homeworkers," 291; McDonald, "Chicanas," 7; *HOT Online*, Abigail and León, "Tenayuca"; "Workers University of Mexico," México Es Cultura: La Cartelera Nacional, Secretaría de Cultura, 3rd and 4th quotations, http://www.mexicoescultura.com/recinto/66427/en/workers-university-of-mexico.html#prettyPhoto; Zamora, Interview, 5th quotation. Tenayuca's spoken Spanish was probably superior to her literacy in that language.

30. Winegarten, *Las Tejanas*, 143; Vargas, "Tejana Radical: Emma Tenayuca and the San Antonio Labor Movement during the Great Depression," in *Texas Labor History*, edited by Bruce A. Glasrud and James C. Maroney (College Station: Texas A&M University Press, 2013), 224; "Workers' Hero," *Workers' World*; "Emma Tenayuca," Jocelyn Cohen, quotations.

31. "Tenayuca," *Aztlan*, 2000, 3rd quotation; Rips, Interview, 9, 1st quotation; Vargas, "Tejana Radical," 224–225, 2nd and 3rd quotations on 224; McDonald, "Chicanas," 8; Zamora, Interview.

32. Vargas, "Tejana Radical," 224, 1st quotation; Rips, Interview, 10, 2nd quotation.

33. Vargas, "Tejana Radical," 224–225, 1st quotation on 224; Blackwelder, "Tenayuca," 201–202; McDonald, "Chicanas," 8; Rips, Interview, 9, 2nd and 3rd quotations; Torres, Interview; Calderón and Zamora, "Manuela Solis Sager and Emma Tenayuca" in *Chicana Voices*, 40.

34. Vargas, "Tejana Radical," 224–225; Blackwelder, "Tenayuca," 202; McDonald, "Chicanas," 8.

35. Poyo, Interview, 1st and 2nd quotations; *HOT Online*, Abigail and León, "Tenayuca," 3rd quotation; Zargoza Vargas, "Tejana Radical," 224.

36. Vargas, "Tejana Radical," 225; McDonald, "Chicanas," 10, 1st quotation; Poyo, Interview, 3rd and 4th quotations; *HOT Online*, Abigail and León, "Tenayuca"; "*La Pasionaria*," *Time*, 2nd quotation; González, "Tenayuca," 218; McDonald, "Chicanas," 10.

37. Patricia E. Gower, "Unintended Consequences: The San Antonio Pecan Sheller Strike of 1938," *The Journal of South Texas* 17, no. 2 (Fall 2004): 94; Rozek, "Entry of Mexican American Women," 24; "La Pasionaria," *Time*, 1st and 2nd quotations; Sonia Hernández, *Working Women into the Borderlands* (College Station: Texas A&M University Press, 2014), 116, 3rd quotation; Roger C. Barnes and James Donovan, "The Southern Pecan Shelling Company: A Window to Depression-Era San Antonio," *South Texas Studies* 11 (2000): 53.

38. González, "Tenayuca," 213, 1st and 2nd quotations; Selden C. Menefee and Orin C. Cassmore, *The Pecan Shellers of San Antonio: The Problem of Underpaid and Underemployed Mexican Labor*, Division of Research, (Washington, D.C.: United States Government Printing Office, 1940) Sect. 24, Introduction, XVII, 3rd quotation, Sect. 25, 4th quotation; Vargas, "Tejana Radical," 226.

39. Keyworth, "Poverty," 9, 13, 1st quotation on 9, 2nd quotation on 13; "*La Pasionaria*," *Time*, 4th and 5th quotations; González, "Tenayuca," 214, 3rd quotation; Gower, "Unintended Consequences," 95, 6th and 7th quotations, as quoted; Anthony Quiroz, "The Quest for Identity and Citizenship: Mexican Americans in Twentieth-Century Texas," in *Twentieth Century-Texas: A Social and Cultural History*, John Storey and Mary Kelley, eds. (Denton: University of North Texas Press, 2008), 48, 9th quotation.

40. Menefee and Cassmore, *Pecan Shellers*, Sect. 17; Blackwelder, *Women in the Depression*, 141; Blackwelder, "Tenayuca," 203–204; Keyworth, "Poverty," 13, 111, 1st quotation; McDonald, "Chicanas," 9, 2nd quotation; Teresa Gutiérrez, "Workers' Hero: Emma Tenayuca," Reprinted from the Aug. 13, 1999, issue of *Workers World* newspaper, 3rd quotation as quoted, http://www.workers.org/ww/1999/emma0819.html; Menefee and Cassmore in the 1940 government report use the term "spontaneous walkout" to describe what happened (Sect. 17).

41. Blackwelder, "Tenayuca," 203–204, 1st quotation on 203, 3rd quotation on 204; Suzanne Mettler, *Dividing Citizens: Gender and Federalism in New Deal Public Policy* (Ithaca: Cornell University Press, 1998), 48, 2nd quotation; Menefee and Cassmore, *Pecan Shellers*, Sect. 18.

42. Blackwelder, "Tenayuca," 204; Rips, "Living History," Insert, 12, 1st quotation; Mariana Pisano, "Legendary Leader," *San Antonio Express-News*, S.A. Life Section, March 12, 1996, 2nd quotation, ETC, MS420, Box 11, Folder 24; Gower, "Unintended Consequences," 92–93, 3rd quotation on 92, 4th quotation on

92–93; Teresa Gutiérrez, "Workers' Hero," *Workers World*; Keyworth, "Poverty," 112; Cannon, "A Careful Balance," 90. Cannon in "A Careful Balance" notes that the shellers recognized that the taint of Communism would work against them and "attempted to distance themselves from the Communist label" (95).

43. *"La Pasionaria," Time*, all quotations.

44. Cannon, "A Careful Balance," 90, 1st quotation; McDonald, "Chicanas," 9–10, 2nd quotation on 9, as quoted, 5th quotation on 10; Gower, "Unintended Consequences," 93, 3rd quotation; Blackwelder, *Women of the Depression*, 143; Keyworth, "Poverty, Solidarity, and Opportunity," 120, 4th quotation; "Emma Tenayuca," UTSA; Vargas, "Tejana Radical," 231–232; Blackwelder, "Tenayuca," 204–205. According to the 1940 Menefee and Cassmore government report cited earlier, "over 1,000 pickets were arrested during the strike" and "tear gas was used on 6 or 8 occasions during the first two weeks of the strike" (Sect. 17).

45. González, "Tenayuca," 214–215, 1st quotation on 214, 4th quotation on 215; Gower, "Unintended Consequences," 94–95, 2nd quotation on 95, 3rd quotation on 94; Poyo, Interview, 5th quotation. In the previously cited "A Careful Balance," Laura Cannon writes that "as long as the Anglo community thought Communists were running the walkout," groups such as LULAC and the Mexican Chamber of Commerce "could not openly support strikers" (90). She notes that, once communism was not an issue any longer, the Mexican-American business community began to indicate support for the workers' wage demands. Cannon also points out that Tenayuca was not the only leader of the strike to be removed because of suspected Communist affiliations. Regarding Tenayuca's religious disillusionment, in a letter to Lupe Anguiano, dated September 6, 1975, the Tejana admits that she "once dropped the church" and that, despite having returned, "at times I feel spiritually bankrupt." This letter can be found in ETC, MSS Box 3, Folder labeled "Anguiano, Lupe 1975."

46. Vargas, "Tejana Radical," 231, 1st quotation, as quoted; Rips, "Living History," 11; Winegarten, *Las Tejanas*, 143; Blackwelder, *Women of the Depression*, 145, 2nd quotation; Laura Cannon Dixon, "Police Brutality Makes Headlines: Retelling the Story of the 1938 Pecan Shellers' Strike" (M.A. thesis, Indiana State University, 2010), 27, 3rd quotation.

47. Blackwelder, *Women of the Depression*, 148; Vargas, "Tejana Radical," 231–232, 1st quotation on 231; Blackwelder, "Tenayuca," 206; McDonald, "Chicanas," 12, 2nd and 3rd quotations, as quoted.

48. Blackwelder, "Tenayuca," 204–205; "The American Civil Liberties Union of Texas: 70 Proud Years of Defending Rights in the Lone Star State," ACLU of Texas, pamphlet, nd, www.aclutx.org [hereinafter cited as "Defending Rights," ACLU pamphlet].

49. Cannon, "A Careful Balance," 97–98, 1st quotation on 98; Menefee and Cassmore, *Pecan Shellers*, Sect. 18, 2nd and 3rd quotations; Blackwelder, *Women of the Depression*, 141, 143; Keyworth, "Poverty," 117, 120–124, passim; Blackwelder, "Tenayuca," 205; Gower, "Unintended Consequences, 98, 4th quotation. Although Julius Seligmann's surname is spelled Seligman in a quotation in this paragraph, a number of sources spell it with two n's, which will be the practice in this chapter.

50. Keyworth, "Poverty, Opportunity, and Solidarity" 124–126, 1st quotation on 124; Gower, "Unintended Consequences," 99, 2nd quotation; Blackwelder, "Tenayuca, 205–206.

51. Vargas, "Tejana Radical," 232–233; Blackwelder, *Women of the Depression*, 149, quotation; Blackwelder, "Tenayuca," 206.

52. Emma Tenayuca and Homer Brooks, "Officers of the Texas Communist Party, Outline Their Vision for Mexican Unification, 1939," excerpt from "The Mexican Question in the Southwest," *Communist*, March 1939, 264–265, reproduced in *Major Problems in Texas History: Documents and Essays*, eds. Sam Haynes and Cary Wintz (Boston: Houghton Mifflin Co., 2002), 380–381, 3rd quotation on 381; Michelle A. Holling, "A Dispensational Rhetoric in 'The Mexican Question in the Southwest,' " in *Border Rhetorics: Citizenship and Identity on the US-Mexico Frontier*, ed. Robert De Chaine (Tuscaloosa: University of Alabama Press, 2012), 76–77, 80, 84n2, 2nd quotation on 80; Calderón and Zamora, "Manuela Solis Sager and Emma Tenayuca," in *Chicana Voices*, 34–35, 1st quotation on 34.

53. Richard B. Henderson, *Maury Maverick: A Political Biography* (Austin: University of Texas Press, 1970), 176–177, 192–193, 1st and 2nd quotations on 176, 3rd quotation on 193; "Defending Rights," ACLU pamphlet, 4th quotation.

54. Henderson, *Maverick*, 214–215; Vargas, "Tejana Radical," 235; González, "Tenayuca," 217.

55. González, "Tenayuca," 217–218, 1st quotation on 218; Rips, "Living History," 11; Vargas, "Tejana Radical," 235; Roberto Botello, "Women's History Month: Emma Tenayuca," reprinted from *People's Weekly World*, March 15, 2008, 2nd quotation, http://cpusa.org/women-s-history-month-emma-tenayuca.

56. Henderson, *Maverick*, 215–216, 1st, 2nd, and 3rd quotations on 215; Blackwelder, *Women of the Depression*, 150; González, "Tenayuca," 217, 4th quotation; Keyworth, "Poverty," 128.

57. González, "Tenayuca," 281, 1st quotation, as quoted; Blackwelder, *Women of the Depression*, 150, 2nd quotation; Henderson, *Maverick*, 225–228, passim.

58. Blackwelder, *Women of the Depression*, 150, 1st quotation; "Tenayuca," *Atzlan*, 2000, 2nd quotation; González, "Tenayuca," 218; Vargas, "Tejana Radical," 236; *HOT Online*, Abigail and León, "Tenayuca," 3rd quotation.

59. Vargas, "Tejana Radical," 235–36, 1st quotation on 235; González, "Tenayuca," 219, 2nd, 3rd, and 4th quotations; Emma Tenayuca, State Chairman, "Communist Party of Texas 1940 State Platform," https://archive.org/stream/CommunistPartyOfTexas1940StatePlatform_153/1940plat4_djvu.txt.

60. Blackwelder, "Tenayuca," 207, quotation; McDonald, "Chicanas," 14; González, "Tenayuca," 218.

61. Blackwelder, "Tenayuca," 207; González, "Tenayuca," 219; "Tenayuca," Biography Resource Center, 1st quotation; Tenayuca to Lupe Anguiano, September 6, 1975, 2nd and 3rd quotations; Vargas, "Tejana Radical," 236, 4th quotation.

62. Poyo Interview, quotation; Zamora, Interview; "Tenayuca, Emma (21 Dec. 1916–23, July 1999)," *American National Biography Online*, www.anb.org/articles/15/15–0132.html; *HOT Online*, Abigail and León, "Tenayuca"; Biography Resource Center; González, "Tenayuca," 221.

63. "Events in the Life of Emma Tenayuca," The Hispanic Experience: Civil Rights Movement, Houston Institute for Culture, Special Feature, http://www.houstonculture.org/hispanic/tenayuca.html; McDonald, "Chicanas," 15, quotation; Blackwelder, "Tenayuca," 207.

64. McDonald, "Chicanas," 15; "Events in the Life of Emma Tenayuca," Houston Institute for Culture; *HOT Online*, Abigail and León, "Tenayuca."

65. "Henry Cisneros," *Encyclopaedia Britannica*, https://www.britannica.com/biography/Henry-Cisneros; Draft, Emma Tenayuca to Honorable Henry Cisneros, August 12, 1986; Henry G. Cisneros, Mayor, to Emma Tenayuca, October 3, 1986, quotation; Henry G. Cisneros, Mayor, to Emma Tenayuca, August 28, 1987. All correspondence cited in this endnote can be found in the Emma Tenayuca Collection, Box 4, Henry Cisneros Folder, Texas Woman's Collection.

66. "Emma Tenayuca, December 21, 1916-July 23, 1999: '*La Pasionaria de Texas*,'" 1st quotation, houstoncpusa-com1.webs.com/documents/emmatenayuca,pdf; "Biography-Emma Tenayuca," 2nd quotation, latinopia.com/latino-history/emma-tenayuca/; Roberto Botello, "Women's History Month: Emma Tenayuca," 3rd quotation, http://cpusa.org/women-s-history-month-emma-tenayuca; Teresa Córdova, Norma Cantú, et al., *Chicana Voices: Intersections of Class, Race, and Gender* (Albuquerque: University of New Mexico Press, 1990), ix, xxi; Office of the Governor [Mark White], to Emma Tenayuca, September 30, 1985, ETC, Box 5, Correspondence, Nasworthy, Carol Folder; *HOT Online*, Abigail and León, "Tenayuca," 4th quotation; Bob Bullock, Comptroller of Public Accounts, to Emma Tenayuca, August 3, 1988, ETC MSS Box 3, Bob Bullock Folder, 5th quotation; Elaine Ayala, "Marker to Honor Labor Leader: Celebration Is Today at Milam Park," updated Wednesday, December 21, 2011, 6th and 7th quotations, http://www.mysanantonio.com/news/local_news/article/Marker-to-honor-labor-leader-2416153.php.

67. Blackwelder, "Tenayuca," 207, 1st quotation; "Tenayuca," *Aztlan*, 2000; Pisano, "Legendary Leader," 2nd quotation.

68. Blackwelder, "Tenayuca," 207, all quotations.

69. "Tenayuca," *Aztlan*, 2000, 1st quotation; Carmen Tafolla, "*La Pasionaria para Emma Tenayuca* (December 21, 1916-July 23-1999)," (San Antonio: Wings Press, 1999), copy at Benson Latin American Collection, University of Texas at Austin, 2nd quotation.

70. McDonald, "Chicanas," 16, all quotations, as quoted.

Photograph of Jovita González. E.E. Mireles and Jovita González Mireles Collection, Box 47, Mary and Jeff Bell Library Special Collections and Archives, Texas A&M University-Corpus Christi.

Jovita González
and Edmundo E. Mireles

*Gente Decente**

WHEN JOVITA GONZÁLEZ MARRIED Edmundo E. Mireles in 1935, she had already achieved more than most Mexican Americans of her generation, male or female. By age thirty, the Tejana was an accomplished folklorist, historian, speaker, author, and teacher. As for her husband, the erudite Mexican-born Mireles was destined to become a renowned pioneer in bilingual education. At a critical time in American history, the notable couple worked together for decades to promote the teaching of Spanish language and culture in public schools.

As Mireles gained prominence on the local, state, and national scenes, his career eclipsed that of his wife. Not until the late twentieth century, after both Jovita and Edmundo were deceased, did the efforts of a few dedicated scholars reawaken appreciation for González's historical importance. Today she is recognized as a ground-breaking Mexican-American woman, even more celebrated than her husband. To understand how and why she became more acclaimed in death than in life, one must examine the individual and collective stories of Jovita González and Edmundo E. Mireles.

***

Jovita González came from a family with proud roots but few financial resources. Her mother, Severina Guerra Barrera, was a

housewife whose Spanish ancestors held an impressive land grant
in the Rio Grande region during the colonial period. Her father,
Jacobo González Rodríguez, was a teacher in Tamaulipas, Mexico.
Their baby girl was born around 1904 on her grandparent's San
Román Ranch in the border region near Roma, Texas. Her early
years on the ranch significantly shaped her life. González and her
sister would go horseback riding with their grandfather, take long
walks with their father, and visit with the *vaqueros* (cowboys).
The girls were fascinated by the cowboys' tales of "ranch lore" and
their border ballads. Also entertaining were stories about ghosts
and witches. These experiences helped the sisters gain pride in
their Hispanic heritage. From their grandmother they also learned
that family roots had been planted in Texas long before the Anglos
arrived, and she impressed upon them that "Texas is our home.
Always remember these words: Texas is ours."[1]

The Spanish language was also an integral part of the family's
identity, and Jovita's father initially did not allow English spoken
in his home. But his pride in being a Mexican American did not
blind him to obstacles facing Tejanos in the early twentieth century.
With the coming of the railroad and increased migration from the
American Midwest, the border region was changing to the disadvantage of Mexican Texans, regarded as inferior by the rapidly
growing Anglo population. These concerns, combined with the
realization that his children were receiving an inferior education
at the small one-teacher, ranch-supported school, convinced their
father of the need to relocate. The senior González decided to move
his family to San Antonio in 1910, but the children's adjustment
to that Anglo-dominated city proved difficult. Fortunately, Jovita
was a talented student who earned the equivalent of a high school
diploma while still in her teens.[2]

Acquiring a high school education was an unusual accomplishment for a Mexican-American woman in that era, but the
Tejana longed for additional learning. Her goal was to attend

The University of Texas at Austin, an institution then admitting only a small number of Mexican Americans. Although they were not prohibited from admission, as were African Americans, "lack of class/academic preparation and other cultural resources" often proved insurmountable obstacles. González had the requisite academic ability, but financial necessity forced her to delay her dream, and she enrolled in a much less expensive Normal school. There she earned a teaching certificate in two years. Then, with the assistance of her uncle, the young woman landed a teaching position in Rio Grande City. She lived there with him and his family to save money for her aspiration of attending the coveted university in Austin.[3]

In the early 1920s, González's hard work enabled her to enroll at The University of Texas at Austin. She studied Spanish under Professor Lilia Casis, who became a role model for the younger woman. Unfortunately, she was forced to return to San Antonio within a year when her funds ran out. There she directed a small school until she received a scholarship in 1924 to cover her major expenses at Our Lady of the Lake College. With this assistance, she earned a Bachelor of Arts degree in Spanish in 1927. Determined to study under Casis, even while enrolled at Our Lady of the Lake, the Tejana managed to take summer courses in Austin with her role model. This afforded González a chance to interact with other noted members of The University of Texas faculty, such as folklorist J. Frank Dobie, who was to play a critical role in her life, and historian Carlos E. Castañeda, who was a friend of the Tejana's family.[4]

Dobie, "the man who had put Texas folklore studies on the map," became the Tejana's mentor for about twenty years. Early in their relationship, the two were formal in their interactions with each other. Later, however, Jovita came to address him as "my godfather" and "*muy amigo mío*" (my very good friend). The famed folklorist had a profound influence on the Tejana. Although she had always been fascinated by folk tales of the border region,

Dobie helped her to understand their importance to other people, and he encouraged her to record those stories in written form. At his urging, González began collecting and writing border history. Her specialty became transforming oral traditions into short stories or sketches that appealed to "readers who preferred a refined quality of literature."[5]

Dobie helped open doors for the Tejana that would otherwise have been closed to a minority woman. González's talents, however, allowed her to take advantage of opportunities that presented themselves. Her mentor was a prominent figure in the Texas Folklore Society (TFS), and because of him, the young woman gained acceptance into that prestigious group. She became part of an "unprecedented dialogue between Anglo and 'ethnic' public intellectuals" that allowed the latter to play a role in preserving Texas's history and culture. González first appeared on the annual TFS program in 1927. Despite her own impressive ancestry, the Tejana chose not to talk about "the landed proprietor who, in my part of the state, forms the better class." Instead, she focused on "the socially alienated *vaquero*." Jovita's formal presentation was accompanied by Mexican cowboys who sang ballads. Not only was the speech well received by the audience, but it also led to her first publication, an article in *Texas Southwestern Lore*, the official journal of the TFS.[6] This possibly was the first time a Mexican American in Texas had published an essay in English, and the Mexican-American folklorist was just getting started. Soon thereafter, she became a regular speaker at the TFS's annual program.

At the 1928 TFS conference, Jovita presented a story entitled "The Woman Who Lost Her Soul," which was also published. The tale involves Don Francisco, who changes as a result of contact with a young woman named Carmen. "Spoiled and very selfish," Carmen has an affair with her best friend's fiancé. The devastated friend, as she lies dying, warns Carmen that "my spirit will torture yours from Hell." Carmen's mother then dies of shame, and people treat the young woman as an outcast. "A living corpse," she believes that her soul is with her "victim in Hell." With the intervention of a priest, Don Francisco learns a valuable lesson about forgiveness of his own daughter, as he and his wife try to help Carmen "become her old self again."[7]

With tales, such as "The Woman Who Lost Her Soul," the Tejana sought "to create tolerance and mutual understanding" between Anglos and Hispanics. That her efforts were effective is evident by the recognition she received early in her career. By the end of the 1920s, González's speeches and publications made her one of the "stars" of the TFS. After serving two terms as secretary, she was elected vice-president of the organization in 1929.[8]

Despite her literary accomplishments, Jovita was determined to continue her formal education. But, again, money was a problem. By 1927, she had taken a position as a Spanish teacher at Saint Mary's Hall in San Antonio. With the help of Saint Mary's director and Professor Dobie, within two years Jovita received the Lapham Scholarship. This finally allowed her to pursue graduate studies in Austin. Being a Tejana at The University of Texas brought mixed blessings, however. As a graduate student under the direction of historian Eugene C. Barker, Jovita had access to a quality education, available to few of her gender or ethnicity. Indeed, she was one of perhaps thirty Mexican Americans from the Rio Grande Valley and one of about 250 from the entire state who attended the university at the time. Outside the classroom, González took time to embrace her Hispanic heritage by joining the Latin American Club, the Newman Club for Catholic students, and the *Junta del Club de Bellas Artes* (Fine Arts Club).[9] Celebrating that same heritage in the classroom proved much more difficult.

Jovita learned hard lessons as a Mexican American woman at a university then controlled by Anglo males. White professors, including Dobie, praised the role of Anglo Americans in Texas's past but ignored the injustices done to Mexico and its people. Minorities were presented as "inferior . . . and wholly unequal to the [other] Texans." Upset by the racist overtones of what was being taught in some of her courses, the Tejana nevertheless understood that to challenge her professors openly would threaten her status as a student and future teacher. Although she kept her tongue in the classroom or avoided certain classes altogether, González found other means by which to express her views. Based on her love and understanding of border people, she proposed to do her master's thesis on social life in three heavily Hispanic South Texas counties, but her major professor declared the topic unsuitable, and it was certainly nontraditional. Acting on González's behalf, Castañeda argued that her work would prove useful "in the years to come as source material." Persuaded, Barker let the Tejana proceed with one of the few theses being written at the time that did not present "Mexicans as a social problem."[10]

In planning her research trips into Cameron, Starr, and Zapata Counties, the graduate student was well aware that women of her day did not normally engage in activities like her undertaking. People in South Texas might well be reluctant to share their histories with her; so she needed them to understand that she was respectable, even though she was pursuing a career path usually reserved for men. Soliciting letters of introduction from Catholic and Episcopal officials and clergy, the Tejana benefitted from being "Maestro Jacobo's daughter . . . and Don Francisco Guerra's granddaughter," as well as "*una persona decente*" (a decent or refined person). To be seen as one of the "*gente decente*" was very important to Jovita González, because the words meant that one had good breeding, as opposed to the less refined and poorly educated "*gente corriente*" (common people). Even though her family was "lower middle class" during her lifetime, she never forgot that her ancestors once had been among the elite. That she worked to preserve the culture and customs of lower class Mexican Texans, a group from which birth set her apart, was only one of several ironies that marked her life.[11]

Another irony was that González's thesis on "Social Life in Cameron, Starr, and Zapata Counties" presented Texas history from a perspective that was notably different from that taught by her major professor, Barker. He and other historians of the time wrote books that, for the most part, justified "Anglo imperialism" as preordained, glorified the defenders of the Alamo, and considered the Texas Revolution to be the beginning of "a new utopia." Countering that interpretation, González pointed out that Spaniards and Mexicans had been in the state long before Anglos arrived and deprived them of their land. She called attention to the positive aspects of the Hispanic heritage in South Texas but also acknowledged the flaws in a system that allowed exploitation of *peónes* (peasants) and domination of women. González's thesis also contained chapters on more current topics such as "Present Mexican Population in the Counties Considered," "Border Politics," and "What the Coming of the Americans Has Meant to the Border People." The Tejana believed the early twentieth century was bringing a "Renaissance to the border counties." A new generation of Tejanos, with "a clearer understanding of the good and bad qualities of both races," was becoming Americanized. Presciently, she wrote that they had strong traditions behind them and "a struggle for equality and justice before the law" in front of them. González concluded her thesis with the hope that this new generation would "bring to an end the racial feuds that have existed in the border for nearly a century."[12]

Despite its controversial nature, "Social Life in Cameron, Starr, and Zapata Counties" helped González meet the requirements for her master's degree. After graduating from The University of Texas in August 1930, she continued to teach at Saint Mary's Hall and to be professionally active. At the annual TFS meeting that year, the folklorist presented what was to become one of her best known tales, "The Devil on the Border." The story features a Tejano, Pedro de Urdemañas, who appears unexpectedly in hell one day and convinces the devil to go to Texas. Unpleasant experiences with chili peppers, a prickly pear cactus, and an angry cow cause a humiliated Satan to rush back home and kick the Tejano out of hell. Since then, González informed her audience, Satan has never returned to the Lone Star State. Urdemañas, on the other hand, "still wanders through the Texas ranches always in the shape of some fun-loving *vaquero*."[13]

By 1930 González's star was shining so brightly that she became the first ever Mexican- American woman to be elected president of the TFS, an office to which she was reelected the next year. Since the organization had few female or Hispanic members, her two terms in its highest office were especially noteworthy. That same year, the Tejana felt secure enough to vent some of her frustrations, and not just remain silent. In an article entitled "America Invades the Border Towns," she criticized Anglos and Hispanics for their roles in the "racial struggle" that gripped South Texas from 1848 to 1930. She described Anglos as "an aggressive, conquering, and materialistic people" but also labeled those of her ethnicity as "a volatile but passive and easily satisfied race." With this published article, her completed thesis, and Dobie's support, the Tejana received a prestigious Rockefeller Grant in 1934. This enabled her to take a year's leave from teaching "to research and write a book on South Texas history and culture." The materials gathered for her book were used later for program presentations at professional meetings and for additional published articles.[14]

Although the professional side of Jovita's life was going remarkably well, she was still unwed at age thirty. Reasons for her delaying marriage perhaps seem obvious, because educational and professional goals had consumed the Tejana's time, energy, and resources for years. And she still held hopes of pursuing a doctorate degree. The severe economic depression in the United States

"To Jovita, whose friendship I have always cherished, E. E. Mireles" reads the inscription on this portrait. Collection 033, Series IX, Photographs, 1957–1975, a matted photo of Edmundo Mireles, age 26, with an inscription to Jovita González. Jovita González Papers, The Wittliff Collections, Texas State University.

also complicated Jovita's life. As a working woman and graduate student, Jovita not only had to support herself, but she also was compelled to help her family as the economy worsened in the 1930s.[15] Not all obstacles to marriage were financial, however. As a proud Mexican-American, González probably aspired to marry within her ethnic group, but for a strong, intelligent, and non-traditional woman to find a compatible mate was problematic. Another reality was that Jovita lived in an era when men were dominant over women in American society. This dominance was even more pronounced in Mexican culture, where wives were expected to be submissive to their husbands. Having already learned hard lessons about silence and submission, González undoubtedly had serious reservations about surrendering her independence.

Regardless of the factors that had kept her single, the Tejana put aside these concerns and married Edmundo E. Mireles in 1935. The two had met while students at The University of Texas and formed a "cherished" friendship.[16] Later, during their long years together, Jovita González would learn that marriage to a strong Mexican-American male bore some resemblance to being a graduate student at The University of Texas. On occasion, she had to make difficult compromises and prudently remain silent.

Who was this man for whom González was willing to make such sacrifices? Mireles, in many respects, was a worthy partner for this accomplished Mexican-American woman. His father, Sostenes, was a merchant in Mexico, where Edmundo was born in late 1905. The circumstances of his upbringing are unclear, but it is certain that the boy grew up in San Antonio, where he was schooled and learned English. As an adolescent, he returned to Mexico with his father to fight in the revolution engulfing their country of origin. After being wounded, Edmundo returned to San Antonio, where he graduated from Main Avenue High in 1926, took classes at San Antonio College, and then transferred

Wedding portrait of Jovita González and Edmundo E. Mireles, 1935. E.E. Mireles and Jovita González Mireles Collection, Box 47, Mary and Jeff Bell Library Special Collections and Archives, Texas A&M University-Corpus Christi.

to The University of Texas to study classical languages. Active in extra-curricular activities and a promising student of Greek and Latin, the scholarly Mireles became president of the Classical Language Club. He also served as editor of the university's first Latino newspaper. After receiving his college degree in 1931, the young man returned to San Antonio to teach at the same high school from which he had graduated and married Jovita González four years later.[17]

The husband and wife had much in common, even though Edmundo was born in Mexico and Jovita in Texas. Both were literate in English, as well as Spanish. Both were alumni of The University of Texas, and given their levels of education and career opportunities, they differed significantly from the vast majority of Texans of their ethnicity. Nevertheless, the two of them took pride in their heritage, as evidenced by their extra-curricular activities in college and their becoming teachers of Spanish. Mireles was no doubt impressed with his wife's accomplishments, possibly even a bit intimidated by them. That González was his equal was apparent. The question of whether such an unusually accomplished Tejana would make a satisfactory wife was another matter altogether. Nonetheless, despite any misgivings they probably shared, their marriage lasted for almost fifty years until "death did them part." With the help of Professor Castañeda at The University of Texas, the newlyweds were hired by the San Felipe School District in Del Rio, Texas. The husband became a high school principal, while the wife taught English and served as department head. Together they played a significant role in public education for the community of San Felipe.[18]

González Mireles aspired to continue with her own education. Expressing interest in doctoral programs at leading universities in California and New Mexico, she requested reference letters from former professors, including Dobie. However, this aspiration was never achieved. Possibly finances were again a factor, but almost certainly marital considerations came into play, as pursuing a Ph.D. would mean prolonged absences from home. One questions whether Mireles would have been supportive of that eventuality. Had there been a major university closer to where they lived, Gonález might well have had the opportunity to pursue a doctorate, but that was not the case in Del Rio or later in Corpus Christi, where they resided for decades.[19]

For a time after her marriage, the Tejana did remain active as a folklorist and author with articles appearing in the mid-1930s. Among her better known works from this period is "Bullet Swallower." This title was Jovita's contribution to *Puro Mexicano* (*Pure Mexican*), a compilation of Mexican folklore edited by Dobie and published in 1935. "Bullet Swallower" is narrated by Antonio, "a landowner by inheritance, a trail driver by necessity, and a smuggler and gambler by choice." As they cross the Rio Grande, Antonio and his companions are confronted by Texas Rangers. The men resist, because "it was not ethical among smugglers to lose the property of Mexicans to Americans." Death would be better than dishonor. During the confrontation, one of the Rangers shoots Antonio, but he survives. Later he boasts that "the bullet knocked all of my front teeth out, grazed my tongue and went right through the back of my neck. Didn't kill me, though." After this episode, the folk hero is called Antonio Bullet-Swallower. As he brags: "It takes a lot to kill a man . . . who can swallow bullets." Also, the Tejana made another presentation mid-decade at the twenty-second annual meeting of the TFS in Austin. She was one of only two Hispanics on the program that year, the other being Adina De Zavala, covered in the previous chapter. Indeed, by the end of 1930s, "González was considered a national expert on the Mexican Americans of the Southwest and was 'one of the first native scholars of Mexican-American cultures and very probably the first woman.'"[20]

While his wife was busy as a teacher and folklorist, Edmundo Mireles endeavored to improve conditions for fellow Hispanics.

He helped found a political group called *Club Político Latino* (Latino Political Club), and he also played an active role in the League of United Latin-American Citizens (LULAC), "a patriotic organization made up of United States citizens of Latin or Mexican descent." Mireles was attracted to LULAC, because it encouraged maintaining pride in one's Mexican heritage but stressed being "a true and loyal citizen of the United States of America" as the best means for achieving full political and civil rights. The emphasis on a "dual cultural approach" was very much in line with Mireles's own philosophy.[21]

In the late 1930s, the Mireleses moved to Corpus Christi, because LULAC members from that coastal city had recruited them. In their new home, Mireles became a fifth-grade teacher at Southgate School, while his wife taught at a high school. She also continued to labor on a long-term project dear to her heart: a historical novel, based in part on research funded by her Rockefeller grant. She wanted to record the culture of South Texas as it had existed before the Anglos arrived in the 1840s and imposed their way of life on those living along the border. Before moving to the Gulf Coast, González had asked Margaret Eimer of Del Rio to serve as co-author of the proposed novel. Perhaps the Tejana believed that a story about "the Mexican side of the war of 1848" would have a better chance of publication with an Anglo's name also appearing on the title page. No doubt the difficulty of completing the novel without assistance, given other demands on her time, likewise influenced the Tejana's decision. In any event, Eimer accepted the invitation but, given the controversial nature of the project, chose to write under the pseudonym Eve Raleigh. For years the two women "worked so hard to finish and get the manuscript on the market" that they were "sick of the thing" when it was finally completed. They nonetheless submitted the novel to three publishers, one of which "admitted that the background is interesting, the plot stirring, [and] the characters alive." But in the end, all three firms sent rejection notices. Discouraged, the co-authors then abandoned the project by the late 1940s.[22]

The unpublished novel focuses on the elite Mendoza y Soría clan during the period when the United States militarily occupied South Texas from 1845 to 1848, with flashbacks to earlier periods. The family head, Don Santiago, is proud and domineering. He and other aristocrats are determined "to resist Anglo intruders to the death." Their sisters and daughters, however, react differently, and some of them form unions with the Anglos, relationships that "become the glue for a new society." The patriarch threatens to disown his favorite child, Susanita, who falls in love with an Anglo army officer, and loses her as a consequence. Similarly, Don Santiago becomes estranged from his artistic second son whom he considers effeminate, when Luis resists his father's dictates. Refusing to accommodate to the new reality, the patriarch also faces the loss of his land to Anglo-American squatters, one of whom declares "We be white folks and this is the United States, ain't it? We got the right of it." As the novel ends, Don Santiago dies "lonely and with no heir, clinging to a handful of dirt from his ranch." His fate symbolizes what lies in store for many Tejanos.[23]

Significantly, Edmundo Mireles was not unhappy that his wife's co-authored manuscript had been rejected for publication. She had wanted to deliver a message about the past, while his focus was on the present. He shared his wife's desire to be regarded as among the "*gente decente*," thereby gaining respect and acceptance, but in his view, her novel put them at risk. He and Jovita were especially vulnerable in their positions as public school teachers in Corpus Christi, where "the walls of racial prejudice" were high. Edmundo also feared that the themes of injustice by Anglo Americans, as presented in his wife's manuscript, would anger "both Anglo bigots *and* Chicano nationalists." Since Jovita had set aside plans to publish the novel, Edmundo insisted on destroying manuscript, despite her objections. Once again, circumstances forced concessions on the

Tejana. She did not openly defy Edmundo but instead secretly saved a copy of her manuscript. She did, however, give up all hope of publishing it in her lifetime.[24]

Probably in reaction to her failed publication, as well as her husband's objection to it, the Tejana "limited her folklore writing and focused . . . [instead] on teaching Spanish and on being a wife." Also, some signs indicate that she was becoming disillusioned with the limited possibilities of folklore to effect meaningful change for people of her ethnicity, which also may have contributed to her becoming more involved in "the battle for educational equity for Mexicanos that her husband championed."[25] Regardless of the reasons for the career shift, public awareness of her earlier achievements as Jovita González faded over time, and the people of Corpus Christi came to regard her as Mrs. Edmundo E. Mireles. Meanwhile, her husband's career was on the ascent. He was the right man in the right place at the right time.

Committed to the teaching of Spanish to English-speaking students, Edmundo de Mireles faced many obstacles. Not the least of these was a law enacted by the Texas legislature in 1918, more than twenty years before the Mireleses moved to Corpus Christi. This legislation required all public school classes, except foreign language courses, to be taught in English. In lower grades, foreign languages could not be taught at all. Passed during World War I, the "English Only" policy grew out of patriotic support for the war effort and fear of ethnic German immigrants. The Lone Star State had a large German population, dating back to the mid-1800s. The original immigrants and their descendants had maintained their native language and culture, which made them objects of suspicion in wartime. This enabled supporters of the 1918 law to insist "that they were defending the culture of those who died at the Alamo" against undesirable foreign influences. However, long after the war ended, the English-Only rule persisted in Texas, but with a new target. Fleeing from the chaos of the 1910

Mexican Revolution, increasing numbers of Mexico's citizens had been drawn to the United States by its geographic closeness, its economic opportunity, and its political stability. Texas's leaders were concerned about immigrants who did not understand English. These concerns bled over to Mexican Americans as well. They, too, were suspect as "men and women, born and reared in the Lone Star State, who speak a foreign tongue and cherish the habits and ways of another country."[26]

"Americanization" of Mexican Americans became a major goal in the Lone Star State. For example, in 1930 the State Department of Education created a special English-Only curriculum for Spanish-speaking children in first and second grades, and the policy "was applied ruthlessly." In extreme cases, Hispanic children could be suspended from school if they spoke a single word in their birth tongue. Besides being made to feel ashamed of their language, Spanish-speaking children had trouble comprehending what was being taught in the classroom. Labeled slow learners, these youngsters were separated from other students. Poor scores on intelligence tests seemed to justify the low opinion of their abilities, and many educators chose to overlook the possibility that English-language tests did not fairly measure the intelligence of minority children.[27]

That Hispanics were darker-skinned than whites was another strike against them. Regarding people of color as inferior, Anglo Americans kept apart from minorities as much as possible. African-American students were prevented by law from attending the same schools as whites, but Mexican-American students with their Spanish and Indian parentage were considered white. They were not subject to legal segregation based on race, but the English-Only policy led to the same practical result, de facto (in effect) "segregated schools for Tejanos." Many of these students were further handicapped by their circumstances of living lived in poverty with poorly educated parents clustered in low-income neighborhoods with substandard schools. Not surprisingly, then, Mexican-American youths had a "shocking failure or drop out rate," which further reinforced notions of their inferiority.[28]

Long overdue changes, however, were on the horizon by the time the Mireleses moved to Corpus Christi near the end of the 1930s. Once again international events and a world war fostered changes in the educational system. This time, however, the reforms would work to the benefit of Hispanic students. With Germany and Japan engaged in aggressive actions abroad, the United States faced possible involvement in another world war. Concerned American officials knew that poor relations between the United States and Spanish-speaking nations in the Western Hemisphere could be exploited by the country's enemies. So the United States government moved to adopt a "Good Neighbor Policy," aimed at improving relationships in Latin America.[29]

Acutely aware that any successful Good Neighbor effort had to begin at home, in 1940 President Franklin D. Roosevelt named Nelson Rockefeller as Coordinator of Inter-American Affairs. Rockefeller's duties included introducing "Good Neighborism" into the nation's public schools. And somewhat surprisingly, Texas became "the most involved and cooperative state" in those efforts. The state's leaders pledged "to bring about a greater interest in our neighbor republics," as well as promote "more tolerance, acceptance, and understanding of Mexican Americans." To help achieve these goals, a state law, passed in 1941, called for the teaching of Spanish beyond the second grade in public schools. Legislators in Austin recognized the change as vital to the interests of their state and the United States.[30]

After more than two decades, English-Only was dead. The State Department of Education was instructed by the Texas legislature to create a "course of study for the teaching of Spanish to all Texas schoolchildren from the third to the eighth grade." And, of course, the state had a pioneer educator who had already created such a curriculum in Corpus Christi—Edmundo E. Mireles. He had long concluded that the future of the United States depended largely on "our ability to understand and influence other nations and to cooperate with them." His belief that "we shall never really know a people until we understand their language" explained why he had learned—and spoke—eight languages. To Mireles, however, language was about biculturalism as much as about bilingualism. Joining Mireles in his crusade was Corpus Christi's school district superintendent, R. B. Fisher. For the 1940–1941 academic year, the two men proposed a Spanish language program to help "the child to speak, read, and write the Spanish language," while also giving "the children the proper knowledge of Latin-American customs, history, and traditions." Students in grades three through eight would participate. However, because the proposed bilingual program was illegal under Texas law at that time, the district had to request special permission from the state. With that accomplished, Spanish instruction began in all Corpus Christi elementary schools in September 1940.[31]

Edmundo E. Mireles served as Coordinator of Spanish for the city's public schools. Initially, he oversaw more than seventy teachers and their more than five thousand students. Faced with a lack of qualified Spanish language teachers, Mireles exhibited a practical side. He insisted that it was "unnecessary to know much Spanish to teach a little." And, the Tejano did everything he could to ensure that teachers knew more than just "a little." He offered popular weekly training seminars and night courses, as well as reviewing lesson plans submitted by the head Spanish teacher in each school.[32]

The educator also worked with his wife and Superintendent Fisher on a textbook entitled *Mi Libro Español: Libro Uno (My Spanish Book: Book One)*. That she became involved in writing this book and in other aspects of her husband's bilingual program was not surprising. After all, she was a native Spanish speaker, an experienced language teacher, and a published author. Apparently, her husband had no objection to her writings when they suited his purposes. In *Libro Uno*, the authors explained that a simple and logical method was being used in the Spanish program to avoid traditional, boring exercises in grammar. As a result, the 6,500 students who had participated were reportedly "eager to continue." Also, the first year of the pilot program "proved that a modern language properly presented is relatively easy for young children." The authors listed the three major objectives of the Spanish language program. They were "to give the child the ability to speak and read a language he hears daily," to help him or her become familiar with "Latin American history and culture, conditions and customs," and "to create a sympathetic attitude toward other peoples and their ways." The thirty lessons in the textbook were designed to accomplish those objectives. Also recommended were that at least twenty minutes a day be spent in the classroom on Spanish instruction and that each school create a Pan American Club to meet about an hour each week. In all, three volumes of *Mi Libro Español* were published for use in Spanish language instruction. The Mireleses in the 1940s also produced a six-part textbook series for the bilingual program called *El Español Elemental (Basic Spanish)*.[33]

Edmundo Mireles was dedicated to the success of the Spanish language program, which he directed for a quarter of a century. And, succeed it did. Praise came from many quarters. A university professor complimented him for "pioneering in a movement which is of vital interest to Americans today and especially to Texans." As evidence of this, requests for copies of Corpus Christi's Spanish language course of study came from as far away as New Jersey. Powerful national figures also recognized the value of the Corpus Christi model. In 1940, Congressman Richard Kleberg of Kingsville, Texas, noted that a "neighborly and friendly relationship between North and South America" was very important.

Because the elementary grades were the best time to learn a foreign language, he declared his support for Mireles's exemplary program. Even more impressive, Good Neighbor Coordinator Nelson Rockefeller wrote Mireles that he "was most interested to hear of your work in teaching Spanish in Corpus Christi." He added, "It is most important for North Americans to know Spanish and for South and Central Americans to know English in order that a deeper understanding and friendship may be achieved." And First Lady Eleanor Roosevelt wrote, "I hope that every school in this country will teach the children to consider Spanish as their second most important language. I am studying Spanish every day I can."[34]

Time magazine in February 1944 featured an article on the Corpus Christi model and the "passionate" Mireles. The educator himself was described as a "Mild-mannered Teacher" who was a mixture of Latin and American. The author noted that Mireles kept "two books on his desk: Shakespeare and Cervantes," which represented the best of literature in English and Spanish. Mireles was quoted as hopeful that bilingual children would lead "adults a long way toward inter-American understanding." Indeed, the article reported that "in Corpus Christi more than 600 adults have enrolled in night Spanish classes in order to keep up with their children."[35]

Despite national attention, probably the greatest impact of the Spanish program was within Texas. In 1942 Thurmond Krueger of the Texas Junior Chamber of Commerce declared that Mireles's language program had "put Corpus Christi and Texas on the map." The intense focus on the Spanish language model was caused in part by the entry of the United States into World War II in 1941. As millions of Americans entered the armed forces, serious labor shortages resulted. One solution was a formal arrangement for Mexico to send workers to its northern neighbor. The historically poor treatment of Hispanics in the Southwest complicated the process, however, because the Mexican government wanted guarantees of protections for its citizens involved in the *bracero* program, which allowed the legal importation of workers from Mexico. Although the program formally began in 1942, Texas's record of discrimination delayed that state's participation until later in the decade. Better treatment of Hispanics became necessary for the sake of the war effort, however, and attempts were made to increase public awareness about the "discrimination being practiced . . . against Mexican nationals." In a powerful newspaper piece, Undersecretary of State Sumner Welles insisted that workers came north to seek good-paying jobs "to better themselves and the members of their family." They helped the "national war effort by relieving labor shortages." He believed many Americans were unaware of discrimination against Mexicans. This mistreatment must end, he declared, or "the term 'good-neighbor policy' will lose much of its real meaning."[36]

The Mireleses shared the concerns of Sumner Welles, as they worked inside and outside of the classroom to promote Pan Americanism. In one aspect of this work, they helped create the non-profit Pan American Council of Texas. Chartered in 1943 to do business in Corpus Christi, the organization was open to anyone over the age of eighteen with an interest "in the study of the Spanish language and the Latin American Republics." Jovita, under the name Mrs. E. E. Mireles, was a charter member, while Edmundo was not only president of the Council but also held a position on the Board of Directors. A formal goal of the Council was to have April 14 observed annually as Pan American Day, beginning in 1943. Spreading to other towns, the organization grew rapidly, and annual fiestas in Corpus Christi attracted thousands of people. Not immodestly, Mireles claimed that the Council was helping "to make this the best community in South Texas."[37]

The coastal city also benefitted in other ways because of the energetic Tejano's efforts. He helped the community at large by serving as Director of the Nueces County Tuberculosis Association, as well as being a member of the Corpus Christi War Housing

Board and Family Service Board. At one point, Mireles decided that he could better serve the people of the coastal region as a public official. He set his sights on a legislative seat in the 71ˢᵗ District, which included Nueces, Jim Wells, and Duval Counties. Although he advertised himself in the Democratic primary as a highly qualified candidate who "brought national recognition to Corpus Christi," his bid for public office failed. Rebounding from this failure, Mireles used the radio to campaign effectively for other Mexican-American candidates running for public office. Urging Latinos to vote "in favor of our own," he insisted that they must be active in the civic and political arenas. For some twenty-five years, he presented radio talks on a number of topics, many of which related not only to politics but also to education. The broadcasts informed Spanish-speaking parents on how to enroll their children in the public schools and explained the process by which low income students could receive free meals at school.[38]

Mireles also used the written word to good effect. In a Spanish-language article written for *Texas Outlook* in 1951, he provided an update on the language program in Corpus Christi. The educator restated his belief "that the greatest means of promoting friend-ship between Anglo Americans and Mexican Americans is for each to learn the language of the other." He reported that the Corpus Christi Spanish Program in its tenth year had 180 teachers and almost 10,000 students, which contributed to the government's efforts to achieve "international peace." Similar information was presented in an English-language piece by Mireles in *The American School Board Journal* two years later. In that article the program was reported to have 229 teachers and more than 10,500 students, notable growth for such a short period of time. That a man as involved as Mireles in multiple undertakings found time to pursue his own higher educa-tion is truly remarkable, but he not only took graduate courses in Austin but also earned a master's degree in Spanish in the early 1950s from a college in Monterrey, Mexico.[39]

While Edmundo was involved in bilingual education, politics, public service, speaking, writing, and studying, Jovita worked as a classroom teacher and by the mid-1950s was the Head Teacher in the Spanish program for Ray High School. She also directed "*pastorelas*, pageants, and Christmastime *posadas* with local Mexican children as . . . pilgrims for the entertainment of a mostly Anglo Audience." However, her activities were overshadowed by those of her renowned husband. In her personal life, the Tejana became distant from "the Mexican American local community." To the Anglos she was "upper crust." To her own people "she was either not known" or seemed "aloof, mixing only with the highly educated people of Anglo and Spanish/Mexican society." Her friends, whether Anglo or Hispanic, were "people of prestige."[40] This is not surprising, especially when one considers her level of education, as well as her desire to be considered a cultured person. Her husband probably approved of Jovita's limiting her social circle to the "upper crust," because he valued respectability, and it benefited his career.

Edmundo Mireles continued to play a key role in educational reforms in Corpus Christi for decades. In the 1950s, city leaders realized that "lack of the English language" placed Latino children at a disadvantage. They often had to repeat the same grade "again and again . . . through no fault of their own." A new summer program was begun in 1956 to prepare "six-year old Non-English speaking children to enter the first grade." The LULAC- supported pre-school training program taught a vocabulary of 500 English words and some 50 common expressions. Of the 152 students who participated in the first year, only three "failed to pass" to the next grade. By 1959, 680 children were enrolled in the rapidly growing program. And, predictably, the coordinator of the Corpus Christi pre-school program was none other than Edmundo Mireles. The Corpus Christi experiment attracted the attention of the Texas Education Agency, as well as state politicians. Mireles later claimed that this led to passage of House Bill 51 in the 56th legislature.

That law established optional "Head Start" pre-school training for non-English speaking students in all Texas school districts. Again, Corpus Christi led the way with Mireles playing a key role.[41]

Thoughtful people at all levels of government recognized that educational needs were not limited to children. The Economic Opportunity Act, passed by the United States Congress in 1964, aimed "to mobilize the human and financial resources of the nation to combat poverty in the United States." Consequently, Corpus Christi began an Adult Basic Education Program (ABE) for people eighteen or older who were unable to make a decent living because of illiteracy in English. Beginning in 1965 with 560 registered adults, the free program had 721 students by its third year of existence. It went far beyond the teaching of English by offering a variety of other subjects as well. By the early 1970s, the aging Edmundo Mireles was Coordinator of the ABE Program for Corpus Christi, yet another in his long line of administrative positions.[42]

As it turned out, Mireles remained active in the workforce longer than his increasingly reclusive wife, who retired in 1967, in part because she suffered "from diabetes and chronic depression." Attempts to write her autobiography, of which only a few paragraphs were devoted to her life following the relocation to Corpus Christi, proved abortive. If she were to be remembered after her death, it would have to be because others recognized the value of her early accomplishments. Fortunately, the "dynamic duo" of Jovita González and Edmundo E. Mireles came to the attention of historian Marta Cotera, who interviewed the couple during the 1970s. Having heard about the unpublished novel that González had written with Eimer, the interviewer asked about it. Edmundo responded that he had destroyed the manuscript, but Jovita made a little gesture that only Cotera could see. The interviewer believed that the Tejana was trying to let her know that a copy of the novel still existed. For reasons that will become apparent, that gesture proved significant after the couple were deceased, following nearly fifty years of marriage. Jovita died in 1983, followed four years later by Edmundo.[43]

Many in Corpus Christi wanted to honor the Mireleses for their tireless service to their community, and naming a school after them seemed a fitting tribute. However, the first two attempts to achieve this goal failed. In the late 1990s, renewed effort came from a committee determined to pursue "Project Mireles." It finally achieved success, and the press announced that a new elementary school was to be named "for the famous educator and his wife." Note that he was described as a "famous educator," while Jovita was simply "his wife." While the issue of naming a school for the Mireleses was under consideration in Corpus Christi, events occurred elsewhere that would make Jovita more than just Edmundo's wife. During their lifetimes, the couple had acquired "printed materials, correspondence, . . . handwritten notes, books, . . . photographs, artifacts, and sound recordings." With no children as heirs, the Mireleses left their estate to an employee, María Isabel Cruz. She, in turn, donated the library and papers to Texas A&M University at Corpus Christi, although some of the couple's materials found their way to the Nettie Lee Benson Latin American Collection at The University of Texas at Austin and to Texas State University in San Marcos.[44] These collections were treasure-troves, which led to Jovita González again becoming a person of well-deserved renown.

The Tejana's resurrection late in the twentieth century was due in part to the efforts of Teresa Palomo Acosta and Cynthia Orozco. At a 1990 conference on "Mexican Americans in Texas History," these two scholars helped raise awareness about what an exceptional woman González had been. Others interested in the life and works of Jovita González included María Eugenia Cotera, whose mother interviewed the Mireleses in the 1970s, and José E. Limón, who had graduated from Ray High School in Corpus Christi. By the early 1990s, Cotera was a graduate student at The University of Texas at Austin, where Limón was a professor.

Working together, the two did research in the Mireles and González papers and found the Tejana's historical novel. Subsequently, Cotera and Limón edited the long-lost work, finally published under the title of *Caballero* in 1996.[45]

Limón's scholarship also led to the publication in the following year of another book-length work by González. "A collection of folklore loosely woven together into a semi-autobiographical novel," *Dew on the Thorn* deals with the ranching elite. This second novel takes place in the early twentieth century at a time of dramatic changes in South Texas. The region has been enjoying peaceful, stable conditions, in part because of the intermarriage of Mexicans and Anglos—a theme first introduced in *Caballero*. And Spanish is celebrated in *Dew* as having again become a respectable language along the border. The major conflict in the second novel results from the arrival in South Texas of a new wave of Anglos, brought by the arrival of the railroad. The newcomers are prejudiced against Hispanics, and Fernando Olivares, a major character in the novel, is a member of one of the racially mixed families. The discrimination that he experiences in Corpus Christi shocks him. "Had he received a slap on the face he could not have felt worse. That his family had been in the country for five generations meant nothing to these Americans." To them, "he was just a Mexican, and a Mexican was something to be treated as an inferior being." Olivares, however, does not submit to discrimination without protest. He fights back through political involvement. Exhorting his fellow Hispanics "to exercise their rights as American citizens," Olivares also advises them "to learn English . . . to send our children to American schools. Not because we are ashamed of our Mexican traditions, but because this will make us know how to protect ourselves against them [the Anglos]."[46]

Dew on the Thorn mirrors the lives of Jovita González and Edmundo E. Mireles. Both were born into a minority group that was treated as inferior, yet neither meekly accepted that situation. While valuing Mexican traditions, the two of them learned English, became Americanized, and were active citizens. Like Fernando Olivares in the novel, the Tejana came from a family that had been in Texas for generations, but she was considered inferior by those who arrived much later than her ancestors. She, however, was determined to make her mark in a world that placed many obstacles in the path of a Mexican-American woman, and she did. Although life forced compromises on González, she persisted as a student, a professional, and a wife. Rather than being ashamed of her people's heritage, she brought their story to Anglos who would not otherwise have been exposed to the rich traditions and history of South Texas. In so doing, she also preserved that heritage for the generations of Mexican Americans to follow. And, in the end, albeit posthumously, she found ways to be heard, despite the best efforts of her husband to silence her.

Edmundo Mireles, on the other hand, bore a strong resemblance to fictional Fernando Olivares in urging Hispanics to be politically active and in trying to gain political office for himself. A brilliant man with tremendous energy, he dedicated his life to bettering the condition of fellow Hispanics. Ultimately, however, he chose to work from within the system and take a less militant approach than some of his ethnicity. Aware that knowledge is power, Mireles focused on education as the best avenue for his efforts. And as a pioneer in teaching Spanish language, culture, and history to young Anglos, he helped reduce ignorance and prejudice in their parents as well. By encouraging native Spanish-speakers of all ages to learn English and helping them to become better educated in general, he improved the quality of their lives. Also, through his involvement in the Pan-American movement, the Mexican American intellectual sought to build bridges among the people and countries in his hemisphere.

***

As individuals and as a couple, Jovita González and Edmundo Mireles were noteworthy. They were an interesting pair, she with her affinity for borderlands folklore and historical fiction, and he with books by William Shakespeare and Miguel Cervantes on his desk. Before they married, she broke barriers as a folklorist, author, and speaker. After they wed, she became eclipsed by her power-house husband, who gained national recognition for his initiatives in bilingual education and Pan-Americanism. The two Tejanos worked together effectively, but he appears to have been the domi-nant partner in the relationship. This was not a total sacrifice on González's part, because she and her spouse did share much in common: the love of their native language, appreciation of their Spanish heritage, the desire to improve Anglo-Hispanic relations, the will to help their people, the calling to teach, the ability to write, and a love of learning. Their shared passions have left a joint legacy that continues to inform and inspire people of all ethnic groups.

Bibliographical Commentary

Works written about and by Jovita González provide insights into many aspects of this remarkable woman's life. Concise starting points are "González de Mireles, Jovita (1904–1983)," by Cynthia E. Orozco and Teresa Palomo Acosta, in the *Handbook of Texas Online* (www.tshaonline.org) and material in *Las Tejanas: 300 Years of History* (2003) by Teresa Palomo Acosta and Ruthe Winegarten. Other secondary works include the following: Leticia Magda Garza-Falcón's *Gente Decente: A Borderlands Response to the Rhetoric of Dominance* (1998) from which this chapter gets its subtitle; "Jovita González Mireles: A Sense of History and Homeland" in *Latina Legacies: Identity, Biography, and Community* (2005), edited by Vicki L. Ruiz and Virginia Sánchez Korrol; *Native Speakers: Ella Deloria, Zora Neale Hurston, and Jovita González* (2010) by María Eugenia Cotera; "*Gente Decente*: Jovita González de Mireles and Edmundo de Mireles" by Harriett Denise Joseph, Alix Riviere, and Jordan Penner in *A Corner of Canaan: Essays on Texas in Honor of Randolph Campbell* (2013), edited by Richard B. McCaslin, Donald E. Chipman, and Andrew Torget; and María Cotera's "Jovita González Mireles: Texas Folklorist, Historian, Educator" in *Leaders of the Mexican American Genera-tion: Biographical Essays* (2015), edited by Anthony Quiroz.

González's posthumous publications deserve special mention. These include *Caballero* (1996), co-edited by José Limón and María Cotera; *Dew on the Thorn* (1997), edited by José Limón; *The Woman Who Lost Her Soul and Other Stories* (2001), edited by Sergio Reyna; and *Life along the Border: A Landmark Tejana Thesis* (2006), edited by María Cotera.

As noted in the chapter, in recent decades more public recognition and scholarly writing have focused on Jovita González than on her husband— a reversal of the situation during much of their lengthy marriage. Nevertheless, some of the sources cited above include information on Edmundo E. Mireles, and Carlos Blanton's *The Strange Career of Bilingual Education in Texas, 1836–1981* (2004) provides considerable coverage on his significance as an educator. The *Handbook of Texas Online* also has an entry, titled "Mireles, Edmundo Eduardo (1905–1987)," by Cynthia E. Orozco. A general internet search can also be productive in locating more information on both of these notable Mexican Americans, but even this approach tends to yield more sources on the wife than on the husband.

For the researcher interested in delving into archival materials, documents related to the Mireleses can be found at the various universities cited in the text of the chapter.

Endnotes

*This term is borrowed from Leticia Magda Garza-Falcón's book, *Gente Decente: Borderlands Response to the Rhetoric of Dominance*, and translates as "people of good breeding."

1. Sergio Reyna, "Introduction," *The Woman Who Lost Her Soul and Other Stories*, by Jovita González (Houston, TX: Arte Público Press, 2000), xi, 1st quotation; Andrea R. Purdy, "Jovita González de Mireles (1904–1983)," in *American Women Writers, 1900–1945: A Bio-Bibliographical Critical Sourcebook*, ed. Laurie Champion (Westport, CT: Greenwood Press, 2000), 143; Leticia Magda Garza-Falcón, Gente Decente: *A Borderlands Response to the Rhetoric of Dominance* (Austin: University of Texas Press, 1998), 258; Rosemary A. King, *Border Confluences: Borderland Narratives from the Mexican War to the Present* (Tucson: The University of Arizona Press, 2004), 28; María Eugenia Cotera, "Jovita González Mireles: Texas Folklorist, Historian, Educator" in *Leaders of the Mexican American Generation: Biographical Essays*, ed. Anthony Quiroz (Boulder: University Press of Colorado, 2015), 120, as quoted. Although sources disagree as to the date of Jovita González's birth, it was probably 1904.

2. *Handbook of Texas Online*, Cynthia E. Orozco and Teresa Palomo Acosta, "González de Mireles, Jovita," http://www.tsha.utexas.edu/handbook/online/articles/view/GG/ fgo34.html; Garza-Falcón, *Gente Decente*, 258; María Eugenia Cotera, "Introduction: A Woman of the Borderlands," *Life along the Border: A Landmark Tejana Thesis*, by Jovita González (College Station: Texas A&M University Press, 2006), 10; Cotera, "Jovita González Mireles," in *Mexican American Generation*, 124. [*Handbook of Texas Online* hereinafter cited as *HOT Online*.] See David Montejano's award-winning *Anglos and Mexicans in the Making of Texas, 1836–1986* (1987) for a detailed explanation of changes taking place in Texas and the impact on relations between Anglo Americans and Texas Mexicans.

3. José E. Limón, *Dancing with the Devil: Society and Cultural Poetics in Mexican-American South Texas* (Madison: The University of Wisconsin Press, 1994): 61–62, quotation; Garza-Falcón, *Gente Decente*, 258.

4. Garza-Falcón, *Gente Decente*, 258; Teresa Palomo Acosta and Ruthe Winegarten, eds., *Las Tejanas: 300 Years of History* (Austin: University of Texas Press, 2003), 94; Cortera, "Introduction: A Woman of the Borderlands," 11; Cotera, "Jovita González Mireles," 129.

5. Limón, *Dancing with the Devil*, 61, 1st and 2nd quotations; Garza-Falcón, *Gente Decente*, 258; Laurie Champion, "Introduction" to *American Women Writers*, xv, 3rd quotation.

6. Sylvia R. Longoria, "González's Works Inspire Local Scholars: Library Yields Unpublished Writings by Famed Historian," *Corpus Christi Caller Times*, August 1, 1999; Cotera, "Jovita González Mireles," in *Leaders*, 127, 1st quotation; Purdy, "Jovita González de Mireles," in *American Women Writers*, 143, 2nd and 3rd quotations; Garza-Falcón, *Gente Decente*, 259.

7. Jovita González, *The Woman Who Lost Her Soul*, 143–145, 151, 1st quotation on 143, 2nd through 4th quotations on 145, 5th quotation on 151.

8. Reyna, "Introduction," xix, 1st quotation; Garza-Falcón, *Gente Decente*, 259, 2nd quotation.

9. Biographical note in "A Guide to the Edmundo E. and Jovita González Mireles Papers, 1921–1993," Southwest Writers Collection, Albert B. Alkek Library, Southwest Texas State University, San Marcos, http://www.lib.utexas.edu/taro/tsusm/00051/00051-P.html; Garza-Falcón, *Gente Decente*, 259; *HOT Online*, Orozco and Acosta, "González de Mireles, Jovita."

10. Garza-Falcón, *Gente Decente*, 1, 260, 1st and 2nd quotations; Limón, *Dancing with the Devil*, 68–69; Cotera, *Mexican-American Generation*, 128; Acosta and Winegarten, *Las Tejanas*, 94; Benjamin Johnson, "Engendering Nation and Race in the Borderlands," *Latin American Research Review* 37 (2002): 269; *HOT Online*, Orozco and Acosta, "González de Mireles, Jovita," 3rd quotation.

11. Garza-Falcón, *Gente Decente*, 88–90, 259, 4th and 5th quotations on 88; María Eugenia Cotera, *Native Speakers: Ella Deloria, Zora Neale Hurston, Jovita González, and the Poetics of Culture* (Austin: University of Texas Press, 2008), 114, 1st and 2nd quotations; *HOT Online*, Orozco and Acosta, "González de Mireles, Jovita," 3rd quotation; Reyna, "Introduction," xix, 5th quotation. Some sources say that she did research in Webb, rather than Cameron county; however, her resultant thesis covered Cameron, Starr, and Zapata Counties.

12. Cotera, "Introduction: A Woman of the Borderlands," 4, 16–17, 20, 1st quotation on 4; Carlos Kevin Blanton, "Deconstructing Texas: The Diversity of People, Place, and Historical Imagination in Recent Texas History," in *Beyond Texas through Time: Breaking Away from Past Interpretations*, eds. Walter L Buenger and Arnoldo De León (College Station: Texas A&M University Press, 2011), 180, 2nd quotation; González, *Life along the Border*, 41–45, 73–81, 109, 116, 3rd quotation on 109, 4th through 6th quotations on 116.

13. Acosta and Winegarten, *Las Tejanas*, 94; Garza-Falcón, *Gente Decente*, 260; Jovita Gonález, "The Devil on the Border," in *Hecho en Tejas: An Anthology of Texas-Mexican Literature*, ed. Dagoberto Gilb (Albuquerque: University of New Mexico Press, 2006), 102–105, quotation. Later "The Devil on the Border" was published in "Tales and Songs of the Texas-Mexicans," *Man, Bird and Beast*, Texas Folklore Society 8.

14. Acosta and Winegarten, *Las Tejanas*, 94; Garza-Falcón, *Gente Decente*, 260; Limón, *Dancing with the Devil*, 67; *HOT Online*, Orozco and Acosta,

"González de Mireles, Jovita"; Purdy, "Jovita González de Mireles," 142, 1st through 3rd quotations; José E. Limón, "Introduction," *Caballero: A Historical Novel*, by Jovita González and Eve Raleigh (College Station: Texas A&M University Press, 1996), xv, xvii, 4th quotation on xv; Reyna, "Introduction," *Woman Who Lost Her Soul*, xi–xiii, xx–xxi.

15. Reyna, "Introduction," *Woman Who Lost Her Soul*, xix.

16. *HOT Online*, Cynthia E. Orozco, "Mireles, Edmundo Eduardo, 1905–1987," http://www.tsha.utexas.edu/handbook/ online/articles/view/MM/fmi90.html. The Wittliff Collections at Texas State University contain a photograph of Mireles that he gave to González before their marriage. Signed E.E. Mireles, the inscription reads: "To Jovita whose friendship I have always cherished." Note that some sources cite Jovita González's married name as González Mireles, but others refer to her as González de Mireles.

17. *HOT Online*, Orozco, "Mireles, Edmundo Eduardo"; Garza-Falcón, *Gente Decente*, 78;
Leaflet with "Vote for E.E. Mireles for State Representative," Edmundo E. Mireles papers (1940–1971), Benson Latin American Collection, General Libraries, University of Texas at Austin (Hereinafter cited as EEM Papers).

18. Garza-Falcón, *Gente Decente*, 77–78; *HOT Online*, Orozco, "Jovita González de Mireles."

19. Cotera, "Jovita González Mireles," *Mexican American Generation*, 134.

20. Garza-Falcón, *Gente Decente*, 82; González, "The Bullet-Swallower," in *The Woman Who Lost Her Soul*, 47–55, 1st through 4th quotations; Cotera, "Jovita González Mireles," *Mexican American Generation*, 130–131, 5th quotation.

21. The League of United Latin-American Citizens, "LULACS," EEM Papers, 1st quotation; *HOT Online*, Orozco, "Mireles, Edmundo Eduardo"; Garza-Falcón, *Gente Decente*, 113–114, 261; Mario T. García, *Mexican Americans: Leadership, Ideology, and Identity, 1930–1960* (New Haven: Yale University Press, 1989), 29–33, 2nd and 3rd quotations on 31. For more information on the creation of LULAC and its philosophy, see Richard A. Garcia, "Alonso S. Perales: The Voice and Visions of a Citizen Intellectual," in *Leaders of the Mexican-American Generation*, ed. Anthony Quiroz, 85–117.

22. Garza-Falcón, *Gente Decente*, 114, 261, 2nd quotation on 114; Limón, "Introduction," *Caballero*, xvi–xvii, xix, xxi. 1st and 3rd quotations on xix.

23. Johnson, "Engendering Nation and Race," 269, 1st and 2nd quotations; González and Raleigh, *Caballero*, 5, 157, 194–195, 3rd quotation on 194–195; Garza-Falcón, *Gente Decente*, 117, 120, 125, 128, 4th quotation on 120.

24. Limón, "Introduction," *Caballero*, xxi–xxii, 2nd quotation on xxii; Garza-Falcón, *Gente Decente*, 95, 112–113, 1st quotation on 95, 3rd quotation on 112.

25. Reyna, "Introduction," *The Woman Who Lost Her Soul*, xiii, 1st quotation; Cotera, "Jovita González Mireles," in *Mexican American Generation*, 133, 2nd quotation; Limón, Introduction, *Caballero*, xiii.

26. Carlos Kevin Blanton, *The Strange Career of Bilingual Education in Texas, 1836–1981* (College Station: Texas A&M University Press, 2004), 65, 67–68, 76–77, 1st quotation on 76, 2nd quotation on 77.

27. Blanton, *Bilingual Education*, 70–71, 76, 82, 1st quotation on 76, 2nd quotation on 82. See Gilbert C. González, *Chicano Education in the Era of Segregation* (Originally published by Associates Presses, 1990; repr. Denton: University of North Texas Press, 2013).

28. Blanton, *Bilingual Education*, 85, 88, 1st quotation on 88, 2nd quotation on 85; Limón, "Dancing with the Devil," 61–62. See Gilbert González, *Chicano Education in the Era of Segregation*.

29. Blanton, *Bilingual Education*, 96.

30. Blanton, *Bilingual Education*, 97–98, 1st quotation on 97, 2nd and 3rd quotations on 98; Senate Bill no. 67, March 4, 1941, EEM Papers.

31. Blanton, *Bilingual Education in Texas*, 100–103, 1st quotation on 100; Edmundo E. Mireles, "Philosophy," 2nd and 3rd quotations, EEM Papers; Edmundo E. Mireles, "Corpus Christi Spanish Program, 1950–1951," 4th and 5th quotations, EEM Papers.

32. *HOT Online*, Orozco, "Mireles, Edmundo Eduardo"; "¿Habla Vd. Inglés?", *Time* (Feb. 14, 1944), 72; Blanton, *Bilingual Education*, 102–103, quotation on 102.

33. Edmundo E. Mireles, R. B. Fisher, and Jovita González Mireles, "Introduction," *Mi Libro Español: Libro Uno* (Austin, TX: Benson & Company, 1941), vii–viii, 1st and 2nd quotations on vii, 3rd through 5th quotation on viii; "To the Teacher," xi . Volumes one and three of *Mi Libro Español* and volumes two and six of *El Español Elemental* can be found in Jovita González Mireles Manuscripts and Works, ca. 1925–1980, Benson Latin American Collection, General Libraries, University of Texas at Austin.

34. Earle Hamilton, February 11, 1941, 1st quotation, William H. Wilson, September 10, 1941, Richard Kleberg, August 1940, 2nd quotation, Nelson Rockefeller, August 11, 1940, 3rd and 4th quotations, and Eleanor Roosevelt (N.d.), 5th quotation, all as quoted in "Comments from Educators on Corpus Christi Spanish Program, 1939–1941," EEM Papers.

35. "¿Habla Vd. Inglés?," *Time*, 72, quotations.

36. Thurmond Krueger, "Letter to School Superintendent of Spanish Program from Junior Chamber of Commerce," February 24, 1942, 1st quotation; Sumner Welles, "Good Neighbor Policy and Discrimination in Southwest," in *Pan American Day Brochure: A United Front* (1944), all other quotations, EEM Papers. See *HOT Online*, Fred L. Koestler, "Bracero Program," http://www.tshaonline.org/handbook/online/articles/ombo01 for a brief entry on the program, but for more detailed information, see Michael Snodgress's "The Bracero Program, 1942–1964," in *Beyond La Frontera: The History of Mexico-U.S. Migration* (New York: Oxford University Press, 2011).

37. Pan American Council of Texas, *Organization, Constitution, By-Laws, Committees, Motion to Incorporate, Charter* (N.p., N.d.), 3, 19–20; Edmundo E. Mireles, "History of the Council," in *Saludos Amigos* (Pan-American Day Dinner Dance Program, 1946), quotation, EEM Papers.

38. Leaflet, "Vote for E.E. Mireles for State Representative" (N.d.), Edmundo E. Mireles, radio talks on behalf of Mexican American candidates, "Radio Talk," on KWBU (July 24, 1948), quotation, EEM Papers; Edmundo E. Mireles, radio spots for the beginning of classes in public schools (1946), Edmundo E. Mireles, "Pláticas de Educación" (N.d.), EEM Papers; *HOT Online*, Orozco "Mireles, Edmundo Eduardo."

39. Edmundo E. Mireles, "Los Niños de Corpus Christi Son Bilingues," *Texas Outlook* (May, 1951), quotations, EEM papers; Edmundo E. Mireles, "The Teaching of Spanish in Our Public Schools," *The American School Board Journal* (November 1953), 33–34, 92; Biographical Note in "A Guide to the

Edmundo E. and Jovita González Mireles Papers," Albert B. Alkek Library, Southwest Texas State University, San Marcos [Hereinafter cited as "Guide to Mireles Papers," Alkek, STSU]. Note that Southwest Texas State University has since been renamed as Texas State University.

40. Corpus Christi Public Schools Division of Curricular Services, "Report of Spanish Department 1955–56," EEM Papers; Garza-Falcón, *Gente Decente*, 97–98, 2nd through 5th quotations on 97, 1st and 6th quotations on 98.

41. Edmundo E. Mireles, "Report to Corpus Christi Public Schools: Summer English Program for Pre-School Non-English Speaking Children" (1962), all quotations, EEM Papers.

42. Govtrack, S.2642 (88th): "An Act to Mobilize . . . in the United States," quotation, https://www.govtrack.us/congress/bills/88/s2642; "Status and Progress Report of Adult Basic Education Program" (November 21, 1967), and "Adult Basic Education, 1969–1970" (N.d.), EEM Papers.

43. Cotera, "Jovita González Mireles," in *Mexican American Generation*, 136–137, quotation on 137; Limón, "Introduction," *Caballero*, xxi–xxii; Garza-Falcón, *Gente Decente*, 261.

44. Jonathan Osborne, "School May Bear Name of Mireles," *Corpus Christi Caller Times*, July 25, 1999, 1st through 4th quotations; Content note, in "Guide to Mireles Papers," Alkek, STSU, 5th quotation; Thomas H. Kreneck, "Foreword," to *Caballero*, x.

45. "A Guide to Edmundo E. and Jovita González Mireles Papers, 1921–1933," The Wittliff Collections, Southwestern Writers Collection, Texas State University, San Marcos, www.lib.utexas.edu/taro/tsusm/00051.html; Garza-Falcón, *Gente Decente*, 74; Kreneck, Foreword, *Caballero*, ix–x; Limón and Cotera, Editors' Acknowledgements, *Caballero*, xi.

46. Johnson, "Engendering Nation," 270; Jovita González, *Dew on the Thorn*, ed. José Limón (Houston: Arte Público Press, 1997), 151–152, as quoted in Johnson, "Engendering Nation," 270.

Congressional Medal of Honor recipient Roy Benavidez served in the U.S. Army from 1955–1976. Photo by James O. Tenney. Roy P. Benavidez Papers, 1943–2007, di_11027, The Dolph Briscoe Center for American History, The University of Texas at Austin.

Raul "Roy" Pérez Benavidez

The Mean Mexican

RAUL "ROY" PÉREZ BENAVIDEZ was an unlikely hero. Born into a Spanish-speaking, economically disadvantaged family during the Great Depression, he suffered the loss of both parents while still a child. The orphan became known for having a quick temper, as insults directed at him personally or slights against Mexican-Americans caused him to react in anger. Given his readiness to fight, the people who cared about Raul were concerned about his future. Even after he enlisted in the military, his belligerence repeatedly got him into trouble and jeopardized the attainment of his career goals. Fortunately, with marriage and maturity, Benavidez learned to channel his aggression in more appropriate directions. Ultimately, his fighting tendencies served him, his comrades, and his country well.

During his lifetime, Roy Benavidez became engaged in a number of conflicts—military and political—which he later referred to as his three wars. Fearless in combat, he risked life and limb on more than one occasion, and more than once he was so gravely wounded that he almost died. True to character, he defied death just as valiantly as he fought his nation's enemies. He not only survived potentially fatal injuries but also heroically helped save the lives of others. The full recognition that Benavidez merited for his exceptional military exploits was not easily attained, however, and he had to fight for that as well. Only years of determined effort gained for him a belated, but well-deserved, Congressional Medal of Honor. Surprisingly, the third "war" in which the veteran engaged was against the same government that he had served so bravely as a soldier during the Vietnam War. When faced with losing badly needed disability benefits, he battled to get them reinstated not only for himself but also for others with disabilities as well.

As he got older, Benavidez strived to serve as an inspiration to others, a goal he still achieves posthumously. Studying the life of this Tejano reminds us that hardships can be overcome, that a person can change for the better, that aggression can be used in productive ways, that unexpected people can aspire to become heroes, and that one should never hesitate to "fight the good fight." There is much to learn from "The Mean Mexican," as he was affectionately called by his brothers-in-arms.

* * *

On August 5, 1935, Raul Pérez Benavidez was born into a life of poverty near Cuero in DeWitt County, Texas. During the United States' most severe depression, Raul's father, Salvador Benavidez, worked as a sharecropper, which meant that he did not own the land on which he farmed but had to give a percentage of his crops to the landlord. Despite his humble circumstances, Salvador's family had been in Texas for generations, and a century earlier his ancestors had participated in the fight for independence from Mexico. Raul's mother, Teresa, was a Yaqui Indian from Northern Mexico, so her social status was even lower than that of her husband at the time of their marriage. Neither of their families approved of the union.[1]

In the late 1930s, after Teresa had given birth to a second son named Rogelio (Roger), Salvador died of tuberculosis. The widow was left with responsibility for supporting two young children. Hoping to find domestic work, Teresa moved with her family to Cuero, a town about seventy-five miles east of San Antonio.

There she married Pablo Chávez, and the couple had a daughter named Lupe. Raul later acknowledged that their stepfather "was not cruel" to his stepsons, but he did not pay them "much attention" either.[2]

Only Spanish was spoken in the Chávez home, which placed young Raul at a disadvantage in his early education. He required special instruction in English before he could attend regular elementary school classes. In the small school he attended, his pranks got him into trouble, so he was sent to St. Michael's Catholic School where the nuns maintained strict control. However, the boy soon had graver problems than learning a new language or being disciplined. When Raul was only seven, his mother Teresa died of tuberculosis. He and Rogelio were orphans, and Chávez was unwilling or unable to accept responsibility for "Teresa's boys."[3]

While Lupe stayed with her father's family, her half-brothers found a new home some seventy miles southwest of Houston in El Campo, Texas, with their uncle, Nicholás Benavidez, and his wife, Alexandria. Despite having eight children of their own, they welcomed their orphaned nephews. The boys' grandfather Salvador played an influential role in their upbringing as well. All of the Benavidez adults endeavored to instill proper values in the children, including the importance of going to church together on Sundays. Despite having a home with his relatives, Raul still faced hardships. As migrant workers, the family spent months every year traveling to places as distant as Colorado to pick crops, such as sugar beets and cotton. Work was a family affair, and the children spent more time in the fields than in school. Education was valued, but so was earning enough money for food and shelter. Raul also worked after school and on weekends to get money for movies and other activities. Among the youth's odd jobs were selling empty soda bottles, running errands, and shining shoes. As his English improved, he also translated for the local taxi driver who needed help communicating with his Spanish-speaking customers [4]

Early along the youth experienced the realities of racial discrimination. As an example, he had to sit upstairs in the movie theater, because the lower level was reserved for Anglos (whites). Also, many restaurants would not serve Mexicans or Mexican Americans. One local cafe had a sign that read "No Mexicans or Dogs. Coloreds around back." At school the treatment of Tejanos was little better, with Anglo children taunting Raul by calling him a "taco bender" and a "greaser." He reacted to the insults by getting into fights. In his own words, "I was turning into a tough, mean little kid." By the time he was ten, Raul "fought anybody who looked at me wrong."[5]

Racism was only one reason why the teenager decided to end his education prematurely. The absences caused by the Benavidez family's migrant lifestyle caused Raul to fall behind in his studies, and deficiencies in English continued to hamper his progress. Raul later admitted to being "embarrassed by his academic struggles." However, probably the most important factor influencing his decision was the need to earn more money for himself and his family. At any rate, the adolescent quit school by the time he was fifteen years old, despite efforts by his teacher to dissuade him.[6]

The dropout went to work at the local Firestone store, where owner Curtis Reese and bookkeeper Art Haddock became important figures in his life. Fond of the Tejano youth, they tried to reinforce the same kind of values that his relatives had stressed. Despite the best efforts by family and friends, however, the teenager seemed destined for trouble because of his explosive temper. Raul's readiness to resort to his fists caused his uncle great concern, so Nicholás encouraged his nephew to become involved in boxing—a more positive outlet for the young man's aggression. The adolescent was "a pretty good fighter"; however, he "had a hard time staying within the rules," and formal boxing matches were governed by rules. He revealed still another character flaw, when he proved a bad sport in the face of defeat. After losing a championship match, Benavidez again became a dropout, this time from the boxing arena.[7]

The fact that the teenager was Mexican American, lacked a high school education, and had a hot temper limited his opportunities. One of the few options open to him was military service. The National Guard attracted him, because it required only the part-time commitment of doing basic training, putting in a specified number of weekends every year, and serving two weeks during every summer—unless the Guard was called out for a national emergency. Although there would be rules to follow, the young Tejano could earn extra money while continuing his employment at Firestone. He would also have an opportunity to complete his education with financial assistance provided by the government. Seeking direction in his life, the physically unimpressive 5'6" 130-pound seventeen-year-old enlisted. After attending boot camp at Fort Knox, Kentucky, he returned to work in El Campo.[8]

During his two years in the National Guard, the young Tejano attained the rank of corporal on two separate occasions but lost his stripes both times because of his volatility. Given his lack of discipline and inability to control his temper, Raul seemed ill-suited to the military. Considering his less-than-stellar record in the National Guard, Raul Pérez Benavidez's decision to make a full-time career of military service must have shocked his family and friends. He later explained that he was determined to "become a soldier and be the best." Whether a poorly educated, orphaned Tejano with a troubled history could survive in the army, much less become "the best," was highly debatable. Certainly, the odds were against him. Nevertheless, the nineteen-year-old took the bus to Houston, where he joined the army in June 1955. In the process, he Americanized his name from Raul to Roy.[9]

Thrilled by the prospect of parachuting from planes, the young enlistee's dream was to train with the Airborne forces. However, the army had a different plan. Following basic training at Fort Ord,

California, the recruit was among the infantry sent overseas in the mid-1950s to help maintain a tenuous peace on the Korean Peninsula after a cease-fire ended the conflict there. This proved a learning experience, as the Tejano realized that the poverty experienced in his youth was nothing "compared to the way those folks lived following the war." As a soldier, he also felt "more a part of something than I ever had in my life." Following his Korean tour of duty, he was sent to Fort Chaffee, Arkansas, but then was posted to Germany, where the Eleventh Airborne Division was based in Augsburg. Perhaps predictably, when finally admitted to parachute school, he got into a fight and lost the coveted opportunity before ever making a single jump. Instead, the soldier was stationed in Berlin for his next sixteen months of duty.[10]

While in Berlin, the Tejano struck a lieutenant for calling him a "little Mexican noncom," among other ethnic insults. Facing disciplinary action, the Tejano corporal reported to the office of a captain trained at West Point. On the wall was a plaque with the following inscription: "I do not lie, cheat, or steal nor tolerate those that do"—the West Point honor code. Also inscribed was the institution's motto, "Duty, Honor, Country." Benavidez answered truthfully when the captain asked whether he had struck the lieutenant and was fortunate that he was only demoted to private first class, rather than receiving more severe punishment. When asked why he had taken such a great risk by confessing, the Tejano replied that "he had been inspired by the West Point plaque." He did not want a military career "based on a lie." Because of this experience, Benavidez finally internalized the meaning of all of "those lectures, the morals, the Bible verses, everything he'd been spoon-fed for years in both Spanish and English." He made a pledge to himself to make the West Point code his own and to make every effort to control his aggression.[11]

Another vow that Benavidez made during this period also proved transformative. For years he had been attracted to Hilaría

From the wedding album of Roy P. and Hilaria Coy Benavidez, June 7, 1959. St. Robert Bellarmine Catholic Church, El Campo, TX. Courtesy of the Roy P. Benavidez Estate.

"Lala" Coy, a young woman whom he considered "by far the prettiest girl" in El Campo. With her combined Hispanic and Irish heritage, the five-foot-seven Tejana had "green eyes, fair skin, [and] light brown hair." The attraction went beyond Lala's physical attributes, however. She also understood him and helped

him get beyond the anger engendered in him by racism and sepa-
ratism. For Benavidez, Lala was "the piece that had been missing
in my life." After corresponding and courting, the couple wed on
June 7, 1959.[12]

The Tejano took his bride to Fort Gordon, Georgia, where
he attended military police training and served as a driver for
several high-ranking officers, including William Westmoreland,
commander of the 101st Airborne. Hoping for another chance,
Benavidez asked Westmoreland for help to get into the Airborne
forces. After enlisting for another term of military service a few
months later, he finally got his wish. He and Lala were sent
to Fort Bragg, North Carolina, where he was again given the
opportunity to attend jump school. This time a more mature
Benavidez made platoon sergeant and became a member of the
82nd Airborne.[13]

While Benavidez was finding his niche in the military, the
United States was becoming engaged in the next stage of a
prolonged conflict with the Soviet Union, which was dominated
by the Communist Party. Communist beliefs in a government-
controlled, classless society with no private ownership of property were the opposite of American democratic political ideas
and capitalistic economic practices. The Soviet Union was intent
on spreading its supremacy, and the United States was equally
committed to prevent that from happening. Each side was willing
to fight, when necessary, as had happened in Korea the previous
decade.

By the 1960s one of the hot spots in this global struggle
was Southeast Asia. Having gained control of North Vietnam,
Communists were fighting to conquer the southern region as well.
Initially the United States took only a limited role in the distant
conflict by sending military specialists—called advisers—to help
train the South Vietnamese forces. By the time that President
John F. Kennedy was assassinated in Dallas, Texas, late in 1963,

there were about 16,000 of these advisers in Vietnam. Assuming the presidential office, Lyndon Baines Johnson was determined to prevent the fall of South Vietnam. Early in 1965 America's involvement escalated as he ordered aerial bombing of selected targets in North Vietnam. In April of that year he also sanctioned the deployment of American combat forces to South Vietnam for defensive operations. While unsure whether military escalation was advisable, the commander-in-chief ultimately committed hundreds of thousands of American troops to the battle in Southeast Asia.[14] Although some went voluntarily to serve their country, many others found themselves drafted into military service in an increasingly controversial conflict.

As the war in Vietnam became more costly in human and economic terms, protests broke out on college campuses. Some young men fled the country rather than submit to mandatory military service, if drafted. When Roy Benavidez got his orders to go to Vietnam in 1965, however, he went because "somebody had to do it." As he later explained, "We couldn't *all* refuse to go . . . [or] run off to Canada."[15] Little did Benavidez realize that his first tour of duty in that theater would leave him wondering if he would ever walk — much less run—anywhere again.

Vietnam was an alien environment, where Americans were pitted against an unpredictable, determined enemy. When Benavidez was on his first combat patrol as a military adviser for a squad of South Vietnamese, he came under sniper fire. An experienced warrant officer, who killed the enemy sniper, mentored the Tejano and taught him survival skills useful in jungle warfare.[16]

In the mid-1960s, the Mexican-American soldier was stationed at Payne Compound in Tam Ky, near the later famous Ho Chi Minh trail. During that tour of duty, he was sent on patrol disguised as one of the Vietnamese. Because of his ethnicity, he resembled the native people closely enough to pass for one of them, especially dressed in the clothing of the enemy Viet Cong—a black pajama-like outfit and sandals. Exactly what happened on the ill-fated mission is uncertain, because Benavidez later had no memory of those events. When a Marine patrol eventually found his unconscious body, they mistook the casualty for one of the enemy because of his distinctive clothes and the Russian-made AK-47 lying beside him. They only realized their mistake when they found the dog tags (identification tags) sewn into his clothing.[17]

Suffering paralysis below the waist, the badly injured Tejano was eventually taken to Clark Air Force Base in the Philippines and then transferred to Brooke Army Medical Center at Fort Sam Houston in San Antonio. Doctors concluded that the trauma to his spinal cord must have been caused by a land mine and advised the wounded soldier that he would never walk again. Therapy was considered a misuse of resources. Instead, he would almost certainly be offered a discharge from the army with disability pay. Benavidez lived in "constant fear" of becoming a civilian confined to a wheelchair. He later regretted that these concerns caused him to treat Lala callously when she made the long drive on weekends to visit her husband, especially given that she was pregnant with their first child. However, Raul could not tolerate the thought of once again becoming no more than "a Mexican pepper belly . . . , a seventh-grade dropout who used to work at the Firestone tire store." While questioning why his Catholic God would let this happen, he determined to prove the physicians' prognosis wrong.[18]

This proved to be one of the most critical battles of Benavidez's life. At night he would maneuver his body out of bed and onto the floor, where he "used his chin, elbows, and forearms to pull himself toward the wall, dragging his legs behind him." His goal was to reach two nightstands that he could use to raise himself to a standing position. Meanwhile, other patients on the ward would give odds as to whether he would succeed. He later acknowledged that many nights "the winners were the ones who bet on my defeat." Eventually the nurses would find him on the floor and help him back into bed, but the Tejano did make noticeable progress.[19]

When finally offered a medical discharge, the patient insisted on demonstrating his improvement. Despite considerable pain, he managed to stand and "took one shuffling step, then two, and finally three along the bed, holding to it for support." Impressed, Benavidez's superiors decided to give him a chance to prove his fitness for active service. Initially on his own and then with therapy, he slowly regained his mobility. Thanks to his tenacity, six months after his admission to Brooke Army Medical Center, the determined soldier was able to walk out of the facility "on shaky legs" with a heavily pregnant Lala by his side.[20]

Benavidez was assigned a desk job with the 82nd Airborne at Fort Bragg, North Carolina, where his wife joined him in July 1966. That same month Hilaria gave birth to their first daughter, Denise. All was not well with the Benavidez family, however, because the new father was becoming addicted to pain killers. His physicians ordered him to stop taking the drugs and begin a major exercise program. Despite experiencing almost constant pain, the Tejano proved a compliant patient, and his overall condition improved. Dissatisfied with office duties, Benavidez vowed to prove his fitness for performing more demanding duties. The paratrooper accomplished that by parachuting from a plane three times in one day, though he reportedly had to forge a signature on the paperwork granting him permission to jump.[21] The soldier's fighting spirit made him unstoppable.

Before his tour in Vietnam in the mid-1960s, Benavidez had applied for the elite Special Forces. Because the paperwork associated with his original application could not be found, the ever-resourceful soldier allegedly forged another set of papers to get the coveted assignment. Despite the questionable legitimacy of his documents, the Tejano qualified to become a Green Beret, one of

America's most respected fighting forces.[22] Not bad for a man who had been told that he would never walk again!

Special Forces training posed challenges for Benavidez who at thirty-one "was older than most of the instructors at the John F. Kennedy Special Warfare Center and School" at Fort Bragg. The dropout was also overwhelmed at times by the difficulty of the material and later wrote that he "didn't even know what the hell study habits were." For that reason, he switched his area of intensive training from "operations and intelligence" to "light and heavy weapons" but later gave his original area of interest another try. That he was constantly in pain was yet another obstacle; yet, the Tejano let nothing stop him and successfully completed his training in March 1968.[23]

Back in fighting form, Benavidez was stationed in Southeast Asia for a second tour of duty in 1968. He volunteered for Studies and Observation Group, known unofficially "as Special Operations Group" (SOG), whose members undertook dangerous missions to gather intelligence about the enemy. During this period, Roy acquired a couple of nicknames, as his buddies began to call him "Tango Mike/Mike," the radio call signal for "The Mean Mexican." Rather than being offended, the more mature Benavidez understood that "everything we said was in fun."[24] And all too soon he had to prove just how mean he could be.

On May 2, 1968, three Green Berets and nine allies were "inserted by helicopters in a dense jungle area west of Loc Ninh, Vietnam, to gather intelligence information about confirmed large-scale enemy activity" along the Cambodian border. The twelve men soon came under heavy attack, declared an emergency, and requested extraction. However, the rescue helicopters also experienced "small arms and anti-aircraft fire." The damaged choppers were forced to abandon the rescue attempt and return to the Forward Operating Base, where Benavidez was monitoring the operation over the airwaves. "Tango Mike/Mike" heard the sound of weapons firing, along with "a voice begging for help." When helicopter pilot Larry McKibben left the forward base for another rescue attempt, the Tejano volunteered for the flight. Benavidez later declared, "When I got on that copter, little did I know we were going to spend six hours in hell."[25]

The Green Berets and their allies were surrounded by hundreds of North Vietnamese by the time the helicopter arrived. McKibben was unable to land, and the trapped team members were "either dead or wounded and unable to move to the pickup zone." Benavidez instructed the pilot to fly over an open clearing so that he could jump out. Although armed only with his "Special Forces knife, a wicked Bowie-style weapon[,]" and a bag of medical supplies, "The Mean Mexican" "ran approximately 75 meters under withering small arms fire to the crippled team." He was shot in the right leg and "his face was covered in blood from wounds made by shards of metal from grenades and mortar rounds." Nevertheless, nothing short of death could stop him from rescuing his comrades, as well as making sure that no critical military documents fell into enemy hands.[26]

Using smoke canisters, Benavidez guided the rescue chopper to where some of the fallen were lying. He "carried and dragged half of the wounded team members to the awaiting aircraft." Despite additional wounds, the Green Beret then provided protective fire and ran beside the aircraft as it went to get the rest of the team. While lifting one of injured men into the aircraft, Benavidez was hit by still another AK-47 round, this time in his lower back. He passed out from the trauma. When he awoke, Benavidez realized that the helicopter had crashed. He got the injured men from the crash site and began to apply first aid. Under heavy fire, he distributed ammunition and water to the others. The weakened Tejano "began calling in tactical air strikes and directed the fire from supporting gunships" so that yet another rescue attempt could be made. Just before the next helicopter arrived, Benavidez was hit again in the thigh but still began putting the injured and dead men into the new rescue aircraft.[27]

As he struggled to get his fallen comrades into the chopper, the injured Green Beret was attacked from behind by a North Vietnamese soldier. Clubbed in the head, the Tejano suffered a broken jaw. He also suffered serious bayonet wounds to the arms and hands. Engaging his attacker in hand-to-hand combat, "the Mean Mexican" used his knife to kill the Vietnamese soldier. Incredibly, the critically injured Green Beret also disposed of two more of the enemy who were storming the helicopter and made one last circuit to insure "that all classified material had been collected or destroyed, and to bring in the remaining wounded." Only then did the Tejano think about saving himself. As he ran for the chopper, a "last round hit Benavidez in the stomach." He ran to the aircraft with his intestines spilling out, "holding them in with his hands."[28]

Roy Benavidez was later credited for getting a total of seventeen injured or dead bodies into the rescue craft, thereby saving "the lives of at least eight men." Those extracted included his fellow Special Forces comrades, members of the downed helicopter crew, and three enemy soldiers "loaded by mistake."[29] Sadly, it seemed unlikely that "the Mean Mexican" would live to be honored for his valor.

Barely alive Benavidez "was truly terrified for the first time" in his life. Unable to move and in indescribable pain, he feared that he would not survive. This was reinforced when the medics onboard the rescue chopper decided not to provide treatment. The Green Beret understood this meant that they considered him to be beyond hope. Despite miraculously surviving the flight back to the Loc Nihn base, the Tejano was mistakenly presumed dead because of the number and severity of his wounds. His broken jaw prevented him from speaking to let the medical personnel know that he was still alive. Benavidez later recounted that he spat "a mixture of blood, spittle, and mucus" on the doctor to get his attention before a body bag was zipped closed around him. Although still alive, however, odds were against the valiant warrior who had been "shot five times, riddled with shrapnel, and bayoneted and clubbed."[30]

Benavidez was taken to Saigon for medical treatment, where surgeons worked for days to remove most of the metal fragments from his body. Regaining consciousness, he found himself bandaged like a mummy with tubes in every opening of his body. Unable to talk or move, the patient faced more operations. Even then, some shrapnel remained. Two foreign objects deemed too risky to extract were left in his heart. For the rest of Benavidez's life, small pieces of metal would occasionally work their way out of his body—reminders of his six hours in hell. From Saigon, the Tejano was taken to Tokyo, Japan, where he was hospitalized until he was strong enough to be sent back to the United States. Upon his return, the elite soldier again became a patient at Brooke Army Medical Center, where he spent almost a year recuperating.[31] Although he did better than anyone would have predicted, he would never fully recover.

Benavidez received several commendations for his acts of heroism on May 2, 1968, including two Purple Hearts and the Vietnamese Cross of Gallantry with Palm (1968) Unit Citation. He was also awarded the army's second highest award, the Distinguished Service Cross. However, when a lieutenant handed the hospitalized hero the DSC "like a grocer gives bubble gum to a polite kid," he objected to the informality. Consequently, General William Westmoreland later personally conferred the medal in a proper ceremony at Fort Sam Houston.[32]

In May of 1969, the Tejano once again left Brooke Army Medical Center. As before, he hoped to continue on active duty. Earlier in his military career, doctors had told him that he would never walk again, but he had proved them wrong. Maybe he could repeat that feat. Sadly, only one jump was necessary to convince even the tenacious Benavidez that his days of parachuting were over.[33] He would stay in the army but he would not see combat again—at least not on the battlefield.

Roy spent three years as the driver for General Robert Linville at Fort Riley, Kansas, and the Benavidez's second child, Yvette, was born during that posting. Unfortunately, the cold weather worsened Benavidez's pain; so, he was transferred to Fort Sam Houston in San Antonio, where he was Lieutenant General Patrick Cassidy's driver. Cassidy reported the Tejano to be "an outstanding chauffeur," who was "loyal, dependable, and dedicated." He also noted that his driver experienced "physical problems due to extensive wounds" but kept "in good shape by physical exercise."[34]

Roy and Hilaria were pleased to return to the Lone Star State. With them came their daughters, and a son named Noel was born in Texas in 1972. Living in San Antonio, the growing Benavidez family was closer to relatives and friends in El Campo, where they would eventually retire. The Green Beret remained in the military until his honorable discharge with the rank of Master Sergeant in 1976 "after twenty years and three months of active, often painful duty." At that time he was qualified as being be 80 percent disabled.[35]

During the years before retirement, Benavidez heard rumors that he had been recommended for a Congressional Medal of Honor for his heroism but had never received official notification to that effect. Because his Special Forces comrades believed that he deserved the highest award the army had to offer, they encouraged him to pursue the matter. While still driving for General Cassidy, he had broached the subject with his superior. Although the general warned his chauffeur that getting a MOH was extremely difficult to accomplish, he began an inquiry to locate Colonel Ralph Drake's original recommendation. The veteran was not surprised to learn that the paperwork could not be found. He knew that, given the avalanche of forms generated by the military during the war in Vietnam, "it was inevitable that a tremendous number would simply disappear."[36]

The Tejano was encouraged by fellow Vietnam veteran Colonel Jim Dandridge to contact his former commander only to learn that Drake thought Benavidez had died from his severe injuries at Loc Ninh. Colonel Drake explained that he had actually submitted the paperwork for a Distinguished Service Cross, not for a Medal of Honor. In fact, he expressed surprise that his subordinate had been awarded even the former, not only because of the secretive nature of the Loc Ninh mission but also because the recommendation "was pretty short of detailed information."[37]

Drake and Dandridge agreed to consider helping the Special Forces veteran secure a Congressional Medal of Honor. Consequently, on April 9, 1974, Drake wrote "a letter to the awards and decorations board at Fort Sam Houston" to recommend that Benavidez's DSC be upgraded. Dandridge managed to collect several letters of support, although not necessarily from actual eyewitnesses. Like General Cassidy, Drake cautioned Benavidez not to expect a favorable outcome, since award recommendations had to be submitted within two years of the actual events under review.[38] Was it indeed too late for Benavidez to receive the recognition he deserved?

As the colonel had warned, the MOH request was denied on this and subsequent occasions. The Senior Army Decorations Board required accounts from eyewitnesses and definite proof of acts of heroism before approving this exalted award. Drake's report about Benavidez's actions on May 2, 1968, had not provided enough detail to confirm his valor. The Tejano's former commander himself acknowledged that he had more urgent concerns at that time than doing "any research on the matter." Also lacking were eyewitness reports, since so many of the participants had been killed. Even some of the survivors "were fighting to forget, not relive" the painful memories of May 2, 1968. The former Green Beret later wrote that he considered abandoning the quest; however, others insisted that he should fight for the award, just as he had fought through six hours in hell to deserve it. Ultimately, the Mexican-American found himself in a prolonged battle that "evolved into a six-year obsession." As a result, Benavidez made "more friends than I even dared dream" but also "a few enemies who would misinterpret my motives."[39]

An encouraging development occurred late in 1974 when President Gerald Ford signed new legislation that suspended the former two-year time limit for making Medal of Honor and other award recommendations. Consequently, the Senior Army Decorations Board reviewed Benavidez's case in 1976 and again in 1977, but both efforts resulted in negative determinations. Representatives of the Department of the Army insisted that "considerable time, effort and expense" had been taken to "insure that Sergeant Benavidez be given a just and fair evaluation." However, the only formal explanation provided for the rejections was "that 'no new substantive information' had been presented," as military policy dictated that no specific reasons be given for approving or denying any particular recommendation.[40]

The distinguished veteran and his proponents had their own opinions as to why the board kept denying him the coveted medal. The events of May 2, 1968, had actually taken place in Cambodia, not Vietnam, a fact the United States government did not want to acknowledge publicly. Also, officials almost certainly hoped to downplay the extent of deadly combat occurring in Southeast Asia at the time. To award Benavidez a MOH would result in publicity about matters best kept quiet. In fact, he, as well as others involved in the events of May 2, were "still under an oath of silence" about the classified mission in question that had "penetrated boundaries of other nations"— yet another obstacle in his path.[41]

The former Special Forces trooper was all too aware that Vietnam veterans had not received the same respect and gratitude as those from earlier wars. The United States had withdrawn from Vietnam without achieving victory, a source of embarrassment to the nation. Also, many Americans thought that their country should never have become embroiled in the conflict at all. There were also allegations of brutal and criminal acts by some U.S. troops in Southeast Asia. These circumstances meant that returning veterans too often had been met with hostility, rather than cheers. Benavidez suspected that these were the real reasons why he was getting the "runaround."[42]

The Tejano's funds and his energy were waning, but he had "faith in the fairness of the system." As he explained, "if I went down, I was going down swinging." On February 22, 1978, Fred Barbee, a friend of the veteran's and also editor of the *El Campo Leader-News*, published an emotional editorial asking if Washington had forgotten about Benavidez's exploits. The two men hoped that "publicity and political pressure" might make a difference. The disabled veteran sent copies of the article to numerous government and business leaders, and newspapers around the world reprinted the *Leader-News* editorial. Letters of support began to arrive from numerous individuals and organizations. Nevertheless, his chances for the medal still remained slim until one man in the Fiji Islands learned of Barbee's article.[43]

In the summer of 1980, "Tango Mike/Mike" got an unexpected telephone call from Brian O'Connor, the desperate man "who had radioed the frantic message seeking evacuation" on May 2, 1968. Each of the severely wounded men thought that the other had died that day. Only through Barbee's editorial had O'Connor learned that the hero who had saved him was alive and residing in Texas.[44]

To help his rescuer receive the recognition he deserved for the exceptional deeds performed a dozen years earlier, O'Connor prepared written statements on Benavidez's behalf. He praised the Tejano for voluntarily placing himself in danger against almost insurmountable odds because of a "sense of duty to get us out of there alive." The survivor admitted that he "was ready to die and I'm sure the other team members [also] realized the futility of continuing." However, Benavidez's resolute courage and spirit inspired them to "hold on for an extra five or ten minutes that then dragged into hours." Contending that the heroic actions bordered "on the realm of the humanly impossible," O'Connor insisted that Benavidez deserved an MOH in 1968 and still merited this honor.[45]

O'Connor's "report hit the Department of the Army like a bomb," as did the public response to Benavidez's situation. Suddenly, the impossible became possible. Late in 1980 the United States Congress passed, and President Jimmy Carter signed, a bill to award the long-sought recognition to the Tejano. The Mexican-American veteran had won another battle but would not receive the medal until February of 1981, when it would be presented by Carter's successor, Ronald Reagan.[46]

By the early 1980s the former Green Beret was—in his own words—"just a fat, middle-aged man." Nevertheless, he realized the significance of the event about to occur. He was going to be "a stand-in for all of the millions" who had served in Vietnam, as well as "the 350,000 who died or were wounded." This honor would signify "a new attitude of respect and understanding toward" the many military personnel whose sacrifices had not been properly appreciated at the time.[47]

The day before the awards ceremony, Benavidez along with dozens of relatives headed to the nation's capital, although the veteran had difficulty getting through the metal detector at the Houston airport because of the shrapnel still lodged in his body. Upon arrival, he, Lala, and their children were impressed by the luxurious penthouse suite at the Marriott Hotel where they were housed. More impressive still were the people they met, including the Secretary of Defense and the Secretary of the Army who had lunch with the family. That evening Drake came to the hotel. With him was O'Connor, whom Benavidez had not seen since 1968. The men embraced and cried. They talked about dead comrades "whom we would never see again, but remember always."[48]

On February 24, 1981, the honoree and his immediate family were taken to the White House, where they met with Ronald and Nancy Reagan. Intimidated in the presence of the president and his wife, the Benavidez adults had difficulty carrying on a conversation. Nine-year-old Raul unintentionally helped break the ice, when he saw the president's jar of jelly beans and asked for some. President Reagan gave the boy the whole container, and everyone began to relax.[49]

The Reagans and Benavidezes went together to the Pentagon for the formal presentation. In full dress uniform, Roy Benavidez stood at attention as the impressive ceremony began. That the Tejano was, as he had envisioned, a symbol of all Vietnam veterans was reinforced by the president's remarks. Reagan made clear his intention to honor not only the medal recipient but also all of the "fighting men who had obeyed their country's call and who had fought as bravely and as well as any Americans in our history." The commander-in-chief expressed his regret that "they were greeted by no parades, no bands, no waving of the flag. . . . There's been no 'thank you' for their sacrifice." Reagan expressed the nation's belated gratitude to these men and women, as he talked at length about the many good works that these Americans had performed in Vietnam such as building hospitals and orphanages.[50]

The president praised the heroism of Raul Benavidez, whose exploits had gone unrecognized for years. Recounting the saga in detail, Reagan explained that the Green Beret had volunteered to help his comrades and had exposed himself to constant barrages of enemy fire. Despite receiving many severe wounds, the Mexican American had provided fearless leadership and had saved at least eight lives. Furthermore, Reagan declared,

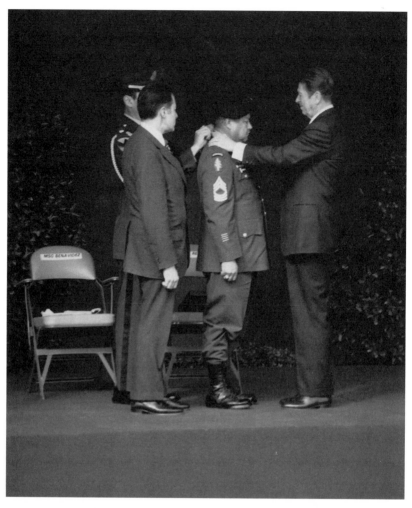

President Ronald Reagan bestows the Congressional Medal of Honor on Roy P. Benavidez, February 24, 1981. Roy P Benavidez Papers, 1943–2007, di_11026, The Dolph Briscoe Center for American History, The University of Texas at Austin.

his "actions in the face of overwhelming odds were in keeping with the highest traditions of the military service, and reflect the utmost credit on him and the United States Army." The former Master Sergeant was warmly thanked for "service above and beyond the call of duty."[51]

As President Reagan spoke, the honoree was hit by vivid memories of May 2, 1968. He could hear the "clatter of machine guns, the howl of jets. . . . I could smell the stench of frying flesh and worst of all, hear again the cries of my dying comrades." When the speech ended, Reagan placed the Medal of Honor around Benavidez's neck. At that historic moment, "Tango Mike/Mike" thought "this is for you guys—Leroy, Frenchy, and the rest who didn't come out of the jungle that day." As Benavidez prepared to salute his commander-in-chief, Reagan grabbed the Mexican-American hero and hugged him. The Tejano was so surprised that he unintentionally stepped on the president's foot.[52]

An exhausted, but triumphant, Benavidez and family headed home the next day. Back in El Campo, they discovered that a big reception had been planned in their honor. More than one thousand people came to the high school gymnasium to honor their local hero. Governor Bill Clements called to congratulate his fellow Texan, and the decorated veteran realized "that a return to any kind of normal life was going to be hard to come by."[53]

While many lauded the Tejano's moment of honor, others reacted differently. Some people in his hometown alleged that he received the medal only because of all the publicity he had generated, not because he truly deserved it. Jealousy may have been a factor, because the El Campo veteran was indeed becoming famous. At any rate, the Mexican American was deeply wounded by these sentiments, some of which were said to his face. However, the mature Benavidez, unlike the hot-headed adolescent he had been, did not strike out against those who maligned him.[54]

The veteran was also upset that people did not appreciate the amount of pain he suffered on a daily basis. In fact, his partial disability benefits had been "boosted to one hundred percent" in 1980. Legally certified as unable to work, he received a check from the Social Security Administration every month, money critical to the Benavidez family's economic well-being. However, there were those who viewed the Tejano as a stereotypical lazy Mexican. These detractors insisted that he should get a job, rather than having the taxpayers support him. That the veteran spent considerable time travelling to make speeches about his military exploits only added fuel to the fire.[55]

Gus Leija, Chairman of the American GI Forum of Corpus Christi, later felt compelled to defend Benavidez from the malice exhibited by some of the people in his hometown, "apparently for no other reason than his being Mexican-American." Quoting a local resident, Leija contended that Benavidez left El Campo "a poor unknown Mexican and came back a hero. Some people resent that." According to Leija, Benavidez only wanted to "survive with dignity and pride."[56]

Fortunately for Benavidez, his supporters greatly outnumbered his detractors. Following his historic trip to Washington, D.C., the Medal of Honor winner was in great demand as a speaker for school assemblies, youth groups, community organizations, and other functions. He not only accepted many invitations for public appearances but also got a GI-style haircut every Friday to look properly military. Indeed, the former Special Forces soldier felt compelled to champion "the cause of his comrades and lost comrades . . . as well as speaking out for America." Upset at the lack of patriotism in the country, he hoped to inspire others, especially young Mexican Americans, to love and appreciate the United States. The motto he lived by and the one he tried to impress upon his audiences was *"duty, honor, and country."*[57]

Benavidez urged children to stay in school and to stay off drugs. Using his own life as an example, he stressed the opportunities that America had to offer. After all, he had been a poor orphan with limited education and now was a Medal of Honor winner who had been hugged by the president of the United States! The Tejano also tried to set an example by going back to school and getting an associate's degree in Political Science. Earlier he had completed his high school education in the military.[58]

While making inspirational speeches, the war hero did not suspect that he would soon be in serious conflict again, this time with the very same government that he had served so loyally. However, in the early 1980s, the Social Security Administration (SSA) began "a cost-cutting review" process that resulted in hundreds of thousands of people losing their disability assistance. Those dropped from the program had the right to appeal the decision, and their monthly checks would continue until the case was decided. If the appeal were rejected, however, the recipient would have to repay the money received in the interim.[59]

In 1983, the MOH recipient was one of many notified that they "had to prove their disability for a second time in order to continue to receive benefits." He subsequently provided various documents and medical records to support his legal appeal. Unpersuaded, the SSA concluded that Benavidez was capable of lifting "a fifty-pound weight," as well as standing, walking, and sitting "for a total of 6 hours in an 8-hour work day." Looking at his body with its many scars and feeling the pain that was always with him, the veteran knew that an injustice was being perpetrated. Once again, he would fight for what was right. However, the battle with the SSA proved humiliating. Skeptical about Benavidez's disability claims, the agency made many demands of him, some of which seemed inappropriate for a distinguished veteran holding multiple medals and commendations. He had to appear before a judge at a formal hearing, be examined by a special physician in Houston, and submit to a psychiatric examination. The Tejano felt as if the government wanted to "pour a little salt in" his wounds.[60]

Results of the psychiatric examination referenced above proved illuminating. According to Dr. Will R. Calhoun, the forty-eight year-old veteran reported being upset by the many malicious comments directed at him. Benavidez also disclosed virtually constant medical problems, as well as being "intermittently troubled with nightmares," waking "up in a cold sweat on occasions," and having difficulty being confined. Regarding his own observation of Benavidez's mental status, Calhoun wrote that the Tejano tended to focus on "his medical problems and the events of the past" but that "his contact with reality is good." Despite there being no evidence of "delusions, hallucinations or confusions," Benavidez was described as having "some subtle defects in his remote memory as well as his recent memory."[61]

Diagnosing the Vietnam veteran as suffering from Chronic Post Traumatic Stress Disorder, Dr. Calhoun reported that "the patient's ability to withstand the stresses and pressures associated with day-to-day work activity is grossly impaired." He alluded to the significance of the Tejano's agreeing "to accept medical retirement from the army which was the one work activity that he was greatly ego-involved with, and he felt unable to perform." According to Calhoun, "if he [Benavidez] only suffered from his medical problems or if he only suffered from his . . . stress disorder, that either one of these would not be severe enough to totally incapacitate him. However, the combination of the two seems to present significant problems and significant impairment."[62]

The above psychiatric report certainly strengthened the veteran's case but was not the only weapon in his arsenal. As in his campaign to get the MOH, publicity played a key role in the outcome of this battle. In April, the *Reader's Digest* published an article titled "A Medal for Roy Benavidez," and the producer of a television program called *Real People* planned an episode about Benavidez's military exploits to be aired on Memorial Day in May of 1983. Newspapers carried stories about this wounded hero being denied his modest benefits. WFAA, a radio station in Dallas, asked him to talk on air about his plight. As his story spread, the Tejano feared being perceived as an object of charity. He only wanted what he deserved as a disabled veteran.[63]

Benavidez was swamped with telephone calls, letters, and visits from others threatened with loss of their benefits— "cripples, mothers with small children, disabled veterans, you name it." They asked the Tejano to be their spokesman, a role with which he was not really comfortable. He simply hoped to "get my benefits restored so I could pay my utility bills, feed and clothe my family, and have enough left over to take a trip now and then to speak." Nevertheless, he soon found himself representing "the common man, in general, and the veteran, in particular. "[64]

Facing negative publicity, government officials hoped to resolve the situation quickly and quietly. While Benavidez was in Washington, D.C. to film the *Real People* episode, he was invited to a meeting at the White House, which became a major media affair. The Tejano was informed privately that the Reagan administration was taking a special interest in his situation, which would be handled with help from private sources. The Mexican American was all too aware, however, that others were in financial jeopardy as well. In front of the cameras, he declared that "these same people who are denying us our benefits are living free at the expense of my buddies, their lives, blood, and limbs." Again he clarified that he did not "want charity—I wanted justice."[65]

The outspoken Medal of Honor winner was asked to appear before The Select Committee on Aging of the House of Representatives in June of 1983 with *Real People* cameras filming the event. With Benavidez was his lawyer, Tom Burch, a former Green Beret and representative of the United Vietnam Veterans Organizations. During stirring testimony, the Tejano protested the injustice being committed against those who went to war to defend their country, as well as "their widows, their sons, their daughters." The Mexican American pointed out the irony "that 'the Administration that put this medal around my neck is curtailing my benefits.'" Near the end of the proceedings, one congressman asked Benavidez whether he would serve in Vietnam "over again, if you knew that these events were going to happen." Without hesitation, the Mexican-American veteran answered, "Yes sir, I would do it all over."[66]

Partly because of the publicity generated by Benavidez's crusade, the Secretary of Health and Human Services announced that "disability reviews would become more 'humane and compassionate.'" This must have been welcome news to all involved in the process, and the Tejanos veteran's testimony ultimately helped many people get their benefits restored. In July 1983 Benavidez received the welcome news that he would continue to receive his disability payments, and less than two years later, the Veterans Administration again affirmed that the Mexican American was 100 percent disabled. Therefore, he was entitled "to a compensation rate of $2,374.00 for a married veteran," which did not include any stipend for children or the $200 he was already "receiving as a Medal of Honor recipient."[67] Yet another battle had been won.

Having been in the spotlight again, Benavidez received even more invitations for public appearances around the country and abroad. That he had a positive impact on his audiences was illustrated when the decorated veteran spoke in Houston. While the Tejano had been serving his country, one man in attendance had been a peace protester on a college campus, because he had believed that "the war was wrong!" As he subsequently wrote to Benavidez, "I can't say I would have had the nerve to do what you did. But what you did made me more proud than I have been in a long time to be an American."[68]

The MOH recipient received many letters and kept them all, which became an issue as far as Hilaria was concerned. Finally, his wife told him to "either rent a storage shed for all of these papers or stack them in your bedroom and *you* live in the storage shed."[69] We do not know which choice he made but suspect that it was the former!

Much was written by and about Benavidez, as well as to him. In 1986, he co-authored a book with Oscar Griffin called *The Three Wars of Roy Benavidez*, dedicated to his family, his "brothers-in-arms," his friends, and the "nation's young people." The former Green Beret also wrote the dedication page for Pete Billac's *The Last Medal of Honor*, published in 1990. He commemorated the veterans who "have a hard time sleeping or being able to cope with life because of the battles they fought." He praised "the nurses, who seem to have been forgotten," as well as expressing his appreciation "to the veterans who gave up their tomorrows so each of us could live our todays." In 1995, with the assistance of John R. Craig, the Tejano penned *Medal of Honor: A Vietnam Warrior's Story*, reissued a decade later as *Medal of Honor: One Man's Journey from Poverty and Prejudice*.[70]

Finally, there came a battle that Benavidez could not win, as his health problems became more serious. In 1998, he was hospitalized in San Antonio after a long illness complicated by anemia and diabetes. In October doctors had to perform a partial amputation of his right leg. The patient seemed to be improving by late November, but then his condition deteriorated. Along with family and friends, a stream of military officers came to pay their respects to the dying man. Roy Benavidez expired at Brooke Army Medical Center on November 29, 1998, at age sixty-three.[71]

The veteran's funeral did not take place for five days, because there were many who wanted to pay their respects. A service was held at St. Roberts Catholic Church in El Campo on December 1, where Fred Barbee's son, Chris, delivered a eulogy. Speaking of the deceased, Barbee noted that "I never saw a mean bone in his body, but I'm sure hundreds of North Vietnamese regulars and Viet Cong would surely disagree." He also chastised those who "felt that Roy should maintain a lower profile than he did" by declaring that "it was his willingness to stand up and be counted that made him special."[72]

The day after the service in El Campo, the body was available for viewing at a funeral home in San Antonio with a rosary in the chapel at Fort Sam Houston scheduled for that evening. Then, on the morning of Thursday, December 3, 1998, a mass was celebrated by family-friend Archbishop Patrick Flores at San Fernando Cathedral, followed by the funeral at the Fort Sam Houston National Cemetery. Some 1,500 family, friends, and admirers were there to bid farewell to this exceptional Mexican American.[73]

Both before and after his death, Raul Benavidez was showered with well-deserved honors, other than the many military decorations and commendations he had received. In 1981, Governor William Clements proclaimed a Roy Benavidez Day during which the veteran was honored in Austin, and the governor also commissioned him an honorary Admiral in the Texas Navy. That same year the Texas Press Association named him Texan of the Year—its highest honor. In the 1980s, several Texas cities, including Galveston and Houston, proclaimed their own Benavidez Day, and he was later named an honorary citizen of Midland. Also, when the Hispanic Hall of Fame was established in 1987, the veteran was informed of his "nomination for induction" as a "unique" individual "whose contributions must be further recognized and published nationwide." Accolades continued into the twenty-first century with the Texas Legislative Medal of Honor being bestowed upon the native son "for his acts of valor and for the way he devoted the rest of his life to the youth of Texas and the United States." Multiple schools were named after him, as well as a National Guard armory, a conference room at West Point Military Academy, and a Special Operations Logistics Complex at Fort Bragg, North Carolina. The United States Postal Service even issued a pictorial stamp to commemorate the Medal of Honor recipient.[74]

One of the greatest posthumous honors occurred in the year 2000, when the United States Navy announced plans to name a ship after the Tejano. The USNS *Benavidez* was one of the "class of ships . . . [that] are capable of coming forward in a vital way when America calls for reinforcement of its combat needs around the world." According to Secretary of the Navy Richard Danzig, this was the spirit that Benavidez had represented. The recently widowed Hilaria declared that "Roy would be proud" and attended the ceremony in July 2001 to christen the vessel. Another tribute that same year seemed particularly fitting as part of the Green Beret's proud legacy. "In 2001, the Hasbro toy company released the Roy P. Benavidez G.I. Joe action figure, the first G.I. Joe to portray someone of Hispanic heritage."[75] He had elevated not only the image of Vietnam veterans but also of Latinos.

Three years later, on Armed Forces Day, a bronze sculpture of the hometown hero was unveiled in the Roy P. Benavidez Park in Cuero, Texas. A memorial foundation had dedicated several years to raising the $50,000 needed to bring the project to fruition. Donations came from numerous individuals and organizations desiring to honor the hero who dedicated his life to "Duty, Honor, and Country."[76]

* * *

Today Raul "Roy" Benavidez would be labeled "disadvantaged," because he was a Mexican American born into poverty and orphaned at an early age. In his youth, he was too fond of fighting and not fond enough of studying. That he would make much of his life seemed doubtful. Joining the army was the right decision for Raul, as was marrying Hilaria. Both brought needed elements of stability, maturity, and purpose into his life. None of this would have made a difference, however, if Benavidez himself had not grown to be a man of great courage and proven determination. More than once, he faced death in the service of his country, and in so doing, he won the respect of his fellow soldiers and of his superiors. During the Vietnam War, he selflessly rescued his comrades at a high price to himself. Afterwards he did not seek charity but only wanted his due, whether it was a Medal of Honor or disability benefits.

Was "The Mean Mexican" a hero? President Jimmy Carter, himself a veteran, and his successor Ronald Reagan thought so. The men whose lives he saved certainly agreed. The children and adults inspired by his speeches considered him heroic, as did the disabled Americans helped by his efforts. Almost certainly, anyone reading his biography would conclude that this outstanding Mexican American deserved the label of hero. One man would disagree, however. Despite his pleasure in talking about his military exploits, Roy Benavidez did not feel that the word applied to him. In his view, "the real heroes are the ones who gave their lives for their country. . . . I just did what I was trained to do."[77]

Bibliographical Commentary

Four books are the major primary and secondary published sources from which to learn about Roy Benavidez's dramatic life. In 1986, he co-authored *The Three Wars of Roy Benavidez* with Oscar Griffin. Almost a decade later, assisted by John R. Craig, Benavidez wrote *Medal of Honor: A Vietnam Warrior's Story* (1995), published again in 2005 as *Medal of Honor: One Man's Journey from Poverty and Prejudice*. Between the original publication dates of these first-person narratives, Pete Billac authored *The Last Medal of Honor* (1990), for which Benavidez penned the dedication. More recently, Eric Blehm authored *Legend* (2015) based on access to family members, accounts by eyewitnesses, and documents from various archives. Combined, these works provide the reader with an impressive amount of information about this heroic Mexican American–much of it from Benavidez's perspective. For the younger reader, Yvette Benavidez Garcia recently published a children's book about her father's early life and military career: *Tango Mike Mike: The Story of Master Sergeant Roy P. Benavidez* (2017).

An internet search for "Roy Benavidez" produces numerous possibilities that range from "[Ronald Reagan's] Remarks on Presenting the Medal of Honor to Master Sergeant Roy P. Benavidez" to "Roy P. Benavidez: Biographical Essay." YouTube videos include one by the ConsHispanicSociety that covers the highlights of Benavidez's life and exploits (5:15) and an autobiographical, inspirational speech (24:50) given by Benavidez himself in 1991. Also, the *Handbook of Texas Online* has an entry by Art Leatherwood entitled "Benavidez, Raul Pérez [Roy,] (1935–1998)" that can be accessed at www.tshaonline.org.

For the more serious investigator, Benavidez's papers are housed at the Institute for Studies in American Military History, Dolph Briscoe Center for American History at The University of Texas at Austin. Donated by the Benavidez family, the collection includes "correspondence, photographs, topical files, military documents, honors and awards, writings, printed materials, LP albums, and memorabilia." See "A Guide to the Roy P. Benavidez Papers, 1943–2007" (www.lib. utexas.edu/taro/utcah/00585/00585-P.html).

Endnotes

1. Roy P. Benavidez, MSG. (Special Forces) Green Beret, U.S.A., Biographical Sketch, [nd], "The Benavidez (Roy P.) Papers, 1943–2007," The Institute for Studies in American Military History, Dolph Briscoe Center for American History, University of Texas at Austin, Box 4Zc194 [Benavidez Papers hereinafter cited as Papers, CAH]; Roy Benavidez with John R. Craig, *Medal of Honor: A Vietnam Warrior's Story* (Washington: Brassey's, 1995), xv, 1–3; Pete Billac, *The Last Medal of Honor* (New York: Swan Publishers, 1990), 20. Although named Raul by his parents, Benavidez later legally changed his name to Roy.

2. "Roy P. Benavidez," Biography Resource Center, http://draweb.utb. edu:2012/servlet/BioRC/hists?c=1&b=&docType=Narrative+Biography; Benavidez, *Medal of Honor*, 4–5, quotations on 5.

3. Benavidez, Biographical Sketch, Papers, CAH; Benavidez, *Medal of Honor*, 5, 7, 11; Eric Blehm, *Legend* (New York: Crown Publishers, 2015), 8–10, quotation on 10.

4. Billac, *Last Medal*, 20; Benavidez, *Medal of Honor*, 8, 12–13; "Benavidez," Biography Resource Center; "Ship's Name to Honor Army Hero Benavidez," *San Antonio Express News*, September 17, 2000, http://www.mishalov.com/ Benavidez.html.

5. "Ship's Name," *San Antonio Express*, 2000; Benavidez, *Medal of Honor*, 6, 9, 15–16, 21, 1st quotation on 16, 2nd and 3rd quotations on 21, 4th and 5th quotations on 9.

6. Richard Goldstein, "Roy P. Benavidez, Recipient of Medal of Honor, Dies at 63," *New York Times*, December 4, 1998, http://www.nytimes. com/1998/12/04/us/roy-p-benavidez-recipient-of-medal-of-honor-dies-at-63. html; Benavidez, *Medal of Honor*, 19, 24; "Raul (Roy) Benavidez," The Beret Project, Tuesday, June 11, 2011, http://beretandboina.blogspot.com/2011/03/ raul-roy-perez-benavidez.html; Blehm, *Legend*, 21, 23, quotation on 23.

7. "Benavidez," Biography Resource Center; Benavidez, *Medal of Honor*, 19–25, passim, quotations on 23.

8. The *Handbook of Texas Online*, Art Leatherwood, "Benavidez, Raul Perez [Roy]," http://www.tshaonline.org/handbook/online/articles/fbetq [The *Handbook of Texas Online* hereafter cited as *HOT Online*]; Benavidez, *Medal of Honor*, 30–31. See Alex Mendoza, "'I Know No Other Country': Tejanos and the American Wars of the Twentieth Century, 1917–1972," *Military History of*

the West 41 (2011): 31–59 for an analysis of the complex and evolving reasons that motivated Tejanos to serve in the U.S. military during the 1900s.

9. "Benavidez," Biography Resource Center; "Ship's Name," *San Antonio Express*, 2000, quotations; Benavidez, *Medal of Honor*, 33–34; Biographical Note, A Guide to the Roy P. Benavidez Papers, 1943–2007, Briscoe Center for American History, The University of Texas at Austin, http://www.lib.utexas.edu/taro/utcah/00585/cah-00585.html; Mendoza, "'I Know No Other Country," *Military History of the West*, 48. According to the estate attorney, Raul Benavidez did not just Americanize his name by beginning to call himself Roy but at some point underwent a legal name change.

10. Sean McCoy, "The Power of One," *Touchstone* (March 2005): 18–20; Benavidez, *Medal of Honor*, 41–46, 1ˢᵗ quotation on 43, 2ⁿᵈ quotation on 46.

11. Blehm, *Legend*, 28–30, 1ˢᵗ quotation on 28, 2ⁿᵈ and 3ʳᵈ quotations on 29, 4ᵗʰ through 6ᵗʰ quotations on 30.

12. Benavidez, *Medal of Honor*, 30, 61–63, 1ˢᵗ quotation on 30, 3ʳᵈ quotation on 62; Roy Benavidez and Oscar Griffin, *The Three Wars of Roy Benavidez* (San Antonio: Corona Publishing Co., 1986), 72–72, 2ⁿᵈ quotation on 72.

13. *HOT Online*, Leatherwood, "Benavidez"; "Benavidez," Biography Resource Center; 82D Airborne Division Certificate of Completion, Roy P. Benavidez, SP5 E5, 12 May 1961, Papers, CAH 4Zc194.

14. Robert Divine, et al., *The American Story*, Combined Volume, 5ᵗʰ ed. (Boston: Pearson, 2013), 973, 992–996.

15. Billac, *Last Medal*, 143, all quotations.

16. "Benavidez," Biography Resource Center.

17. "Benavidez," Biography Resource Center; Benavidez and Griffin, *Three Wars*, 70–71; Benavidez, *Medal of Honor*, 85.

18. Benavidez and Griffin, *Three Wars*, 70–71; Benavidez, *Medal of Honor*, 85, 87–89, 96, 1ˢᵗ quotation on 96; Blehm, *Legend*, 46, 48–49, 2ⁿᵈ quotation on 49.

19. Blehm, *Legend*, 49–50, 1ˢᵗ quotation; Benavidez and Griffin, *Three Wars*, 79–81, 2ⁿᵈ quotation on 81.

20. Benavidez and Griffin, *Three Wars*, 81–83, 1ˢᵗ quotation on 82; Blehm, *Legend*, 50–51, 2ⁿᵈ quotation; Benavidez, *Medal of Honor*, 98.

21. Benavidez, *Medal of Honor*, 99–103, passim.

22. Benavidez and Griffin, *Three Wars*, 120–122; Blehm, *Legend*, 53–54.

23. Blehm, *Legend*, 57, 1ˢᵗ quotation; Benavidez and Griffin, *Three Wars*, 123–126, 2ⁿᵈ through 4ᵗʰ quotations on 124, 5ᵗʰ quotation on 125.

24. Benavidez, *Medal of Honor*, 121–125, passim, 1ˢᵗ quotation on 121, 2ⁿᵈ through 4ᵗʰ quotations on 125.

25. Richard Goldstein, "Roy P. Benavidez, Recipient of Medal of Honor, Dies at 63," *New York Times* Archives, December 4, 1998, 4ᵗʰ quotation, http://www.nytimes.com/1998/12/04/us/roy-p-benavidez-recipient-of-medal-of-honor-dies-at-63.html; Ronald Reagan, "Remarks on Presenting the Medal of Honor to Sergeant Roy P. Benavidez, February 24, 1981," 1ˢᵗ and 2ⁿᵈ quotations, wysiwyg://18//http://www.reagan.utexas.edu/resource/speeches/1981/22481d.htm; Blehm, *Legend*, 151–171, passim; "Benavidez, Roy Perez," http://www.nightscribe.com/Military/benevidez.htm, [hereinafter cited as "Benavidez," nightscribe]; Benavidez, *Medal of Honor*, 139–140, 3ʳᵈ quotation on 139. As Blehm notes on pages 99 and

121 of *Legend*, this was a top secret mission and the men involved were sworn to secrecy, at least in part because U.S. troops were not publicly acknowledged to be in Cambodia at the time.

26. Reagan, "Remarks," 1st and 3rd quotations; "Benavidez, Roy P.," findagrave.org/state/46.html, 4th quotation; Benavidez, *Three Wars*, 206, 2nd quotation; "Roy P. Benavidez, Patriot," Military Order of the Purple Heart, Texas Capital Chapter 1919, Austin, Texas, http://www.purpleheartaustin.org/Benavidez.htm; "Benavidez," Biography Resource Center; Billac, *Last Medal of Honor* (New York: Swan Publishers, 1990), 27–29.

27. Reagan, "Remarks," 1st quotation; Benavidez, *Three Wars*, 213–214; Blehm, *Legend*, 204–205; "Benavidez," nightscribe, 2nd quotation;

28. Reagan, "Remarks," 1st quotation; McCoy, "The Power of One," 25; "Benavidez," Biography Resource Center, 2nd and 3rd quotations.

29. Reagan, "Remarks," 1st quotation; "Benavidez," findagrave, 2nd quotation.

30. Benavidez and Griffin, *Three Wars*, Prologue, 1–2, 4–5, 1st quotation on 1; Billac, *Last Medal*, 78–80; Ross Perot, Foreword, *Medal of Honor*, vii–viii, 2nd quotation. Pages 84–85 of Billac's *Last Medal* contain illustrated drawings with a "Front View" and a "Rear View" of Benavidez's body with the many wounds suffered on May 2, 1968.

31. Billac, *Last Medal*, 18–20, 81–83; Benavidez, *Medal of Honor*, 153.

32. Department of the Army Headquarters, United States Army Vietnam, General Orders Number 3572, 24 July 1968, Award of the Distinguished Service Cross, RA25865154 Staff Sergeant E6, Papers, CAH 4Zc194; Benavidez, Biographical Sketch, Papers, CAH; Billac, *Last Medal*, 87–88, quotation on 87.

33. Benavidez, *Medal of Honor*, 152–153.

34. Enlisted Efficiency Report, Benavidez, Roy P SFC, 5th USA Spt Elm . . . by Patrick F. Cassidy, LTG, USA, 30 September [197?], Papers, CAH, 4Zc194, all quotations; Benavidez, *Medal of Honor*, 152.

35. Benavidez, *Medal of Honor*, 152–154; "Medal of Honor Recipient Master Sergeant Roy Benavidez," www.Psywarrior.com/Benavidez.html; Benavidez, *Three Wars*, 250, quotation; U.S. Army Military Personnel Center, Alexandria, Virginia, 27 August 1976, James A. Windsor, Lt. Col, GS, Chief, Retirement Branch, Orders D41-2, Papers, CAH.

36. Benavidez, *Medal of Honor*, 153, 237–238, quotation on 238. Sources present conflicting versions as to whether Colonel Ralph Drake had recommended Benavidez for a MOH after the events of May 2, 1968. According to "A Guide to the Roy P. Benavidez Papers, 1943–2007," Briscoe Center for American History, Benavidez learned that Drake had recommended him twice without success for a MOH. However, in both *Three Wars* (239) and *Medal of Honor* (154) Benavidez writes that Drake told him the original recommendation was for a Distinguished Service Cross, not a Medal of Honor.

37. Benavidez and Griffin, *Three Wars*, 239, quotation; Benavidez, *Medal of Honor*, 154.

38. FACT Sheet, Subject: Request for Upgrade of the Distinguished Service Cross to the Congressional Medal of Honor for MSG Roy Benavidez, Papers, CAH, 4Zc194; Benavidez, *Medal of Honor*, 154–155; Benavidez and Griffin, *Three Wars*, 241–24, quotation on 241. See also letter from Ralph R. Drake to Commander, Fifth U.S. Army, Attn: Awards & Decorations, 9 April 1974, in *Three Wars*, 241–243.

39. Benavidez, *Medal of Honor*, 155, 2nd quotation; Benavidez and Griffin, *Three Wars*, 239–240, 279, 1st quotation on 239, 3rd quotation on 279, 4th and 5th quotations on 240.

40. William C. Moore, Brigadier General, USA, Director of Personnel Management Systems, to Joseph D. Martin, 22 June 1977, Papers, CAH, 4Zc194, 1st and 2nd quotations; Dudley T. Bunn, Colonel, Department of the Army, to Ms. Mack J. Webb, 12 April 1977, Papers, CAH 4Zc194; Benavidez and Griffin, *Three Wars*, 245, 256–257, 3rd quotation on 256.

41. Benavidez, *Three Wars*, 253–258; Blehm, *Legend*, 240–241, 1st quotation on 241; Fact Sheet, Subject: Request for Upgrade of the Distinguished Service Cross, Papers, CAH, 2nd quotation.

42. Benavidez and Griffin, *Three Wars*, 257, quotation.

43. Clipping, "TV Cameras Visit El Campo," [no other information, probably *El Campo Leader-News*, 1978], Papers, CAH, 4Zc194; Benavidez and Griffin, *Three Wars*, 255–259, 1st quotation on 257, 2nd and 3rd quotations on 259; Benavidez, *Medal of Honor*, 156; Ruben Bonilla, Jr., Office of National President, LULAC, Apr. 1, 1980, to the President, Papers, CAH. For a copy of Barbee's article from the El Campo *Leader News*, see *Three Wars*, 255–259. Examples of correspondence between Benavidez and officials such as Senator John Tower can be found in the Benavidez Papers, CAH.

44. Goldstein, "Benavidez," *NYT*, quotation; Benavidez, *Medal of Honor*, 157.

45. Congressional Medal of Honor Eyewitness Statement for Roy Benavidez MSG Retired, Brian T. O'Connor, SP/4 Retired, July 24, 1980, Papers, CAH 4zc194; Additional Statement, Brian T. O'Connor, SP/4 Retired, [part of date missing, probably July 24 or 25] 1980, Papers, CAH, 4Zc194, all quotations.

46. Benavidez and Griffin, *Three Wars*, 262–263, quotation on 262.

47. Benavidez and Griffin, *Three Wars*, 266–267, 1st quotation on 266, 2[nd,] 3rd, and 4th quotations on 267.

48. Arthur Wiese, "Benavidez Remembered 'Buddies' at Ceremony," *Houston Post*, Feb. 25, 1981, Papers, CAH, 4Zc194; Benavidez, *Medal of Honor*, 158; Benavidez and Griffin, *Three Wars*, 263–264, quotation on 264.

49. Benavidez and Griffin, *Three Wars*, 267.

50. Benavidez, *Medal of Honor*, 158; Ronald Reagan, "Remarks on Presenting the Medal of Honor to Master Sergeant Roy P. Benavidez," all quotations, wysiwyg://18/ http://www.reagan.utexas.edu/resource/speeches/1981/22481d.htm.

51. Reagan, "Remarks," all quotations.

52. Benavidez and Griffin, *Three Wars*, 270, 1st and 2nd quotations; Benavidez, *Medal of Honor*, 161. A photograph of President Reagan hugging Roy Benavidez and the honoree accidentally stepping on the president's shoe can be found in Billac's *Last Medal of Honor*, 95.

53. Benavidez and Griffin, *Three Wars*, 271, quotation.

54. Benavidez and Griffin, *Three Wars*, 272–276, passim.

55. Benavidez and Griffin, *Three Wars*, 276–278, quotation on 177; Billac, *Last Medal*, 18–19. Letters to editors that can be found in the Benavidez Papers at the Briscoe Center for American History emphasize the resentment that some people expressed about his receiving disability benefits.

56. Gus Leija, "Prejudice Seen," Letter to the Editor, *El Campo Leader-News*, 16 May 1984, Papers, CAH, 4ZC194, all quotations.

57. TRC-Disability Determination Request for Psychiatric Examination, Will R. Calhoun, M.D., Psychiatrist, Benavides [*sic*], Roy P., June 2, 1983, Papers, CAH, 4Zc195, 1st quotation [Hereinafter cited as TRC-Disability Determination Request, Papers, CAH]; "Roy Perez Benavidez," http://www.houstonisd.org/Page/91541; Billac, *Last Medal*, 17–18, 97; Benavidez, *Medal of Honor*, 171–172; Benavidez and Griffin, *Three Wars* 279–280; "Master Sergeant Roy P. Benavidez Memorial," 2nd quotation, http://www.markbyrd.com/RPB_memorial.htm; The Benavidez Papers at the Center for American History at UT Austin contain ample correspondence and other documents that testify to the many requests that Roy received to make public appearances, as well as his acceptance of numerous of those invitations.

58. Billac, *Last Medal*, 18, 20, 99; Benavidez, *Medal of Honor*, 171–172.

59. Goldstein, *NYT*, quotation; Benavidez and Griffin, *Three Wars*, 281–281; Billac, *Last Medal*, 149.

60. Social Security Notice, Department of Health and Human Services Social Security Administration, to Roy P. Benavidez, Feb. 22, 1983, Papers, CAH, 4Zc195, 3rd quotation; Blehm, *Legend*, 257–258, 1st quotation; Benavidez and Griffin, *Three Wars*, 181, 281–282, 2nd quotation on 181; Billac, *Last Medal* 19; Goldstein, "Benavidez," *NYT*, 3rd quotation.

61. TRC-Disability Determination Request, Papers, CAH, all quotations.

62. TRC-Disability Determination Request, Papers, CAH, all quotations.

63. Benavidez and Griffin, *Three Wars*, 282–283; Billac, *Last Medal*, 250–252.

64. Billac, *Last Medal*, 150, 1st quotation; Benavidez and Griffin, *Three Wars*, 284, 287–288, 2nd quotation on 288, 3rd quotation on 284. That Benavidez's efforts affected others can be readily illustrated. As an example, see a letter from Frances Rockledge of Manchester, Connecticut, to Benavidez on September 14, 1983 [Benavidez Papers, CAH, Box 4Zc199]. Disabled "for about ten years," Rockledge explains that she has a daughter "whose survival depends on me." She expresses appreciation to the veteran for his having responded to an earlier letter of hers and thanks him for his "thoughtfulness and help."

65. Billac, *Last Medal*, 151; Benavidez and Griffin, *Three Wars*, 284–285, 1st quotation on 285, 2nd quotation on 286.

66. Blehm, *Legend*, 258, 1st quotation; Billac, *Last Medal*, 151; Benavidez and Griffin, *Three Wars*, 286–288, 3rd and 4th quotations on 288; Goldstein, "Benavidez," *NYT*, 2nd quotation.

67. Goldstein, "Benavidez," *NYT*, 1st quotation; *HOT Online*, Leatherwood, "Benavidez"; Veterans Administration, February 26, 1985, to Roy P. Benavidez in Reply Refer to: 362/213B, C 29-283-595, Papers, CAH, 2nd and 3rd quotations.

68. "Born: August 5, 1935 Died: November 29, 1998," section titled "Retirement," http://www.post639.com/msg_roy_benavidez.htm; Letter from Charlie Thop, Houston, Texas, to Roy Benavidez, n.d., printed in Billac, *Last Medal*, 184, all quotations.

69. Billac, *Last Medal*, 97, quotation.

70. Benavidez and Griffin, *Three Wars*, Dedication, n.p., 1st and 2nd quotations; Billac, *Last Medal*, Dedication, n.p., 3rd, 4th and 5th quotations; Benavidez and Craig, *Medal of Honor*, 1995; Roy Benavidez and John R. Craig, *Medal of Honor: One Man's Journey from Poverty to Prejudice* (Washington, D.C.: Potomac Books, 2005).

71. "MOH Recipient, Roy Perez Benavidez," http://members.aol.com/lilsispam/taps.htm; [Benavidez Obituary], *San Antonio Express-News*, 29, http:www.mishalov.com/Benavidez.html. Sources differ as to whether Roy Benavidez said any last words as he lay dying and what those words might have been.

72. Copy of Eulogy by Chris Barbee, Dec. 1, 1998—6 p.m., Wake at St. Robert's Catholic Church, Papers, CAH, 4Zc194, all quotations.

73. "Born . . . Died," section titled "Death," www.post639.com; "MOH Recipient, section titled "Funeral Arrangements," http://members.aol.com; "Benavidez," www.houston.isd.org.

74. "State Leaders to Honor Benavidez in Austin Tuesday," El Campo *Leader-News*, Mar. 28, 1981, Papers, CAH, 4Zc194; "Roy Benavidez Receives Medal of Honor for Bravery," *Twin City News*, Rochester, Texas, June 18, 1981, http://tcn.stparchive.com/Archive/TCN/TCN06181981PO1.php; "Texas Press Group Honors Countian as Texan of 1981," *Wharton Journal-Spectator*, June 25, 1981, Papers, CAH, 4Zc194; Proclamation, Office of the Mayor [E. "Gus" Manuel], City of Galveston, 1981, Papers, CAH, 4Zc195; Proclamation, Kathryn J. Whitmire, Mayor of the City of Houston, 8 May 1987, Papers, CAH, 4Zc195; "Greetings: Honorary Citizen of Midland, Texas," Carroll Thomas, Mayor, July 13, 1991, Papers, CAH, 4Zc194; Letter from Oscar Moran, National President, League of United Latin American Citizens, March 17, 1987 to Roy P. Benavidez, Papers, CAH, 4Zc199, 1st, 2nd, and 3rd quotations: "Born . . . Died," www.post639.com; "Master Sergeant Roy P. Benavidez Memorial," 4th quotation, http://www.markbyrd.com/RPB_memorial.htm; Goldstein, "Benavidez," *NYT*. The section entitled "Awards, honors, and recognitions" in the previously cited "Born: August 5, 1935, Died: November 29, 1998" at www.post639.com provides lists of Benavidez's major military decorations and other honors received.

75. "Navy Names New Roll-On/Roll-Off Ship for U.S. Army War Hero," September 15, 2000, 1st quotation, http://www.rpbfoundation.org/navy%20ship.htm; "Ship's Name," *San Antonio Express News*, September 17, 2000, 2nd quotation, http://www.mishalov.com/Benavidez.html; Sig Christenson, "Navy's Newest Ship Is Solid—Like Its Namesake," San Antonio, web posted: July 22, 2001, 3rd quotation, http://www.hcvc.org/2001archives/july2001.html; Benavidez," www.houstonisd.org.

76. Mike Scovel Studios, "Veteran's Memorials and Military Artwork," http:mikescovel.powerweb.com/VeteransMemorials.htm; "Bronze Sculpture Honoring Roy Benavidez Nears Completion," Cuero, TX (PRWEB), April 29, 2004, http://www.prweb.com/releases/2004/04/prweb122096.htm; "Cuero Honors Hometown Hero," MyPlainview, November 11, 2004, http://www.myplainview.com/news/article/Cuero-honors-hometown-hero-8832085.php.

77. Goldstein, "Benavidez," *NYT*, quotation.

Irma Rangel takes the oath of office for the Texas House of Representatives in 1977. Irma Lerma Rangel Collection, A2003-042.0010, South Texas Archives, James C. Jernigan Library, Texas A&M University-Kingsville.

Irma Lerma Rangel

Latina Legislator

BORN IN KINGSVILLE, TEXAS, on May 15, 1931, Irma Rangel helped pave the way for future generations of Latinas.[1] Despite the many obstacles she faced as a Mexican-American woman, she let nothing stand in the way of fulfilling her goals. During her lifetime, the Tejana gained education, position, power, and respect. She used these not for her own benefit, but rather to make it easier for others to achieve their dreams as well.

Rangel lived at a time when important changes were occurring in her state and in the nation. Tired of being second-class citizens on the basis of gender, ethnicity, or race, minority groups within the United States were demanding better treatment and increased opportunities. Not one to be a bystander, the Tejana took a leading role in implementing reforms in the Lone Star State. Although her primary focus was to benefit minorities, the lives of other Texans were improved as well. In her successive roles as teacher, lawyer, and legislator, she had an impact that is hard to overemphasize.

In her personal life, Rangel had more than her share of hardships. As a young woman, she had to overcome the death of her fiancé, and she never married despite living into her seventies. Later in life, she was confronted by a number of serious health crises, any one of which could have broken the spirit of a lesser person. Rather than indulge in self-pity, however, she worked tirelessly until she

literally was on her deathbed to make Texas a better place for all of
its citizens. This woman of courage can truly serve as an inspiration
for all of us.

* * *

Irma's father, Presciliano Martínez "P.M" Rangel, was of humble
origins. An orphan at age five, he had little opportunity for formal
education. Although he worked in agriculture as a cotton picker,
P.M. wanted to improve his circumstances and through his own
efforts attained marginal literacy. With time, he became a businessman who owned "a bar, two barbershops, and several other stores."
His wife, Herminia Lerma, also overcame a difficult background.
Orphaned herself after she finished fifth grade, she had to drop
out of school. Before she was twenty, Herminia married P.M, and
the couple eventually had three children: Irma, Olga, and Minnie.
During the Depression, "Big Minnie" spent weekends peddling
"clothes from ranch to ranch outside of Kingsville." On occasion,
young Irma accompanied her mother to sell candy to the customers'
children. As a result of Big Minnie's efforts and her husband's
encouragement, she eventually became the proprietor of a dress
shop. Serving as role models, P.M. and Big Minnie showed their
children that hard work and strong determination were among the
keys to success.[2]

Another source of inspiration to their daughters was their
parents' refusal to submit to discrimination. As improved economic
circumstances enabled the Rangels to build a new home, they
purchased a lot in an Anglo (white) neighborhood near Texas
College of Arts and Industries in Kingsville (now Texas A&M
University-Kingsville). Local residents felt threatened not only by
the possibility of having "Mexicans" as neighbors but also by P.M.'s
work with other activists to elect minorities to the Kingsville city
council and school board. Anglos in Kingsville failed to make any
real distinction between Mexicans and Mexican Americans with

both groups considered undesirable to have as neighbors. And minority activists who were challenging the status quo were even less desirable. A petition was circulated in an attempt to keep the Rangels out of the neighborhood. Nevertheless, with support from "one very good person," P.M. and Big Minnie built the house that Irma considered her home for more than half a century.[3]

The Rangels also raised their children to have empathy "for people who are less fortunate, less successful, or less able." P.M. even took his daughters to pick cotton for a week so that they would experience for themselves how hard it was to work in the fields, as so many economically disadvantaged Hispanics had to do. Still another life lesson that the girls learned from their parents was "that not everyone can succeed without help." Irma internalized these values and devoted her life to helping others.[4]

P.M. and Big Minnie instilled in their children the value of education, and Irma went to school longer than most Tejanas did in the mid-twentieth century. She not only completed high school but also attended college in her hometown of Kingsville. As she later commented, "When I was at A&I, you could count the Hispanic students on two hands." Despite being part of a minority with traditionally limited access to higher education, the young woman graduated with a bachelor's "degree in business administration and teacher certification" in 1952.[5]

In the early 1950s, Rangel's dreams seemed to be nearing fulfillment in her personal life, as well as in her academic pursuits. The Tejana was engaged to a Navy pilot, when tragedy struck. In 1954 the young aviator died as the result of a plane crash. This loss deeply affected the young woman, who lived for almost another half century but never married—and not for lack of opportunities. The Tejana later articulated her reasons for remaining single. For one, she had mixed feelings about wives and mothers being in the workforce. "If a woman can manage to undertake a profession without ignoring the needs of the family—fine. But the family's needs must always come first," she contended. Rangel also readily acknowledged that she was a "very independent woman" and that "the older you become, the more particular you get." The men of her acquaintance tended to be "overly possessive," she observed, and wanted to tell her "what to do." She, on the other hand, had been raised to think for herself. Considering herself "a very content woman," she did not need the security of marriage, especially at the cost of her independence. [6]

There is little doubt the Tejana's life and priorities would have been different had her fiancé lived. Instead, she turned her energies to a succession of careers. Because few professions were open to Mexican-American women, she worked for fourteen years in the field of education. After teaching in South Texas at Robstown and Alice, she went to Venezuela, where she served first as a bilingual teacher and subsequently as a principal. Upon returning to the United States, Rangel spent a few years in the classroom in Menlo Park, California, where she co-authored a textbook. During that period, she also returned to Venezuela as part of the Teachers Corps to instruct educators in Caracas on methods for teaching modern math.[7]

The classroom soon became too confining for Irma Rangel, especially when Mexican-American activists in the mid-1900s became more determined to gain greater rights and recognition for people of their ethnicity. Adopting the term Chicano, some favored a more militant approach to tackle long-existing problems such as "racism, oppression, and poverty." Their aspirations included the attainment of equal educational opportunities and more effective political involvement. Among those most in need of assistance were farm workers, who were poorly paid, poorly housed, and poorly treated. A sympathetic Irma was involved in a farm workers' march in 1966. Marching was not enough for the Tejana, however. Rangel aspired to become a lawyer, because she believed that the legal professional would enable her to do more for her ethnic community. Even though she had been out of school for years and would be the only woman in her class, she enrolled at St. Mary's University School of Law from which she graduated in 1969.[8]

Following graduation, the freshly minted attorney spent two years working for Federal District Judge Adrian Spears in San Antonio—one of the first Hispanic women to serve as a law clerk for a federal judge. In 1971 she became an assistant district attorney in Nueces County, where she supervised five employees. Again, the young professional was one of the first of her gender and ethnicity to hold that position in the Lone Star State. Also, she insisted on receiving the same pay as a man would, even though women commonly received lower wages than their male counterparts for doing the same work.[9]

Although Rangel's tenure in the district attorney's office was not long, the experience had a profound impact on her life and views. As the only woman serving as a prosecutor in Corpus Christi, she had responsibility for all cases involving incest and rape. She found it very difficult to explain to victims who became pregnant in those situations that under existing laws they could receive a prison sentence of two to ten years should they get an abortion. She was also deeply affected by her investigation of a woman who "attempted to abort herself with a coat hanger . . . and then she died." Despite being a devout Catholic, she began to question the wisdom of anti-abortion laws.[10]

In 1973 Rangel left the district attorney's office to work in private practice in Kingsville, where she and a friend, Hector García, soon formed their own firm. The only Tejana lawyer in her hometown, and one of only a few in the state, she quickly became involved in local politics. Just one year after moving back to Kingsville, Rangel "made political history by becoming the first woman to serve as Kleberg County Democratic Chair." She not only devoted herself to the practice of law and involvement in politics but also did volunteer work to benefit her community. While still residing in Corpus Christi, the Latina had served on the Board of Directors of both Family Counseling Services and the Young Women's Christian Association. And after returning to her hometown, she became a board member for Family Guidance Services and for the Kingsville Planning and Zoning Board.[11]

Irma's varied experiences made her ever more aware of the many challenges faced by families living in poverty. The Tejana became convinced that the government did not do enough to help people in need, especially those living in her region of South Texas with its heavily Hispanic, low-income population. Vocal in expressing her opinions, the Texas Democrat began to attract attention, especially of other Mexican-American women. An important turning point in Rangel's life occurred in 1975, when she attended a conference in Austin that focused on the theme of women in public life. Notable at the proceedings was the small number of minority women featured on the stage. During the conference, members of the Texas Women's Political Caucus and the Mexican American Women's Caucus approached the Tejana attorney about running for the state House of Representatives. They stressed that more women, especially those of her ethnicity, needed to be involved in politics. Also, the timing seemed favorable, as the incumbent from her district was under federal investigation for alleged illegal activities.[12]

Rangel's decision was a difficult one, because the Texas House of Representatives and Senate were historically controlled by white males. Conducting a political campaign was an expensive proposition, and raising money could prove difficult. Adding to the challenges she faced was the fact that no Mexican-American woman had ever been elected to the State Legislature, although Rangel later claimed to have been unaware of that fact when debating whether to run. She readily admitted that she had "never been at the Capital." To the Tejana, however, not trying would be worse than losing. Consequently, she resigned her position as Kleberg County's Democratic Chair in early 1976 "to seek the position of State Representative, 49th District."[13]

To kick-start her campaign, Rangel got $1750 in "seed money" from the Texas Women's Political Caucus. Among other groups that contributed $100 or more were Texas Education Political Action Committee ($100), Southwestern Bell ($196.03), and Beer Wholesalers Political Action Committee ($300). LIFT, a trial lawyer's organization, gave $1000. Notably, women and men of more humble means did their part as well with donations of as little as $1.00. Female migrant farm workers helped raise funds on her behalf. The Tejana contended that they supported her candidacy because "they knew I had been involved with the farm workers' march in 1966 and that I was compassionate toward their problems and concerns." She also received the support of important Hispanic groups such as the American G.I. Forum and the League of United Latin American Citizens (LULAC).[14]

Despite help from a number of sources, the odds were against Rangel who was only one of several Democrats making a serious bid for the legislative seat. Her opponents included an Anglo woman who reportedly "had the political and finan- cial support of the powerful King Ranch"—a major force in in South Texas. The Tejana also realized that she was handi- capped by having only recently returned to her hometown after an absence of almost two decades. She later "credited her parents' and sister's popularity and good reputations for helping her overcome this obstacle." P.M. was a trusted member of his community, who had been "very active in the local Democratic Party and the Good Government League." Called "her greatest supporter" by the candidate, he helped with introductions, gave her the benefit of his expertise, and provided a $1000 contribu- tion to her campaign. Older sister Herminia ("Little Minnie") had also been active in local politics. A pharmacist, she was the "first Mexican American woman to become the President of the School Board" in Kingsville. Undoubtedly, "the local prominence of her parents and sister were an asset when Rangel began running for political office."[15]

Perhaps because the Tejana came to be seen as a strong contender, her opponents began to use mud-slinging tactics. Playing off the fact that she was not married and that she had been involved with the farm workers, she was accused of being a lesbian and of having "burned the American flag." Irma handled the spurious charges, especially the former, with a combination of respect and humor. While denying the allegations, she clarified that there was "nothing wrong" with being a lesbian and that she was "not going to go to bed" with the men questioning her sexual orientation to prove that she was straight. She stood on her qualifications and argued that being gay "wouldn't make me any less capable." Certainly, Irma Rangel in 1976 demonstrated tolerant attitudes toward homosexuals that were enlightened for her time.[16]

Thanks to an effective grassroots campaign, Rangel made the runoff in the Democratic primary and won that contest "by almost a two-to-one margin." Victory in the general election was then assured, because there was no Republican opponent seeking that legislative seat. When subsequently elected to the Texas House of Representatives in 1976, she became the first Tejana elected to serve in that body. By the time she took office the following year, the new legislator was well aware of the responsibility she faced. As she told a reporter, "I felt like I was really going to have to deliver. If I didn't succeed, they were going to say, 'All Mexican American women are failures.'" And, succeed she did, even though "early on, it was difficult for her to make a mark in the legislature." Although discouraged at times, Irma never quit. She went on to serve an impressive fourteen terms as a state representative until her death in 2003, twenty-seven years after she won her first election bid. By that time she was fifth in seniority in the Texas House of Representatives.[17]

EL DIA 5 DE JUNIO ELIJA A
IRMA
RANGEL
REPRESENTANTE ESTATAL
DEL DISTRITO NO. 49

★ Abogada por más de 5 años.
★ Educadora por más de 10 años
★ Creedora en la representación por el
   pueblo y para el pueblo.

Anuncio político pagado por Hector R. Garcia,
Tesorero de Campaña, 123 N. 7th, Kingsville

ELECT ON JUNE 5TH
IRMA
RANGEL
STATE REPRESENTATIVE
49TH DISTRICT

★ A Lawyer for over 5 years.
★ An Educator for over 10 years.
★ A lifetime believer of representation
   for and by the people.

Pol. Adv. paid for by Hector R. Garcia,
Campaign Treasurer, 123 N. 7th, Kingsville

A sample of Irma Rangel's campaign literature in both English and Spanish. Texas Woman Biofile, "Rangel, Irma," 3 9351 005320686. Courtesy of the TWU Libraries Woman's Collection, Texas Woman's University, Denton, TX.

During her decades in office, Rangel would serve on numerous House committees, responsible for matters ranging from "Judicial Affairs" to "Business and Industry" to "Higher Education" to "Border and International Affairs." She was vice-chair of four committees and chair of one. From 1993–1995, she was also the "first and only woman to serve as Chair of the Mexican American Legislative Caucus," a group composed of Hispanics in the Texas House. The Tejana legislator became a role model who "paved the way for others to follow." By the late twentieth century, more than thirty women were serving in the state legislature, a number that included eight Latinas. As one source noted, "these women must credit Irma Rangel for blazing the trail for Latina leadership in state politics"—though Emma Tenayuca had tried to do the same decades earlier.[18]

How did Irma Rangel manage to get re-elected term after term, especially as Texas's population grew over time and district boundary lines were redrawn on more than one occasion? Part of her secret was that she presented herself not as a politician but as a "public servant." When running for office, the Tejana campaigned in the "old-fashioned way" and let the people know that she considered it a privilege to represent them. She would meet with the local press, have coffee and pastry in private homes, attend functions in her district, and call on city and county officials to gain support. The legislator viewed her constituents as "not just votes, but real people with real concerns, hopes, and dreams." She also reportedly had a special "ability to make people feel better about themselves, their lives, their government and their future." As a single woman, she was "married to her mission of making South Texas a better place to live," which influenced at least a majority of people in her district to vote for her time and time again.[19]

That Rangel was repeatedly re-elected did not mean that she lacked serious opposition or vocal critics. In both 1985 and 1987, *Texas Monthly* labeled her as "furniture," a term the magazine used for lawmakers "who, by virtue of their indifference or inactivity, were indistinguishable from their desks. . . ." Added to that was the legislator's tendency to be an independent thinker, which did not always make for popularity within her district. As an example, despite economic decline in the state in the 1980s, Rangel supported a measure that imposed a tax increase. Insisting that "it was the responsible thing to do," she declared that the state's educational needs could not be met "with peanuts. It must be done with money." Although the Representative's stand garnered letters of support from educators, many of her other constituents were displeased at the prospect of higher taxes.[20]

Rangel did face a potentially serious challenge in her bid for reelection in 1988. Her opponent, J.M. "Chuy" Alvarez, ran a dirty, mud-slinging campaign that led one reporter to label him "the head clown" because of his "circus-like" antics and "lack of professionalism." Ultimately, Alvarez's tactics backfired. Coming to Rangel's defense, the local press declared that "nothing could be farther from the truth" than calling her furniture and urged their readers to vote for the incumbent in the upcoming election. Even with this endorsement, however, Rangel won by a margin of less than 200 votes.[21]

Having survived Alvarez's bid for her seat in 1988, Rangel's popularity grew as she sought to be returned to the state legislature every two years. Anyone who ran against her for her party's nomination faced an uphill battle, and at times no one tried. In both 1994 and 1996, the Tejana received more than 60 percent of the votes in the Democratic primary and 100 percent in the general elections. In the last two elections of the century, she garnered all of the votes cast in both primary and general elections, as she had also done in 1992.[22]

A hard-working Representative with a personal touch, Rangel did her best to deliver on issues important to her district, despite occasional claims of *Texas Monthly* to the contrary. The Latina understood that Mexican-American, African-American, and Anglo-American students living in poverty suffered from a number of disadvantages, especially in the area of educational opportunities. They typically went to inferior public schools, had frequent absences, and experienced higher drop-out rates. Additionally, many Latinos faced additional barriers, because Spanish was their primary language. Minority youth tended to make lower grades in school and get lower scores on standardized tests. Along with poor whites, they were also less likely to get a high school diploma or be admitted into colleges and universities. The cost of higher education was likewise a substantial barrier for these students. These realities distressed Rangel who believed that "the way people break out of cycles of poverty is through education."[23]

The Representative "fought tirelessly, right up until her death, to make the dream of a college degree the reality for thousands upon thousands of students." Early along in her legislative career, she opposed a bill aimed at funding the state highway system and insisted that the money should instead be used for better purposes such as education. As she eloquently stated, "This is about students. . . . When we cheat students, we cheat the state of Texas. We cheat the economy and we cheat ourselves, too."[24]

Besides students, women and the poor particularly benefitted from Rangel's initiatives. Based on her experiences as a prosecutor in Corpus Christi, she opposed anti-abortion bills that came before the legislature, especially those penalizing women who became pregnant because of rape or incest. The Tejana clearly stated her conviction that men did not have the right to tell a woman what to do with her own body. And she used the abortion issue effectively in her first term in office, when a bill was pending that would provide employment and education for low-income mothers with dependent children. She challenged her fellow Representatives to support the measure by saying, "All right guys, you want us to have babies, then help us support them." The bill passed. Another early success involved a measure to facilitate donations of food to the needy by businesses within the state. The Tejana also helped to "create centers for victims of domestic abuse."[25]

Because Rangel's constituents kept returning her to the legislature, she gained seniority in the House which brought appointments to important committees. These memberships facilitated her efforts to improve conditions for people in the state, but especially South Texas. Certainly, Irma was not the only person whose attention was focused on the border region which was experiencing tremendous growth during the latter decades of the twentieth century. In terms of access to higher education, however, South Texans continued to lag far behind the rest of the state. Colleges and universities north of San Antonio received much greater funding, as well as being authorized to offer more degrees and programs than those to the south. Addressing these inequities, a class-action lawsuit was filed in Texas in 1987 with the support of the Mexican-American Legal Defense and Educational Fund (MALDEF). *LULAC v. Richards* demanded equality "in quantity and quality of academic programs" at universities in South Texas, as compared to the rest of the state. A lower court ruled in favor of MALDEF, but the Texas Supreme Court later reversed that decision.[26]

Despite the ultimately unsuccessful outcome of *LULAC v. Richards*, the 71st Texas legislature "felt the heat." Legislators "decided that it would be in the best interest of the state to enhance the South Texas/Border Region." The result was the South Texas Border Initiative, which began in 1989 but continued in various phases into the next century. Under this initiative, significant new funding was provided "for academic programs and facilities" in border institutions of higher education. Rangel had served in the Texas House of Representatives for about a decade when the MALDEF lawsuit was filed, and she played a key role in maximizing the opportunities it provided. In 1993 she was credited with helping to get more than $450,000,000 budgeted for higher education in the border region. And the amount of special item funds allocated for South Texas post-secondary institutions from the 1990 through 2003 fiscal years totaled $880 million.[27]

Increased attention and funding brought dramatic results. For the first time, both The University of Texas System and the Texas A&M System established a major presence in the extreme southern section of the state. Several existing institutions of higher education were incorporated into these systems. As an example, Pan American University at Edinburg became the University of Texas-Pan American. Rangel's alma mater, Texas A&I Kingsville, became Texas A&M University-Kingsville. The number of students attending colleges and universities in South Texas increased significantly with more degree options available to them. As William Cunningham, chancellor of the U.T. System noted in 1997, "Young people are reaping rewards from the state's wise decision to make new investments in higher education in the region."²⁸ Certainly, Irma Rangel was one of the legislators who deserved credit for closing the gap in higher education in the state.

The Tejana's influence in that arena increased in the mid-1990s, when she was named Chair of the House Higher Education Committee. Serving in that powerful position for years, she "led the charge to ensure educational opportunities for all children" and adults in Texas. One of the issues that the legislator tackled involved criteria used to admit students to state colleges and universities. Traditionally, higher education had been available primarily to affluent white students and others who could afford it. However, in the second half of the twentieth century, colleges and universities in Texas began to use race and ethnicity as a factor in determining who could attend and who would receive financial aid. The intent was to insure that certain numbers (or quotas) of minority students were allowed access.²⁹

While the new practices did help Latinos and African Americans achieve greater educational equality, they simultaneously alienated some whites, who felt that they were now the ones facing discrimination. Opponents of so-called racial preferences charged that colleges and universities admitted minority students with lower grades and national test scores than white students, who were sometimes denied admission. The result was another lawsuit, *Hopwood v. Texas.* Cheryl Hopwood was one of four white students who sued the law school at The University of Texas at Austin in 1992. The claimants, whose applications for admission had been rejected, "challenged the school's system of racial preferences." They alleged themselves to be victims of discrimination, because they were better qualified than African Americans and Hispanics who had been admitted. The *Hopwood* case took several years to make its way through the court system. In 1996 the U.S. Fifth Circuit Court of Appeals in Louisiana ruled in favor of the white students on the grounds that "the 14ᵗʰ amendment forbids state universities from using race as a factor in admissions." Subsequently, Texas's Attorney General Dan Morales "directed all public universities to adopt race-neutral policies for admissions, financial aid, and scholarships." While Hopwood and her fellow petitioners no doubt celebrated, the court's ruling was a setback for minorities hoping to attend the more prestigious institutions of higher education in the Lone Star State.[30]

Representative Rangel was one of many Texans distressed by the outcome of the *Hopwood* case. They feared it would hurt "the ability of colleges and universities in Texas to continue to attract African-American and Hispanic students." And the federal court's decision indeed "led to huge declines in minority applications and admissions." As one example, undergraduate "applications from blacks and Hispanics to the University of Texas-Austin dropped by about one-quarter [25 percent] each." Critics asserted that the state's flagship university once again seemed to be selecting most of its freshmen from wealthier suburban high schools or from expensive private schools. Similarly, of 791 graduate students first granted admission to the Fall 1997 class at the UT Law School, only 23 in total were Mexican-American and African-American—almost a 40 percent decline.[31]

Opponents of the *Hopwood* decision sought to "find ways of making sure that Texas colleges and universities are available and accessible to all Texas students." Consequently, more than two dozen institutions sent representatives to a conference held at Texas A&M University on November 12, 1996. Interested state leaders attended as well, including Irma Rangel. Almost five hundred people participated in the deliberations held at College Station. At the conference, a panel recommended a plan to increase minority enrollments in higher education. The proposal called for high school students in the top 10 to 15 percent of their graduating classes to be admitted automatically to state colleges and universities. The panelists also advised "that colleges and universities can work together . . . to recruit minority students, looking at geographic factors and class rank rather than standardized tests."[32]

Some minority lawmakers proceeded to act on the conference recommendations. As the Higher Education Committee Chair, Irma Rangel "helped to organize, and closely cooperated with, the task group that authored" House Bill 588. She also played a leading role in convincing her fellow legislators of its merits. Passing by a narrow margin in 1997, this significant piece of legislation mandated that public colleges and universities in Texas "automatically admit all students graduating in the top 10 percent of their high school class." The Tejana argued that the plan rewarded students for their hard work and motivated them to succeed. Also, the new approach would help achieve college enrollments more "representative of the state population as a whole."[33]

The Ten Percent Plan did prove effective in increasing minority enrollment on college campuses. Praising Texas for its innovation, one Harvard Law faculty member noted that it sent "the message that access and diversity are not the enemy of excellence." George W. Bush, governor of Texas at the time the plan was adopted, received considerable credit for the legislation. Whether the credit was deserved was a matter of debate. Some sources alleged that Rangel "saw Bush only when he signed the bill, [and that] Bush never publicly supported it until after it became recognized as successful." To set the record straight, the Latina legislator "took it upon herself to meet with reporters and editorial page writers" to clarify that the governor "had little to do with passing the bill."[34]

Despite its positive aspects, the Ten Percent Plan provoked criticism and produced unintended consequences. Critics charged that it discouraged students from taking rigorous courses and encouraged them to attend less competitive schools, while some higher education administrators complained about having limited flexibility in selecting their students. Also, flooded with applications from top ten-percent seniors, The University of Texas at Austin and Texas A&M University at College Station experienced serious growing pains. In the early 2000s, strained resources caused the former to stop admitting new and transfer students for a brief period. However, in 2003, a Supreme Court ruling "allowed some race-based affirmative action" in college admissions. After UT Austin agreed to "start considering race again for those students now admitted automatically," the university in 2009 received permission to restrict automatic admissions to 75 percent of the incoming freshman class. This effectively meant that only the top 7 percent of high school graduates were assured admittance. Abigail Fisher, a white woman, legally challenged the UT "race-conscious admissions program." The Supreme Court's ruling in *Fisher v. University of Texas* was handed down in June 2016—almost two decades after the enactment of the Ten Percent Plan. Justice Anthony Kennedy, author of the majority decision, made note of the plan's strengths and weaknesses, but stated that it "did not alone produce sufficient diversity." Therefore, "admissions officials may continue to consider race as one factor among many in ensuring a diverse student body." [35]

When enacted in 1997 the Ten Percent Plan applied only to undergraduate admissions, a cause of concern at the time. Medical schools, for example, continued to rely heavily on scores from standardized national exams to determine which candidates to accept. Applicants "with lousy grades and low test scores" were automatically rejected, despite other qualifications. While there were strong arguments supporting those practices, minorities were again placed at a disadvantage, because of their tendency to score lower on standardized tests. Rangel was particularly disturbed that in Texas graduate schools as late as the year 2000, "[only] 4 percent of students in doctoral programs were black. Six percent were Hispanic. . . ." The legislator was determined "to give graduate schools a tool to admit a more diverse group of students."[36]

In the early 2000s, Rangel helped secure a law to improve graduate-level minority enrollments in Texas. No longer were scores on standardized exams to be the major basis for admission. When used, test scores were to be compared only with those of "students from similar socioeconomic backgrounds." Whether the applicant was bilingual, was from a low-income background, had to work while going to school, had to help raise children, or participated in community activities were other factors to be considered. Instructed to seek "geographic diversity" among their students, admissions committees had to look at where an applicant had gone to high school, as well as the region where the prospective student currently lived. Also, consideration had to be given to whether the applicant's hometown suffered from "a shortage of professionals in the medical or law fields."[37]

Like the Ten Percent Plan, the new law proved polarizing. By helping more Hispanics, African Americans, and other under-represented minorities get into graduate programs, it was applauded by groups such MALDEF. Predictably, opponents argued that these groups were again being given an unfair advantage over better qualified whites. A different type of concern was expressed by the Director of Admissions at The University of Texas Southwestern Medical Center. He asserted that entrance exam scores had long been viewed as the best way to determine which students were more likely to "make it through the curriculum and become outstanding physicians." Changing that practice could cause problems. Also, the Dean of Graduate Studies at UT Austin complained that admissions committees found it difficult to follow the new, less objective, guidelines.[38]

Despite criticism of the new undergraduate and graduate admission criteria, Irma Rangel was committed to both. However, her attempts to accomplish even more were not always fruitful. In 1999—years before the above-mentioned 2003 and 2016 Supreme Court decisions—the Latina legislator introduced a bill to the House Higher Education Committee "to allow the consideration of race, ethnicity and national origin in college admissions." Strong negative reaction ensured, in part because of considerable opposition in Texas to reinstating racial preferences. Rangel's proposed legislation was considered an attempt to circumvent the federal ruling in the *Hopwood* case, an accusation which she denied. Nevertheless, the bill was "left pending in committee."[39]

More successful was another measure that Rangel sponsored in 1997. Passed into law, it allowed tuition exemptions for public school teachers' aides studying to become certified teachers. Rangel's legislation not only provided opportunities for many who could not otherwise have afforded to pursue higher education but also addressed the teacher shortage in Texas. Eighteen years later, this program was credited with having benefitted 46,000 educators, and the State Board of Educator Certification noted "an exceptionally high teacher-retention rate for the home-grown teachers" produced.[40]

Rangel knew all-too-well that for many other students aspiring to attend college, cost was a major obstacle. Expenses related to higher education had been escalating in the 1980s and 1990s without a corresponding increase in the funding provided by the state. To compensate, institutions were raising tuition and fees with more of the burden being borne by students and their families. One consequence reported by the Texas Guaranteed Student Loan Corporation was that "an increasing percentage of low-income high school graduates are either deferring or altogether forgoing post-secondary education." As always, Representative Rangel believed in tackling problems head-on. The state had a duty, in her opinion, to make financial assistance available to students who could not otherwise afford the rising costs of higher education. Toward that end, she co-authored a bill introduced at the 1999 legislative session. The resulting legislation created the Toward Excellence and Success (TEXAS) Grants Program. As originally created, the program helped "approximately 11,000 low-income students from across the state to go to college" by providing $100 million in financial aid.[41]

Despite the TEXAS Grant Program and other state efforts, a report presented to the Texas House Committee on Higher Education late in 2000 revealed serious problems within the state's educational system, and not just in the area of access. The National Center for Public Policy and Higher Education had done a study on universities across the United States. Each state was graded in five categories: "preparation, enrollment, affordability, graduation rates, and the economic and social benefits of the states' education policies." Texas's results were embarrassingly low.[42]

The Lone Star State received no grade higher than a C in the National Center's report. Texas received "C grades for preparing schoolchildren for higher education, affordability of higher education and the social benefits to the state as a result of its residents' level of education." Worse, the state received only D- for enrollment and D+ for graduation rates. One of the reasons for the depressingly low scores was the difference in college enrollment rates between whites and minorities—still a reality in the early twenty-first century. Whites continued to attend college at a much higher percentage than did other races. The two lowest grades Texas received were caused in part by the state's inability to provide adequate financial aid to economically disadvantaged students.[43] Irma Rangel had figured that out long before this report was issued!

As Rangel's committee considered the National Center's report, the related long-running issue of standardized testing was also a hot topic, specifically the Texas Assessment of Academic Skills (TAAS). Administered to specified grades in the public schools, the mandated test that covered academic subjects such as reading and math was required for graduation from high school. Rangel strongly opposed such exams on principle. She insisted that they were punitive and created a barrier for minority students. The Latina legislator was not alone in those opinions. In the late 1990s, the GI Forum in a lawsuit against the Texas Education Agency alleged that using TAAS as a high-school graduation requirement "unfairly discriminates against Texas minority students" and "violates their rights to due process." U.S. District Judge Edward Pardo acknowledged that for years "Hispanic and African American students have performed significantly worse than majority students on this exit exam." Nevertheless, he also labelled it an effective measure of a "student's mastery of the skills and knowledge . . . Texas has deemed graduating high school seniors must possess." Pardo ruled that the disparities in scores were not a result of flaws in the exam and that TAAS did not violate the Civil Rights Act. According to the judge, "the state was within its power to use the TAAS as one way to remedy underachievement by minority students."[44] Consequently, GI Forum members, Representative Rangel, and other involved parties would have to seek other avenues to address the issue of high-stakes testing.

Early in 2001 a "Texas Latino Testing Conference" was held in Austin, Texas. Rangel was a keynote speaker at the forum, which brought together nationally known figures who had "played a major role in public policy debates on education." The conference's Concept Statement declared that the question under consideration was whether the educational system in Texas with its "high-stakes testing" allowed fair opportunities for "underprivileged, mostly African and Latino youth" to move through the pipeline from elementary school to secondary to college.[45]

The "no-testing crowd" reacted strongly against a plan put forth by former Texas governor and recently elected U.S. President George W. Bush. Committed to the concept of standardized testing, he wanted examinations not only to determine an individual student's progress but also to be used to grade schools. Bush's proposal would require elementary students in grades three through eight to take mandatory tests in reading and math with results for each school being made public. Bonuses would go to high-performing schools, while those at the other extreme would be given additional funds to help improve their scores. In the name of accountability, schools that continued to be deficient would face serious consequences, including "corrective action" or "restructuring." As a former teacher and principal, Rangel not only opposed Bush's plan but also introduced a bill into the state legislature to eliminate TAAS.[46]

Ironically, the Latina got her wish, but not in the way that she intended. The Texas legislature did eliminate TAAS in the early 2000s, only to replace it with The Texas Assessment of Knowledge and Skills (TAKS). The new more rigorous assessment program would cover even more subjects and be administered in more grade levels. Of special concern to opponents was the requirement that students would have to "pass exit level tests in four content areas— English language arts, mathematics, science, and social studies–to graduate from a Texas public high school."[47]

Despite Rangel's inability to prevent the enactment of TAKS, she had one of her proudest accomplishments in 2001. Although other parts of the state had professional schools to train physicians, pharmacists, dentists, and others, South Texas lacked those same facilities. The Tejana authored a successful house bill to create a School of Pharmacy at Texas A&M University-Kingsville, referred to in the press as "the first professional school in South Texas."[48]

Even though gains were being made, the Texas Association of Chicanos in Higher Educaton (TACHE) expressed concern that advances in educational opportunities for minority students had not been matched by increases in the numbers of Hispanic faculty on college campuses. TACHE called this a "silent crisis," given studies projecting that Hispanics would become the state's largest ethnic group by 2030. Breaking the silence, a past-president of the organization declared that "campuses do not have a tradition of acceptance of Hispanic faculty, administrators, or their culture.

Every step has been a battle." The article also noted the most commonly cited reason was the lack of qualified minorities. [49]

Praising the members of TACHE as "role models and wonderful mentors to our Hispanic students," Rangel endorsed their mission as critical in ending discrimination. That mission included urging the state government to facilitate an increase in the number of under-represented groups in graduate schools and requiring "Texas public colleges and universities to make a strong commitment to faculty and staff diversity, one that reflects the student population." As Rangel noted, "Here we are in the new millennium, and there are people out there who still question our academic credentials." She continued, "I think still a lot of people don't put confidence in our ability. I have tried to convince them we are capable."[50]

When Rangel said, "we are capable," she referred not only to Latinos in general but to women of her ethnicity in particular to whom she hoped to serve "as a role model and inspiration." To motivate more of them to aspire to public service, she hired Latinas as her administrative assistants, including Myra Leo who worked for her from 1985–1994 and served as her Chief of Staff. The Representative was also involved in the Hispanic Women's Network of Texas (HWNT), which was created in the 1980s "to advance the educational, cultural, social, legal and economic well-being of all Hispanic women." At the tenth annual HWNT conference in 1996, Rangel and Christine Hernández (Democrat, San Antonio) conducted a workshop on "Latinas in the Political Arena: Getting Ready for the 21st Century."[51]

Making Mexican Americans part of her staff or presenting workshops at conferences were not overly controversial activities. Some women's rights issues, however, plunged Rangel into the middle of heated debate. As already noted, she had strong opinions about a woman having the legal right to terminate a pregnancy. In her seventh legislative term, the Latina representative had again demonstrated the courage of her convictions when she "and nineteen of the 25 women in the House helped defeat an effort to criminalize abortion."[52]

Another controversial topic on which Irma took a stand did not involve women's rights, but rather human rights—the issue of the death penalty. At the turn of the century, Texas increasingly captured attention for leading the nation in the number of executions. One case that generated headlines involved African-American Gary Graham (also known as Shaka Sankofa), who had been convicted of capital murder in the early 1980s and was still on death row a decade later. Many people doubted his guilt, and his supporters formed a movement to seek "justice" by stopping the execution. Among actions undertaken on his behalf were public meetings, public marches, and prayer vigils. When a list was published of "public figures" who opposed the execution, Irma Rangel was among those named. Nevertheless, Graham was executed in June 2000.[53]

Rangel did not support women's rights, help low income mothers and children, increase educational opportunities, and take other principled positions to gain personal acclaim. Nevertheless, by championing the causes in which she believed, the Tejana earned numerous forms of recognition. Honors for this exceptional public servant began early in her career and continued after her death. Many awards came from her local community, from fellow Hispanics, or from women's organizations; however, she also gained acclaim in the broader arena and from other minorities as well which makes her even more noteworthy.

Among her most significant accolades were being named Texas Mexican-American Woman of the Year by the Women's Political Caucus in the late 1970s, being selected as Latina Lawyer of the Year by the Hispanic National Bar Association in the early 1990s, and being honored as a Texas Woman of the Century by the Women's Chamber of Commerce of Texas in the late 1990s. Certainly, a high point of Rangel's career was being admitted into the Texas Women's Hall of Fame by Governor Ann Richards in 1994.[54]

The late twentieth century brought many kudos other than those listed above. MALDEF bestowed upon Rangel the Matt García Public Service Award for "public servants who exemplify dedication and commitment to the Mexican-American community." The 75th Legislative Black Caucus made her the recipient of the G. J. Sutton Award "for her efforts to promote equal opportunity and treatment in education for minorities." The Tejana was not only the first female but also "the first Mexican American legislator to receive this award." Rangel became a recipient of the Mirabeau B. Lamar Medal "for exemplary service to Texas Higher Education" from the Association of Texas Colleges and Universities, another first for a Mexican-American. Likewise, she became "the first Hispanic in the state to receive the Margaret Brent Women Lawyers of Achievement Award from the American Bar Association's Commission on Women in the Profession."[55]

Irma Rangel must have taken special pride in one of the last honors accorded to her during her lifetime: the creation of the Moreno/Rangel Legislative Leadership Program by the Mexican American Legislative Foundation in the early 2000s. Named for the two longest-serving Latinos in the state legislature, the program was designed to provide select undergraduate and graduate students the "opportunity to gain first-hand experience by working in the Texas House of Representatives."[56]

What kind of person was this woman who received so many awards and honors during her lifetime? A friend, Ramiro Cavazos of San Antonio, called her "a great role model and one of a kind." According to Cavazos, "she had a lot of chutzpah [nerve/guts], she was single, she played golf and drove a Cadillac and she was irreverent, but she never backed down from a good fight and she never forgot where she came from." Another acquaintance commented that Rangel "didn't take herself seriously but was serious about her work." After going on the campaign trail with Irma, a relative bragged that she "instantly filled a room with her great smile and trademark sugary way of talking." Even though she was a public figure, Irma was approachable. Everywhere she went, the representative "was immediately recognized and greeted with smiles and *abrazos* (hugs)." Even strangers got a feeling of warmth from her.[57]

Irma was quite a character. Despite her sugary speech, she was capable of "salty" language when she felt the occasion called for it. Curse words aside, Rangel displayed a maternal side. She "had a habit of calling people 'baby.'" Perhaps because she never had a family of her own, the Latina became a kind of den mother for some of the newer members of the Texas House of Representatives. "Always there to lend a hand or smile," Rangel took "'most of the Hispanic women [legislators] under her wing." She could be counted on for "moral support" and "a complimentary word."[58]

While the Tejana had her soft side, she also had a well-deserved "reputation for being tough" and even intimidating on occasion. Staff member Myra Leo attributed this in part to her "burden of always having to be a pioneer, always having to do better, of coming from the generation that had to be the 'first.'" Rangel's parents, especially her mother, had raised her with the awareness that to succeed as a Latina she was going to have to perform at a much higher level than others. Taking that lesson to heart, Irma "worked long hours and strived for perfection"—and expected others to do the same. That her intensity paid off is evidenced by her record in the state legislature.[59]

Rangel's greatest battles did not occur in the political arena, however. This woman of great courage fought a deadly enemy for years toward the end of her life. Faced first with ovarian and then inflammatory breast cancer, the Latina "was always cheerful . . . and fearless." Determined to keep serving her constituents despite her health crises, Irma was like the "Energizer Bunny." She just kept on

Irma Rangel in pink suit and hat continues to perform her responsibilities as a state legislator while she faces one of several battles with cancer. Irma Lerma Rangel Collection, A2003-042.0011, South Texas Archives, James C. Jernigan Library, Texas A&M University-Kingsville.

going. When treatment in San Antonio caused her hair to fall out, Irma reacted by wearing colorful hats to the state legislature. "One day, fellow female lawmakers walked into the House sporting hats in a show of support. With them were two males . . . also wearing women's hats."[60]

Because she had overcome two forms of cancer, Irma's friends and supporters were shocked in November 2002 to learn that she had brain cancer. Ironically, that was the same month that she won re-election for what would prove to be her last term as a state representative to District 43, composed at that time of "Kleberg, Kenedy, Willacy, Brooks, Jim Hogg, and part of Cameron counties." Once again Irma made trips to San Antonio, this time for for radiation treatments, and again she worked to fulfill her duties in Austin.[61]

Irma's last term proved especially challenging, and not just because her health was failing. Texas, a traditionally conservative state dominated by Democrats after Reconstruction ended in the 1870s, was undergoing a dramatic political transformation. As the twentieth century progressed, the Democratic Party had become more liberal. Nationally, Democrats sponsored reforms such as Civil Rights to protect the rights of minorities and Medicare to give additional benefits to senior citizens. The Republican Party was simultaneously shifting to the right with a more conservative orientation on these and other issues. As a result, Republican candidates began to attract more votes in the Lone Star State and swept the elections in 2002. With Republican ascendancy, Rangel's influence and that of her party waned. The Tejana was replaced as Chair of the Higher Education Committee and relegated to the position of vice chair instead. Significantly, however, she was "the only Democrat from previous years who was asked to continue in a leadership position" in the Texas House of Representatives.[62]

Another cause for concern to Irma Rangel, besides the declining power of her party, was a severe financial crisis facing Texas. Revenue coming into the state treasury was projected to be billions of dollars less than what was needed to cover expenditures. The Republicans had pledged not to increase taxes; so, major cuts were being proposed in the state budget, especially in the area of higher education. If those reductions were enacted, South Texas would be especially hard-hit with some of Rangel's accomplishments in jeopardy.[63]

Privately, the public servant was getting tired and discouraged. Early in 2003, she told a friend that she was serving her last session in the legislature, a pronouncement that he viewed with skepticism. There had been other occasions when "she would be very frustrated, and . . . she would say, 'I'm not coming back. I hate this place.'" Eventually she would change her mind, he said, because she felt a sense of responsibility to her constituents.

Indeed, that sense of duty was so strong that Rangel worked in the legislature almost to the day of her death.[64]

Publicly, the Latina would not give up nor would she let others do so. In spring 2003, she met with college presidents from South Texas universities. She challenged these administrators to let the legislators know what they "really needed." "'Just come at us,' she challenged. 'What's the worst that can happen? You get turned down or you get some of what you requested. How can we live with ourselves if we do anything less, when our region needs so much.'"[65]

Considering Rangel's activities during the 78th session of the Texas legislature, one would never imagine she was in serious physical decline. Perhaps it was a sense of urgency that led her to write or co-author at least twelve bills on a variety of topics, particularly education. Still opposed to standardized testing, the Tejana filed House Bill 3375, designed to enact "repeal of the Texas Academic Skills Program." Covering reading, writing, and math skills, TASP had been used in the Lone Star State for more than a decade to evaluate a student's readiness for college-level work. Students who failed any subject area of the exam had to take remedial (developmental) courses that not only had a high attrition rate but also cost taxpayers well-over $100 million a year by the early 2000s. Because minority students failed the test at a notably higher rate than whites, the representative favored replacing TASP with "the Success Initiative," a plan allowing each institution of higher education to "decide the readiness of its applicants." Another measure Rangel authored toward the end of her life presented "a strategy to ensure that public institutions of higher education employ faculty and staff who reflect the population of Texas." This corresponded with previously discussed efforts by TACHE to that end.[66] Sadly, the representative did not live to see the above bills through the legislative process.

On March 17, 2003, a group of public school employees from around the state visited the capital. They planned to meet with several legislators to discuss issues of concern. One of their stops was the office of Representative Rangel, but they found the door locked. The visitors were saddened to learn that Irma had collapsed and had been taken to the hospital, where she was in a coma. Later that day "an announcement was made at the Texas legislature . . . that Representative Rangel from Kingsville was . . . not expected to make it through the night."[67]

On Tuesday, March 18, 2003, Irma Rangel lost her battle with brain cancer. A rosary was held in Austin on March 20 at Our Lady of Guadalupe Church, where a moving funeral mass was conducted the next morning with hundreds in attendance. Then, mourners followed the flag-draped casket in "a walking procession from the church to the Texas State Cemetery." Fittingly, a special memorial service was also held almost two weeks later on the Texas A&M University-Kingsville campus. Many in Austin, Kingsville, and else-where recognized that the Lone Star State had lost one of its most dedicated public servants.[68]

* * *

Irma Rangel made her mark. One cannot calculate the number of lives on which she had a positive impact, first as an educator, then as an attorney, and, finally, as a legislator. During her more than twenty-six years of public service, she advised her fellow legislators to "Vote your conscience, you won't go wrong."[69] By following her own conscience, this Latina came to be loved by some, appreciated by many, and respected even by her opponents.

If a measure of a person's life is how they are regarded in death, Irma Rangel's worth cannot be questioned. In the state legislature, her loss was keenly felt. "A glass vase with 27 long-stemmed yellow roses, one for each year, Rangel served, sat atop her desk as colleagues wept openly." A reporter noted that even her political adversaries shed tears. Tom Craddick, Speaker of the Texas House, described Rangel as "a groundbreaker among Mexican Americans and women." Corpus Christi Democrat

Vilma Luna sponsored House Bill 518, which called Rangel a "champion of social justice." The measure passed unanimously. Republican Governor Rick Perry spoke of the Tejana's "years as a dedicated public servant" and "ordered flags flown at half-staff at state buildings in Rangel's memory." Perry also asked for the new Texas A&M University-Kingsville school of pharmacy to be named after her, a recommendation endorsed by the legislature. At the national level, the United States House of Representatives adopted a formal resolution to honor Rangel "for her contributions to American society as a Texas legislator." And on a more personal note, Dr. Juliet García, President of the University of Texas at Brownsville, expressed a deep sense of personal loss. Although saddened at her friend's death, Dr. García celebrated "a life well-lived with ethical values beyond reproach and a will to survive the insurmountable."[70]

When Irma Rangel died, many mourners wanted to send flowers to her funeral. Her family asked instead that donations be made in her memory to the P. M. Rangel Family Scholarship Fund at Texas A&M-Kingsville or to the Breast Cancer Research Program at the University of Texas Health Science Center in San Antonio.[71] Through these contributions Irma Rangel continued posthumously to help worthy students attend college and to fight the battle against cancer. What a fitting legacy for this memorable Tejana!

Bibliographical Commentary

Print coverage of Irma Rángel can be found in sources on more general topics, such as Nancy Baker Jones and Ruthe Winegarten's *Capitol Women: Texas Female Legislators, 1923–1999* (2000); José Angel Gutiérrez, Michele Mélendez, and Sonia Adriana Noyola's *Chicanas in Charge: Texas Women in the Political Arena* (2007); and Sonia García, et al., *Políticas: Latina Public Officials in Texas* (2008). Categorized as juvenile literature, Sammye Munson's *Our Tejano Heroes: Outstanding Mexican Americans in Texas* (1989) has a short biographical chapter on Rangel, and Anna Butzer's *Irma Rangel* (2014) is a brief children's book in the Great Women in History series.

Online sources are plentiful. Of particular interest is an oral interview that José Angel Gutiérrez conducted with Irma Rangel on April 10, 1996. Located in the Tejano Voices Collection, Center for Mexican American Studies, the University of Texas at Arlington, both the oral interview and a transcribed version can be accessed at http://library.uta.edu/tejanovoices/interview.php?cmasno=047. A sampling of the many online obituaries, tributes, and news articles related to Rangel include the following: Juliet V. García, "Open Letter from the President," University of Texas at Brownsville, March 19, 2003; "Obituary, Irma Rángel," The Austin Chronicle Politics: Naked City, March 21, 2003; "Irma Rangel's Legacy," Corpus Christi Caller.com, March 20, 2003; Jo Ann Castro, "Mourners Pay Tribute to the Late Irma Rángel, *La Prensa*, April 6, 2003; "In Memoriam: It Was Always about the Students," *The Texas Observer*, April 11, 2003; and "A Texas Lawmaker Dies of Brain Cancer," News 8 Austin, Your News, April 30, 2003. The *Handbook of Texas Online*, available through the website of the Texas State Historical Association (www.tshaonline.org), has an entry entitled "Rangel, Irma Lerma" by Britney Jeffrey. The *Handbook* also covers related topics, including Cynthia Orozco's "Mexican American Legislative Caucus" and Judith McArthur's "Women and Politics."

For anyone wanting to consult archival materials, the Irma Lerma Rangel Collection has been catalogued and made available to researchers. It is housed at the South Texas Archives and Special Collections, James C. Jernigan Library, Texas A&M University-Kingsville.

Endnotes

1. Birth Certificate, Box 1, Folder A2003-042.005, Irma Lerma Rangel Collection, South Texas Archives, James C. Jernigen Library, Texas A&M University, Kingsville, Tx. [The Rangel Collection is hereinafter cited as IRC].

2. Ibid.; Sonia R. García, et al., *Políticas: Latina Public Officials in Texas* (Austin: University of Texas Press, 2008), 35–36; Carmina Danini, "Texas State Representative Irma Rangel, 1931–2003," *San Antonio Express-News,* March 19, 2003, http://www.ibcmemorial.org/412.html; the *Handbook of Texas Online,* Britney Jeffrey, "Rangel, Irma Lerma," 1st quotation, http://www.tshaonline.org/hadbook/online/articles/fra85 [*Handbook of Texas Online* herinafter cited as *HOT Online*]; "Upbringing Shaped Rangel's Career," *Corpus Christi Caller,* Jan. 30, 1994, Box 1, Folder A1989-039.002, IRC, 2nd quotation; Irma Rangel, interview by José Angel Gutiérrez, April 10, 1996, University of Texas at Arlington, Center for Mexican American Studies, transcript, 3, http://library.uta.edu/tejanovoices/interview.php?cmasno=47. [Gutiérrez interview with Rangel hereinafter cited as Rangel Interview.]

3. Rangel Interview, 2–5, quotation on 2.

4. McDougal Littell, "Irma Rangel: Legislator," *Celebrating Texas,* Unit 9, Chapter 32, Section 2, all quotations, http://www.celebratingtexas.com/tr/lsl/114.pdf.

5. "Rep. Rangel Named Distinguished Alumnus for 2001," *Javelina Alumni,* Summer 2001, Texas A&M University-Kingsville, 1st quotation, http://www.

tamuk.edu/javalumni/tusk/2001/summer/rangel.shtml; García, *Políticas*, 36, 2nd quotation; Rangel Interview, 22.

6. Danini, "Rangel," *Express-News*; Rangel Interview, 21–22, 2nd through 5th quotations on 21, 6th quotation on 22; "Views on Women's Liberation Are Far from Radical," *Corpus Christi Caller-Times*, June 20, 1971, Box 4, Folder A2003-042.002, IRC, 1st quotation.

7. Rangel Interview, 7–8. Sources disagree as to the exact dates that Rangel served as a teacher or principal in each location. In her oral interview with Gutiérrez, she said that she spent a total of fourteen years as an educator, seven of which were in Venezuela.

8. Nancy Baker Jones and Ruthe Winegarten, *Capitol Women* (Austin: University of Texas Press, 2000), 204. Arnoldo de León, *Mexican Americans in Texas: A Brief History*, 3rd ed. (Wheeling, IL: Harlan Davidson, Inc., 2009), quotation on 139; García, *Políticas*, 36; "Kingsville Woman to Head Division in DA's Office," newspaper clipping, no name, February 5, 1971, Box 4, Folder A2003-042.002, IRC. For a concise overview of the Chicano Movement in Texas, see de León, *Mexican Americans in Texas*, 135–150. For extensive coverage of the movement in San Antonio, Texas, see David Montejano's *Quixote's Soldiers: A Local History of the Chicano Movement, 1966–1981* (Austin: University of Texas Press, 2010).

9. García, *Políticas*, 36; "Kingsville Woman to Head Division," 1971; *HOT Online*, Jeffry, "Rangel"; Theresa Palomo Acosta and Ruthe Winegarten, *Las Tejanas* (Austin: University of Texas Press, 2003), 267–268.

10. Rangel Interview, 30, quotation.

11. García, *Políticas*, 37; Benjamin Márquez, *Democratizing Texas Politics: Race, Identity, and Mexican American Empowerment, 1945–2002* (Austin: University of Texas Press, 2014), 112, quotation; Biographical materials, Box 4, Folder A2003-043.003, IRC.

12. Littell, "Irma Rangel"; Jones and Winegarten, *Capitol Women*, 204; Rangel Interview, 9.

13. "First Hispanic Woman Elected to Legislature Reflects," *El Turista*, *McAllen Monitor*, Nov. 8, 1994, Box 4, Folder A2003-042.023, IRC; Rangel Interview, 11, 1st quotation; Letter, Irma Rangel to Honorable Calvin Guest, January 27, 1976, 2nd quotation, Box 233, Folder A2003-043.003, IRC.

14. Acosta and Winegarten, *Las Tejanas*, 268, quotations; Handwritten List of Donations for 1976 Campaign, Box 233, Folder A1998-039.002, IRC.

15. García, *Políticas*, 36, 38–39, 2nd quotation on 38, 3rd and 6th quotations on 36; Jones and Winegarten, *Capitol Women*, 204–205, 1st quotation on 205; Rangel Interview, 6, 10, 5th quotation on 6; Sydney Rubin, "South Texas Lawmakers Value Independent Roles," *San Antonio Express*, Feb. 16, 1983, 4th quotation, Box 4, Folder A2003-042.003, IRC; Handwritten List, Box 233, Folder A1998-039.002.

16. Rangel Interview, 20–22, 1st through 3rd quotations on 30, 4th quotation on 22.

17. García, *Políticas*, 39–40, 1st quotation on 40; Acosta and Winegarten, *Las Tejanas*, 190; Danini, "Rangel," *San Antonio Express*, 2nd and 3rd quotations; "Irma Rangel," Terms of Service, Texas Legislators: Past and Present, Legislative Reference Library [hereinafter cited as LRL], http://www.lrl.state.txus/mobile/memberDisplay.cfm?memberID=227; "Rangel Laid to Rest on Friday,"

Your News, News 8 Austin, April 30, 2003, http://www.news&austin.com/content/your_news/?SecID-278&ArID=65581.

18. "Rangel," Committee Information, LRL; "Representative Irma Rangel, May 15, 1931-March 18, 2003," The Mexican American Legislative Caucus, 1st and 2nd quotations, http://www.malc.org/Rangel.htm; Jones and Winegarten, *Capitol Women*, 285–286; García, *Políticas*, 34, 3rd quotation.

19. García, *Políticas*, 47; Augustín Rivera Jr., "Irma Rangel's Legacy," Caller.com, *Corpus Christi Coastal Bend South Texas News, Information, Events Calendar*, all quotations, http://www.caller.com/cr/cda/article_print/1,1250,CCCT_879_1825912,00. Html.

20. "Rangel," Texas Monthly's Best and Worst Legislators, LRL, 1st quotation; "Furniture," *Texas Monthly*, July 2003, 2nd quotation, www.texasmonthly.com/politics/furniture/ , 2nd quotation; "Rep. Rangel, Alvarez Discuss Issues," *Kingsville Record*, Feb. 28, 1988, 3rd and 4th quotations, Box 233, Folder A2003-042.013; As examples of the letters of support, see Dorothy L. Griffin to Rangel, Aug. 10, 1987; Dr. Andy Hicks to Rangel, Aug. 11, 1987, and Dr. Roger Bulger to Rangel, Aug. 14, 1987; these can be found in Box 233, Folder A2003-042.020, IRC.

21. "A Herald Editorial," *Rio Grande City Herald*, Feb. 18, 1988, Box 233, Folder A2003-042.013, IRC; "Step Right Up!", *The South Texan*, February 19, 1998, 1st through 3rd quotations, Box 233, Folder A2003-042.013, IRC; Clipping, *Kingsville Record*, March 6, 1988, 4th quotation, Box 234, Folder A2003-042.010, IRC; Advertisement, *Falfurrias Facts*, Feb. 25, 1988, Box 234, Folder A2003-042.010, IRC; García, *Políticas*, 40.

22. "Irma Rangel," *The Texas Tribune*, www.Texastribune.org/directory/Irma-rangel

23. Phyllis McKenzie, *The Mexican Texans* (College Station: Texas A&M University Press, 2004), 76–77, 104, 110–111; de León, *Mexican Americans in Texas*, 128–130; M. Levin, "Educational Reform for Disadvantaged Students: An Emerging Crisis," NEA Professional Library, 1986, http://eric.ed.gov/?id=ED273694; "Texas Lawmakers Seek Explanation of Average Higher Educational Rankings," *Black Issues in Higher Education* 17, issue 23 (Jan. 4, 2001): 1, ProQuest document ID 67224915, http://pathfinder.utb.edu:2072/pqdweb?index=13&did=000000067224915%SrchMode=1&s; Carlos Blanton, *The Strange Career of Bilingual Education in Texas, 1836–1981* (College Station: Texas A&M University Press, 2004), 154–155; Joyce Luhrs, "Texas Test Hurts Hispanics," *The Hispanic Outlook in Higher Education* 6, issue 7 (Nov. 24, 1995): 6, Proquest document ID 494408321, http://pathfinder.utb.edu:2072/pqdweb?index=16&did=000000494408321&SrchMode=1&s. . . . See Gilbert G. González, *Chicano Education in the Era of Segregation* (Denton: University of North Texas Press, 1990), for detailed information on topics such as "intelligence Testing and the Mexican Child."

24. "Representative Irma Rangel," MALC, 1st and 2nd quotations; Jones and Winegarten, *Capitol Women*, 205.

25. Rangel Interview, 31–32, 1st quotation on 32; García, *Políticas*, 40, 42; Jones and Winegarten, *Capitol Women*, 205, 2nd quotation.

26. Chuck Owen, "A Wakeup Call: Funding Fight Brings Attention to South Texas Education, LMT Business, quotation, http://www.lmtonline.

com/lmtbusiness/b2.htm; "Presentation on South Texas Border Initiatives," Teri Flack, Deputy Commissioner Texas Higher Education Coordinating Board, before the House Border and International Affairs Committee, March 6, 2003, http://216.239.37.100/search?q+cache:mYdXdKRVtSOJ:www.thecb.state. tx.us/cfbin/Arch . . . .

27. Owen, "Wakeup Call," 1st quotation; "Presentation on South Texas Border Initiative," Flak, 2nd quotation; "Expansion of U.T. Degree Programs Continues in South Texas/Border Region," U.T. System News Release, November 13, 1997, 3rd quotation, http://www.utsystem.edu/news/1997/SoTXBrdrDegrees11-12-97. htm; "Representative Irma Rangel," MALC.

28. "Presentation on South Texas Border Initiatives," Flak; "Expansion of U.T. Degree Programs," quotation. In 2015, the University of Texas-Pan American at Edinburg and the University of Texas-Brownsville were dissolved with their campuses becoming part of the University of Texas Rio Grande Valley, a new entity created by the Texas legislature.

29. "Rep. Rangel Named Distinguished Alumnus"; "Representative Irma Rangel," MALC, quotation; Randolph B. Campbell, *Gone to Texas: A History of the Lone Star State*, 2nd ed. (New York: Oxford University Press, 2012), 470; Claudio Sánchez, "How the Cost of College Went from Affordable to Sky-High," NPR Special Series, Paying for College, March 18, 2014, www.npr.org/2014/03/18/2908680131/ how-the-cost-of-college-went-from-affordable-to-sky-high; "Texans Seek to End Use of Racial Quotas and Racial Preferences: Ward Connerly Lends His Support to Texas Battle," Adversity.Net Special Report, Last Updated July 29, 1999, http://www. adversity.net/texas/initiative.htm +87.

30. "Texans Seek to End Use of Racial Quotas and Racial Preferences"; "Education Quotas: Texas," Adversity.net, http:www.adversity.net/education_3_texas.htm; "Hopwood v. Texas," "*Hopwood v. Texas*," CIR The Center for Individual Rights, Washington, D.C., 1st and 2nd quotations, https://www. cir-usa.org/cases/hopwood-v-texas/; "Education Quotas: Texas"; "Texas Passes Diversity Legislation," *Black Issues in Higher Education*, Issue 7 (May 29, 1997):6, 3rd quotation, ProQuest Document ID 13582724, http://pathfinder. utb.edu:2072/pqdweb?index=8&did000000013582724&/SrchMode=1&si. . . ; Campbell, *Gone to Texas*, 470. At the time that the *Hopwood* decision was issued, it applied only to three states: Texas, Louisiana, and Mississippi.

31. "State and University Officials Will Gather at Texas A&M," Office of University Relations, Texas A&M University, Nov. 6, 1996, 1st quotation, http://www. tamu.edu/univrel/aggiedaily/news/stories/archive/110696-1.html;   "*Hopwood*, Proposition 209, and Beyond," *FairTest Examiner*, Spring 1997, all remaining quotations, http://www.fairtest.org/examarts/spring97/hopwood.htm; Lani Guinier and Gerald Torres, "Leadership from the Bottom Up," minerscanary, http://www.miner-scanary.org/mainart/leadership.shtml.

32. "Texas College and Universities Will Need to Work with Legislators . . . ," Office of University Relations, Texas A&M University, Nov. 13, 1996, all quotations,   http://www.tamu.edu/univrel/aggiedaily/news/stories/archive/ 111396-4.html.

33. García, *Políticas*, 45, 1st quotation; "Memorial: Irma Rangel," 2nd quotation, http://cfapps.caller.com/obits/obittemplate.cfm?ID=5693&FirstName=Ir ma&MName=&La. . . . ; "Irma L. Rangel: Texas State Representative," Women in

Government, 3rd quotation, http://magazines.ivillage.com/goodhousekeeping/myhome/friends/articles/0,,287164_2905.

34. Lani Guinier, "An Equal Chance," RaceTalks Initiatives, Apr. 23, 1998, 1st quotation, http://www.law.harvard.edu/faculty/guinier/racetalks/nyed2. htm; Excerpt from *The Chronicle of Higher Education*, June 23, 2000, in Notes on Bush as Governor of Texas, 2nd quotation, http://www.sierrafoot.org/soapbox/Bush_Texas.html; Myra Leo, "In Memoriam: It Was Always about the Students," *The Texas Observer*, April 11, 2003, 12, 3rd and 4th quotations.

35. Amy Scott, "'Top 10 Percent' Rule for College Admissions Faces a New Challenge," Marketplace, May 23, 2016, 1st and 2nd quotations, https://www.marketplace.org/2016/05/18/wealth-poverty/top-10-rule-faces-new-challenge-texas; Adam Liptak, "Supreme Court Upholds Affirmative Action Program at University of Texas," *New York Times*, June 23, 2016, 3rd through 5th quotations, https://www.nytimes.com/2016/06/24/us/politics/supreme-court-affirmative-action-university-of-texas.html. The author's daughter was an incoming freshman at UT Austin in summer 2000, and at a campus meeting for incoming freshmen university officials announced the temporary suspension of new and transfer students.

36. Linda K. Wertheimer, "Diversity Law Complicates Grad School Policies," *Dallas Morning News*, Feb. 25, 2002, all quotations, http://aad.english.ucsb.edu/docs/lwertheimer.html.

37. Wertheimer, "Diversity Law," *Dallas Morning News*, all quotations.

38. Wertheimer, "Diversity Law," *Dallas Morning News*, quotation; "MALDEF Applauds Passage of New Standards for Texas Graduate School Admissions and Scholarships," *La Prensa* 12, issue 51 (San Antonio, June 24, 2001), ProQuest Document ID 468640351, http://pathfinder.utb.edu:2072/pdqweb?index=10&did=000000468640351&SrchMode=1&s. . . .

39. "Texas Initiative 2000?," Texans Seek to End . . . Racial Preferences, adversity.net, 1st quotation; "Bill Filed to Overturn Hopwood Affirmative Action Ruling," *Fort Worth Star-Telegram*, February 27, 1999, http://www.star-telegram.com/news/doc/1047/1:STATE72/1:STATE72022799.html; "Bill: HB 1106, Legislative Session: 76(R)," Texas Legislature Online: History, 2nd quotation, http://www.legis.state.tx.us/billlookup/History.aspx?LegSess=76R&Bill=HB1106&Sort=D.

40. Crystal Pollard, "Bilingual Education Program for Future Teachers to be Implemented at SWT," The Daily University Star Online, http://www.universitystar.com/98/10/16/news/html; "Texas AFT Calls for Restoration of Tuition Scholarships for Educational Aides," Texas AFT, Feb. 11, 2015, quotation, http://wwww.texasaft.org/texas-aft-calls-restoration-tuition-scholarships-educational-aides/.

41. Sánchez, "How the Cost of College Went from Affordable to Sky High"; "Economic Returns from Higher Education in Texas," Texas Guaranteed Student Loan Corporation, nd, 1st quotation, https://www.tgslc.org/pdf/Hocken.pdf; "Rep. Rangel Named Distinguished Alumnus," 2nd quotation; "Overview: TEXAS Grant," Texas Higher Education Coordinating Board, February 2012, www.thecb.state.tx.us/download.cfm?downloadfile=7C7CD8D4. . . . The TEXAS Grant program proved so successful that it lasted long after Rangel's lifetime and grew significantly with hundreds of thousands of students ultimately receiving the benefit of these grants.

42. Thomas Meredith, "Higher Education Committee Looks at Reasons, Solutions for 'C' Rating," *The Daily Texan* 101, no. 70 (December 12, 2000), quotation, http://tspweb02.tsp.utexas.edu/webarchive/12-12-00/2000121201_s02_Higher.html.

43. "Texas Lawmakers Seek Explanation," quotation; Meredith, "Higher Education Committee."

44. *Texas Assessment of Academic Skills (TAAS) Examination Requirements for High School Graduation Discrimination against Minority Students*, Texas Education Agency, 2000, all quotations, https://marces.org/mdarch/htm/m031923.htm; *Texas (State): True or False: Does Testing Unfairly Discriminate against Minorities*, Education Quotas: Texas, adversity.net, http://www.adversity.net/education_3_texas.htm; Tamara Henry and Martin Kasindorf, "Testing Could Be the Test for Bush Plan," Floridians for School Choice, Feb. 27, 2001, http://www.floridians.org/newsf/01/0227011.html.

45. "Re: TX Latino/testing conference," ARN, all quotations.

46. Henry and Kasindorf, "Testing Could be the Test"; "The New Rules: An Overview of the Testing and Accountability Provisions of the No Child Left Behind Act," Frontline, PBS, KMBH, all quotations, http://www.pbs.org/wghb/pages/frontline/shows/schools/nochild/nclb/html.

47. Chapter 1, "Historical Overview of Assessment in Texas," *Technical Digest*, 2008–2009, quotation, tea.texas.gov.WorkArea/DownloadAsset.aspx?id=2147494058.

48. García, *Políticas*, 48, quotation.

49. Jeff Simmons, "Organizations: TACHE Determined to Boost Hispanic Faculty; Full-Court Press on Five-Point Agenda," *The Hispanic Outlook in Higher Education* 2, issue 7 (Jan. 8, 2001), all quotations, ProQuest document ID 494422411, http://pathfinder.utb.edu:2072/pdqweb?index=12&did=000000494422411&SrchMode=1&s.

50. Simmons, "Organizations: TACHE," all quotations.

51. MAD of Texas News, January 1988, 1st quotation, Box 235, Folder A20003-042.019, IRC; Jones and Winegarten, *Capitol Women*, 205; "Non-Attorney Professionals, Myra Leo," Attorney Profiles, Hughes & Luce, LLP, http://www.hughesluce.com/AttyProf/Attys/AttorneyBio.asp?ID=353; "Hispanic Women's Network of Texas Holds Annual Conference," *La Prensa* 8, issue 20 (San Antonio, Nov. 17, 1996): 9A, 2nd and 3rd quotations, ProQuest Document ID 46865390, http://pathfinder.utb.edu:2072/pqdweb?index=19&did=000000468653901&SrchMode=1&s.

52. Jones and Winegarten, *Capitol Women*, 205, quotation.

53. "Background: History of the Death Penalty in Texas," Texas Execution Information Center, www.txexecutions.org/history/asp; "Stop the Execution of Gary Graham!", quotations, http://www.ccadp.org/garygraham.htm.

54. Danini, "Texas State Representative Irma Rangel"; "Upbringing Shaped Rangel's Career," *Corpus Christi Caller*, Jan. 30, 1994, Box 1, Folder A1989-039.002, IRC.

55. "State Rep to Get Top Honor," *Kingsville Record*, nd, 1993, 1st quotation, Box 4, Folder A2003-042.018, IRC; "Rep. Rangel Named Distinguished Alumnus," TUSK, 2nd and 3rd quotations; Danini, "Texas State Representative Irma Rangel," 4th quotation; "Previous Margaret Brent Women Lawyers of Achievement Award

Recipients," American Bar Association, www.americanbar.org/groups/women/
initiatives_awards/margaret_brent_awards/pasthonorees.html.

56. "Representative Irma Rangel," MALC, quotation.

57. Danini, "Texas State Representative Irma Rangel," 1st through
3rd quotations; Augustin Rivera Jr., "Irma Rangel's Legacy," Corpus Christ
Coastal Bend South Texas News, Information, Events Calendar, Caller.com,
4th and 5th quotations, http://www.caller.com/cr/cda/article_print/1,1250,C
CCT_879_1825912,00.html.

58. Peggy Fikac, "Irma's Story: Farewell to Irma," *Express-News* Austin
Bureau, Mar. 22, 2003, 1st through 3rd quotations, http://www.ibcmemorial.
org/412.html; Jones and Winegarten, *Capitol Women*, 205–206, 4th through
6th quotations.

59. Leo, "In Memoriam," 1st and 2nd quotations; Rangel Interview, 61;
García, *Políticas*, 41, 3rd quotation.

60. García, *Políticas*, 49; Danini, "Texas State Representative Irma Rangel,"
all quotations.

61. "Names and Events in the News," Issue 11–04–02, Nov. 22, 2002, http://
www.ktcinet.com/aaup/Wanda/Nov_22_2002.htm; Danini, "Texas State Representative Irma Rangel," quotation.

62. Campbell, *Gone to Texas*, 472–473; "Gallego Shifted to Insurance, Reform
Committees," *Pecos Enterprise*, Pecos, Tx, January 31, 2003, http://www.pecos.
net/news.arch2003/013103p.htm; García, *Políticas*, 49, quotation.

63. Matt Flores, "Texas Educators Are on Edge at the Top," *San Antonio Express News*, Feb. 25, 2003, http://216239.39.100/search?q=cache:xjy_
QA1bbkJ:www.utimco.org/extranet/WebData/N.

64. Fikac, "Irma's Story: Farewell to Irma," quotation.

65. Open Letter from the President, [Juliet V. García], The University of
Texas at Brownsville and Texas Southmost College, Mar. 19, 2003, all quotations.
Upon the death of Irma Rangel, President García sent this letter in an email to all
UTB/TSC employees, and the author has a print copy in her possession.

66. "Bills Authored/Joint Authored by Representative Rangel, 78th Legislature," *Texas Legislature Online*, 1st, 2nd, and 4th quotations, www.capitol.state.
tx.us/tlo/reports/author/78R/A4240.HTM; Michelle Kay, "Lawmakers Hope
to Kill College Test," *Austin American-Statesman*, statesman.com, Apr. 21,
2003, 3rd quotation; Joyce Luhrs, Texas Test Hurts Hispanics, *The Hispanic
Outlook in Higher Education* 6, Iss. 7 (Nov. 24, 1995) ProQuest document ID
494408321, http://gateway.proquest.com/openurl?url_ver=Z39.88-2004&res_
dat=xri:pdq&rft_val_fmt=info:ofi/fmt:kev:mtx:journal&genre=article&rft_
dat=xri:pqd:did=000.

67. "Members Gather in Austin March 17 to Lobby State Legislators,"
Corpus Christi American Federation of Teachers (ccaft), http://www.ccaft.org/
lobby-day.htm; "'A Tough Lady to the End,' Irma Rangel, 1931–2003," Scripps
Howard (SH), March 19, 2003, Box 1, Folder A2003-042.035, IRC; García,
"Open Letter from the President," quotation.

68. News 8 Austin Staff, "A Texas Lawmaker Dies of Brain Cancer," Mar. 18,
2003, in Your News, Apr. 30, 2003, quotation, http:www.news8austin.com/
content/your_news/?SecID=278&ArID=65260; Fikac, "Irma's Story: Farewell
to Irma."

69. Danini, "Texas State Representative Irma Rangel," quotation.

70. Danini, "Texas State Representative Irma Rangel," 1st, 2nd, 4th and 5th quotations; "The Austin Chronicle Politics: Naked City," Mar. 21, 2003, 3rd quotation, http://www.austinchronicle.com//issues/dispatch/2003-03-21/pols_naked3. html; "Governor- Press Release – March 19, 2003," Austin, http://www.governor.state.tx.us/divisions/press/pressreleases/PressRelease.2003-03-19.2419; Ty Meighan, "$45M in A&M Bonds are OK'd," *Corpus Christi Caller-Times*, Apr. 18, 2003, www.caller.com/ccct/local_news/article/01641,0; Fikak, "Irma's Story: Farewell to Irma," 6th quotation; García, "Open Letter from the President," 7th quotation.

71. "Irma Rangel, Obituary," Statesman.com, published in *Austin American-Statesman*, March 30, 2003, http://www.legacy.com/obituaries/statesman/obituary.aspx?n=irma-rangel&pid=1590141.

Selena performs during a show at La Villa Real in Mission, Texas, in November 1993. Rick Vasquez, *The Monitor*, McAllen, Texas.

Selena
The Tragic Tejana

AT THE TIME OF her tragic death in 1995, twenty-three-year old Selena Quintanilla-Pérez was not only an award-winning star in the Tejano music industry but also gaining appeal among a wider audience. The term "meteoric" had been used to describe her rapid rise in popularity, even though she began singing as a child. Sadly, that word is an appropriate description of Selena's life. Like a meteor, she flashed brightly across the sky and then was gone. Ironically, the shocking events surrounding the Tejana's murder and its aftermath gained for her a kind of immortality, but at a much greater cost than anyone should have to pay. Posthumously, she has remained a marketable commodity with a strong fan base ready to purchase Selena music and products. Those closest to her disagree among themselves, even to the point of litigation, as to the most appropriate ways to memorialize her. Selena's dramatic story has all of the elements of a *telenovela*, a Latin American soap opera, and illustrates that truth indeed can be stranger—and sadder—than fiction.

***

To understand the chain of events that determined the course of Selena's life, one must first look at her father, an aspiring musician in his youth. In the 1950s, Abraham Quintanilla Jr. became one of three vocalists in Los Dinos, slang for the Boys. Initially performing English-language music, the group was unable to get bookings in desirable venues, no doubt handicapped by their ethnicity.

Changing tactics, Los Dinos turned to Latino audiences. Unfortunately, "English oldies" had little appeal to Mexican Americans, who wanted to hear Tejano music—"fiery Spanish-language music" created and performed along the Rio Grande border in northern Mexico and South Texas. In the mid-1960s, Los Dinos transitioned to Texas-Mexican music. They recorded a few Spanish albums for the Falcón label, had some hits at the regional level, and "received a significant amount of airplay." Nevertheless, the group disbanded in 1974, and Quintanilla recognized the need to find more stable employment. Music remained his first love, however, a passion that was to have a great impact on his children, especially his youngest daughter, Selena.[1]

When Selena was born in Lake Jackson, Texas, on April 16, 1971, Quintanilla was working at a chemical plant. By that time, he and his wife Marcella (Pérez) had two other children, Abraham III (nicknamed A. B.) and Suzette. While Selena was still young, the father of three became unemployed, at which point he decided to open a Mexican restaurant called Papa Gallos. Despite his later occupations, the Tejano's heart remained in the world of music, and he taught his son to play the guitar. One source claims that "Selena was jealous of the attention" that A.B. was getting from their father, so she picked up a microphone and began to sing. Recognizing his daughter's exceptional talent, he reportedly saw "a way to get back into the music business." Buying some used instruments, Abraham formed a family band. The young Selena was the vocalist, A.B. played bass, and a cousin played drums. When the latter moved away, Papa Abraham decided to have older daughter Suzette become the drummer. To promote the group, he placed a small platform and dance floor in his restaurant where they appeared live. They also began to perform at weddings in the Lake Jackson area.[2]

An unfortunate downturn in the oil industry depressed the local economy, causing Papa Gallos to close its doors about a year after opening. In financial crisis, the family looked to the music business as a way "to put food on the table." Learning from his experience with the original Los Dinos, Selena's father decided early on that she needed to sing songs in Spanish. He was convinced that Mexican-American audiences would respond more positively to music in their native language. However, the Quintanilla children had not learned fluent Spanish in the home, so Selena did not understand the meaning of the words she was singing. In her late teens, however, she took a greater interest in learning her ancestral language, which helped the Tejana gain pride in her heritage and realize how "lovely" her culture was.[3]

Selena y Los Dinos turned professional in 1981, and the Quintanillas moved to Corpus Christi the following year. Performing "in rural dance halls and urban nightclubs," they played "tejano music for tejano audiences." Selena remained the vocalist with Suzette still on drums. Brother Abe III wrote the songs, and Father Abraham served as the band's manager. Some sources allege that the three Quintanilla children did not aspire to careers in music, that they preferred playing outside to rehearsing indoors. Their father, however, supposedly insisted that he was doing what was best for them and that someday they would be grateful. Regardless, entering the music industry at an early age had a major impact on Selena's life. As the young Latina later said, "When I was eight[,] I recorded my first song in Spanish, a country song. When I was nine[,] we started a Tex-Mex band." Being a child star made leading a normal life problematic.[4]

Presumably for reasons of her career, Abraham took Selena out of school after the eighth grade. To continue her education, the adolescent took courses by mail and received her high school diploma in 1989. Selena then studied business administration, also by correspondence, through Pacific Western University. While pursuing her studies, she continued to perform. When the Tejano group La Mafia experienced success appearing in Mexico,

Los Dinos followed their lead. The young Tejana "conquered the hearts of Mexicans across the border as well as in . . . the United States."[5]

Besides performing live in the 1980s, Selena y Los Dinos began to record their music. Selena had a short, disappointing relationship with Freddie Records at the beginning of the decade, but in 1985 she signed with a bigger label, Cara Records. The following year, Los Dinos entered into a contract with Manny Guerra of GP records, a decision that led to their first hit. "Dame un beso" ("Give Me a Kiss") reached #1 on the El Paso Tejano list and also earned an award for Record of the Month in New Mexico. In 1987, Selena won the prestigious Tejano Music Award for "Female Entertainer of the Year"— only the first of many times that she would be so honored. The group's version of "La Bamba" also reached #20 on Billboard Latin charts. That same year, Selena appeared with Johnny Canales on his television program based in Corpus Christi but broadcast all over Latin America and the United States.[6]

By this point, major record companies aspired to add Selena y Los Dinos to their list of performers. The Quintanilla family's opportunity came when they signed with the major Capitol/EMI label. This company saw Selena not only as being a great Texas-Mexican artist but also as having the potential to "be a major star in Mexico and the South American market." Under EMI in 1989, the band released its first CD, appropriately entitled *Selena y Los Dinos*. One of the songs, "Contigo quiero estar" ("I want to be with you") reached # 8 on Billboard's Mexican regional chart, the highest ranking of any of the group's songs to that date. The Long Play was also reported to be the first by a woman in the Tejano music industry to sell 50,000 units. Noted for bringing for "a certain charm, innovative spirit, and new perspective" to the genre, Selena was acclaimed as "the dominant female vocalist in a predominantly male industry."[7]

Significantly, 1989 became a turning point in Selena's career. At the Tejano Music Awards, she was named both "Female Entertainer of the Year" and "Female Vocalist of the Year." By the end of the decade, Selena was recognized as "*la Reina de la Onda Tejana*" (The Queen of Tejano Music), while retaining her image as "a woman of the people." EMI worked hard to promote "The Queen," and Selena was transformed—from the Tejana "girl-next-door" into a very different persona. She became a marketable commodity, just like the products she was touting. The companies with which Selena was associated exploited her growing sexuality, as on stage and in photo sessions, she wore tight, revealing clothing to make her a "Madonna-like Latina sex queen."[8]

Selena's fame, fortune, and awards indicated that she was overcoming obstacles posed by her gender. Certainly, she benefitted from the accomplishments of a few ground-breaking predecessors such as Lydia Mendoza, Chelo Silva, and Laura Canales, but Selena was "probably the first female to introduce charisma and choreography into Texas-Mexican music." While performing, she "twisted, turned, and twirled." She made Tejano music "fun to dance to" and "enjoyable to watch." Certainly, men enjoyed watching Selena, but her appeal was broader. She added a female view on love to Tejano songs with their traditional macho orientation. Her lyrics told of strong, independent Latinas, of women capable of surviving a failed relationship and standing up for themselves. Such messages had great appeal to Selena's female fan base.[9]

Another challenge for the Tejana was to present an image "of both sexuality *and* family values" simultaneously. Again she succeeded. Off stage the young woman came across as a well-mannered "working-class Mexican American girl who obeyed her parents." The common people adored her. Young Latinas saw Selena as a role model, a girl from the *barrio* (poor Hispanic neighborhood) who had made good. Her success instilled hope and pride in them. She showed "that the color brown was sexy, trendy, and beautiful." Indeed, Selena was very conscious of her ethnicity. "If a person in our condition thinks that he is inferior, he is. But one has to be positive," she declared. The singer labeled racism as a sad worldwide problem, but was proud to be Mexican American, despite the hardships involved.[10]

Fortunately, the Tejano music industry was changing in the 1990s, partly as the result of the growing Hispanic population in the United States. Immigration from Mexico was increasing dramatically, and more Latinos were migrating from other parts of the Americas as well. Also, a "more educated, prosperous and bilingual Latino middle class" had money to spend and an affinity for ethnic music. Large recording companies such as Capitol/EMI and Sony *Discos* (Sony Records) recognized the profitability of broadening the appeal of Tejano music "first to an international Spanish-speaking market and then to the English speaking-one." They promoted two distinct types of songs, Colombian *cumbias* and *baladas* (ballads), which were popular in Spanish-speaking countries. This redirected the focus of Tejano music, previously based heavily on regional ensembles such as *conjuntos* (accordian-based groups) and *orquestras Tejanas* (Tejana orchestras). While marketing the new sound, major labels also competed to find groups that could crossover into the English language market.[11]

Three Tejano groups, La Mafia, Mazz, and Selena y los Dinos, set the "standards and provided the leadership for venturing into new markets. . . . Each contributed something special to *música tejana* [Tejano music] and helped forge its distinct sound." Though *orquestra* dated back to earlier decades, Selena's role was especially significant, as she "introduced pop, rap, rock, dance, and *mariachi* influences into Tejano music." Her recordings of *cumbias*, such as "Techno-Cumbia" and "Como La Flor" ("Like the Flower"), became hits both regionally and nationally. At the same time, Selena wisely chose not to abandon the more traditional "*rancheras*," which had a polka beat. Instead, she made them more spirited. Selena y Los Dinos released albums with half *cumbias* and half *rancheras*. With this combination of old and new, the singer dominated the Tejano market in the early 1990s, and her success influenced major record companies to sign more women, a trend that continued throughout the decade.[12]

Corporate marketing, lively performances, and excellent songs propelled Selena's success. By 1994, she "had taken the Tejano music industry by storm and was on the verge of becoming an international artist. . . ." Her album sales set records. With her 1992 LP *Entre a Mi Mundo* (*Come into My World*), she became the first female in the Tejano music industry to sell more than 100,000 units. This LP was also #1 in Billboard's regional Mexican charts. In 1994, *Amor Prohibido* (*Forbidden Love*) made quadruple platinum with over 400,000 units sold. The title track "reached number one on Billboard's Latin chart to become the biggest hit of her career. The album remained at number one or two on Billboard's Latin top fifty for 1994."[13]

Other factors contributed to Selena's success. In the 1990s, the venues where Tejano groups could perform multiplied, as did the number of awards for which they qualified. Previously, these ensembles had performed primarily at patriotic festivals, private parties, and public dances. This changed as Latino ensembles were invited to big arenas in major cities. As an example, more than 33,000 fans came to hear Selena y Los Dinos when they appeared live at the Alamodome in San Antonio. In 1993 Selena and other Latino performers appeared at "The Go Tejano Rodeo" in Houston with almost 67,000 people in the audience. Los Dinos continued to break attendance records at various concerts during the first half of the decade.[14]

As early as the mid-1980s, the National Academy of Recording Arts and Sciences, which sponsored the Grammy Awards, had added a new category for regional/Mexican music. Selena garnered many of these awards, year after year. Her trophies included a 1994

Grammy for Best Mexican-American Album for *Selena Live*. Also, the Tejano Music Awards ceremony was gaining in prominence. In a single year, the Latina received "six of 15 awards, winning for an unprecedented seven consecutive years."[15]

With surging record sales, major public appearances, and numerous music awards came increased opportunities. Selena signed a contract with the Coca Cola Company, as well as making profitable deals with Dep Corporation, AT&T, and Southwestern Bell. In 1995 she also made a small appearance in the film *Don Juan de Marco*. The income from Selena's music career and business deals made her a wealthy woman. By the mid-1990s, *Hispanic* magazine estimated the young woman's worth at approximately $5,000,000.[16] Obviously, her singing had done more than just put food on the table.

In 1994 *Texas Monthly* named Selena one of the twenty most influential Texans, and to her credit, the songstress recognized the responsibility that accompanied fame. Considering herself a "public servant," she used her celebrity to benefit a number of causes. The Latina encouraged young people to avoid drug and alcohol abuse. Helping the Coastal Bend AIDS Foundation, making pro-education videos, and publicizing a Houston area abuse shelter were among her other public service efforts.[17]

Selena's growing celebrity was featured in a *Texas Monthly* article in September 1994. Author Joe Nick Patoski labeled the eight-piece Los Dinos band "a favorite of the tejano dance-hall circuit" and "the biggest act in Tejano music." Noting that *música tejana* had become popular on the international scene, Patoski wrote that "The rise of tejano has paralleled Selena's success." As evidence that the two went hand in hand, for the previous seven years Selena had "won either the entertainer of the year or the female vocalist of the year award at the Tejano Music Awards." A year earlier, she also garnered "a Grammy for best Mexican-American performance." And her album sales each hovered around the three-quarter million mark. Patoski reported that Selena's song "Amor Prohibido" was "selling two thousand copies a day in Mexico alone."[18]

The same article commented on the two-sided image projected by Selena. Calling the Latina the perfect example of "the good girl," Patoski wrote of her natural beauty before she put on the heavy makeup worn for public performances. Once Selena went on stage, a remarkable transformation happened. Wearing "a halter top and tight pants," she worked her body to excite the crowd and even tossed a pair of her panties to the audience. Nevertheless, it was Selena's voice that commanded attention. Patoski marveled that it was "as fragile as fine crystal when wrapped around a ballad or roaring like a tiger when thrust in front of a pounding *cumbia* rhythm."[19]

Near the end of his article, Patoski talked of plans for Selena's first English-language album, "her bid to cross over to the pop mainstream" and appeal to an English-speaking audience. He recognized this as the greatest challenge of her career. Even if she succeeded, Patoski wrote, Selena vowed to remain faithful to the Tejano fans responsible for her success. Her philosophy was that "a person should never be satisfied with what they've accomplished. . . . Better to try than not to try at all."[20]

By the time that Patoski's article was published in *Texas Monthly*, Selena was taking major steps in her personal life, as well as in her career. On April 2, 1992, in a secret ceremony at the county courthouse in Corpus Christi, she had married the Los Dinos guitarist, Christopher Pérez. The media reported that Abraham Quintanilla Jr. had opposed the marriage, because he believed that his daughter was too young. Nevertheless, Selena became Chris's bride. Although this was a step toward independence, the songstress remained close—literally and figuratively—to her family. The newlyweds "lived next door to her parents" in a "modest working-class Corpus Christi neighborhood."[21]

Another alleged source of conflict was the creation of Selena's own clothing line in 1992, a long-time ambition of the singer's. Two years later she opened boutiques named Selena Etc. in Corpus Christi and San Antonio. Possibly concerned "that fashion would distract her from music," Abraham Quintanilla Jr. was said to be less than enthusiastic about these enterprises. Nevertheless, Selena, was determined to design and market attractive apparel.[22]

The Tejana proposed opening a factory in Monterrey, Mexico, to produce the clothing for her stores. During several trips across the border, she met cosmetic surgeon Dr. Ricardo Martínez. Although he was about twenty years older than she, the physician became Selena's friend and she his patient. *People Weekly* reported that much gossip ensued. Rumors spread that he had performed a liposuction procedure on the singer to enhance her curves. More damaging were stories of a romantic relationship between her and Martínez, who was also married. Calling Selena "an honest and respectable woman," the doctor vehemently denied these allegations. He also alleged to *People Weekly* that Selena had complained about lack of cooperation from her father and husband in establishing the factory in Mexico. Quintanilla responded by admitting that Selena wanted more support from him and Chris than she was getting. In his defense, Abraham insisted that he did not know anything about that type of business. He also explained that Chris's "world is music, not fashion."[23]

Perhaps trying to be more supportive, Abraham reportedly recommended that his daughter hire Yolanda Saldívar to help with her growing business enterprises. In her mid-thirties, Saldívar had helped organize Selena's fan club of which she became president. The two women with their shared "humble Mexican-American roots" seemed to be a good fit, and Yolanda became Selena's personal assistant. Resigning as head of the fan club, Saldívar not only went with Selena on trips to Mexico but also became manager of the clothing store in Corpus Christi. The two Latinas developed a close personal relationship. In fact, one news reporter later wrote that Yolanda considered Selena to be "the only friend" she had.[24]

Although Selena liked and trusted Saldívar, not everyone shared those sentiments. In one instance, a clothing designer who had been working for Selena decided to terminate the business relationship, evidently because of Saldívar's unacceptable behavior. He claimed that she upset other employees by screaming at them and was driving him crazy. Bad blood also developed between Yolanda Saldívar and Abraham Quintanilla Jr. The exact reasons for the estrangement are subject to interpretation, as is the actual chain of events that led to the murder of Selena Quintanilla-Pérez by Yolanda Saldívar on March 31, 1995. What is clear is that questions began to arise about Saldívar's management—or mismanagement—of funds from the fan club and the boutique. According to Chris Pérez, the Quintanillas believed that Saldívar had misappropriated as much as $30,000. The result was a confrontation in which Selena demanded her bank records back from the store manager and decided to terminate the woman's employment.[25]

On March 11, a distraught Saldívar reportedly bought a .38-caliber revolver at a store in San Antonio. The Tejana presented herself as a nurse taking care of a dying patient and claimed to need protection because of "death threats" from the patient's family. On March 13, the day that she picked up the gun, Saldívar had her lawyer prepare a letter of resignation to present to Selena. Oddly, the woman returned the gun a few days later with the explanation that her father had given her another pistol, a .22 caliber handgun. Nevertheless, Saldívar allegedly went back to the store on March 26 to purchase the original firearm again.[26]

Adding to the confusion was an incident on March 31 in which Selena went with her estranged employee to a medical center in Corpus Christi. Saldívar claimed to have been raped a few days earlier and possibly accused Selena's father of being the perpetrator.

When a physical examination failed to substantiate Yolanda's claims, Selena concluded that the story was a fabrication. In this tense atmosphere, the two Latinas left the clinic and went to Saldívar's room at the Days Inn. After angry words were exchanged, Yolanda shot Selena in the back.[27]

Immediately after the shooting, an hysterical Saldívar got into a pickup truck in the motel parking lot. When police blocked the vehicle, the disturbed woman remained there for more than nine hours "with the murder weapon pointed at her head." A hostage negotiation team attempted to persuade her to surrender. As the tense hours passed, Saldívar kept saying, "I didn't mean to do it." Blaming Abraham Quintanilla Jr. for the tragedy, she declared that he "made me do it. He was out to get me . . . This man was so evil to me. My father even warned me about him. My father said I should get out before I get trapped." Saldívar repeated her claim that Quintanilla had raped her and told hostage negotiator Larry Young that "I had a problem with her [Selena] and I just got to end it."[28]

The negotiators promised Saldívar that her lawyer and mother would be waiting if she surrendered, which she finally did. Apparently, neither promise was kept. Yolanda Saldívar signed a confession in which she admitted her guilt, a document that later proved controversial. Both the accused and her lawyer insisted that she had declared the shooting an accident, but that declaration was not in the written confession she signed. This omission became a major legal issue in the subsequent trial. Notably, Texas Ranger Robert Garza testified that he heard Saldívar complain that the document "said nothing about the shooting being an accident." Questions also were raised as to whether Saldívar's original intent had been to kill herself rather than Selena on that fatal day at the end of March.[29]

The Quintanilla family did not question Saldívar's guilt. Early in April, a Spanish-language publication, *La Voz de Houston* (*The Voice of Houston*) printed Abraham's version of the fatal events. Selena's father declared that there had been suspicion of possible financial mismanagement by Saldívar. He claimed that the fan club's new president had reported numerous complaints from those who had paid their membership fees but had not received the merchandise promised—"*La camiseta y una grabación de la artista*" (the T-shirt and a Selena recording). These and other irregularities had led the Quintanillas to demand that Saldívar surrender the financial records from the fan club and the boutique.[30]

In the same article, Abraham said that Selena and Chris had confronted Saldívar at the hotel the night before the singer was killed, and the manager had handed over some of the business records, but not all. According to Quintanilla, Selena had fired Saldívar that same night. He claimed that the disgruntled employee had called on Friday, March 31, to tell Selena that the rest of the records were at the hotel, and his daughter went to get them. As reported in *La Voz de Houston*, a heated discussion then occurred between the former friends at the Days Inn, and Selena was shot when she tried to leave. The wounded singer ran to the hotel lobby, where the clerk hid her behind the counter and called the police. When authorities arrived, Saldívar was already in the truck in the parking lot. Meanwhile, Selena was transported by ambulance to the Memorial Medical Center, where she was declared dead at 1:05 p.m.—just weeks away from her twenty-fourth birthday. Her father explained that the Quintanillas had learned about these tragic events only when they received a telephone call from a radio station. Selena's family wanted to see justice done.[31]

Mike Westergren, the judge assigned to the sensational case, also wanted to ensure that justice was served. Although the trial was originally scheduled for Nueces County where the shooting had occurred, "Selena's appeal has always been strongest in South Texas, where she lived and worked." The judge ordered the venue changed to Houston, where "finding a fair jury would be easier." Determined to conduct an orderly trial, Westergren banned cameras from the courtroom. Nevertheless, hundreds of English and Spanish-language newspaper, television, and magazine reporters flocked to Houston to provide coverage of the high-profile case. The Spanish-language networks Univisión and Telemundo carried detailed daily reports on the trial.[32]

District Attorney Carlos Valdez conducted the prosecution of Yolanda Saldívar. Ironically, he came from the same Corpus Christi neighborhood in which Selena had been raised. He, too, wanted justice served, which led to a charge of first degree murder. Recognizing the notoriety of the case, Valdez ostensibly relied heavily on his chief prosecutor, an experienced attorney named Mark Skurka. Elissa Sterling, who had tried cases in Judge Westergrens's court, also became a member of the prosecution team.[33]

Douglas Tinker, a defense attorney with a good acquittal record, was appointed by Judge Westergren to represent Yolanda Saldívar. In fact, the same year that Selena was killed, Tinker was recognized by the State Bar of Texas's criminal justice section "as the state's outstanding criminal defense lawyer." He requested the aid of Spanish-speaking Arnold García from Jim Wells County. Many other lawyers also offered their services, and Tinker accepted the assistance of Fred Hagan, possibly because he had money to help fund the defense. Not surprisingly, the defense team received threats for daring to represent Selena's accused murderer. Unintimidated, Tinker insisted that "the shooting was an accident" and emphasized that critical information had been omitted from Saldívar's confession. Hoping to shift some of the blame onto Quintanilla, Tinker alleged that Selena's father was jealous of his daughter's relationship with the accused. The attorney insisted that Abraham and Yolanda had been involved in a power struggle, during which Abraham told Selena that Saldívar was a homosexual. Also, Abraham reputedly had opposed Selena's intention "of expanding her fashion business" into Mexico, because it would hurt the band.

Tinker hoped to prove that hostility between Yolanda Saldívar and Abraham Quintanilla led the accused woman to buy the gun for self-defense. The attorney insisted that his client had not intended to kill Selena.[34]

Probably to diffuse the anticipated "blame the father strategy," District Attorney Valdez called Quintanilla as the prosecution's first witness. On the stand, Selena's father "forcefully denied ever threatening Saldívar, calling her a lesbian, or raping her, as she claimed on the hostage audio tapes." When prosecutors had first told him of the rape claim, he testified that he had responded by declaring "Have you ever seen the woman?" Tinker chose not to cross examine Selena's father, a decision later justified by saying that he did not want "to put him through it." However, critics of the defense attorney's strategy contended that he was afraid an attack on Abraham could backfire and "stir up sympathy for him." Instead, the defense focused on the claim that the shooting was an accident and that Saldívar's written confession was flawed.[35]

Skurka proved skillful in presenting the prosecution's case. A picture of Selena was prominently placed in view of the jury as a visual reminder of the talented young woman whose life had ended so tragically. The prosecution team "called both friendly and hostile witnesses before the defense could" and kept "the jurors focused on the victim." They used the testimony of hotel employees to portray "Selena's screams and her last steps and words immediately following the shooting." One of these witnesses testified that Saldívar yelled "Bitch" at Selena just before shooting her.[36]

Tinker reportedly liked the composition of the jury and believed that at least a few members would prove sympathetic to the defendant. Summoning only three defense witnesses, he recalled only two people who had testified for the prosecution before resting his case. Saldívar was not put on the stand to testify, a decision that later elicited criticism. Tinker also chose not to ask the judge to consider a lesser charge of voluntary manslaughter, an omission that he might have regretted later, given the outcome of the trial.[37]

Despite the defense's best efforts, the jury deliberated less than three hours. On October 23, 1995, they found Yolanda Saldívar guilty of murder in the first degree. Three days later, the Latina was sentenced "to the maximum of life in prison with no possibility of parole for 30 years." Tinker made clear his intent to appeal. In the meantime, the convicted woman had to be placed in protective custody when she was taken to prison. This was perhaps predictable, because the *State of Texas v. Yolanda Saldívar* "was the most closely watched murder trial in Texas in years." For fourteen days, "Selena's ghost hung over the courtroom and the hundreds of fans keeping vigil outside." One writer reported that the outcome of the trial helped restore trust in the legal system. "It proved to Texas' largest minority group that the criminal justice system, flawed as it may be, really does work."[38]

How had Selena's family and fans reacted to the events of March 31, 1995? Twenty-six-year-old widower, Chris Pérez, appeared emotionally devastated in the months following his wife's death. Keeping a low profile, Selena's mother said little publicly. During the trial, however, when a hotel employee began describing "Selena's last moments, an overwrought Marcella had to leave. The next day, she was admitted to the coronary unit of St. Joseph's Hospital for observation." Also heartbroken, Abraham Quintanilla Jr. reacted very differently from his wife. Presiding at many press conferences, he was criticized for seeking the spotlight. He announced the establishment of the Selena Foundation to handle the many donations being sent by individuals and corporations. The Mission Statement expressed the following goals: "to offer the motivation that every child needs to complete their education, to live moral lives, to love their families, to respect human life and to sing whatever song they were born to sing." Funds from the foundation were dedicated to philanthropic causes as varied as the March of Dimes, the Special Olympics, hospitals, schools, and scholarships.[39]

Selena's death did not end Abraham Quintanilla Jr.'s involvement in the music industry but forced him to direct his management services to other talented recording artists. By year's end, he introduced a "new discovery, twelve-year-old Jennifer Peña," who looked somewhat like a young Selena but proved not to have the magnetic star power of his daughter. He also announced that he would be executive producer for a movie about Selena's life—as seen from her father's point of view. Underway as well were what proved to be abortive plans for another Los Dinos tour. One year after the murder, band members reunited for an emotional jam session in one of the recording studios at Q Productions, Quintanilla's Corpus Christi-based entertainment company. However, they realized that Selena was as irreplaceable in their professional as in their personal lives.[40]

Abraham Quintanilla Jr. faced public accusations that he was trying to profit from his daughter's death. Matters deteriorated even more when court records showed that Selena's estate "was only worth $164,000 and that Chris Pérez had given up his right to administer the estate to Abraham." What had happened to Selena's fortune? Why was so little left for her husband? As these and other questions were raised, Quintanilla became "increasingly hostile to the media." For his part, Pérez defended the decision to surrender control to Abraham. The bereaved widower said that Selena did not have a lawyer when she was alive and that he felt no need for a lawyer after she was dead. He trusted his father-in-law. As Chris noted, he had already suffered a loss much greater than money. "Why should I worry about losing something? I have already lost what I always wanted. I would trade everything I had if I could have her back."[41]

Selena's fans shared her husband's sentiments. As one Texas disc jockey predicted at the time, "Years from now, we'll all remember where we were and what we were doing when Selena died." Indeed, as news spread about what had happened to the beloved singer, reactions were intense. In Corpus Christi, hundreds went to the Days Inn parking lot where they cried at the loss of their idol. Also, "A long procession of cars passed the lower-middle class home where Selena lived. Many fans placed balloons and notes . . . in a chain-link fence in front of her property." Later, when Selena's casket was placed on display at the Bayfront Convention Center, tens of thousands came to view it. About six hundred people attended the singer's Jehovah's Witness funeral, which was private. Many more would have gone had they been allowed.[42]

In San Antonio, the "acknowledged capital of Tejano music," two memorial services were quickly organized. At a mall on the south side of the city a large crowd of all ages gathered to play

A memorial mural located on the outside wall of a convenience store in the Molina subdivision in Corpus Christi, where Selena spent her childhood. This mural does not have an artist signature. Photo by Bob Prager, Bob Prager Selena Portfolio, Mary and Jeff Bell Library, Special Collections and Archives Department, Texas A&M University-Corpus Christi.

Selena's recordings, wave candles, say prayers, and cry together. Similar vigils, memorials, and masses were held all over the Southwest. Street murals were painted in Selena's honor in poor Hispanic neighborhoods in cities such as Corpus Christi and Laredo. And within six months after the singer's death, an estimated six hundred babies in Texas alone were named after her.[43]

During the fourteen days of Yolanda Saldívar's trial, angry fans waited outside the courthouse. They expressed their feelings on T-shirts that read *Justicia* (Justice) or *Cien anos* (One hundred years), the prison sentence they hoped the defendant would receive. Some carried signs demanding that she be hanged; others called her a pig. So much hatred was directed toward the accused that one magazine writer called her "a marked woman" and wondered "whether the 35-year-old Saldívar is safer in prison or out."[44]

That so many people, particularly Latinos, loved Selena was recognized by George W. Bush, governor of Texas at the time of the murder. Bush proclaimed April 16—the star's birthday—as "Selena Day" in the Lone Star State. According to the governor, she "represented 'the essence of the culture of South Texas.'" He expressed admiration for the Tejana's "firm belief in family values," as well as her role in the fight against drugs and her work to stop the spread of AIDS. And on "Selena Day" in 1995, less than one month after the tragic shooting in Corpus Christi, tens of thousands of people around the state and nation commemorated what would have been Selena's twenty-fourth birthday. Reacting to Governor Bush's proclamation, State Senator Carlos Truan called the internationally known Tejana a young, ambitious singer who "overcame ethnic and cultural barriers." In doing so, he cited Selena as "an example that inspired millions of people." In the senator's prophetic words, she "would continue being one of the most brilliant jewels of Texas."[45]

Not everyone thought that Selena was such a brilliant jewel or that her death was a great tragedy. On his New York radio show,

Howard Stern ridiculed her fans for their emotionalism and declared that "Spanish people have the worst taste in music." His remarks created a backlash, as furious Hispanics organized a boycott of Stern's sponsors. In the end, the radio personality issued a public apology "given only in Spanish," but it was dismissed publicly by some as "insulting" and "insincere."[46]

The loss felt by Selena fans created endless opportunities for exploitation. Within hours of the fatal incident at the Days Inn, "the first signs of commercialism over Selena's death emerged." Abraham Quintanilla Jr. was furious at "vultures" who were selling unauthorized merchandise, such as T-shirts, albums, and videos, in places as distant as Argentina, Japan, and England. He did everything possible to stop the marketing of these illicit products. Particularly upsetting was a sketch "of Selena as a singing skeleton holding a microphone" that sold for thousands of dollars; however, the Quintanillas were able to prevent copies from being made. Faced with the reality of tremendous demand for Selena-themed items, her father eventually accepted legal advice "'to put things out because if we don't others will, and then we'll have to fight them in court.'"[47]

Several unauthorized Selena biographies appeared, the first a bilingual volume written in only a few weeks by Clint Richmond and published by Pocket Books. *Selena!* made the *New York Times* list of best sellers. The staff at the press admitted to having known "little about Tejano music before the book was produced." And a senior editor acknowledged that the firm was seeking profitable opportunities to mine the subject even more.[48]

Ramiro Burr, a writer for the *San Antonio Express-News*, bemoaned the exploitation of Selena. "It's hard to separate the good guys from the bad guys," he wrote. Nevertheless, his own paper had marketed a posthumous poster of the singer, and Burr himself was selected by Abraham Quintanilla Jr. to write an official Selena biography. When later removed from the project, the author filed a lawsuit but dropped it, presumably because Selena's father apologized. Quintanilla's next choice was award-winning Victor Villaseñor, who did not fare any better than Burr. The release of this "official" book was canceled, reportedly because Quintanilla concluded that it "was not what he had had in mind."[49]

Texas Monthly author Joe Nick Patoski considered himself an expert on Selena. While writing a book called *Selena: Como la Flor* (*Selena: Like the Flower*), he insisted that he was not exploiting her death. To the contrary, he accused the Quintanilla family of "capitalizing on the singer's legacy." The author admitted, however, that "the tragedy is, no one would be interested in this book if she were alive."[50]

Magazine publishers wanted their share of the proceeds from Selena mania. Uncertain of Selena's national appeal, *People Weekly* opted for its "first-ever split-run cover story." More than 400,000 Selena issues were distributed in the Southwest. After these sold out, *People* printed a special tribute issue, "only the third time in the magazine's history, with Jacqueline Kennedy Onassis and Audrey Hepburn preceding Selena." In two subsequent runs, its tribute issue sold more than 900,000 copies. *Texas Monthly* likewise did something out of the norm when it "devoted two covers to a single subject," Selena. The first issue sold an estimated 80,000 copies, high numbers for that magazine. Although the editors voiced concern about exploiting the singer's murder, *Texas Monthly* author Patoski opined "that Selena wouldn't have merited a cover in life."[51] And more coverage would follow.

Besides publications, "tribute" albums also flooded the market. Record labels with any connection to Selena, no matter how small, used her name to sell their wares. The company with official permission to distribute Selena's music was Houston-based Southwest Wholesale. While employee Bob Olivio claimed that he did not "personally approve of many of the Selena-themed products" sold by his firm, he admitted that "we're in the business of supply and demand." And, Selena merchandise was in big demand.[52]

A dramatic example that Selena was perhaps even more marketable in death than in life was the album on which she was working when she was murdered. *Dreaming of You* contained some English songs, some bilingual songs, and "a few remixed versions" of Selena's earlier hits. Lines of people waited to buy the CD when it went on sale in mid-July 1995. By the end of the first day, more than 175,000 copies had sold, which made the deceased "the fastest selling female artist in music history." By the end of the month, *Dreaming of You* had achieved double platinum status, and it was number one on Billboard's pop charts. As one record shop manager noted, "Sales are magnificent."[53]

Selena posthumously added to her already impressive list of honors. At the Tejano Music Awards (TMA) in 1996, she was again named "Female Vocalist of the Year" and "Female Entertainer of the Year." "I Could Fall in Love" was "Tejano Crossover Song of the Year." Also, at that ceremony Selena y Los Dinos won for "Song of the Year," "Showband of the Year," and "Overall Album of the Year." Later in the 1990s, Selena was recognized by *Billboard Magazine* as "The Best Latin Artist of the Decade"— an incredible accomplishment when one remembers that she only lived for half of that period.[54]

Public fascination with Selena's life and death appeared boundless. *Entertainment Tonight* and *Dateline NBC* aired short stories on the Tejana singer. In December 1996 ET presented "The Selena Murder Trial," a two-hour program based on actual court transcripts. In 1998 the A & E network premiered "Selena: Murder of a Star," which looked at her life, "the events that led up to her murder, and the case against Yolanda Saldívar." While Selena was being featured on the small screen, a major movie was also in production about her life. Again "accused of jumping on the Selena bandwagon"— a charge that he vehemently denied—Abraham Quintanilla Jr. served as executive producer. He selected Esparza/Katz Productions to make the film, "because they know the culture." Quintanilla "hand-picked the best Hispanic talent in Hollywood," including Gregory Nava of *El Norte* (*The North*) and *Mi Familia* (*My Family*) fame as the film's director. Edward James Olmos was chosen to play Selena's father. More than 20,000 young women auditioned for the role of Selena, which launched the career of another exceptionally talented Latina, Jennifer López, when the movie was released in 1997.[55]

The same year, Corpus Christi honored its fallen star, but only after considerable controversy. Mexican American leaders in the coastal city had favored creating a permanent Selena memorial, but opponents questioned whether the Tejana merited such recognition, especially if it were to be at taxpayers' expense. The debate became heated with city officials receiving faxes and phone calls, many of which had "ugly, racist" overtones. In the end, the Devary Durrill Foundation funded a bay front monument by local sculptor H.W. Tatum. Featured was a life-sized bronze statue of Selena with her face turned toward the water, as well as a sculpted white rose—her favorite flower. A plaque carried the following inscription: "Her stage is now silent. Yet, her persona enriched the lives of those she touched and her music lives on. . . ." Called *Morador de la Flor* (translated as Overlook of the Flower or View-point of the Flower), the monument that was dedicated in May of 1997 proved a major tourist attraction, along with other Selena-related sites in the city.[56]

The attraction of some Selena sites in Corpus Christi proved problematic for her parents and husband. Immediately following the Tejana's death, the parade of "tourists, rubberneckers, and late-night vigilists" to their street began—and it did not stop. Given that the family members were in mourning, the constant attention was difficult to bear. Suzette Quintanilla observed that her mother and father could not even go outside their house, because people were so often present. To regain some sense of

Mirador De La Flor (Overlook of the Flower) pavillion is located in Corpus Christi. The statue of Selena was sculpted by H. W. Tatum Jr. and serves as a memorial to the fallen singer. By Simiprof - Own work, CC BY-SA 3.0, https://commons.wikimedia.org/w/index.php?curid=24438469.

privacy, the Quintanillas and Chris Pérez decided to move from their neighborhood, probably a wise decision since Selena's popularity did not abate.[57]

In the new millennium, special tribute was paid to the deceased Tejana at the 2001 TMA ceremony when Governor Rick Perry of Texas fittingly presented the Selena Lifetime Achievement Award to her brother A. B. Quintanilla III. The following year, EMI announced that it was "reissuing its 10-title Selena catalog" to mark the singer's twenty years in the music industry. The albums would contain bonus material, including videos and photos. Some "liner notes" with comments from A.B. Quintanilla, Suzette Quintanilla, and Chris Pérez were also promised.[58]

In effect, life and business went on after March 31, 1995, for everyone except Selena Quintanilla-Pérez. While continuing with his career, husband Chris Pérez had transitioned from Tejano music to Spanish-language rock. Selena's brother A. B. enjoyed growing success with his "Kumbia Kings" group. By 2000, His *Amor, Familia y Respeto* (*Love, Family, and Respect*) had sold about one million copies. In 2003, "No Tengo Dinero" ("I Don't Have Any Money") was # 5 on Billboard's Latin Tracks chart. And just two years later, A.B. received a platinum record for his album *Fuego* (*Fire*). Sister Suzette Quintanilla Arriaga became manager of the Selena boutique, which enjoyed impressive sales after the Tejana died, but insisted that the family was not selling Selena merchandise just to make "a fast buck." Rather, it was "a matter of keeping her image alive" with items ranging from Selena dolls to Forbidden Love perfume.[59]

That Selena's family and fans did indeed succeed in "keeping her image alive" became obvious a decade later. The Tejana was remembered in some ways that seemed a fitting tribute and others that appeared overly commercial. As the tenth anniversary of Selena's death neared, fans went online to connect and comfort each other. They also kept busy "selling and buying her memorabilia on eBay" and elsewhere. Some made a pilgrimage to Corpus Christi to pay their respects. "With much care and love," Marcella Quintanilla placed white roses around her daughter's tomb to prepare for the many admirers expected to visit the site.[60]

Among memorabilia that fans could buy in 2005 were plastic soft drink cups displaying pictures of Selena, which were on sale at Circle K convenience stores. Also involved in the promotional activity was the Coca Cola Company for which the singer had helped market products. Each cup carried the name of the Selena Foundation along with its mission statement. Since the foundation was known for helping "innumerable children in crisis," Selena probably would not have objected to this method of raising money.[61]

On sale also were numerous publications commemorating the talented Tejana. As an example, the March 20005 issue of *People en Español* (*People in Spanish*) not only featured Selena on the cover but also included a lengthy section entitled "10 años de lágrimas y recuerdos" ("Ten Years of Tears and Memories"). As stated in those pages, the Spanish-language version of the magazine "perhaps would not exist if it were not for Selena" and the profitability of the issues published a decade earlier on the occasion of her murder. On a more personal note, the memorial issue reported that Abraham Quintanilla Jr. had a museum dedicated to Selena in his offices of Q Productions in Corpus Christi. Items on display included his daughter's Porsche, awards, costumes, and photos. Brother A. B. informed readers that the Quintanilla family had still not recovered from the loss of their beloved family member.[62]

That same year, A.B. also announced that a film covering the creation of his Kumbia Kings group would include real-life footage of his sister's funeral. Also, he planned to use new technology to record a duet with Selena—something he had never done while she was alive. Denying that he was trying to profit from his sister's death, A.B. instead criticized others for exploiting her memory.[63]

In memory of their beloved Selena, the Quintanillas worked with Univisión to present a live televised star-studded tribute concert in April of 2005. "Selena Vive!" ("Selena Lives!") was held in Houston, where the Tejana had appeared in her last concert. Los Dinos was reunited for the event, in which artists such as Pete Astudillo, Gloria Estefan, and Thalía performed songs made famous by the murdered singer. Funds from ticket sales went to the Selena Foundation, and later a soundtrack of the concert went on sale. Also available for purchase in 2005 was a collection titled *Unforgettable: Ultimate Edition*. The set of two CDs and two DVDs contained fifteen of Selena's standards and an equal number of concert recordings. For $39.98, the buyer also received more than a dozen videos, as well as "*Selena Remembered*, the Edward James Olmos documentary chronicling her life and career."[64]

That Selena's popularity continued long after the tenth anniversary of her death testifies to her lasting impact. In March of 2011, the United States Postal Service issued a series of collector stamps to commemorate "Latin Music Legends." Selena was one of five people honored. Artist Rafael López received the commission to create "semi-realistic portraits that showed each performer's personality with brilliant colors." Noting Selena's unique stage presence, he declared that she "was beautiful to paint." Tens of millions of the commemorative stamps were issued in anticipation of strong demand.[65]

Little more than a year later, the April 2012 Spanish language edition of *People* magazine again featured the Tejana on the cover with the caption "Selena Para Siempre" ("Selena Forever"). Also noted was that "la dinastía Quintanilla continue" ("the Quintanilla dynasty continues"). The magazine announced the release of a history-making CD, *Enamorada de Ti* (*In Love with You*), featuring living artists such as Selena Gómez and Christian Castro performing Selena's greatest hits along with the deceased songstress. A Capitol Latin executive vice-president explained that the company's goal was to give people "the sensation that she is alive, singing *en vivo.*" The recording company also revealed plans to release two additional Selena CDs by the end of 2013—one in English and another in Spanish. Besides recording projects, the Quintanilla family were reported to be involved in a number of other endeavors "*mantener vivo el legado de Selena*" ("to keep the legacy of Selena alive"). These ranged from a credit card with Selena's image to a mini-series based on her life.[66]

The magazine provided personal reactions from Selena's family members on the seventeenth anniversary of her death. Abraham bemoaned that he still had "*una herida en el corazón que jamás se va a curar*" ("a wound in the heart that will never heal itself"). Selena's father consoled himself with the conviction that "*mi hija vive por medio de su música*" ("my daughter lives by means of her music"). Marcella spoke sadly of goals such as superstardom that her daughter would have achieved had she not been died so tragically. Brother Abraham admitted to suffering from depression since the murder. For her part, Suzette lamented that Selena was cheated of her dream of becoming a mother. [67]

The man who likely would have fathered Selena's children, Chris Pérez, was also featured in the magazine, along with excerpts from his new book: *Para Selena, con amor* (*To Selena with Love*). According to Chris's mother, the writing project was cathartic for her son. Previously, she said, he would not talk about Selena; however, he could finally enjoy the good memories of his wife. Although having achieved closure of a sort, Chris Pérez declared that "*Selena estará en mi vida hasta el día que yo muero*" ("Selena will be in my life until the day that I die").[68]

Pérez later partnered with a Latino production company to develop a television series based on the above memoir. Suing to halt the project, Abraham Quintanilla, Jr. accused his former son-in law of violating "the Estate Properties Agreement contract he signed after Selena's death back in 1995. . . ." The lawyers representing

Selena's father contended that Pérez had signed away his rights in return for "twenty-five percent (25%) of the new profits [to be] derived from the exploitation of the Entertainment Properties. . . ." Consequently, they alleged that "Quintanilla Jr. is the only person with ownership and all proprietary rights in the name, voice, signature, photograph, and likeness of Selena." The resolution of this litigation remains uncertain.[69] What is certain is that Selena would have been distressed to know that two men whom she loved would be at odds over her estate long after her death.

That countless others share the love that Abraham Quintanilla Jr. and Chris Pérez had for Selena is easily demonstrated. The name of the online website selenaforever (www.selenaforever.com) speaks for itself. It provides links to pictures of the songstress, lyrics of her music, newspaper articles about the murder trial, a blog focused on Selena, and other topics related to the beloved Tejana. Also included is information about the Selena Museum, housed at Quintanilla's Q-Production.

When a special " 'Selena at 40' Remembrance Page" was created on the Selenaforever site to commemorate what would have been the singer's fortieth birthday (April 16, 2011), fans eloquently expressed their feelings. Pledging her loyalty "until the end of time," Corrine wished that Selena were "here today to make more beautiful songs" and "to celebrate . . . with family, friends, and fans." Selena was her "inspiration because she believed in a dream and had the courage to make her dream come true." Sergio from Buenos Aires asked, "what would be the best gift today for Selena?" In response, he quoted the singer's own words: "I only want that you remember me with love." The Argentinian assured Selena that she was "not merely '*fotos y recuerdos*' (Photos and memories, a Selena song)," but that she would "always live through the love and caring of your people."[70]

That Selena has such enduring appeal is truly remarkable, but the diversity of her fan base also merits recognition. Addison, who described himself as "a 17 year old black boy," wrote that "I love rap, but I fell in love with Selena and her music." Caitlin, a self-described "white girl from Florida," affirmed that "Selena is truly a 'legend'—the epitome of the word. She proved that even the impossible is possible. Her death is a tragedy, but *what a gift her life was*."[71]

Not surprisingly, Latinas profess an especially strong connection with the deceased musician. In one striking example, Gianna eloquently acknowledged Selena's influence on her life with the following post:

> She was a Mexican-American, but did not grow up speaking Spanish and I am Mexican-American, but I didn't grow up speaking Spanish either.
>
> People have told me that I am not Mexican, because I wasn't born in Mexico or don't speak much Spanish. Both Mexicans and non-Mexicans have told me that.
>
> Who are they to tell me what I am and what I'm not?
>
> It still hurt to hear people say that to me, but seeing how Selena became a fluent Spanish speaker, [*sic*] inspires me. I am slowly learning and hope to become fluent. . . .
>
> A beauty so breath-taking and a smile so contagious. The old and the young naturally fall in love with her. . . . Her legacy will last.[72]

Part of that lasting legacy is the inspiration and hope that Selena has provided to the Lesbian, Gay, Bisexual, and Transgender community. Drawn by "her fashion, her music, and her flare," Latinos from these groups particularly embrace her, because they come from a culture that does not embrace them. The ambiguous lyrics to "Amor Prohibio" ("Forbidden Love") resonate, because the song could be referring to "a love that is forbidden due to a person's sexuality, race or class." Her being shot in a hotel room by a woman rumored to be a lesbian infatuated with her "resembles the murder scenes of hate crimes against transgender and non-gender conforming youth of color. . . ." For these and other reasons, members of the LGBT community have brought the Tejana into the fold, as they impersonate Selena in drag, host tributes in her memory, and find other ways to honor their icon.[73]

To try to explain the Selena phenomenon, a number of scholars, of differing ages and from varied disciplines, have chosen to study the deceased celebrity. The impressive list includes José E. Limón, Deborah Paredez, Deborah R. Vargas, and Raul Coronado Jr. They examine myriad themes that range from the Tejana's role in public culture to the significance of her performance art to the economic and racial aspects of her commercialization. As a result, Selena "is studied in classrooms across the U.S."[74]

Fans do not need scholarly explanations of Selena's continuing appeal. They feel it instinctively. That is why well over 150,000 of them have made the pilgrimage to Corpus Christi in just three years for an annual event known as *Fiesta de la Flor* (Fiesta of the Flower), inaugurated in 2015. Dedicated to celebrating the Queen of Tejano Music, the festivities, which grow more impressive each year, are hosted by the city's Convention and Visitors Bureau with the support of corporate sponsors and the Quintanilla family. The most recent celebration, held on March 24–25, 2017, included guest appearances by noted Latino stars, performances by bands such as A.B. Quintanilla's Elektro Kumbia, artisans from around the Americas, an art museum exhibit of "Selena videos, pictures, and music," and too many other attractions to mention. In just three years, the impact on the local economy has totaled approximately $40,000,000, and plans are underway for *Fiesta de la Flor* 2018.[75]

Indeed, every year that passes, Selena's family and devotees have more reasons to celebrate her growing list of accomplishments. In 2016, the Tejana was inducted into the Texas Women's Hall of Fame, her wax figure was added to the Madame Tussauds Hollywood exhibit, and an official Selena brand of cosmetics was introduced internationally. In 2017 at the Billboard Latin Music Awards, she was named "Top Female Latin Albums Artist of the Year" for the second consecutive time. That same year she received the rare privilege of having a star placed on the Hollywood Walk of Fame.[76] What these latest achievements prove yet again is that death has not silenced the voice or ended the career of the unstoppable force known simply as Selena.

***

Selena's importance to Hispanics and her impact on Tejano music cannot be overstated. The vivacious singer not only served as a role model for her people but also was "the voice of a young Latino generation." Her appeal reached across age, ethnic, and gender lines, as she helped break barriers in the music industry. Though Selena's career—while she was alive—only lasted about fifteen years, she achieved more in that time than most artists blessed with much longer life spans. She accumulated music awards, graced magazine covers, endorsed major products, became an entrepreneur, and achieved single-name status. Her widespread popularity and commercial potential did not end with her demise, but instead intensified. The accomplishments of Selena's life, coupled with the tragic circumstances of her death, made her a legend. As one Tejano music executive aptly summarized, "*Rock* has Elvis Presley, . . . *country* has Hank Williams. We have Selena and her music."[77]

Indeed, Selena was and is unforgettable. She lives on in the memories of those who knew her—and those who wish that they had. She lives on in the hearts of those who loved her. She lives on in her *cumbias* and *rancheras*. And her beat goes on.

Bibliographical Commentary

Unlike some of the other *Mexicanos* and Tejanos profiled in this book for whom easily accessible sources are more limited, material on Selena is over-whelmingly abundant. Some of the many print sources featuring the singer are discussed in the narrative text of the chapter, as well as being referenced in the endnotes. Also deserving of mention is a children's bilingual picture book, written by Patty Rodríguez and Ariana Stein with illustrations by Citlali Reyes. Titled *The Life of/La vida de Selena*, the biography is scheduled for release in March 2018.

The *Handbook of Texas Online* contains a biographical entry by Cynthia E. Orozco at http://www.tshaonline.org/handbook/online/articles/fquxg. Titled "Quinta-nilla Pérez, Selena [Selena] (1971–1995)," it includes links to six of Selena's songs on iTunes. Also of special interest are websites located at www.q-productions.com and www.selenaforever.com. Founded in the early 1990s by Abraham Quintanilla Jr., the Q Productions entertainment company in Corpus Christi maintains the official Selena website that provides links to the Selena Museum, assorted merchandise, and a free-access Selena radio station. The selenaforever site has links to Selena's song lyrics, the murder trial files, and other many other topics. Also accessible there are the online Guestbook and Remembrance Page, discussed in the chapter. Anyone wanting to learn more about Selena-related places to visit in Corpus Christi or about Fiesta de la Flor events can consult the following sites: http://www.loveselena.com/Presents/SelenaLocations.html, http://www.visitcorpuschristitx.org/trip-ideas/must-see/extend-your-fiesta-de-la-flor-experience/, http://www.fiestadelaflor.com/ and http://www.visitcorpuschristitx.org/trip-ideas/must-see/fiesta-de-la-flor-a-history/.

Endnotes

1. Welcome to Dreaming of You: A Tribute to Selena, 1st quotation, http://www.texmexqueen.com/selboi2.htm; Guadalupe San Miguel Jr., *Tejano Proud: Tex-Mex Music in the Twentieth Century* (College Station: Texas A&M University, 2002), 71, 74–75, 3rd quotation on 74; Joe Nick Patoski, "Selena," *Texas Monthly* 22 (September 1994), 2nd quotation, ProQuest document ID: 7237231, http://gateway.proquest.com/openurl?url_ver=Z39.88-2004&res_dat=xri:pqd&rft_val_fmt=info:ofi/fmt:kev:mtx:journal&genre=article&rft_dat=xri:pqd:did000000007237231&svc; Manuel Peña, *Música Tejana* (College Station: Texas A&M University Press, 1999), 203.

2. *Handbook of Texas Online*, Cynthia E. Orozco, "Quintanilla Pérez, Selena (1971–1995)," http://www.tsha.utexas.edu/handbook/online/articles/QQ/fquxg.hmtl [*Handbook of Texas Online* hereinafter cited as *HOT Online*]; S. C. Gwynne, "Death of a Rising Star," *Time* 145 (April 10, 1995), ProQuest document ID: 1899104, http://gateway.proquest.com/openurl?url_ver=Z39.88-2004&res_dat=xri:pqd&rft_val_fmt=info:ofi/fmt:kev:mtx:journal&genre=article&rft_dat=xri:pqd:did=000000001899104&svc. . .; Dreaming of You: A Tribute to Selena, quotations; Ricardo León Peña Villa, "Selena ídolo y amor de todos," *El Diario La Prensa*, (March 31, 2000), New York, ProQuest document ID:

480732091, http://gateway.proquest.com/openurl?url_ver=Z39.88-2004&res_
dat=xri:pqd&rft_val_fmt=info:ofi/fmt:kev:mtx:journal&genre=article&rft_dat=
xri:pqd:did=00000480732091&svc.

3. Dreaming of You: A Tribute to Selena; Joe Nick Patoski, "Selena," *Texas Monthly*, quotation; "Selena," *People Weekly* 44 (December 25, 1995): 105, ProQuest document ID: 9152471, http://gateway.proquest.com/openurl?uri_
ver=Z39.88-2004&res_dat=xri:pqd&rft_val-fmt=info:oft/fmt:kev:mtx:journal&
genre=article&rft_dat=xri:pqd:did=000000009152471&svc. . . ; Villa Peña, "Selena ídolo y amor de todos."

4. *HOT Online*, Orozco, "Quintanilla Pérez, Selena," 1st quotation; Patoski, "Selena," *Texas Monthly*, 2nd quotation; Peña, *Música Tejana*, 203–204; Welcome to Dreaming of You: Tribute to Selena; Gwynne, "Death of a Rising Star," *Time*, 145, 3rd quotation.

5. *HOT Online*, Orozco, "Quintanilla Pérez, Selena"; Barbara Kantrowitz et al., "Memories of Selena," *People Weekly*, April 1, 1996, ProQuest document ID: 9399964, http://gateway.proquest.com/openurl?url_ver=Z38.88-2004&res_
dat=xri:pqd&rft_val_fmt=infor:ofi/fmt:kev:mtx:journal&genre+article&rft_dat=
xri:pqd:did=000000009399964&svc. . . ; San Miguel, *Tejano Proud*, 105–106, quotation on 106. Sources disagree as to whether Selena actually completed eighth grade before being withdrawn from school.

6. Peña, *Música Tejana*, 204.

7. Milexis J. Rodríguez, "A Tremendous Loss," *Hispanic* 8, no. 4 (May 1995), ProQuest document ID: 1670203, http://gateway.proquest.com/
openurl?url_ver=Z39.88-2004&res_dat=xri:pqd&rft_val_fmt=info:ofi/fmt:kev:
mtx:journal&genre=article&rft_dat=xri:pqd:did=000000001670203&svc. . .;
Peña, *Música Tejana*, 204–205, 1st quotation; San Miguel, *Tejano Proud*, 117, 2nd and 3rd quotations.

8. *HOT Online*, Orozco, "Quintanilla Pérez, Selena," 1st and 2nd quotations; Peña, *Música Tejana*, 204–206, 3rd quotation on 205, 4th quotation 206.

9. San Miguel, *Tejano Proud*, 24, 42–43, 85, 90, 117–118, all quotations on 90; Peña, *Música Tejana*, 64.

10. San Miguel, *Tejano Proud*, 206–207, 2nd quotation on 206, 1st quotation on 207; Catherine Vásquez-Revilla, "Thank You, Selena," *Hispanic* 8, no. 4 (May 1995), 96, 3rd quotation, ProQuest document ID: 08983097, http://gateway.proquest.com/openurl?url_ver=Z39.88-2004&res_
dat=xri:pqd&rft_val_fmt=info:ofi/fmt:kev:mtx:journal&genre=article&rft_dat=
xri:pqd:did=000000001670202&svc; Villa Peña, "Selena ídolo y amor de todos," 4th quotation.

11. San Miguel, *Tejano Proud*, xiii, 7, 118–119, 204, 1st quotation on 118, 2nd quotation on 204: Peña, *Música Tejana*, xi, 184, 189, 207.

12. San Miguel, *Tejano Proud*, 104, 106–110, passim, 118, 1st quotation on 104, 2nd quotation on 108.

13. San Miguel, *Tejano Proud*, 1st quotation on 108, 2nd quotation on 110.

14. San Miguel, *Tejano Proud*, 110, 120–124.

15. San Miguel, *Tejano Proud*, 123–124; Selena: Biography, http://launch.
yahoo.com/artist/artistFocus.asp?artistID=1023965, quotation.

16. *HOT Online*, Orozco, "Quintanilla Pérez, Selena."

17. *HOT Online*, Orozco, "Quintanilla Pérez, Selena."

18. Patoski, "Selena," *Texas Monthly*, all quotations.

19. Patoski, "Selena," *Texas Monthly*, all quotations.

20. Patoski, "Selena," *Texas Monthly*, all quotations.

21. Mario Tarradell, "*Viva Selena!*" Arts Day, *Dallas Morning News*, March 31, 2005; Kantrowitz et al., "Memories of Selena," *People Weekly*, 1st quotation; Patoski, "Selena," *Texas Monthly*, 2nd quotation. Sources disagree as to whether Selena's married name should be written as Quintanilla Pérez or Quintanilla-Pérez.

22. Kantrowitz, "Memories of Selena," *People Weekly*, quotation; *HOT Online*, Orozco, "Quintanilla Pérez, Selena."

23. Kantrowitz, "Memories of Selena," *People Weekly*, quotation.

24. Kantrowitz, "Memories of Selena," *People Weekly*; "Caso Selena: Declaran culpable a Saldivar," *La Voz de Houston*, October 25, 1995, ProQuest document ID: 491792601, http://gateway.proquest.com/openurl?url_ver=Z39.88-2004&res_dat=xri:pqd&rft_val_fmt=info:ofi/fmt:kev:mtx:journal&genre=article&rft_dat=xri:pqd:did=00000049179261&svc. . . ; Joe Nick Patoski, "The Sweet Song of Justice," *Texas Monthly* 23 (December 1995), all quotations, ProQuest document ID: 8680212, http://gateway.proquest.com/openurl?url_ver=Z39.88-2004&res_dat=xri:pqd&rft_val_fmt=info:ofi/fmt:kev:mtx:journal&genre=article&rft_dat=xri:pqd:did=000000008680212&svc. . . .

25. Kantrowitz, "Memories of Selena," *People Weekly*; "World Premiere Presentation: 'Selena: Murder of a Star,'" *La Voz*, Denver, Colo., November 25, 1998, ProQuest document ID: 482245011, http://gateway.proquest.com/openurl?uri_ver=Z39.88-2004&res_dat=xri:pqd&rft_val_fmt=info:oft/fmt:kev:mtx:journal&genre=article&rft_dat=xri:pqd:did=000000482245011&svc. . . ; "Selena," *People Weekly*; Patoski, "The Sweet Song of Justice," *Texas Monthly*.

26. Patoski, "The Sweet Song of Justice," *Texas Monthly*, quotation.

27. Patoski, "The Sweet Song of Justice," *Texas Monthly*; [Isis Sauceda?], "Chris Pérez: 'Selena me cuida,'" *People en Español*, April 2012, 100.

28. Patoski, "The Sweet Song of Justice," *Texas Monthly*, all quotations; [Sauceda?], "Chris Pérez: 'Selena me cuida,'" *People en Español*, 102.

29. Patoski, "The Sweet Song of Justice," *Texas Monthly*, quotation.

30. "Trágico homicidio de estrella Hispaña: Cronología de los hechos detienen a presunta responsible," *La Voz de Houston*, April 5, 1995, quotation, ProQuest document ID: 491793301, http://gateway.proquest.com/openurl?url_ver=Z39.88-2004&res_dat=xri;pqd&rft_val_fmt=info:ofi/fmt:kev:mtx:journal&genre=article&rft_dat=xri:pqd:did=000000491793301&svc.

31. "Trágico homicidio de estrella Hispaña," *La Voz de Houston*, April 5, 1995.

32. Patoski, "The Sweet Song of Justice," *Texas Monthly*, all quotations.

33. Patoski, "The Sweet Song of Justice," *Texas Monthly*.

34. Patoski, "The Sweet Song of Justice," *Texas Monthly*, all quotations.

35. Patoski, "The Sweet Song of Justice," *Texas Monthly*, all quotations.

36. Patoski, "The Sweet Song of Justice," *Texas Monthly*, all quotations.

37. Patoski, "The Sweet Song of Justice," *Texas Monthly*.

38. Patoski, "The Sweet Song of Justice," *Texas Monthly*, 2nd through 4th quotations; "Woman Who Murdered Singer Gets a Sentence of Life in Prison," *New York Times*, October 27, 1995, A28, 1st quotation, ProQuest document ID: 8639067, http://pathfinder.utb.edu:2072/pqdweb?index=94&did=000000008639067&SrchMode=1&s . . .; Glen Castlebury, "High Profile Inmates a Security Concern

for Texas Prisons," Corrections.com: Where Criminal Justice Never Sleeps, http://www.corrections.com/articles/9494-high-profile-inmates-asecurity-concern-for-texas-prisons.

39. Patoski, "The Sweet Song of Justice," *Texas Monthly*, 1st quotation; Support the Selena Quintanilla-Pérez Foundation, http://www.texmexqueen.com/foundation.htm; The Selena Foundation, Q-Productions, 2nd quotation, http://www.q-productions.com/selenafoundation.html.

40. Patoski, "The Sweet Song of Justice," *Texas Monthly*, quotation; Isis Sauceda, "Selena eternal," *People en Español*, April 2012, 90.

41. Patoski, "The Sweet Song of Justice," *Texas Monthly*, all quotations.

42. "Selena," *People Weekly* 44, 1st quotation on 105; Gwynne, "Death of a Rising Star," *Time*, 2nd quotation on 91; Péña, *Música Tejana*, 210; HOT Online, Orozco, "Quintanilla Pérez, Selena."

43. Gwynne, "Death of a Rising Star," *Time*, quotation on 91; "Selena," *People Weekly* 44; Patoski, "The Sweet Song of Justice," *Texas Monthly*.

44. Patoski, "The Sweet Song of Justice," *Texas Monthly*, all quotations.

45. "El Governador de Texas Proclama el 'Día de Selena,'" *La Voz de Houston*, April 19, 1995, all quotations, ProQuest document ID: 491785341, http://gateway.proquest.com/openurl?url_ver=Z39.88-=-2004&res_dat=xri:pqd&rft_val_fmt=info:ofi/fmt:kev:mtx:journal&genre=article&rf_dat=xri:pqd:did=000000491785341&svc.

46. Peña, *Música Tejana*, 1st quotation on 213; Jerry Crowe, "Latinos to Stern: Apology Is Not Accepted," *Los Angeles Times*, April 19, 1995, all remaining quotations, http://articles.latimes.com/1995-04-11/entertainment/ca-53295_1_howard-stern.

47. Peña, *Música Tejana*, 210; Tony Cantu, "Cashing in on Selena," *Hispanic* 9, no. 6 (June 1996), 1st and 3rd quotations, ProQuest document ID: 9746988, http://gateway.proquest.com/openurl?url_ver=Z39.88-2004&res_dat=xri:pqd&rft_val_fmt=info:ofi/fmt:kev:mtx:journal&genre=article&rft_dat=xri:pqd:did=000000009746988&svc; Raul Coronado Jr., "Selena's Good Buy: Texas Mexicans, History, and Selena Meet Transnational Capitalism, *Aztlan: A Journal of Chicano Studies* 26, no. 1 (November 2001), 2nd and 4th quotations on 61.

48. Cantu, "Cashing in on Selena," *Hispanic*, quotation.

49. Cantu, "Cashing in on Selena," *Hispanic*, all quotations.

50. Cantu, "Cashing in on Selena," *Hispanic*, all quotations.

51. Cantu, "Cashing in on Selena," *Hispanic*, all quotations.

52. Cantu, "Cashing in on Selena," *Hispanic*, quotation.

53. Chito de la Torre, "Selena: Fastest Selling Female," *La Prensa*, July 28, 1995, all quotations, ProQuest document ID: 468953321, http://gateway.proquest.com/openurl&url_ver=Z39.88-2004&res_dat=xri:pqd&rft_val_fmt=info:oft/fmt:kev:mtx:journal&genre=article&rft_dat=xri:pqd:did=0000004 68953321&svc. . . . As explained in this source: "In the US Latin Market, a platinum record is earned when an artist sells at least 100,000 units." According to the "Selena Facts" listed on the Selena Forever website, the *Dreaming of You* album had sold more than 5,000,000 copies by mid-May 2014.

54. Ramiro Burr, "Emilio, Selena Dominate Tejano Awards," *Billboard*, New York (April 6, 1996), ProQuest document ID: 9404552, http://gateway.proquest.com/openurl?uri_ver=Z39.88-2004&res_dat=xri:pqd&rft_val_fmt=info:oft/fmt:

kev:mtx:journal&genre=article&rft_dat=xri:pqd:did=000000009404552&svc. . . ;
Selena Quintanilla Pérez, Biography, www.starpulse.com/Music/Perez,_Selena_
Quintanilla/Biography/.

55. *HOT Online*, Orozco, "Quintanilla Pérez, Selena"; Tom Gliatto,
"The Selena Murder Trial: The E! True Hollywood Story," *People Weekly*,
December 23, 1996, ProQuest document ID: 10521034, http://gateway.
proquest.com/openurl?url_ver=Z39.88-2004&res_dat=xri:pqd&rft_val_
fmt=info:ofi/fmt:kev:mtx:journal&genre=article&rft_dat=xri:pqd:did=00
0000010521034&svc. . . ; "World Premier Presentation: Selena: Murder of
a Star," *La Voz*, 1st quotation; Cantu, "Cashing in on Selena," *Hispanic*, all
remaining quotations; Richard Corliss, "¡Vive Selena!", *Time* 149 (March 24,
1997), ProQuest document ID: 11268814, http://gateway.proquest.com/
openurl?uri_ver=Z39.88-2004&res_dat=xri:pqd&rft_val_fmt=info:oft/fmt:
kev:mtx:journal&genre=article&rft_dat=xri:pqd:did=000000011268814
&svc; María Morales, "10 años de lágrimas y recuerdos," *People en Español*,
March 2005, 125.

56. Coronado, "Selena's Best Buy," *Aztlan*, 87, 1st quotation; "Selena Lives
in the Hearts of South Texans," Caller.com, Your Visitors Guide, 2nd quotation,
www.caller2.com/visitors/things_to_do/selena.html; Corpus Christi, Texas: Selena
Memorial, www.stxmaps.com/go/selena-memorial.html.

57. Jeff Winkler, "Amor Prohibido," *Texas Monthly*, September 2015, quotation, http://www.texasmonthly.com/the-culture/amor-prohibido/.

58. Selena Forever: Selena Awards, www.selenaforever.com/SelenaAwards/
Selena_Awards.html; Leila Cobo, "EMI Fuels Selena Legacy with Reissues,"
Billboard, New York, August 17, 2002, all quotations. ProQuest document ID:
149317311, http://gateway.proquest.com/openurl?uri_ver=Z39.88-2004&res_
dat=xri:pqd&rft_val_fmt=info:oft/fmt:kev:mtx:journal&genre=article&rft_dat=
xri:pqd:did=000000149317311&svc.

59. Joe Nick Patoski, "Tuned Out," *Texas Monthly* 28 (May 2000),
ProQuest document ID: 53297803, http://gateway.proquest.com/openurl?uri_
ver=Z39.88-2004&res_dat=xri:pqd&rft_val-fmt=info:oft/fmt:kev:mtx:journal&
genre=article&rft_dat=xri:pqd:did=000000053297803&svc. . . ; Rose Ybarra,
"Tuning into Tejano," Entertainment, *Brownsville Herald*, April 27, 2003, D 11;
Amado Felix Cruz, "'No quiero aprovecharme de la tragedia de mi hermana':
A.B. Quintanilla," *TV y Todo* 1, no. 9, supplement to *Brownsville Herald*, May 21,
2005, 4; Cantú, "Cashing in on Selena," *Hispanic*, all quotations; Tarradell, "Viva
Selena!," *Dallas Morning News*.

60. Morales, "Selena: 10 años de lágrimas y recuerdos," *People en Español*,
124, 128–129, 1st quotation on 124, 2nd quotation on 128.

61. Morales, "Selena: 10 años de lágrimas y recuerdos," *People en Español*,
125; Circle K Coca Cola cup in possession of author, quotation from cup.

62. Morales, "Selena: 10 años de lágrimas y recuerdos," *People en Español*,
124–126, quotation on 125.

63. Oscar Vargas C. and Sara Sánchez, "¡Junto a A.B. Quintanilla en una
película!", *Furia Musical USA*, 2005, 64–65; Cruz, "'No quiero aprovecharme de
la tragedia de mi hermana': A.B. Quintanilla," 4.

64. Rose Ybarra, "Selena ¡Vive!," *Brownsville Herald*, February 4, 2005,
1, A12; "Selena ¡Vive!," *Vista Magazine*, May 2005, supplement to *Brownsville*

Herald, 3; Tarradell, "Viva Selena!," *Dallas Morning News*; Mario Tarradell, "Selena: *Unforgettable: Ultimate Edition*," Arts Day, *Dallas Morning News*, May 19, 2005, 12E, quotation

65. "Selena, Other Latin Stars Honored with New Commemorative Stamps," caller.com, quotations, www.caller.com/news/2011/mar/16/stamps-hed-help-hery/.

66. Isis Sauceda, "Selena Eterna," *People en Español*, 1st quotation on cover, 2nd quotation on 92, 3rd quotation on 90.

67. Isis Sauceda, "Selena Eterna," *People en Español*, 92, all quotations; [Isis Sauceda?],"A.B. Quintanilla: de nuevo a la batalla," *People en Español*, April 2012, 94.

68. [Sauceda?], "Chris Pérez: 'Selena me cuida'," *People en Español*, 96, quotation.

69. "Selena's Dad Sues Late Singer's Husband Chris Perez Over TV Series," *Billboard*, Dec. 5, 2016, 1st quotation, http://www.billboard.com/articles/columns/latin/7694309/judge-allows-lawsuit-against-selena-widower-proceed; Diana Marti, "Selena Quintanilla's Father Files Lawsuit Against Her Widower Chris Perez," *E News*, Dec. 6, 2016, 2nd and 3rd quotations, http://eonline.com/news/813906/selena-quintanilla-s-father-files-lawsuit-against-her-widower-chris-perez.

70. Corrine, "'Selena at 40': Remembrance Page," quotations 1–4; Sergio Ernesto Rodríguez, Buenos Aires, Argentina, translated by Bernie, Feb. 27, 2011, quotations 5, 6, and 7, http://www.selenaforever.com/selena_at_40/Selena_at_40_Remembrance_Page.html. Although most comments posted on the Selenaforever website are from fans in the United States, there are also postings from places such as Canada, Sicily, the Netherlands, and Japan.

71. Addison Sarter, 1st and 2nd quotations, Caitlin Willard, 3rd and 4th quotations, http://www.selenaforever.com/selena_at_40/Selena_at_40_Remembrance_Page.html.

72. Gianna, quotation, http://www.selenaforever.com/selena_at_40/Selena_at_40_Remembrance_Page.html.

73. Mala Muñoz, "Selena: Her Living Legacy and What It Still Represents Today," *VIBE*, July 1, 2016, 1st quotation, https://www.vibe.com/2016/07/selena-quintanilla-living-legacy-today/; Alejandra Molina, "LGBT Group to Host Tribute for Selena in Santa Ana," *The Orange County Register*, e.edition, March 29, 2015, 2nd quotation, http://www.ocregister.com/2015/03/29/lgbt-group-to-host-tribute-for-selena-in-santa-ana/; Deborah Paradez, *Selenidad: Selena, Latinos, and the Performance of Memory*, e-book (Durham: Duke University Press, 2009), Preface, Chapter 5, 3rd quotation in Chapter 5.

74. Jorge Rivas, "These People Have PhDs in Selena," *Splinter*, March 27, 2015, quotation, http://splinternews.com/these-people-have-phds-in-selena-1793846661.

75. "Fiesta de la Flor: A History," by Visit Corpus Christi Texas, http://www.visitcorpuschristitx.org/trip-ideas/must-see/fiesta-de-la-flor-a-history/; "Fiesta de la Flor 2017," by Visit Corpus Christi Texas, quotation, www.visitcorpuschristi.org/trip-ideas/must-see/fiesta-de-la-flor; "CVB Releases Economic Impact Numbers from Fiesta de la Flor 2017," 3 kiii tv South Texas ABC, March 3, 2017, www.kiiitv.com/news/local/cvb-releases-economic-impact-numbers-from-fiesta-de-la-flor-2017/427261040.

76. "Fiesta de la Flor: A History," Visit Corpus Christi Texas; Romeo, "Selena Wins Top Latin Albums Female Artist of the Year at 2017 Billboard Latin Music Awards," April 28, 2017, https://tejanonation.net/2017/04/28/selena-wins-top-latin-albums-female-artist-of-the-year-2017-billboard-latin-music-awards; Libby Hill, "Tejano Star Selena Will Receive a Star on Hollywood's Walk of Fame 21 Years after Her Death," June 29, 2016, http://www/latimes.com/entertainment/gossip/la-et-mg-2017-walk-of-fame-selena-2010629-snap-story-htm.

77. Tarradell, "Viva Selena!", *Dallas Morning News*, 1st quotation; Morales, "*Selena: 10 años de lágrimas y recuerdos*," *People en Español*, 2nd quotation on 130.

Conclusion

ACCORDING TO THE UNITED States Census Bureau, "'Hispanic or Latino' refers to a person of Cuban, Mexican, Puerto Rican, South or Central American, or other Spanish culture or origin regardless of race." That the number and influence of Hispanics/Latinos in the United States is growing at a rapid rate is irrefutable. In the 2010 Census, 50,477,594 Hispanics accounted for "more than half of the growth in the total population of the United States between 2000 and 2010." A striking illustration of their increasing influence is the role that Latino voters played in helping President Barack Obama to win reelection in 2012, a fact noted by politicians, journalists, and commentators, regardless of their political leanings.[1]

Census figures also reveal that the Mexican population, which increased by 54 percent from 2001–2010, was the largest Hispanic group in the country with 31,798,258 people in that category. Significantly, Texas in 2010 had a Hispanic population of 9,460,921, of whom 7,951,193 reported themselves to be of Mexican culture or origin.[2]

As mentioned throughout this work, the fact that Texas has the second largest Mexican population in the United States reflects its history and geography. From the 1500s to 1821, Texas was part of the Spanish Empire, and Spain left an imprint on the province, which is still evident in the twenty-first century. The period during which Texas subsequently functioned as part of the newly independent Mexican nation was relatively brief

(1821–1835/6), but the Mexican influence was significant nevertheless. When Texas began to function as an independent republic in the mid-1830s, Tejanos found themselves residents of the new predominantly Anglo nation—for better or worse. An even more dramatic change came for the Tejano population when the United States annexed Texas a decade later, and the resultant U.S.-Mexican War (1846–1848) cemented the Rio Grande as the international boundary.

Because of Texas's proximity to Mexico, millions of immigrants have come to the Lone Star State either legally or illegally to join the original Tejanos and their descendants. The eleven men and women profiled in this book are only a small sampling of those worthy of note, but none had a greater impact than Antonio López de Santa Anna, the most powerful figure in Mexico from the 1830s through the 1850s. Exhibiting qualities of opportunism and ruthlessness, the Napoleon of the West made decisions that influenced Anglo Texans and some Tejanos to rebel in 1835, led to their Declaration of Independence in March of 1836, and caused the defeat of the Mexican Army at San Jacinto in the following month. Santa Anna's policy of showing no mercy to his enemies during the revolution, combined with two expeditions he dispatched to invade the Republic of Texas in 1842, had dire consequences for Tejanos, including Juan Seguín. Later in that decade, the caudillo's military failures contributed to his nation's defeat in a war that not only settled an international boundary dispute but also cost Mexico half of its national territory. As a consequence, tens of thousands of his countrymen found themselves living on U.S. soil, a condition that did not bode well for them. Arguably, Santa Anna played an even greater role than that of the celebrated Stephen F. Austin or Sam Houston in shaping the future of Texas. But in the process, he earned the enmity of generations of Texans.

Father and son Erasmo and Juan Seguín faced difficult choices as Tejanos at a turning point in history, choices that ultimately labeled them traitors to Mexico. A man with deep family roots in Spanish Texas, the esteemed Erasmo befriended Stephen F. Austin, assisted Anglo-American colonization, helped draft a Mexican constitution, and supported Texas's revolutionary cause. As for the younger Seguín, none other than Sam Houston attested to his heroism in the fight for Texas's independence, and he was accorded the solemn responsibility of interring the ashes of the defenders of the Alamo. While some of his own actions contributed to his subsequent downfall, he definitely fell victim to his ethnicity, as anti-Mexican sentiment intensified within the young Republic. Faced with increasing animosity, Juan Seguín took his family across the Rio Grande to Mexico, where he also was less than welcome because of his earlier role in the Texas Revolution. As the price for remaining a free man so that he could care for his family, the Tejano contended that he had no choice but to participate in an invasion of Texas and later fight against the United States. However, as stated eloquently by a recent author: "Juan did not betray Texas, . . . Texas betrayed him."[3] Not until more recent times have the sacrifices of the Seguíns, especially the son, been truly appreciated and this duo received the acclaim they deserve. The Texas Education Agency now appropriately mandates that Erasmo and Juan Seguín are among "significant individuals" whom public school students must study.[4]

Juan Nepomuceno Cortina, another man with a long family history in the region, did not admire or aid the American settlers in Texas. Instead, he was infuriated by a growing Anglo population that was not only seizing land and power but also abusing *Mexicanos* and Tejanos in the process. Intent on punishing those whom he labelled as evil, he thrust the border region into a state of chaos. Although the sincerity of his motives has been debated for one hundred and fifty years, the minimally literate son of a prominent Mexican family became a champion of his people and, in turn, an enemy to Anglo Americans. This complex man robbed, raided, and killed, thereby earning notoriety on both sides of the Great River. Ironically, the antagonism he incurred proved costly to the lives and property of the very people he aimed to protect. Whether Cortina was a crusader or a criminal, hundreds of *campesinos* (peasants) flocked to his cause—a stark illustration of the frustration felt by many of his countrymen in nineteenth-century Texas.

With a life that spanned the mid-1800s to the mid-1900s, blue-eyed Adina De Zavala is an unusual case, because she was more Irish than Hispanic and possibly did not even think of herself as a Tejana. Nevertheless, her surname and ancestry placed her in that category, and she benefited from being Lorenzo de Zavala's granddaughter. Operating within Anglo society, she was committed to fostering appreciation for Texas's rich history and her family's part in it. During her long life, this outspoken woman helped educate children, form important organizations, honor heroic figures, and save important landmarks. She earned the title of "Angel of the Alamo" for her courageous—and almost outrageous—efforts to prevent destruction of the Long Barrack. However, when she lost the struggle to maintain custody of the historic site, it evolved into a shrine that purportedly glorified Anglo heroes and negatively stereotyped Mexicans. Even though she was not always successful in her endeavors, however, anyone who visits San Antonio today to tour the Alamo or the misnamed "Governor's Palace," another historic edifice she helped to save, must recognize how much of Texas's past would have been lost without the efforts of this dedicated preservationist.

With racially mixed parentage and an Indian surname, Emma Tenayuca was certainly aware of and shaped by her ethnicity. Like Juan Cortina, she became angry over the mistreatment of her people, particularly the exploited working poor. More militant than Adina De Zavala, the bright adolescent found herself drawn to labor activism during the Great Depression as an effective device for change. Whether inspiring workers with her oratory skills or participating in a strike herself, she fought for causes in which she believed. Similar in some ways to Juan Cortina, she was lauded by the underclass who appreciated her efforts on their behalf but faced attack after attack from the Anglo establishment for the same reason. With the passion of youth, the young Communist did not always exercise the best judgment, as she later admitted. Her decisions led to occasional arrests, an unsuccessful marriage, economic hardship, and temporary exile. Only with time was she able to return to the Lone Star State where she would be lauded for her earlier advocacy of *Mexicanos* and Tejanos whom she viewed as one people, with a common history and common cause. Emma Tenayuca served as— and continues to be—an inspiration to other Latinos fighting for rights and justice.

The less militant Jovita González shared with Adina De Zavala the desire for respectability, as well as a commitment to the rich heritage of Texas. Early in her career the highly educated González made her mark as a folklorist, author, and speaker. Her potential seemed unlimited, despite obstacles placed in the path of a Mexican-American woman of limited financial resources. Marriage, however, compelled her to make compromises. Her husband, Edmundo E. Mireles, was Mexican by birth but lived in Texas for most of his life. He, too, aspired to be among the *"gente decente"* (people of good breeding). The scholarly intellectual was committed to bilingualism, biculturalism, and Pan-Americanism as the keys to promoting better relations between Hispanics and Anglos, as well as between the United States and Latin America. Mireles developed a model program for teaching Spanish to elementary school children, and his wife collaborated in that effort. He also endeavored to help Hispanic children acquire English, the language of power. While "Mrs. Mireles" shared her husband's career goals, she also produced important Mexican-American literary works that were not seen in print until after her death—in part because of actions taken by her husband. Posthumously, both Mireleses have gained well-deserved recognition for their contributions, but Jovita González has regained her own identity as a significant figure in Mexican-American literature.

Orphaned at a young age, Raul "Roy" Benavidez became an angry adolescent who lashed out at those who insulted him because of his ethnicity. His belligerence concerned those who cared about him and jeopardized his early military career. Fortunately, the combination of a good marriage and growing maturity enabled "The Mean Mexican," as he was called by his army buddies, to channel his aggression in more positive ways. As an elite Green Beret during the Vietnam era, he twice almost died in service of his country. On the second occasion, Benavidez performed superhuman feats to save comrades who were in desperate circumstances. The physical and mental toll of these experiences eventually led to his retirement from the army with disability benefits. He then engaged in a different type of battle to acquire a well-deserved, and long overdue, Congressional Medal of Honor that recognized not only the Tejano's heroism but also paid homage to the underappreciated veterans of a controversial conflict. In yet another struggle, he had to combat the Social Security Administration to preserve his hard-earned disability benefits. Victorious in his "three wars," as he called them, Benavidez spent his later years endeavoring to inspire Latino youth by teaching them that anyone, regardless of their beginnings, can make a difference. He certainly did.

Irma Rangel also made a difference. First a teacher and then a lawyer by profession, she used the state legislature as her battleground. As the first Latina elected to the Texas House of Representatives, she understood that her actions would be under scrutiny but was determined to succeed. The Tejana accepted the challenge of making her mark in a political institution traditionally controlled by Anglo males. During a legislative career that spanned more than twenty-five years from the 1970s to the early 2000s, Rangel achieved many firsts, while serving as a role model and mentor for other Latinas. The Mexican-American legislator understood that education opened doors otherwise closed to those from disadvantaged backgrounds and worked to provide greater opportunities for the people of Texas in general and for minorities in particular. Whether opposing standardized testing, supporting the Ten Percent Plan, or fighting for adequate funding, she served her constituents term after term, despite recurrent battles with cancer. Professionally and personally, she left a legacy that continues to benefit many Texans in the twenty-first century.

Selena Quintanilla's story is an especially poignant one. That a young Tejana who did not speak fluent Spanish gained fame as a Tejano singer is ironic. That her very successful career was perhaps more the fulfillment of her father's dreams than her own is another irony. Whatever propelled her onto the stage, however, her own talent and charisma made her a multiple award-winning vocalist. And her impact went far beyond becoming the Queen of Tejano Music. For many Mexican Americans, "she was a game changer for their identity, proof that the way they looked and sounded was good enough."[5] Inspired fans on both sides of the border idolized the vivacious, sexy—yet wholesome—songstress, who was crossing over into the English-language market when murdered at the age of twenty-three by a former friend and employee. Selena's sudden death produced shock waves that reverberated internationally. The tragedy also provided ample opportunity for exploitation on many fronts. In the more than two decades since her death, the Tejana has continued to win awards, grace magazine covers, inspire books, gain new devotees, and have commercial appeal. Embraced as an icon by the LGBT community, she also has attracted the attention of serious scholars who endeavor to explain the Selena phenomenon.

The saddest irony of all is that Selena's music and marketability live on, though she does not.

A commonality shared by the eleven people discussed above is that they were all fighters in one sense or another. Santa Anna, Juan Seguín, Juan Cortina, and Roy Benavidez fought for their respective causes in a literal sense, while Erasmo Seguín and Edmundo Mireles battled effectively in the political and educational arenas, respectively. One man was undeniably self-serving: Santa Anna. Whether another, Juan Cortina, was self-serving as well remains a matter of heated rhetoric. The term heroic certainly applies to Juan Seguín and Roy Benavidez, although their wars were more than a century apart. As for the Tejanas who had to navigate a male-oriented culture in an Anglo-dominated society, they, too, responded by fighting for their beliefs. Although differing widely in personality and approach, these five women demonstrated remarkable fortitude. Each charted her own path, but collectively they had an impact in fields as wide-ranging as labor activism and the Tejano music industry—often breaking barriers in the process. Over a period of almost two centuries, these notables made a difference, and their stories illustrate the significance of *Mexicanos* and Tejanos in the history of the Lone Star State.

Worth noting is that the men profiled, whatever their time and place, were all married—some more than once. They were often privileged by unions that advanced their careers, provided needed stability, allowed considerable freedom, and gave them heirs. The pragmatic Antonio López de Santa Anna twice wed by proxy young women with significant dowries. First wife, Inés García, not only brought wealth that enabled her husband to gain land and status but also capably managed their properties during his frequent absences. She also bore his children. Although he miscalculated the negative impact of taking young María Dolores de Tosta as his bride too soon after the death of the popular doña Inés, Santa Anna did reap financial benefits from this second union. Evidence also indicates that he participated in at least one bogus wedding ceremony, and tales of other sexual indiscretions abound, including his fathering several illegitimate children. Certainly, his husbandly status did not restrict his amorous activities.

Like Santa Anna, Juan Cortina did not practice monogamy in any sense of the word. At twenty-one he wed a young cousin, María Dolores Tijerina, but only after having fathered a child with Rafaela Cortéz, a widow several years his senior. That daughter died young. Although family lore contends that Cortina deserted his first wife, biographer Jerry Thompson postulates that María Dolores died early in the marriage. Cortina then resumed his liaison with widow Cortéz, which led to the birth of a second daughter, his sole heir. Their relationship was formalized in 1850, and during their many years of marriage, Rafaela "stood by her soldier-husband . . . , tolerated more than one mistress, and survived a series of devastating wars on the frontier." After her death in 1877, the widower took the much younger María de Jesús López as his bride.[6] Apparently, age had not dimmed his ardor.

Erasmo Seguín's spouse, María Josefa Becerra, bore him three children, as well as assuming responsibility for family and business when her husband was occupied with affairs of state. One questions whether he could have accomplished so much for Mexico or Texas without this capable woman as a helpmate. Son Juan at age nineteen wed María Gertrudis Flores de Abrego, "a member of one of San Antonio's most important ranching families."[7] Their fruitful alliance resulted in ten children, which placed considerable responsibility on the husband and father. During the Texas Revolution, the Tejano soldier made sure that his family reached safety in East Texas and went to get them as soon as possible after the fighting ended. When compelled to relocate to Mexico in the 1840s, Juan Seguín cited the need to provide for his family as a justification for enlisting in the Mexican army, participating in an invasion of Texas, and fighting against American troops in the U.S.-Mexico War.

Although they had no children, Edmundo Mireles met his intellectual match in Jovita Gónzalez who worked alongside him in the educational system, in writing textbooks, in penning articles, and in the Pan-American movement. His career benefitted from the partnership, and he was not displeased when one of her book submissions was rejected for publication. Concerned that the controversial content might jeopardize their positions in the school district and their social standing in the community, he went so far as to destroy the manuscript. Mireles obviously considered himself the ultimate arbiter of their fates, and Jovita chose not to defy her husband openly.

Roy Benavidez openly credited his marriage to Hilaria "Lala" Coy as transformative. He considered her the prettiest girl in their hometown, but the attraction went far beyond her physical appearance. She understood him and was the missing piece in his life. Her love helped him make the transition from combative Tejano into a mature Special Forces warrior. Supportive of Roy's career, Lala made the sacrifices required of an army wife, as she moved from military post to military post, maintained home and family while he served his country, and remained by his side during injuries and disabilities. Throughout his various battles, her constancy empowered this Congressional Medal of Honor recipient.

In stark contrast to the above, being a woman of Mexican or Mexican-American descent, especially an educated, successful, or militant one, seemingly made marriage problematic—at least for the five Tejanas herein. Two remained single. Three wed, but one later divorced. All but one remained childless.

Born during the turbulent Civil War period, Adina De Zavala was reportedly enamored of a young man who did not return the sentiment but rejected the overtures of an older man interested in her. At any rate, her resultant single status almost certainly contributed to her having the time and energy for her many causes and allowed the strong-willed preservationist to do what she pleased without having to answer to a possibly disapproving husband. One cannot help but question whether marriage would have suited a woman who went to teachers' meetings only when convenient, did not hesitate to stand up to authority, and demonstrated the desire to be in control.

Activist Emma Tenayuca was passionately attracted to Communist Homer Brooks, whom she married while in her early twenties. However, her often-absent husband seemed more dedicated to his ideology than to his wife. According to the Tejana, Brooks cooperated in removing her from a position of leadership in the pecan shellers' strike, which seemed a betrayal. She also claimed that he overrode her concerns about holding a controversial Communist rally at the San Antonio Municipal Auditorium which caused serious negative consequences for the Tejana. Perhaps not surprisingly, the marriage ended in divorce. Tenayuca never remarried but did have a son whom she raised as a single parent.

In a very different scenario, childless Jovita González and her husband, Edmundo Mireles, were together for half a century. Before their union, her accomplishments included receiving a prestigious Rockefeller Grant to research a nontraditional topic and earning a master's degree from The University of Texas at Austin. After marriage, her aspirations to pursue a doctorate remained unfulfilled, even though Mireles did complete his master's at a college in Mexico. A suitable partner for the powerhouse educator, she worked beside him to advance mutual goals but sacrificed some of her independence and identity in the process, including secreting away a copy of the book manuscript of which her husband disapproved. That Edmundo devoted tremendous amounts of energy to his career and community, which perhaps left limited time for his spouse, was another marital reality. Increasingly reclusive, "Mrs. Mireles" became depressed later in life, and one suspects frustration was a contributing factor.

The two most recent of these Tejanas, Irma Rangel and Selena Quintanilla-Pérez, are also a study in contrasts. The former planned to wed, but her fiancé's death led her to become a career woman instead. As she got older, Rangel noted that men of her acquaintance were controlling and that she was not willing to sacrifice her independence in return for security. She also opined that a woman's primary responsibility was home and family, not a profession. Given that attitude, marriage might well have prevented her from attaining a law degree, becoming a longtime state legislator, or attaining many "firsts." Whether she would have been happier in that event is unknowable. The famous Selena Quintanilla, on the other hand, married fairly young, presumably against her father's objections. She not only continued to pursue a skyrocketing singing career but also worked with husband Chris Pérez in the music industry. Rumors linked her to a Mexican physician, although both forcefully denied having more than a friendship. Her untimely death leaves unanswered questions as to whether Selena and Chris would have lived happily ever after. Could she have been the only one of the five Tejanas to succeed in having marriage, children, and career? Thanks to Yolanda Saldívar, those answers will never be known. What is certain is that single, married, or divorced, all five of these exceptional women stood "heads above the crowd."[8]

The Tejano Monument on the grounds of the Texas State Capital in Austin, Texas. Photograph by Carol M. Highsmith. The Lydia Hill Texas Collection of Photographs in Carol M. Highsmith's America Project, Library of Congress, Prints and Photographs Division.

Regardless of their gender or marital status, the eleven Hispanics under consideration helped to shape Texas history, as did countless other Spaniards, *Mexicanos*, and Tejanos. In the early twenty-first century, a noteworthy step was taken to recognize these groups who helped to make "the state what it is today." In 2001, visionary Mexican Americans in South Texas formed a not-for-profit organization to erect "a monument on the Texas State Capitol grounds that honors the legacy of Tejanos." Members of Tejano Monument, Inc. devoted years to addressing challenges that included gaining the state legislature's cooperation and acquiring significant funding. The organization also surmounted a statutory restriction to secure the desired placement in front of the Texas State Capitol in Austin. Dedicated in an elaborate ceremony on March 29, 2012, the Tejano Monument, sculpted by Armando Hinojosa, consists of ten statues on a granite base with five plaques. The life-size figures depict a Spanish explorer, Tejano *vaquero* (cowboy), and a *ranchero* (ranching) family, while the interpretative tablets cover major periods from 1519 through the twentieth century. This impressive tribute has been cited in the media "as a milestone in the history of Tejanos."[9]

That the Lone Star State publicly honored its Hispanic heritage during a decade when anti-Mexican sentiment was becoming more pronounced within the United States is significant, as are the lives of the eleven notables featured in this book. All were of Mexican "culture or origin," to use the U.S. Census Bureau's term. Each of them was affected by their ethnicity, albeit in different ways. Some reacted in anger against prejudice and discrimination, even to the point of becoming estranged from the majority population. Others embraced their heritage but put a priority on fitting into the larger society. Some were noble by any definition, others less deserving of admiration, but all are worthy of study.

Endnotes

1 "The Hispanic Population: 2010: 2010 Census Briefs," U.S. Department of Commerce, U.S. Census Bureau, issued May 2011, 2–3, 15, 1st quotation on 2, 2nd quotation on 15, www.census.gov/prod/cen2010/briefs/c2010br-04.pdf; Mark Hugo López, "Latino Voters in the 2012 Election: Obama 71%; Romney 27%," Pew Research Center, Hispanic Trends, Nov. 7, 2012, http://www.pewhispanic.org/2012/11/07/latino-voters-in-the-2012-election/?/beta=true&utm_expid=53098246-2.Lly4CFSVQG2lphsg. . . .; Cindy Y. Rodriguez, "Latino Vote Key to Obama's Re-election," CNN, Nov. 9, 2012, http://www.cnn.com/2012/11/09/politics/latino-vote-key-election/; Elise Foley, "Latino Voters in Election 2012 Help Sweep Obama to Reelection," huffingtonpost.com, www.huffingtonpost.com/2012/11/07/latino-voters-election-2012_n_2085922.html. According to the Pew Hispanic Center exit polls, Latinos composed 10 percent of those who voted in the 2012 presidential election, and 71 percent cast their ballots for Barack Obama.

2 "The Hispanic Population," 2–3; "Race and Hispanic or Latino Origin: 2010," 2010 Census Summary File 1, U.S. Census Bureau, American FactFinder, http://factfinder.census.gov/faces/tableservices/jsf/pages/productview.xhtml?src=CF

3 Robert Kerwin, "Juan Nepomuceno Seguín" (master of arts thesis, December 2008, University of Texas-Pan-American), Abstract, iii.

4 Texas Education Agency, TAC Chapter 113, Texas Essential Knowledge and Skills for Social Studies, "Subchapter A. Elementary," http:ritter.tea.state.tx.us/rules/tac/chapter113/ch113a.html; TAC Chapter 113, "Subchapter B. Middle School," quotation from section 113.19, http://ritter.tea.state.tx.us/rules/tac/chapter113/ch113b.html

5 Allie Jaynes, "Why Selena Still Matters," AJ+ On the News, April 22, 2005, quotation, http://medium.com/aj-news/why-selena-still-matters-e3cb62d1b644.

6 Jerry Thompson, *Cortina: Defending the Mexican Name in Texas* (College Station: Texas A&M University Press, 2007), 12–13, 236, 241, 256n4, quotation on 236.

7 *Handbook of Texas Online*, Jesús F. de la Teja, "Seguín, Juan Nepomuceno," quotation, https://tshaonline.org/handbook/online/articles/fse08.

8 At the University of Texas at Brownsville/Texas Southmost College in Brownsville, Texas, over a number of years in the late 1990s and early 2000s the term "Heads above the Crowd" was used to recognize people who attained notable accomplishments.

9 "Especially Texan: The Tejano Monument," email from Legacy of Texas info@legacyoftexas.com to author, Oct. 11, 2017, 1st and 3rd quotations; "Historical Note," Tejano Monument, Inc. Records, 1972–2013, Nettie Lee Benson Latin American Collection, The University of Texas at Austin, 2nd quotation, http://www.lib.utexas.edu/taro/utlac/00352/lac-00352.html. As explained in Andrés Tijerina's "Tejano Monument" entry in the *Handbook of Texas Online*, an existing statute prohibited locating monuments on the "'historic' south grounds of the Capitol." Lobbying by Tejano Monument, Inc. led to passage of HB4114, sponsored by Trey Martinez-Fisher and signed by Governor Rick Perry in 2009. The new law allowed for the monument to be placed on the south lawn.

Glossary

The definitions below borrow heavily from the following sources: Arnoldo de León's *They Called Them Greasers* (1983), Merriam-Webster.com, and Dictionary.com.

Anglo: Non-Mexican American, English-speaking white person

Chicano: Person of Mexican descent or origin who lives in the United States (Chicana denotes a female)

Criollo: important classification during the Spanish colonial period, refers to pure-blooded Spaniards born in the Americas (translates as creole)

Hispanic: Someone of Latin American descent or origin who lives in the United States, often used interchangeably with Latino

Latino: Someone of Latin American descent or origin who lives in the United States, often used interchangeably with Hispanic (Latina denotes a female)

Mexican: someone who is from Mexico or has Mexican ancestry

Mexican American: a person of Mexican descent or origin who resides in the United States, but used at times specifically to reference U.S. citizens of Mexican descent or origin

Mexicano: translates as Mexican (*Mexicana* denotes a female)

Mestizo: a person of mixed Spanish and Indian ancestry

Peninsular: important classification during the Spanish colonial period, refers to pure-blooded Spaniards born in Spain

Tejano: A Mexican residing in Texas, regardless of place of birth (Tejana denotes a female)

Texian: term used in nineteenth century to denote Anglo Texans

Index

Abrego, María Gertrudis Flores de, 63, 373
Acosta, Theresa Paloma, 234
Adams, Francisco "Frank" Tenayuca, 195
African Americans, 2, 96, 62, 211, 225, 295, 298–303, 305 (*see also* slavery)
Agriculture, 20, 55, 62, 113–114, 180, 246–248, 286–287, 291; labor, 180, 246–47, 286–87, 291–92. *See also* slavery; *Bracero* Program
Alamo, 5, 7–8, 26–34, 71–73, 76–77, 97, 130–32, 136–46, 149–50, 155–57, 159, 215, 224, 367–68; Battle of, 5, 26–34, 48n40, 71–77, 97; and Juan Nepomuceno Seguín, 71–73, 76–77, 367; and Adina De Zavala, 7–8, 130–32, 136–146, 148–49, 155–59, photo page will change, 367–68
"Alamo Crusader," 132
Alcalde, 58, 64, 66, 95, 118
Allred, James, 145, 189
American Civil Liberties Union, 188, 195
"America Invades the Border Towns," 216
American GI Forum, 268, 305
Amor Prohibido. See Forbidden Love
Ancient Government Palace, San Antonio. *See* Spanish Governor's Palace
"Angel of the Alamo," 7–8, 132, 146, 368. *See also* Zavala, Adina De
Anglos (Anglo Americans), 2–6, 13, 19–20, 21–22, 26, 28, 54, 59, 61,

65–66, 68–70, 73, 75–76, 78–79, 83, 95–98, 100, 102, 106–08, 111, 141, 151, 158–59, 171, 180–81, 187, 210, 212–13, 215–16, 222–23, 225, 231–32, 235–37, 286, 248, 286, 291, 295, 366–68, 369, 371, 379; defined, 379
annexation (Texas to U.S.), 2, 12–13, 39, 82, 91n72, 93, 97, 136, 146, 366
Arista, Mariano, 98
Arizona, 40–41
Arkansas, 64, 250
army. *See* military
Arredondo, Joaquín de, "The Butcher," 15, 19, 23 57–58
Astudillo, Pete, 351
Austin, Moses, 46n19, 58–59
Austin, Stephen F., 5, 19–22, 24, 37, 46n19, 54, 59, 61–70, 76, 84, 366–67. *See also empresario*
Austin, TX, 106, 108, 116, 142, 211, 213, 221, 226, 231, 234, 274, 290, 298–99, 301–02, 305, 311, 314, 375, 377
Avila, Leandro, 186
Aztec Empire, 1

Barbee, Chris, 273
Barbee, Fred, 263, 273
Barbieri Coppini, Elizabeth di, 137–138
Barker, Eugene, 213–215
Becerra, María Josefa, 37, 373
Benavidez García, Yvette, 260, 276
Benavidez, Hilaria "Lala" Coy, 250–51, 255, 260, 272, 275, 374

Benavidez, Nicolas, 247–48
Benavidez, Noel, 260, 264
Benavidez, Raul, 265
Benavidez, Raul (Roy) Pérez,
  7, 244–276, 370, 372, 374;
  overview, 7, 245–46; ancestry,
  birth, and parents, 246; siblings,
  246–47; is orphaned, 246–47;
  early education, 247; relocates
  to El Campo, 247; extended
  family, 247; early jobs, 247–48;
  experiences discrimination and
  becomes aggressive, 248; at
  Firestone, 248; enters National
  Guard, 249; enlists in U.S. Army
  and Americanizes name, 249,
  278n9; military posts assigned
  to, 250, 252, 255, 260; aspires
  to Airborne forces, 249; bad
  behavior and disciplinary action,
  250; impact of West Point
  Honor Code, 250; marries Lala,
  250–52; enters 82nd Airborne,
  252; posted to Vietnam, 253;
  special mission and severe
  injuries, 253–54; rejects medical
  discharge, 254–55; overcomes
  painkiller addiction, 255; returns
  to paratroopers, 255; challenges of
  Special Forces training, 255–56;
  heroic actions near Loc Ninh,
  256–59; severe injuries, 257–59;
  military commendations, 259;
  and quest for Congressional
  Medal of Honor (MOH),
  260–64, 278–79n25, 279n36,
  280n43; awarded MOH, 264–67;
  honorable discharge in 1976, 260,
  267; celebrated, 267; criticized,
  267–68, 280n55; additional
  education, 268–69; battle with
  SSA, 269–71, 280n55, 281n64;
  and House of Representatives
  hearing on disability, 271–72;
  public appearances, 268, 272,
  281n57; autobiographical and
  other literature on, 273; illness and
  death, 273; eulogy and funeral,
  273–274; posthumous honors,
  274–75; assessment, 275–276,
  370, 372; impact of marriage on
  life and career, 374
Benavidez, Rogelio (Roger), 246–47
Benavidez, Salvador, 247
Benavidez, Teresa, 246–247
Benavidez Prochazka, Denise, 255, 264
Béxar, 15, 25–26, 29, 34, 55, 63–64,
  70–71, 75, 77. See also Alamo;
  San Antonio
Bexareños, 64, 75–76
Béxar County, 168
bilingual education, 6, 209, 227–29,
  232, 237, 288, 369
Billac, Pete, 273
Billboard, 328, 331, 346, 356
Black Bean Episode, 39
Bonaparte, Joseph, 14
Bonaparte, Napoleon, 13–15, 56
border (borderlands), 1, 9, 14, 19,
  63, 93–95, 99–100, 102, 107–08,
  110–13, 115, 116–19, 121–22,
  124, 210–12, 214–16, 222, 237,
  293, 297, 328, 334. See also
  boundary; Rio Grande
boundary, 2–3, 5, 36, 39–40, 78,
  97–99, 294, 366. See also border
Bowie, James, 25–26, 77, 159
Bracero Program, 229–30, 341n36
Brooke Army Medical Center
  (Fort Sam Houston), 254–55,
  259, 273
Brooks, Homer, 183–84, 186, 188,
  190–92, 375
Brownsville Raid, October 1859.
  See Cortina, Juan Nepomuceno
Brownsville, TX, 95, 101 103–09,
  116, 118, 121–122, 124, 315
Buena Vista, 40

Buffalo Bayou, 32, 73, 132
Bullock, Bob, 197
Burnet, David G., 30, 36, 137, 147
Burr, Ramiro, 344
Bush, George W., 300, 305–06, 343

Caballero, 222–224, 233, 375
Cabrera, Tomás, 106–07
Calhoun, Will, 269–270
California, 40, 97–99, 220, 250, 288
Camargo, MX, 95, 98, 119
Cambodia, 262, 256–258
Cameron County, 101, 117, 214–15,
    239n11, 311
Campbell, Randolph B., viii, 1, 29
Canales, Antonio, 78
Canales, Johnny, 328
Canales, Laura, 329
Canales, Servando, 121
Capitol Latin, 351–52
Carroll, Andrew, 156
Casa Blanca Ranch, 82, 84
Cassidy, Patrick, 260
Castañeda, Carlos, 211, 214, 220
Castañeda, Francisco, 23
Castro, Christian, 351
Catholicism. *See* Roman Catholicism
Cavazos, Francisco, 95
Cavazos, Refugio, 95
Cavazos, Sabas, 100, 102, 121
Census, U.S., 365, 377
Census of 1777 (Spanish Texas),
    19, 57
Centralists (MX). *See* Conservatives
Cerro Gordo, 41
Chicano, 181, 197–98, 223, 288,
    306–07, 313, 317n8, 379;
    defined, 379; movement, 288
"Christmas in Old San Antonio,"
    154–55
Cinco de Mayo, 113
City Federation of Women's Clubs,
    San Antonio, 148–49

City Federation of Women's
    Clubs, 148
Civil Rights Act, 305
Civil War (U.S.), 92–3, 111, 114–16,
    121, 132–33, 153, 158. *See also*
    Confederacy
Clareño Massacre, 112
Clark Air Force Base, 254
Clements, William, 264, 274
Club Político Latino, 222
Coahuila, 21–22, 61, 64, 67
Coahuila-Texas, 21, 61–63, 66
Coastal Bend AIDS
    Foundation, 332
Coca Cola Company, 332, 350
cockfighting, 18, 100
colleges. *See* higher education; entries
    for individual institutions
"Come and Take It," 23, 69
Committee on Alamo and Mission
    Improvements, 140
Communism (Communist Part), 175,
    181, 183–84, 186–89, 190–93,
    195, 252, 369, 375
"Como la flor" (song), 330
Confederacy, 111–115, 122, 133, 135
Congress of Industrial Organizations
    (Committee for Industrial
    Organizations), CIO, 186–188
Congress of Patriotism, 139
Conservatives (MX), 16–17, 19,
    20–21, 23, 41, 68–69, 78, 98,
    103–04, 113
Constitution of 1824, MX, 20–21,
    24, 52, 62, 66, 68, 96
"Contigo quiero estar" (song), 328
Coordinator of Inter-American
    Affairs, 226
Coppini, Pompeo, 137–140
Coronado, Raul, Jr., 355
Corpus Christi, 6, 208, 219, 221–24,
    226–35, 268, 289–90, 296,
    327–28, 333–35, 338, 342–43,
    347–48, 350, 355

corridos, 124
Cortina, Carmen, 95
Cortina, José María, 95, 102
Cortina, Juan Nepomuceno, 3, 6,
  92–124, 368–69, 372–73;
  images, 92, 120, 123; overview,
  93–94; family 94–95; youth,
  95–96; mother, 94–95, 101–02,
  110–11, 113; in U.S.-Mexican
  War, 98; American citizenship, 100;
  accusations against, 100, 106; and
  U.S. Quartermaster Corps, 100; and
  El Rancho de San José, 100; and
  land dispossession, 100–101; and
  Anglo Americans in Brownsville,
  101; and War of the Reform,
  103; and enmity toward Anglos,
  104; defense of Hispanics, 104;
  and Brownsville Raid, 104–05;
  issues Proclamations, 105, 108;
  Brownsville response, 106–08;
  Cabrera incident, 106–107; Tobin's
  Rangers, 107–108; and U.S. mail,
  107–108; and Ford, 108, 110,
  112–13, 117, 122; and troops
  under Heintzelman, 108, 110;
  defeat at Rio Grande City, 109;
  defeat at La Bolsa, 109; and Robert
  E. Lee, 110; Green's report on First
  Cortina War, 110; exile, 110–111;
  Second Cortina War, 111–112; and
  U.S. Civil War, 111–12, 114–15;
  and French invasions, 111–12,
  115–16; and Juaristas, 112–13,
  115–16, 118; pro Cortina
  petition; 116–17, 118–19; and
  Robb Commission, 117; Mexican
  response, 117–18; as alcalde, 118;
  imprisonment and return to power,
  119, 121; remarriage, 121; death,
  burial and obituary, 122; scholarship
  on, 122, 124; music about, 124;
  assessment 119, 122, 124; impact of
  marriages on life and career, 373

Cortina, María Estéfana
  Goseascochea. *See* Goseascochea,
  María Estéfana
Cortina(s), Trinidad, 95
Cos, Martín Perfecto de, 23–25, 29,
  32–33, 68–70, 75
Cotera, María, 233
Cotera, María Eugenia, 234–35
Council of National Defense of
  Texas, 147
Craddick, Tom, 314
Craig, John, 273
criollo, 14, 16; defined, 379
Crockett, David "Davy," 26, 28,
  77, 142
Cruz, María Isabel, 234
Cuba, 39, 365
Cuero, TX, 246, 275
cumbias, 330–31, 356
Cunningham, William, 297

Dallas, TX, 252, 270
"Dame un beso" (song), 328
Dandridge, Jim, 261
Dateline NBC, 346
Daughters of the Republic of
  Texas (DRT), 136–37,
  139–45, 146, 155–59. *See also*
  Zavala, Adina De; Driscoll,
  Clara; Alamo
David G. Burnet Elementary School,
  137, 147
Days Inn (Corpus Christi), 336–37,
  342, 344
De la Peña diary. *See* Peña, José
  Enríque de la
Democratic Party, 82, 141, 195, 291,
  307, 312
deportation, 3, 11n4, 182, 190
De Zavala Daughters and Sons of
  the Heroes of the Republic of
  Texas, 145
"Devil on the Border," 216

Dew on the Thorn, 235–36
De Zavala Daughters, 135–36, 138
Díaz, Porfirio, 93, 119–122
discrimination. *See* race, racism
diseases (health issues), 18, 21, 25,
 66–67, 74, 133, 155, 173, 182,
 184, 193, 230, 233, 246–47,
 254–60, 270, 352
Distinguished Service Cross, 259, 261
Dittmar, Mattie, 147
Dobie, J. Frank, 124, 211–14, 216,
 220–21
Dreaming of You, 346
Driscoll, Clara, 139–42, 144–45,
 155–56, 158, 160
Driscollites, 142, 144
DRT. *See* Daughters of the Republic
 of Texas
Daughters of the Republic of Texas,
 136–37, 139–45, 155–57, 159
Duval County, 231

East Texas, 19, 57, 74–5, 373
economy (economic situation), U.S.,
 2–3, 20, 71, 87n26, 96, 172,
 174, 176, 216, 218, 225, 233,
 245, 252–53, 296, 326, 355;
 Mexican, 16, 22, 40, 53, 172,
 224–25, 233; Texas, 53, 65, 71,
 87n26, 96, 107–08, 124, 172,
 176, 225, 287, 294, 304, 307;
 Karl Marx, 175; personal and
 regional, 59, 71, 87n26, 107–08,
 124, 174, 176, 216, 218, 245,
 267–68, 286, 302 304, 307,
 355, 369
Edinburg, TX, 297
education: and the Seguíns, 63,
 84, 367; and Adina De Zavala,
 134, 151; and Emma Tenayuca,
 175–176, 195; and Jovita
 González Mireles, 210–17,
 220–21, 227–28, 232, 374;

and Emundo E. Mireles, 220,
 224–29, 231–33, 236–37, 372,
 374; and Raul "Roy" Benavidez,
 247–49, 259, 268–69; and Irma
 Rangel, 286–88, 371; and Selena
 Quintanilla-Pérez, 327, 332,
 340–41; and minorities, 210–211,
 224–26, 232–33, 247–49, 286,
 293, 288–89, 293–307, 308–09,
 312–13, 371
educators/teachers, 6–7, 63, 132,
 134–35, 137, 153, 158–159,
 195, 209–11, 214, 216, 221–24,
 226–27, 229, 231, 233–34, 236,
 248, 285, 287–88, 295, 303, 306,
 314, 369–70, 375
Edwards, Emily, 148
Eimer, Margaret, 222–23, 233
El Campo Leader-News, 263
El Español Elemental, 228, 241n33
Ellis, Anna, 151
empresarios (colonization agents), 19,
 21–22, 24–25, 54, 59, 66–67, 69.
 See also Austin, Stephen F.; Filisola,
 Vicente
"Enamorada de Ti" (song and
 album), 351
English Only Policy, 224–226
Entertainment Tonight, 346
"Entre a mi mundo" (song), 331
Escandón, José de, 94
Esparza, Gregorio, 26
Esparza/Katz Productions, 347
Espíritú Santo Land Grant, 95, 101
Estefan, Gloria, 329
ethnicity, 2, 4–7, 9, 64, 169–70, 175,
 177, 181, 183, 212–13, 216, 218,
 220, 237, 285, 288–90, 306,
 315, 367–68, 370. *See also* African
 Americans; minorities; race; racism

Fair Labor Standards Act, 189
Fannin, James W., 27, 30–31, 72

Federal Bureau of Investigation
(FBI), 193
Federalists (MX), 15, 17, 20, 22–24,
30, 68, 70, 78, 96–97, 103, 112,
115–16, 131
Ferdinand VII of Spain, 14
Ferdinand Maximilian, 93,
115–116, 135
Fiesta de la Flor, 355, 357
Filibusters, 15, 56–58
Filisola, Vicente, 25, 34, 74
First Cortina War. *See* Cortina, Juan
Nepomuceno
Fisher, Abigail. *See Fisher v University
of Texas*
Fisher, R.B., 227–28
Fisher, W.S., 39
Fisher v University of Texas, 301
Floresville, TX, 82
folklore, 8, 147, 224, 235
Folk Lore Association of Texas, 147
folklorist, 122, 124, 209, 211, 215,
221, 237, 369
Forbidden Love, album, 331; song,
333, 354–55; perfume, 349
Ford, Addie, 121
Ford, John S. "Rip," 108–10,
112–14, 117, 121–22
Fort Brown, 101, 114
Fort Knox, KY, 249
Fort Ord, CA, 249
Fort Riley, KS, 260
Fort Sam Houston, 254,
259–61, 274
"Fotos y recuerdos" (song), 353
Fowler, Will, 42
France, 14–15, 38, 55–56,
93, 112, 131. *See also*
Ferdinand Maximilian;
Napoleon III
"Freedom's Champion," 131
French Revolution of 1789, 22
frontier, 116–17, 373
Fuego (album), 349

Galveston, TX, 132–34, 274
García, Arnold, 338
García, Hector, 289
García, Juliet, 315
Garza, Robert, 336
Genet, Honoré, 138
"*gente decente*," 8, 11n5, 209, 214,
223, 237, 369
G I Joe action figure, 275
Giraud, Beatrice, 192. *See also*
Tenayuca, Emma
Glavecke, Adolphus, 104–105, 121–22
Goldfinch, Charles, 124
Goliad, 5, 27, 30–33, 70, 72, 92, 97
Gómez, Selena, 351
Gómez Farías, Valentín, 21–22
Gonzales, TX, 23–24, 27, 30, 69
González Mireles, Jovita, iii, 6, 8,
208–16, 218, 224–28 230, 232–37,
369–70, 374–75; overview, 8,
209; ancestry, 209–10; parents
and birth, 210; early childhood
and pride in heritage, 210; family
relocates to San Antonio, 210;
education, 210–11, 213–15; and
J. Frank Dobie, 211–12, 213–4,
216; and folklore, 211–13,
215–16; teaching, 211, 215; and
Our Lady of the Lake College,
211; desires respectability, 214;
writes "America Invades the
Border Towns," 216; Rockefeller
Grant, 216; single status, 216–18;
marriage to E.E. Mireles,
218, 230; commonalities with
Mireles, 220; as teacher in San
Felipe (TX), 220; aspires to
doctorate, 220; moves to Corpus
Christi, 222; teaches, 222;
presentations and publications
after marriage, 221; and *Caballero*
manuscript with Margaret
Eimer, 222–24; limits activities
other than teaching, 224, 232;

co-authors textbooks, 227–28, 241n33; and Pan Americanism, 232; retirement, attempts autobiography, 233; María Cotera and *Caballero* manuscript, health issues, 233; death, 233; earlier interview with María Cotera, 233–34; María Isabel Cruz, estate and papers, 234; posthumous recognition, 234–35; "Mexican Americans in Texas History Conference," 234; *Caballero* is published, 234; *Dew on the Thorn* is published, 235–36; assessment, 235–37, 369–70
González Rodríguez, Jacobo, 210, 214
Good Government League, 291
Good Neighbor Policy, 226, 229–30
Goseascochea, María Estéfana, 94–5, 100–02, 104, 110–11, 122
Graham, Gary, 308
Grand Old Opera House, San Antonio, 147
Griffin, Oscar, 273
Guerra Becera, Severina, 209
Gunter Hotel, San Antonio, 179 182
Gutiérrez-Magee Expedition, 15, 56–58
Gutiérrez de Lara, Bernardo, 15, 56.

Hagan, Fred, 338
Harrisburg, TX, 32
Havana, Cuba, 39. *See also* Cuba
Head Start (House Bill 51), 232–33
Hepburn, Audrey, 345
Here Is Where: Discovering America's Great Forgotten History, 156
Hidalgo, Miguel, 14, 56, 58
higher education (colleges and universities), 9, 124, 130, 134, 176, 182–83, 192, 195, 211, 214, 218–220, 232, 234, 254, 272, 286–89, 295–307, 310, 312–15, 327, 375. *See also* education; entries for individual colleges and universities
Higher Education Committee (Texas House), 298, 300, 303, 312
Hispanic, defined, 365, 379
Hispanic Hall of Fame, 274
Hispanic National Bar Association, 308
Hispanic population in U.S. and Texas, 2010 Census, 365
Hispanic Women's Network of Texas, 307
History of the Alamo and Other Missions in San Antonio, 145
Hogg, Jim, 311
Hollywood Walk of Fame, 356
homosexuality, 292, 338, 354–55, 371
Hopwood, Cheryl. *See Hopwood v Texas*
Hopwood v Texas, 298–99, 303
Houston, Sam, 5, 24–25, 28–37, 72–76, 78–9, 81, 97, 108, 366–67
Houston, TX, 136, 183, 192, 247, 250, 264, 269, 272, 274, 331–2, 337–38, 345, 351
Hugo, Charles. *See* Hugo & Schmeltzer
Hugo & Schmeltzer, 138–140
Huston, Felix, 75–76

ILGWU (International Ladies' Garment Workers Union), 181
immigration (immigrants), 1–2, 4, 10, 20, 62, 65, 67, 171–72, 176–77, 186, 224–25, 330, 366
Inca Empire, 1
independence, vii, 1–5, 13–19, 21, 24–25, 28, 30, 33, 36, 38, 45n9, 46n19, 53–54, 56–59, 62–63, 69–71, 77–78, 93, 97–98, 131,

136, 172, 246, 365–67; of Mexico
from Spain, vii, 1, 4, 13–14,
16–19, 45n9, 46n19, 53, 56–59,
63, 93, 172, 365; of Texas from
Mexico, 2–3, 5, 13, 15, 21, 24,
29–30, 33, 36, 38, 54, 62, 69,
70–71, 73, 77–78, 93, 97–98,
131, 136, 246, 366–67; of
Confederacy, 111–112, 133.
See also Santa Anna, Antonio López
de; Seguín, Erasmo and Juan
Nepomuceno; Texas Revolution;
Cortina, Juan Nepomuceno
Indians, 1, 16, 61–62, 170–71,
225, 368
International Ladies' Garment
Workers Union (ILGWU), 181
International Workers' Day, 183
Interstate Index: A Journal of Progress,
San Antonio, 147
Ireland, 132
Irma Lerma Rangel College of
Pharmacy. *See* Rangel College of
Pharmacy
Irma Rangel Collection, 284,
311, 316
Iturbide, Agustín de, 16–17

Jackson, Andrew, 37–38
Jalapa, Vera Cruz, MX, 14, 16, 17
Jehovah's Witnesses, 342
Johnson, Lyndon B., 253
Júarez, Benito, 112–13, 115–116

Kearney, Milo, 124
Kennedy, John F., 252
Kennedy Onassis, Jacqueline, 345
Kilday, Paul, 190
King, Sarah, 154
King Ranch, 291
Kleberg, Richard, 228
Kleberg County, 289, 291, 311

Korea, 250, 252
Krueger, Thurmond, 229
Ku Klux Klan, 191
Kumbia Kings, 349–350

"La Bamba" (song), 328
labor, 3, 8, 133, 170, 173–4, 177–91,
193, 199, 222, 233, 229–230,
247, 287–288, 291–92, 307, 369.
See also Tenayuca, Emma; labor
organizations; slavery; workers;
workers' strikes; workplace
environment and wages
labor organizations (unions), 170,
177–79, 181, 183, 186–190,
223. *See also* specific labor
organizations/unions
Lamar Medal, 309
Lamar, Mirabeau B., 78, 131, 309
Lapham Scholarship, 213
La Prensa, 188
Latino/a, defined, 365 379
Law of April 6, 1830, 46n21,
65–66
League of Women Voters, 195
League of United Latin American
Citizens. *See* LULAC
Lebrón, Manuela Pérez de, 14
Lee, Robert E., 110
Legion of Honor (medal), MX, 24
Leija, Gus, 268
Leo, Myra, 307, 310
lesbian, 292, 339, 354–55. *See also*
homosexuality
LGBT, 355, 371. *See also*
homosexuality; lesbian
Liberals (MX). *See* Federalists
Limón, José, 234–35, 355
Lions Club, 148
Loc Ninh, 256, 258, 261
Long Barrack, 138–39, 141, 145,
155–56, 164n42, 368. *See also*
Alamo; Zavala, Adina De

Looney, Everett, 182
López, Jennifer, 347
López, Rafael, 351
Los Angeles, CA, 193
Los Dinos, 325–27
Louisiana Territory, 55
LULAC, 175, 222, 232, 240n21, 291, 296–97; *LULAC v Richards*, 296–97
Luna, Vilma, 315
Lynch's Ferry, 32

Madame Tussauds of Hollywood, 356
Madison's Regiment, Texas Cavalry (Civil War), 133
Mafia, 327, 330
Magee, Augustus, 15, 56–58
Main Avenue High (San Antonio), 218
MALDEF, 297, 302, 309
Manga de Clavo, 18, 21, 23, 38–39
Manifest Destiny, 39, 97. *See also* Polk, James K.; U.S.-Mexican War
Margaret Brent Women Lawyers of Achievement Award, 309
mariachi, 330
marital status, 6–9, 18, 25, 27, 39, 55, 57–58, 63, 77–78, 95, 110–11, 113–14, 122–23, 132, 137, 152–53, 173–74, 184, 192, 195, 209–10, 216, 218, 220–24, 227, 233–44, 236, 245–47, 255, 271–72, 286–88, 294, 326, 333, 340–41, 369–70, 372–76
marriage. *See* marital status
Masonic Cemetery (San Antonio), 158
Martínez, Antonio, 84
Martínez, Ricardo, 334, 374, 376
Matamoros, MX, 98, 100–01, 105–6, 113–15, 118–19, 121
Maverick, Elizabeth, 154
Maverick, Maury, 189–92
Maverick Green, Rena, 148–149
Mazz, 330
McGibben, Larry, 257

Mcnelly, Leander H., 118–119
Mean Mexican. *See* Benavidez, Raul (Roy) Pérez
Medal of Honor, 7, 244, 246, 260–62, 265–68, 271–74, 276, 370, 374
Medina River, Battle of, 15, 57. *See also* Gutiérrez-Magee Expedition
Menchaca, Antonio, 73
Mendoza, Lydia, 329
Menger Hotel, San Antonio, 139–40, 147, 156
Mestizo, defined, 379
Mexican, defined, 379
Mexican American, defined, 379
Mexican-American Legal Defense Fund, *see* MALDEF
Mexican American Legislative Caucus (TX), 294
Mexican Cession, 40, 99. *See also* U.S.-Mexican War
Mexicano, defined, 279
Mexican population in U.S. and Texas, 2010 Census, 365
"Mexican Question in the Southwest," 190
Mexican Revolution, 172, 225
Mexican War. *See* U.S.-Mexican War
Mexico, 1–6, 13–15, 19–20, 22–23, 37–43, 53–54, 57, 61–64, 66–68, 70–71, 74, 79, 81–84, 93, 95–100, 103, 105, 109–19, 124, 135, 170–72, 246, 326, 333–34, 366–67, 373. *See also* Constitution of 1824; independence; Mexican Revolution; U.S.-Mexican War; Santa Anna, Antonio López de, Seguín, Erasmo and Juan; Cortina, Juan
Mier, 39
Milam, Ben, 136. *See also* Milam Park
Milam Park, San Antonio, 174, 197
Mi Libro Español, 227–228, 241n33

military: Spanish, 14–15, 56–58;
Mexican, 5, 12, 18–19, 21–23,
24–34, 36, 39–40, 63, 68–74,
79, 81–82, 97–99, 103, 113–116,
119, 136, 159, 366, 373; Texan,
5, 24–28, 30–36, 39, 69–78, 97;
U.S., 6–7, 39–40, 82, 98–99,
106, 108, 110, 114, 193, 249–50,
252, 256–267, 270, 273, 275–76,
374; other, 15, 56–58, 68, 96–97,
103, 112–116, 119, 133. *See also*
Cortina, Juan N.; Santa Anna,
Antonio López de; Seguín, Juan
N.; Benavidez, Raul "Roy" Pérez
Military Plaza, San Antonio,
146, 188. *See also* Spanish
Governor's Palace
Miller, James B., 66
minorities, 3–4, 9–10, 53, 70,
83, 169, 171, 180, 214,
225, 235, 285–87, 295, 299,
300–01, 302, 304, 308–9,
312, 340, 371. *See also* African
Americans; education; ethnicity;
race; racism
Mirador de la Flor (Overlook of the
Flower), 347–348
Mireles, Edmundo Eduardo, xiii,
8, 209, 217–224, 226, 227–37,
369–70, 372, 374–75; overview,
6; family, 218; and Mexican
Revolution, 218; education,
218–21, 231; teaching in San
Antonio, 220; friendship with
Jovita González and marriage,
281, extracurricular activities at
UT, 219; principal in San Felipe
(TX), 220; and *Club Político
Latino* (Latino Political Club),
222; and LULAC, 222; moves
to Corpus Christi, 222; teaches,
222; opposes *Caballero*, 223–24;
and bilingual education and Pan
Americanism, 224–28, 230;

co-authors textbooks, 227–28,
241n33; praise for Spanish
language program, 228–229;
runs for legislature, 231; reports
on Spanish language program,
231; earns Master's degree,
232–33; and Corpus Christi
Adult Education Program (ABE),
233; María Cotera and *Caballero*
manuscript, 233–34; death, 234;
posthumous honors, 234; María
Isabel Cruz, estate and papers,
234, 235–37, 369–70, 372; on
impact of marriage on life and
career, 375
Mireles, Jovita González.
See González Mireles, Jovita
Mireles, Sostenes, 218
Mission San José, San Antonio,
137–38
missions, San Antonio, 55, 88n46,
139, 141, 145, 155, 156
Missouri, 19, 59, 64
Mississippi, 64
Molina subdivision (Corpus Christi),
333, 342
Monclova, 68
Monterrey, 231, 334
Morales, Dan, 299
Moreno/Rangel Legislative
Leadership Program, 309
Morris, George, 104–05
Municipal Auditorium Riot
(San Antonio), 191–93. *See also*
Tenayuca, Emma
museums, 138–39, 142, 145,
148–49, 350, 353, 356

Napoleon III, France, 112–13,
115–16
Napoleon of the West. *See* Santa
Anna, Antonio López de
Natchitoches, LA, 59

National Association for Chicano
Studies, 197
National Center for Public Policy and
Higher Education, 304
National Recovery Administration
(NRA), 177
Nava, Gregory, 347
Neill, James, 25–26
Neutral Ground Agreement
(1806), 56
Newman Club, 213
New Mexico, 40, 42, 78
New Orleans, LA, 36, 63, 77
New York City, 133
North Carolina, 252, 255, 274
Nueces County, 230, 289, 337
Nueces River, 39, 97–98, 117
Nuevo Laredo, MX, 63, 83
Nuevo Santander, 56, 94

O'Connor, Brian, 263–65
Olivio, Bob, 345
Olmos, Edward James, 347, 351
orquestra, 330–31
Orozco, Cynthia, 234
Our Lady of the Lake University,
195, 211

Pacific Western University, 327
Palo Alto, 98
Pan American Council, 147, 230
Pan-American movement
(Pan-Americanism), 228, 230,
236–37, 369, 374
Pan-American University at Edinburg.
See University of Texas Pan
American-Edinburg
Panteón de Dolores, 122
Para Selena con Amor (book),
352–53
Paradez, Deborah, 355
Paredes, Americo, 124

Peace Party (TX), 23–24
pecan shellers, 174–75, 181–82,
184–90, 203n40, 204n45. *See also*
Emma Tenayuca chapter
Peña, José Enríque de la, 28–29, 31,
48n41, 74
Peninsulares, 14; defined, 379
Peña, Jennifer, 341
People magazine (*People Weekly*), 334,
345, 350–351
Pérez, Christopher, 333–35, 337,
340–42, 349, 352–53, 376
Perry, Rick, 315, 349, 378
Plan of Casa Mata, 18
Plan of Vera Cruz, 17
Polk, James K., 39–40, 97–98
Porfiristas. *See* Díaz, Porfirio
Presley, Elvis, 356
Project Mireles, 234
Protestants, 64–65
Puebla, 113
Puerto Rican, 365

Q Productions, 341, 350, 357
Querétaro, MX, 116
Quintanilla, Jr., Abraham, 325–28,
333–41, 344–47, 351–53,
365, 371
Quintanilla, Abraham "A.B.", III,
326–27, 349–50, 352–53, 35
Quintanilla, Marcella (Pérez), 326,
340, 350, 352
Quintanilla, Suzette, 326–27,
347, 349
Quintanilla-Pérez, Selena, 9, 325–56,
371–72, 375–376; awards, 9,
328–29, 331–32, 346, 350, 356,
371; overview, 9, 325; parents,
325–26; birth and siblings,
326; early career and father's
influence, 326–28; Selena y Los
Dinos become professional, 327;
education, 327; public image,

329–31; impact and significance, 330; songs and albums, 330–31; corporate contracts and estimated income, 332; civic engagement, 332; and coverage in magazines, 332–34; marriage, 333; clothing line, 334; and Dr. Ricardo Martínez, 334; and Yolanda Saldívar, 334–36; murder, 336; trial, 336–340; media coverage, 337–38; impact of murder on family and fans, 336, 340–43, 347–49; "Selena Day," 343; and Howard Stern, 344; unauthorized merchandise, 344; books about, 345; tribute albums, 345–46; television programs on, 246; movie, 346–47; Corpus Christi monument, 347–48; "Selena Lifetime Achievement Award," 349; family business after death, 349–50; and 10th anniversary of death, 349–50; Selena Museum, 350; tribute concert, 351; commemorative postage stamp, 351; coverage in *People* in 2012, 351–52; Abraham Quintanilla Jr. sues Christopher Pérez, 352–53; websites and fan comments, 353–54; and LGBT community, 354–55; scholarship on, 355; *Fiesta de la Flor*, 355; assessment, 356, 371–72; summary on marriage and impact on life and career, 376

race, 3–4, 7, 16, 54, 69, 76, 83, 89n59, 91n76, 102, 106, 159, 171–173, 175, 215–16, 223–225, 235, 248, 251–52, 285, 288, 298–99, 301, 303–4, 330, 355, 365, 368
racism, 3–4, 7, 16, 54, 76, 79, 83, 102, 159, 173, 175–76, 215–216, 224–25, 235–36, 248, 251–252, 273, 285, 288, 298–99, 304, 330, 355, 377
Raleigh, Eve. *See* Eimer, Margaret; *Caballero*
Rancheras, 330–31, 356
ranching (ranches), 55 58, 70, 74, 82, 96, 100, 104, 107, 134, 210, 223, 286, 291. *See also* rustling
Rangel College of Pharmacy, 307, 315
Rangel Family Scholarship Fund, 315
Rangel, Hermina "Big Minnie" Lerma, 286–87
Rangel, Irma Lerma, 8, 284–316, 370–71, 375–76; overview, 8–9, 285–86; birth, parents, and siblings, 285–87; education, 287, 289; engagement and death of fiancé, 287; as teacher and principal, 288, 317n7; becomes a lawyer, 289; community engagement, 290; runs for Texas House of Representatives, 290–91; allegations against and response, 292; as first Tejana elected, 292; committee and other memberships, 293–94, 296; labeled "furniture" by *Texas Monthly*, 294; commitment to education, 295–307; opposition to anti-abortion legislation, 289, 296, 307–308; and death penalty, 308; honors during lifetime, 308–310; battles with cancer, 310–13; death and funeral, 314; posthumous honors, 314–315, 370–71, 322n65; single status on life and career, 375–76
Rangel, Minnie, 286, 291
Rangel, Olga, 286
Rangel, Presciliano Martínez, 286–287, 291, 315
Ray High School (Corpus Christi), 232, 234
Reader's Digest, 270

Reagan, Ronald, 264–67, 271, 276
rebellion(s), 2, 14–17, 21–24, 26, 53,
    57–58, 93, 96, 107–09, 119, 122,
    138, 366
"Red Baiting." *See* Tenayuca, Emma
Reeves, Charles M., 142
Reform Laws (MX), 103
Regidor, 64
"Remember the Alamo" (song),
    130, 145
Rendón, Minnie, 186–87
Republic of Texas, 7, 36, 53–55,
    75, 83–4, 93, 131, 135–37, 144,
    159, 366
Republican Party, 111, 132, 312
Revilla, Nuevo Santander, 56
Richmond, Clint, 344
Rio Grande City, 109, 211
Rio Grande (river), 2–3, 5–6, 23, 26,
    36, 38–40, 55, 71, 78, 80, 95,
    97–99, 101, 103, 106–09,
    111–13, 116–17, 119, 122, 124,
    210, 221, 326, 366–67
Rio Grande Valley, 95–96, 100,
    107–08, 118, 214, 319n28
Robb Commission, 117
Robstown, 288
Rockefeller, Nelson, 226, 229
Rockefeller Grant, 216, 222, 375
Roma, TX, 210
Roman Catholic Church. *See* Roman
    Catholicism
Roman Catholicism, 2, 16–17, 19,
    62, 65, 96, 103, 134, 137–38,
    180, 187, 191, 193, 213–214,
    254, 273, 289
Roosevelt, Eleanor, 229
Roosevelt, Franklin D., 182, 226
royalists, 14, 16, 56–57
Roy P. Benavidez Papers,
    1943–207, 277
Ruiz, Manuel, 113
Runaway Scrape, 30, 72
rustling, 100, 102, 106, 117–19

Salcedo, Manuel, 57
Saldívar, Yolanda, 9, 334–40, 343,
    346, 376
Saltillo, MX, 25, 49, 55, 64–65, 67
Sam Houston Normal Institute.
    See Sam Houston State University
Sam Houston State University, 134
San Antonio, TX, 24, 56, 246,
    296, 307; and San Antonio de
    Béxar (Béjar), 15, 26, 55; and
    Republican Army of the North,
    15, 57; and Arredondo, 15, 57;
    and Antonio López de Santa Anna,
    15, 25–31, 38, 68–69, 71–73,
    97, 136, 138; the Seguíns, 5, 53,
    55, 58–59, 62–66, 69, 71–79,
    81–82, 84, 374; Texas Revolution,
    24–26, 29, 31, 70–71; and 1842
    expeditions, 38, 78–79; and Adina
    De Zavala, 134, 136–38, 144–51,
    153–54, 158, 368; and Emma
    Tenayuca, 169–178, 180–195,
    197–198, 375; and Jovita
    González, 211, 213, 220; and
    Edmundo Mireles, 218, 220; and
    Raul "Roy" Benavidez, 254–55,
    260, 273–74; and Irma Rangel,
    289, 310–11, 315; Selena, 331,
    334–35, 342. *See also* Alamo
San Antonio Art League, 147
San Antonio College, 218
San Antonio Conservation Society,
    148, 151
San Antonio de Padua (church), 138.
    See also Zavala, Adina De; Alamo;
    Driscoll, Clara
San Antonio de Valero, 138. *See also*
    Zavala, Adina De; Alamo
San Antonio Express-News, 84,
    148, 344
San Antonio Municipal
    Auditorium, 375
San Antonio River, 62, 176, 192
San Antonio School Board, 134

San Antonio Woman's Parliament, 154
San Antonio Women's Club, 147
San Antonio Women's Hall of Fame, 197
San Antonio Women's League, 147, 154
San Felipe, 23–24, 63
San Francisco, CA, 195
San Francisco State University, 195
San Jacinto, 32–36, 73, 75, 82, 97, 132, 140, 366
San Jacinto River, 32, 73
San Juan mission complex, 137–138
San Luis Potosí, 25
San Marcos River, 57
Sanokofa, Shaka. *See* Graham, Gary
Santa Anna, Antonio López de, 2, 5, 12–43, 54, 67–74, 79, 82, 93, 96–9, 103, 112, 131, 136, 138, 366, 372–73; overview, 5, 13–14; role in Texas and Mexican history, 42; hatred of, 5, 98, 113–114; birth and ancestry, 14; as royalist in Spanish army, 14–16; Arredondo as model, 15; Napoleon Bonaparte as model, 13, 15; and filibusters, 115–16; and Mexican independence, 16; and Augustín de Iturbide, 16–17; issues Plan of Vera Cruz, 17; marriage to Inés García and children, 18; *Manga de Clavo*, 18, 21, 23, 38; and Spanish invasion of Mexico (Tampico), 18; The Age of Santa Anna, 13, 19; supports republican government, 20; as president of Mexico, 20–1, 49n67, 96; as commander of Mexican army, 21; responds to Texans' petition, 21–22, 67; becomes Centralist, 22–23, 54, 67–68, 93, 96; suppresses rebellion in Zacatecas, 23, 68, 97; as commander of Mexican army

during Texas Revolution, 5, 24–34, 71–72, 136, 138; as prisoner in Texas, 34–37, 74; and Andrew Jackson, 37–38; returns to Mexico, 38; loses leg, 38; back in presidency, 38; and Santa Fe Expedition and invasions of Texas, 38–39, 79; in exile in Cuba, 39; marriage to María Dolores Tosta, 39; and James Polk, 40; and U.S.-Mexican War, 40, 99; again in exile, 40–41; returns to power in Mexico, 41–2; death, 42; obituary, autobiography, 43; publications about, 5, 42–43, 366; assessment, 42–43, 366, 372; commentary on impact of marriages on life and career, 372–73
Santa Anna: A Curse upon Mexico, 42
Santa Anna: Aurora y ocaso de un comediante, 42
Santa Anna no fué un traidor, 42
Santa Fe Expedition, 38–39, 78–79, 81–82
Santiago Tlateloco Prison, 121
Scheina, Robert L., 42
Scott, Winfield, 99
"Sea of Mud," 34
Seal, Start (Portrait of Adina De Zavala), 156–57
secession, 111–112, 133
Second Battle of the Alamo 139, 141–46. *See also* Zavala, Adina De; Driscoll, Clara; Daughters of the Republic of Texas
Seguín, TX, 78, 83–84
Seguín, Bartolomé, 55
Seguín, Erasmo, 5, 52–55, 57–59, 61–62, 64–66, 70, 73, 78, 82–84, 366–67, 372–73; overview, 5, 53–54; ancestry, 55; offices held, 55, 58, 60–62; marriage to María Josefa Becerra, 58; children, 58; as postmaster of San Antonio,

58, 62; supports Anglo-American
colonization, 53–54, 59–60;
and ranching, 58, 62–63; and
Constitution of 1824, 60–62;
and petition of 1833, 66; expelled
by Gen. Martín Perfecto de Cos,
70; supports Texas Revolution, 54,
62–63, 70–71; and Sam Houston,
81; compensation from Republic
of Texas, 78; death, 82; and racial
discrimination, 83; burial place
unknown, 84; and Texas Education
Agency, 84; assessment, 53–54,
83–84, 366–67, 372; impact of
marriage on life and career, 373
Seguín, Juan José María Erasmo de
Jesús. *See* Seguín, Erasmo
Seguín, Juan Nepomuceno, 5–6,
53–55, 58, 60, 63, 64, 66–84,
87n26, 89n51, 196, 366–67,
372–73; overview, 5–6; ancestry,
55; parents, 58; formal education,
63; marriage to María Gertrudis
and children, 63; helps run post
office, 63; business/trade, 63–64,
77, 87n26; and Veramendi, and
Austin, 54, 65, 76; as *regidor*
(city councilman), 64; as acting
alcalde, 64; and petition of 1833,
66–67; begins military career,
68–70; as judge, 71; as captain
of cavalry, 71; supports Texas
Revolution, 54, 70–71; at Béxar/
Alamo, 71–72; during "Runaway
Scrape," 72, 74; at Battle of San
Jacinto, 73–74, 89n51; and Sam
Houston, 72–74, 75–76, 81;
takes possession of San Antonio,
74–75; receives promotion, 75;
conflicts with Felix Huston,
75–76; land speculation, 76;
buries ashes of Alamo defenders,
76–77; as Senator during
Republic of Texas, 54, 77–78,
90n63; town named after, 78,
90n65; and Lamar, 54, 76, 79,
83; and Santa Fe Expedition,
78–79; as mayor of San Antonio,
78, 81; and Mexican invasions of
1842, 79, 81; moves to Mexico,
54, 81; service in Mexican Army,
81–82; participation in Mexican
invasion, 54, 81; participation in
U.S.-Mexico War, 54, 82; *Casa
Blanca* Ranch, 82; Justice of the
Peace, 82; and Democratic Party,
82; judge of Wilson County, 82;
memoirs, pension, 82; death,
83; and racial discrimination, 83;
publications on, 84; monument,
84; and Texas Education Agency,
84; assessment, 53–54, 83–84,
366–67; impact of marriage on
life and career, 373
Seguín, Santiago, 55
Selena. *See* Quintanilla-Pérez, Selena
Selena Lifetime Achievement
Award, 349
Selena y Los Dinos, 327–28, 330–333,
341, 346, 351
Selena Museum, 350, 353
Seligmann, Julius, 184–85, 189
Senior Army Decorations Board,
261–62
Sevier, Mrs. Henry. *See* Driscoll, Clara
sharecroppers, 246. *See also*
agriculture; labor
Six Flags over Texas (theme park), 135
"Six Flags That Have Floated Over
Texas," 135
Silva, Chelo, 329
Skurka, Mark, 338–39
slavery, 20, 61–62, 65, 74, 97, 108,
111, 115, 133. *See also*
African-Americans
Smith, Harvey, 149, 151
"Social Life in Cameron, Starr, and
Zapata Counties," 214–215

Social Security Administration (SSA), 267, 269, 370
Socialism, 174, 181
Soldaderas, 25
Sony Discos (Sony Records), 330
South America, 1, 228, 334
Southern Pecan Company, 184–85, 189
South Side, San Antonio, 170–71, 195, 342
South Texas, 95, 100–104, 108, 113–14, 116–17, 124, 214–16, 230, 233, 235–36, 288, 290–91, 294, 296–97, 306, 312–13
South Texas Archives, 284, 311
South Texas Border Initiative, 297
Southwestern Bell, 291, 332
Southwest Texas State University. See Texas State University
Soviet Union, 192, 252
Spain, vii, 1, 3, 4, 13–19, 42, 53, 55–59, 63, 93, 135, 138, 146, 155, 172, 237, 365, 367, 377, 379; Spaniards, 1, 14, 16, 57, 84, 138, 215, 377; Spanish empire, 1, 14, 19, 58, 135, 172, 365
Spanish Governor's Palace, San Antonio, 146–151, 155, 159, 368
Special Olympics, 341
Starr County, 116, 214–16, 239n11
State of Texas v Yolanda Saldívar, 337–40
stereotypes, 95–96, 159, 185, 268, 368
Sterling, Elissa, 338
Stern, Howard, 344
Stillman, Charles 101
St. Gerard's Catholic School (San Antonio), 195
St. Joseph's Hospital (Houston), 340
St. Louis, 142
St. Mary's Cemetery, San Antonio, 155, 158
St. Mary's University School of Law, 289

St. Michael's Catholic School (Cuero), 247
strikes. See workers' strikes
"Sweetheart of Texas," 146

Tafolla, Carmen, 198
Tag Day, 147
Tamaulipas, 113, 115–16, 121, 201. See also Matamoros
Tango Mike/Mike. See Benavides, Raul (Roy) Pérez
Tatum, H.W. Jr., 347
Taylor, Zachary, 98. See also U.S.-Mexican War
taxes, 61, 171, 294–5, 102, 181, 312
teachers. See educators; Zavala, Adina De; Tenayuca, Emma; Gónzalez Mireles, Jovita; Mireles, Edmundo E.; Rangel, Irma Lerma
Teachers Corps, 288
"Techno-Cumbia" (song), 330
Tejada, Sebastián Lerdo de, 119
Tejano, 2–6, 10, 20, 26, 32–33, 53–55, 59–62, 65–66, 69–79, 83–84, 96–97, 102–112, 171–74, 180, 186, 198, 210, 215, 223, 225–26, 248, 366–67, 370, 372, 377, prejudice and hostility toward, 2–3, 5, 20, 55, 76–79, 79, 83, 96, 102, 107, 109–10, 108, 180, 248, 367, as defined, 379
Tejano music, 9, 325–32, 342, 344, 346, 349, 355–56, 371–72
Tejano Music Awards (TMA), 329, 331–33, 346, 349
Telemundo, 338
Tenayuca, Emma, 8, 168–72, 174–76, 178–99, 294, 368–69, 375; overview, 8, 169–70; birth and ethnicity, 170; childhood, 171–72; grandfather's influence, 170–71, 175, 176; and Plaza de

Zacate, 174–75; and anarchism and socialism, 174–75; and auxiliary chapter of LULAC, 175; education, 175–76, 179, 195; and racism, 175–77; early activism, 178–82, 202n23; and Workers' Alliance, 181–83; arrest and trial, 182; employment and Roman Catholic Church, 180; health issues, 182; marriage to Homer Brooks, 183–84, 188; continuing activism, 184–188, 203n40, 204n45; criticized for Communist affiliation, 187–88; and Maury Maverick, 188, 191–92; "The Mexican Question in the Southwest," 190; riot at Municipal Auditorium, 191–92; blacklisting, 192; divorce, 192; relocates to Houston, 192; as state chairman of Communist Party of Texas, 193; breaks with Communist Party, 192–93; health, 193; and FBI, 193; in World War II, 193; relocates to California, 193; son, 194–95; returns to San Antonio, 195; organizational affiliations, 195; teaching career, 195; and Henry Cisneros, 195–97; death and funeral, 197–98; assessment, 197–99, 368–69; summary on impact of marriage and divorce on life and career, 375
Tennessee, 24, 26
Ten Percent Plan, 300–302
Terrell, TX, 134
Texas A&M University System, 297
Texas A&M University-College Station, 234, 300–01
Texas A&M University-Corpus Christi, 208, 219, 234, 300–01
Texas A&M University-Kingsville (formerly Texas College of Arts and Industries), 284, 286, 297, 306, 311, 314–15

Texas Academic Skills Program (TASP), 313
Texas Assessment of Academic Skills (TAAS), 304–06
Texas Assessment of Knowledge and Skills (TAKS), 306
Texas Association of Chicanos in Higher Education (TACHE), 306–07, 313
Texas Centennial, 145
Texas College of Arts and Industries. See Texas A&M University-Kingsville
Texas Congress, Republic of Texas, 54, 77–78
Texas Declaration of Independence, 30
Texas Education Agency, 84, 232, 305, 367
Texas Folklore Society (TFS), 8, 212–13, 215–6, 221
Texas General Land Office, 157
Texas Health Science Center (San Antonio), 315
Texas Heroes Day, 137
Texas Historical and Landmarks Association (THLA), 146, 148, 150, 154
Texas Historical Board, 151
Texas Historical Commission, 156
Texas Infant Dress Company, 181
Texas Junior Chamber of Commerce, 229
Texas Latino Testing Conference, 305
Texas Legislative Medal, 274
Texas Monthly, 294–95, 332–33, 345
Texas Navy, 274
Texas Outlook, 231
"Texas Patriot," 131
Texas Press Association, 147, 274
Texas Revolution, 5, 13, 23, 27, 30–33, 38, 54, 63, 68–73, 78, 81, 83, 96–7, 131–32, 136, 144, 215, 367, 373. See also independence

Texas Southwestern Lore, 212
Texas Southwestern Medical
    Center, 302
Texas State Historical Association,
    154–55
Texas State Teachers' Association, 134
Texas State University (formerly
    Southwest Texas State University),
    217, 240, 242, 234
Texas Women's Hall of Fame, 197,
    309, 356
Texas Women's Political Caucus,
    290–91
Texas Woman's Press Association, 154
Texas Woman's University, 194,
    196, 293
Texians, 2, 5, 20, 22–23, 25, 33,
    54, 60–62, 64–65, 67, 69–70,
    73, 76, 81–83, 96–97, 379;
    defined, 379
Thalia, 329
Thirteenth Amendment, U.S.
    Constitution, 133
Thompson, Jerry, 124
Time magazine 185, 229
Tinker, Douglas, 338–340
Tornel, José María, 30
Tosta, María Dolores de, 39, 372
Toward Excellence and Success
    (TEXAS) Grants Program,
    303–04, 320
Travis, William B., 26–27, 71–72, 77
Treaties of Velasco, 36–37
Treaty of Guadalupe Hidalgo, 40, 99
Twin Sisters (cannon), 32
Tyrell, Julia, 132

unions. *See* labor; labor organizations
UCAPAWA (United Cannery,
    Agricultural, Packing, and Allied
    Workers of America), 186, 188
United Daughters of the Confederacy,
    133. *See also* Confederacy

United States Census Bureau, 365
United States Congress, 98, 233,
    264, 315
United States Navy, 275, 287
United States Postal Service, 274, 351
United States Supreme Court, 101,
    297, 301–02
United States Veterans
    Administration, 272
University of Houston, 192
University of Texas, 8, 123–24,
    211, 213, 215, 218–20, 234,
    244, 266, 298, 301, 315, 375
University of Texas-Austin, 211–13,
    215, 218–20, 234, 298–99,
    301–02, 375
University of Texas at Austin School
    of Law, 299
University of Texas at Brownsville,
    124, 315
University of Texas Health Science
    Center, 315
University of Texas-Pan American-
    Edinburg, 297
University of Texas Rio Grande Valley,
    319n28
University of Texas Southwestern
    Medical Center, 302
University of Texas System, 297–98
University of the Incarnate Word, 130
Univisión, 338
Urrea, José, 31–32, 34
Ursuline Academy, Galveston, TX, 134
U.S.-Mexican War, 39–41, 82,
    97–100, 102, 366, 373; and
    Santa Anna, 39–41, 98–99; and
    Juan Seguín, 82, 373; and Juan
    Cortina, 98–101; and James K.
    Polk, 39–40, 97–98

Valadés, José de, 33
Valdez, Carlos, 338–339
Vargas, Deborah R., 355

Vásquez, Rafael, 39, 79, 81
Venezuela, 288
Vera Cruz, MX, 14, 16–18, 36
Veramendi, Juan Martín, 63
Viet Cong. *See* Vietnam
Vietnam, 7, 246, 252–53, 255–65,
    270, 272–73, 275–76, 370
Vietnam War. *See* Vietnam
Villaseñor, Victor, 345

Walnut Spring, TX, 78. *See also*
    Seguin, TX
war, 2–3, 23–25, 37–40, 54, 56, 82,
    93–94, 97–100, 102–3, 110–11,
    114, 115–16, 133, 146, 222,
    224, 226, 230, 245–46, 253,
    263, 370, 372–73. *See also* Texas
    Revolution, U.S.-Mexican War,
    Civil War, World War I, World War
    II, Vietnam
War Party (TX), 23–24
Washington, D.C., 37–38, 52, 106,
    108, 182, 263, 268, 271
Washington-on-the Brazos, 28, 30, 71
weapons, 23, 27, 32, 69, 107,
    114–15, 177, 179, 256–57, 270
Webb, Walter Prescott, 124
Webster, Michael, 124
Welles, Sumner, 230
West, Emily D. (Yellow Rose of
    Texas), 34
West de Zavala, Emily, 132
West Point Military Academy, 56,
    250, 274
West Side Unemployed Council,
    San Antonio, 182
Wester, Thomas, 194
Westergren, Mike, 337–38
Westmoreland, William, 252, 259
WFAA, 270
*Who's Who among the Women
    of San Antonio and Southwest
    Texas*, 154

Williams, Hank, 356
Woll, Adrián, 39, 81–82
"Woman Who Lost Her Soul,"
    212–13
women, 4, 7, 9, 15, 25, 28, 93, 99,
    134–36, 137, 140, 145–149,
    152–54, 169, 171, 173–75,
    177–78, 181, 184, 193, 195,
    197–98, 214–15, 218, 222–23,
    225, 265, 288–92, 294, 296,
    307–11, 314, 329, 331, 334–35,
    347, 356, 366, 372–3, 376;
    violence against, 15, 57, 68,
    99, 178, 296. *See also* chapters
    on Adina De Zavala, Emma
    Tenayuca, Jovita González
    Mireles, Irma Lerma Rangel,
    and Selena Quintanilla-Pérez;
    entries on individual women and
    women's organizations
Women's Army Corps, 193
Women's Chamber of Commerce of
    Texas, 308
Women's Political Caucus,
    290–91, 308
Woman's Texas Council for National
    Defense, 154
Woods, J.M., 84
workers, 3, 8, 169–70, 172–75,
    177–90, 193–94, 198, 229–30,
    233, 246, 287. *See also* chapter
    on Emma Tenayuca; labor;
    labor organizations/unions;
    workplace environment and wages;
    workers' strikes
Workers' Alliance (WA), 181–83,
    186, 188–90
workers' strikes, 8, 177–80,
    183, 185–89, 193, 368–69.
    See also Tenayuca, Emma;
    labor organizations
Workers' University (MX), 181
workplace environment and wages,
    172–74, 177, 179–89, 193, 198

Works Progress Administration (WPA), 182
World War I, 147–148, 224
World War II, 4, 192, 193, 229

Young, Larry, 336
Young Women's Christian Association, 290
Yucatán, 18, 131

Zacatecas, MX, 23–24, 68
Zapata County, 111–12, 214–15
Zavala, Adina De, 7, 30, 130–60, 221, 368–69, 374–75; overview, 7–8; ancestry, 131, 136, 152; parents and siblings, 132; and the Civil War, 132–33, 161n4; education, 134–35, 161–62n9; childhood, 133–34; as teacher, 134–35; conflict with school board, 134–35; reverence for the past, 135; founds De Zavala Daughters, 135–36; and De Zavala Chapter of DRT, 136–37; preservation of San Antonio missions, 137–38; and saving the Long Barrack, 138–141; and "The Second Battle of the Alamo," 141–46; health issues, 143; book on Alamo, 145; and Texas Historical and Landmarks Association, 146, 154; and the Spanish Governor's Palace, 146–151; San Antonio Conservation Society, 148–49; and *Interstate Index: A Journal of Progress*, 147; and San Antonio's bicentennial, 151; and Texas Centennial, 151; ethnicity and views on, 151–52; changes spelling of name, 132; remaining unmarried, 152–53; in *Who's Who*, 154; and Texas State Historical Association, 155; death and burial, 155; estate, 166n69; posthumous honors, 155–58; posthumous treatment by DRT, 155–58; obituary, 159–160; assessment, 132, 158–160, 368; summary on single status and impact on life and career, 374–7
Zavala, Mary, 132
Zavala Point, 132
Zavala y Sáenz, Miguel Lorenzo Justiano de, 30, 131–33, 140, 147, 151–52